Lawrence A. Wise    2/9/02

# FUNDAMENTALS OF DISTRIBUTED OBJECT SYSTEMS

**WILEY SERIES ON PARALLEL AND DISTRIBUTED COMPUTING**
# Series Editor: Albert Y. Zomaya

# FUNDAMENTALS OF DISTRIBUTED OBJECT SYSTEMS

## The CORBA Perspective

Zahir Tari

Omran Bukhres

A Wiley-Interscience Publication

**JOHN WILEY & SONS, INC.**

New York • Chichester • Weinheim • Brisbane • Singapore • Toronto

Library of Congress Cataloging-in-Publication Data is available.

ISBN 0-471-35198-9 (cloth : alk. paper)

Printed in the United States of America

10 9 8 7 6 5 4 3 2 1

*In the memory of my father Si'Hmanou Tari*
*To my mother Takh'lit Madaoui*

*In the memory of my role model, my father,*
*Abdussalam Ali Bukhres*

# Contents

# Foreword

Innovations have been occurring at a predictable rate in certain technology domains for many years. For example, Moore's Law—where the capacity of general-purpose computer chips has doubled every 18 months—is still going strong after three decades. More recently, the speed of IP networks has been improving at an even faster rate—known as Metcalf's Law—where bandwidth increases by a factor of ten every two years. At this point there is even a "bandwidth index," similar to indices that track the price/performance of other commodities, such as petroleum or electricity. The steady advance in these technologies is remarkable and is due in no small part to decades of synergistic research, development, and education by academic, industrial, and government partners around the world.

There are, however, important domains—particularly software-intensive distributed systems in telecommunications, health care, aerospace, and online financial services—that are not improving at the same rate as Moore's Law or Metcalf's Law, due to a variety of inherent and accidental complexities, such as partial failures, distributed deadlock, and non-portable programming APIs. Consequently, although computer and network hardware keeps getting smaller, faster, cheaper, and better at a predictable pace, complex distributed software systems seem to get bigger, slower, more expensive, and buggier, and the innovation cycles are hard to predict.

An appropriate metaphor for the challenges of software-intensive distributed systems appears in the movie *Apollo 13*, starring Tom Hanks. After an explosion in the command module forces the crew into the lunar module, the carbon dioxide levels grow dangerously high due to a broken air scrubber. At this crucial moment, a manager at Johnson space center walks into a room full of engineers and scientists sitting around a table and dumps out a bag containing common components—such as toothpaste, Tang, and duct tape—found on the lunar module. He tells the group they've got eight hours to take these components and assemble an air scrubber that will fit into the appropriate opening, and if it is not right the first time, everyone is going to die!

Increasingly, developers of complex software-intensive distributed systems—especially large-scale mission-critical "systems of systems"—are facing challenges analogous to those of the Apollo 13 engineers and scientists. In particular, time-to-market pressures and competition for consumers and personnel have created a situation where distributed systems must be developed using a large number of commodity-off-the-shelf (COTS) components, which are not developed in-house and whose quality can thus rarely be controlled directly. Yet, just like the Apollo 13 engineers and scientists, we must quickly and robustly master the principles, patterns, and protocols necessary to thrive in a COTS-centric environment because our livelihood—and sometimes even our lives—depend upon our success.

Over the past decade, various techniques and tools have been developed to alleviate many accidental and inherent complexities associated with distributed software systems. Some of the most successful of these techniques and tools center on distributed object computing (DOC) middleware, which resides between applications and the underlying operating systems, protocol stacks, and hardware devices to simplify and coordinate how these components are connected and how they interoperate. Just as communication protocol stacks can be decomposed into multiple layers, so too can DOC middleware be decomposed into the following layers:

- *Infrastructure middleware*, which encapsulates and enhances native OS communication and concurrency mechanisms to create object-oriented (OO) network programming components, such as reactors, acceptor-connectors, monitor objects, active objects, and component configurators. These components help eliminate many tedious, error-prone, and non-portable aspects of developing and maintaining networked applications via low-level OS programming API, such as Sockets or POSIX pthreads. Widely-used examples of infrastructure middleware include Java virtual machines (JVMs) and the ADAPTIVE Communication Environment (ACE).

- *Distribution middleware*, which use and extend the infrastructure middleware to define a higher-level distributed programming model. This programming model defines reusable APIs and components that automate common end-system network programming tasks, such as connection management, (de)marshaling, demultiplexing, end-point and request demultiplexing, and multithreading. Distribution middleware enables distributed applications to be programmed using techniques familiar to developers of standalone applications, i.e., by having clients invoke operations on target objects without concern for their location, programming language, OS platform, communication protocols and interconnects, and hardware. At the heart of distribution middleware are Object Request Brokers (ORBs), such as Microsoft's Component Object Model (COM)+, Sun's Java remote Method Invocation (RMI), and the OMG's Common Object Request Broker Architecture (CORBA), which is a key focus of this book.

- *Common middleware services*, which augment distribution middleware by defining higher-level domain-independent services, such as event notifications, logging, multimedia streaming, persistence, security, global time, real-time scheduling and end-to-end quality of service (QoS), fault tolerance, concurrency control, and transactions. Whereas distribution middleware focuses largely on managing end-system resources in support of an OO distributed programming model, common middleware services focus on managing resources throughout a distributed system. Developers can reuse these services to allocate, schedule, and coordinate global resources and perform common distribution tasks that would otherwise be implemented in an ad hoc manner within each application.

- *Domain-specific services*, which are tailored to the requirements of particular domains, such as telecommunications, e-commerce, health care, process automation, or aerospace. Unlike the other three OO middleware layers—which provide broadly reusable "horizontal" mechanisms and services—domain-specific services are targeted at vertical markets. Domain-specific services are the least mature of the middleware layers today, due partly to the historical lack of distribution middleware and common middleware service *standards*, which provide a stable base upon which to create domain-specific services. Since these services embody knowledge of application domains, however, they can significantly increase system quality and decrease the cycle-time and effort required to develop particular types of distributed applications.

As these DOC middleware layers mature they are becoming COTS products that are readily available for purchase or open-source acquisition. COTS DOC middleware has become essential in software development organizations that face stringent time and resource constraints since it helps amortize software life-cycle costs by leveraging previous development expertise and concentrating research efforts that improve quality and performance. Ultimately, this R&D process will result in software-intensive distributed systems that get smaller, faster, cheaper, and better at a predictable pace, just as computer and network hardware do today.

The following factors have helped improve the quality and performance of COTS DOC middleware products during the past decade:

- *Maturation of DOC middleware standards*—DOC middleware standards have matured considerably in recent years. For instance, the OMG has adopted specifications for CORBA that reduce ORB footprint, improve fault tolerant behavior, reserve real-time connection and threading resources, and expose various types of QoS policies to applications.
- *Maturation of DOC middleware patterns and frameworks*—A substantial amount of R&D effort has focused on patterns and frameworks for DOC middleware and applications. As these patterns mature and become instantiated in COTS framework components, they have helped improve the efficiency, scalability, predictability, and flexibility of DOC middleware.

Until recently, however, it has been hard to instructors and students to learn how to use DOC middleware effectively without dedicating substantial time and effort. One problem has been that DOC middleware APIs, capabilities, and best practices have existed largely in the programming folklore, the heads of expert developers, or scattered throughout articles in trade magazines and web sites. Another problem is that existing books on DOC middleware and CORBA are intended as guides for industry practitioners rather than as textbooks for students. Thus, many important theoretical and fundamental distribution issues are not covered in these books.

In a highly competitive information technology economy, educating students to become effective distributed software developers is increasingly important. Premium value and competitive advantage is accruing to individuals, universities, companies, and even countries that can quickly master the principles, patterns, and protocols necessary to integrate COTS middleware to create complex DOC applications that cannot be bought off-the-shelf yet. Success in this endeavor requires close collaboration between researchers and practitioners, which is why I'm delighted that Zahir Tari and Omran Bukhres have written *Fundamentals of Distributed Object Systems: The CORBA Perspective* to help educate researchers and developers of next-generation information technologies.

This book uses CORBA to illustrate the theory and practice of distribution middleware and many common middleware services, as follows:

- The coverage of CORBA's distribution middleware is split into two parts: (1) *fundamental aspects of the CORBA reference model*, such as the CORBA interface definition language (IDL), object references, and standard interoperability protocols and (2) *advanced CORBA features*, such as portable object adapters, client caching, and enhanced communication protocols. This material provides much more than a rehash of the standard CORBA APIs—it also describes the key technical concepts, underlying theoretical foundations, and common solutions related to challenges encountered when developing and integrating interoperable software.
- The coverage of common middleware services focus on a wide range of CORBA's objects services, such as the CORBA Naming, Trading, Events, Transaction, and Query services. For most of these services, this book describes the corresponding architectures and basic elements. It also shows how such services can be implemented and presents lessons that can be learned and generalized when developing domain-specific services and distributed applications.

By study, mastering, and applying the material in this book, you'll be able to design and implement distributed applications more rapidly and effectively.

We are fortunate that Zahir and Omran have found time in their busy professional lives to write an outstanding textbook on DOC middleware and CORBA. If you want thorough coverage of the DOC middleware technologies that are shaping next-generation distributed systems read this book. I've learned much from it, and I'm confident that you will too.

Douglas C. Schmidt
University of California, Irvine

# Preface

CORBA, the acronym for the Common Object Request Broker Architecture, is the result of a standardization consortium, called OMG (Object Management Group), involving more than six hundred international software companies. OMG aims to produce and set up an architecture and a set of standards for open distributed systems enabling interoperability across different hardware and software vendor platforms.

This book presents the theoretical and technical views of the CORBA technology, including the architecture (the Object Management Architecture), the main technical issues (e.g., adaptor, interoperability, caching) and the different services for the management of heterogeneous and distributed objects (naming, trading, query and transaction management). We also present the technical foundations of the main issues related to the design and implementation of large-scale distributed applications, and give details about how specific parts of a CORBA system can be designed.

This book will be valuable to the reader who is interested in understanding the foundations of the CORBA technology and whose aim is to perform advanced research on one of the technical issues related to such a technology (caching, trading, etc.). Or the reader may just want to learn how to program advanced distributed applications, and therefore the aim is to understand the basic "programming techniques" for building heterogeneous distributed applications. The reader may want to find out as much as possible about the CORBA technology and to get a "technical" inside view of its different aspects (architectural, design etc.).

The eleven chapters of this book provide answers to questions that most people are asking, including our students at RMIT and Purdue University:

- What is CORBA?
- Why do we need CORBA?
- What do we need to know in order to understand the "inside" of CORBA?
- What do we need to know in order to implement distributed applications?

Our aim is to provide detailed and technical answers to these questions. The book is organized into three parts. The first part describes the CORBA basics, such as the foundations of distributed systems, CORBA Architecture details, and CORBA programming. This part provides the first step in understanding all the aspects related to the CORBA technology as well as how to implement distributed applications by using different CORBA components such as the Static Skeleton Interface, Dynamic Invocation Interface, Dynamic Skeleton Interface, and Interface Repository. The second part covers specific issues related to CORBA, including Object Adaptor, Interoperability, Caching and Load balancing. Finally, the last part describes some important CORBA services, such as naming, trading, transaction and query services.

## HOW TO USE THE BOOK

There are many ways to use this book on distributed objects. Basically there are three blocks of chapters, with each referring to a certain level of technicality for CORBA. Block I involves introductory chapters that, as ordered in the figure below, provide a good understanding of the basics of distributed objects. Readers familiar with concepts of distributed systems can skip Chapter 1 and start from Chapter 2 and cover Chapters 3, 5, and 7. These four chapters of the first block cover all the necessary details on the main concepts related to CORBA distributed object systems: the CORBA chapter covers architectural concepts and issues of distributed object systems; Chapter 3 explains how to implement CORBA-based applications; Chapter 5 explains how different distributed object systems communicate with each other, and finally, Chapter 7 explains how objects identified by their "object names" can be used by applications.

After the concepts illustrated in the chapters of Block I are well understood, we suggest readers move to another level of technicality. The chapters of Block II provide a more advanced view of distributed objects.

**Block I**

| | |
|---|---|
| Chapter 1 (Introduction to Distributed Systems) | (2 Hours) |
| Chapter 2 (Introduction to CORBA) | (3 Hours) |
| Chapter 3 (CORBA Programming) | (6 Hours) |
| Chapter 5 (CORBA Interoperability) | (2 Hours) |
| Chapter 7 (Naming Service) | (2 Hours) |

**Block II**

| | |
|---|---|
| Chapter 4 (Object Adaptors) | (3 Hours) |
| Chapter 8 (Trading Object Service) | (3 Hours) |
| Chapter 9 (Event Service) | (3 Hours) |

**Block III**

| | |
|---|---|
| Chapter 6 (CORBA Caching) | (3 Hours) |
| Chapter 10 (Object Transaction Service) | (4 Hours) |
| Chapter 11 (Object Query Service) | (3 Hours) |

Chapter 4 goes into details on one of the major components of CORBA systems—the Object Adaptors. The remaining chapters of Block II address the issues of service retrieval in large-scale distributed systems as well the communication across heterogeneous distributed systems.

Block III contains chapters that need to be read after the basic and advanced concepts of distributed objects are well understood. They require a deep understanding of different aspects covered in Blocks I and II, including programming aspects and architectural aspects. Chapter 6 shows how distributed object applications can be made efficient by extending client proxies. Chapter 10 covers issues of robustness and reliability of transactions in distributed object applications. Chapter 11 explains how CORBA and Database technologies can be (partially) integrated.

For undergraduate students, all the chapters of Block I will need to be covered in detail. The instructor can add additional chapters from Block II according to the order of how they are listed in the figure. Some chapters of the second and third blocks can be assigned as reading material, for example, Chapters 8, 9, and 6.

For postgraduate students, we suggest covering a few chapters of Block I to be covered in the first two or three lectures. Chapters 2 and 5 can be such chapters. If students are familiar with Java, then some of the implementation concepts of programming can be covered as an assignment (e.g., an assignment covering both DII, DSI and the look up of the Interface Repository, where students will build a complex application using such concepts). The remaining lectures will need to cover the chapters of Block II and Block III.

## ORGANIZATION OF THE BOOK

Part I is dedicated to the basics of CORBA and contains technical concepts necessary for a good understanding of distributed systems and distributed object systems. Chapter 1 introduces the main elements of distributed systems and aims at providing readers with appropriate background to better understand the remaining chapters of this book. Detailed descriptions of existing distributed system technologies, such as Socket, Remote Procedure Call, Remote Method Invocation, are also provided. Chapter 2 is the first step into the CORBA world. It draws a general picture of CORBA and describes in more detail the main elements of the CORBA architecture, such as Interface Definition Language (IDL), Object Request Broker (ORB) and Interface and Implementation Repositories. The concept of object binding is presented in the CORBA context, and different approaches supported by existing CORBA-compliant systems are explained, such as the binding of transient object references and the binding of persistent object references. Chapter 3 demonstrates how to design and implement distributed object applications using a Java-based CORBA system, OrbixWeb. It is the only chapter of this book that provides program codes. A step-by-step implementation of a complete application is proposed: first, basic programming techniques are illustrated and later more advanced ones are proposed, such as programming with DII (Dynamic Invocation Interface), programming with DSI (Dynamic Skeleton Interface) and programming with the Interface Repository.

Part II is about advanced topics in CORBA—adaptors, interoperability and caching. CORBA adaptors provide interface flexibility and management. Chapter 4 describes the main issues related to the design of adaptors and later discusses the two architectures: BOA and POA. Both these architectures are explained and compared to each other with regard to a set of criteria, such as object/servant management, object grouping, request redirection and multi-threading. At the end of the chapter, a POA extension to deal with database issues, such as persistence of object references, is given. Chapter 5 explains the inter-ORB communication protocol which is based on the standard IIOP (Internet Inter-ORB Protocol). An ORB can implement additional communication protocols. The structure of IOR (Interoperable Object References), which enables invocations to pass from one ORB to another, is discussed. Chapter 6 is about CORBA performance. It discusses how to make CORBA applications efficient by caching remote objects and therefore make them locally accessible through appropriate proxies. Caching relates to the way proxies (e.g., client proxy and server proxy) and the ORB perform invocations. Chapter 6 describes a specific design for CORBA caching. A FIFO-based removal algorithm is discussed, and this uses a double-linked structure and hash table for eviction. A variation of optimistic two-phase locking for consistency control is proposed. This protocol does not require a lock at the client side by using a per-process caching design.

Part III is about the Common Object Services Specification (COSS). CORBA provided a standard for several distributed services. This part describes some of the important CORBA services, such as the Naming Service, Event Service, Trading Service, Object Transaction Service, and Object Query Service Chapters 7 and 8 describe the CORBA Naming and Trading services, respectively. These services provide appropriate functionalities to share information available in different servers. Users can browse, retrieve, and update object references by using the different operations of the interface provided by the Naming or Trading Services. Chapter 7 enables a transparent access to objects and offers facilities to retrieve objects based on their names. Chapter 8 provides "matchmaking" services for objects. Each object is recorded with appropriate information and the role of the trader is to find the best match for the client, based on the context of the request service and the offers of the providers. Chapter 8 starts with an illustrative example and shows how a trader can be used to locate services. The different steps of this example are illustrated with JTrader, a Java-based CORBA Trading Service. Later sections describe the elements of the CORBA trader architecture as well as the issues related to efficiency and scalability of CORBA Traders (e.g., clustering, query propagation). Chapter 9 covers the CORBA Event Service, which offers sophisticated communication between ORB objects. This chapter provides details of the following aspects: the event architecture, the different communication semantics (e.g. synchronous, asynchronous, and deferred invocations), and the different communication models (Push/Pull and hybrid models). A few implementations of the CORBA Event Service are described. Chapter 10 is about the CORBA Object Transaction Service (OTS). This service is one of the essential parts of most of distributed systems, including those supporting business applications such as OLTP (On-Line Transaction Processing). This chapter starts with a background on transactions, including the different transaction models (such flat and nested models), different concurrency control and commit protocols. Later, a detailed discussion on the CORBA OTS is provided, and this covers the description of the different elements of this service. The last section overviews two implementations, one related to the Iona's product and the other one is the Microsoft counterpart of the OTS, called MTS (Microsoft Transaction Service). Chapter 11, the last chapter of Part III, describes a service which can be qualified as a "data-oriented" service, that is, the Object Query Service. This service enables integration of databases by using a standard query language (such as the ODMG's Object Query Language, denoted as OQL). The first two sections of this chapter describe the main query processing techniques used in distributed databases. This may help the reader to understand the important issues as well as solutions related the processing of heterogeneous databases. Later sections provide a detailed description of the elements of CORBA's Object Service.

# Acknowledgments

We gratefully acknowledge all the people directly or indirectly involved in the preparation of this book. Many people from RMIT and Purdue helped tremendously. In particular, we would like to thank our former students who have reviewed some sections of this book and made valuable suggestions for improvement. Special thanks go to RMIT students:

- Suryadinata Setiawan, who implemented the CODAR database adaptor, and made contributions to Chapters 1, 2, 3, and 4, as well as reviewed questions, exercises, and answers to both of them for all chapters in the book.
- David Lin, for his work on CORBA caching, including the design of the caching model and the implementation and testing of the model.
- Greg Craske and Kiran, who did extensive work on the CORBA Trading Object Service, and in particular, for the issues of clustering and query routing.
- Sunny Bains for his work on the CORBA Event Service, including the design and implementation of the typed and untyped event channels.

We would like to thank our graduate students Christina Davenport, Srinivasan Sikkupparbathyam, Marcelo Areal, Eric Lynch, and Lara Atallah for their readings and tremendous feedback. We also would like to thank Frank Oreovicz and Michelle Boshears for their qualified English editing.

The most important support that made this whole book possible came from our families. We would also like to thank our respective employers for providing us with an appropriate environment and their support for this book.

And as always, a special expression of deep and sincere gratitude goes to Allah almighty for all his help and guidance.

Z. TARI
O. BUKHRES

# Acronyms

| | |
|---|---|
| BOA | Basic Object Adaptor |
| COM | Microsoft's Component Object Model |
| CORBA | Object Request Broker Architecture |
| COSS | Common Object Services Specification |
| DCE | Distributed Computing Environment |
| DCOM | Microsoft's Distributed COM |
| FIFO | First In First Out |
| GIOP | General Inter-ORB Protocol |
| HTTP | Hypertext Transfer Protocol |
| IDL | Interface Definition Language |
| IIOP | Internet Inter-ORB Protocol |
| LRU | Last Recently Used |
| ODMG | Object Database Management Group |
| OQS | Object Query Service |
| OODBMS | Object Oriented Database Management System |
| OMA | Object Management Architecture |
| OMG | Object Management Group |
| ORB | Object Request Broker |
| OTS | Object Transaction Service |
| O2PL | Optimistic 2PL |
| 2PL | Two Phase Locking |
| POA | Portable Object Adaptor |
| RDBMS | Relational Database Management System |
| RMI | Remote Method Invocation |
| RPC | Remote Procedure Call |
| STR | Service Type Repository |
| TCP/IP | Transport Control Protocol/Internet Protocol |
| TOS | Trading Object Service |
| UML | Unified Modeling Language |

# PART I

# BASICS OF CORBA

# CHAPTER 1

# Introduction to Distributed Systems

The advent of computers was motivated by the need to perform complex data calculations and processing quickly. Once their usage to perform these tasks is ubiquitous, the next computing breakthroughs are spurred by the necessity to collaborate with other computers via a network. The earliest solutions are based on a model called *centralized systems*, in which a single computer with one or multiple CPUs processes all incoming requests. However, reasons such as cost, reliability, and the separate nature of the divisions that makes up organizations using the systems causes this model to be less attractive. Another model, called *distributed systems*, addresses these issues with its distribution. Instead of having one single powerful computer, distributed systems employ multiple computers communicating to each other via a common network. The independent, distributed, and sometimes heterogeneous nature of these computers also underlies the importance of having a distributed system software to provide a common view of the systems.

This chapter serves as a brief introductory overview of distributed systems. The first section explains the basic ideas of distributed systems. The second section compares different solutions of a distributed system software, called middleware: Sockets, RPC, RMI, DCOM, and CORBA.

## 1.1  BASICS OF DISTRIBUTED SYSTEMS

A distributed system is a collection of autonomous computers linked by a network and equipped with distributed system software [22]. A distributed system is the opposite of a centralized system, which consists of a single computer with one or multiple powerful CPUs processing all incoming requests. The distributed system software enables the comprising computers to coordinate their activities and to share system resources. A well-developed distributed system software provides the illusion of a single and integrated environment although it is actually implemented by multiple computers in different locations. In other words, the software gives a *distribution transparency* to the systems.

### 1.1.1 Architectures

The definition and implementations of distributed systems evolve from the system where remote terminals or minicomputer, independently carrying out some operations and periodically communicating with mainframes in batch mode. Between the late 1970s and the early 1980s, the notion of distributed systems was synonymous with *distributed processing*, that is, a request processing technique where a request is broken into subtasks which will be processed by multiple machines. During this period, a distributed system was interconnected in either the *star, hierarchical*, or *ring* structure. As shown by Figure 1.1, each remote terminal in star structure is connected to the central computer via a modem. Figure 1.2(a) depicts a distributed system with hierarchical structure.

One or more locations have their own minicomputers. Each minicomputer at these locations is connected to a central computer via leased phone lines. The minicomputer periodically sends the required summary data, for example, daily sales, to the central computer. Figure 1.2(b) illustrates a distributed system interconnected in a ring structure consisting of autonomous computers linked in a peer-to-peer fashion. Examples of peers are mainframes, mid-range machines and PCs.

Distributed system types of this period range from *functional distribution, centrally controlled, integrated systems*, to *non-integrated systems*. A distributed system with functional distribution has some of its functions distributed, but not the capability to process a complete transaction. The system employs intelligent terminals or controllers to perform message editing, screen formatting, data collection, dialogue with terminal operators, some security functions, and message compaction. A centrally controlled distributed system is viewed as a collection of peripheral small computers, which might be capable to completely process. Each of them is sub-

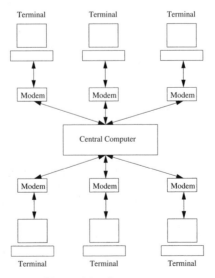

**Figure 1.1** Star structure.

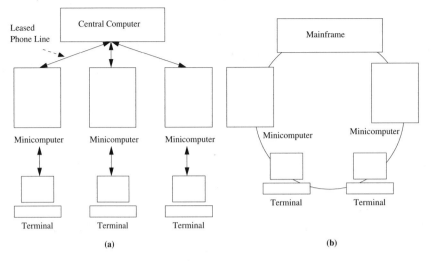

**Figure 1.2**    (a) Hierarchical structure; (b) ring structure.

ordinate to a higher level computer in the overall system structure. An integrated distributed system consists of separate systems which have an integrated design of the data located in different systems, and possibly of the data in different programs as well. A non-integrated distributed system comprises independent systems which are connected by a computer network.

The meaning and implementations of distributed systems started to change in the period between mid to late 1980s. The idea of distributed systems represents a system ranging from a separate, geographically dispersed applications cooperating with each other, to a single application formed by the cooperation of geographically dispersed but relatively independent, stand-alone, and component programs. A distributed system of this period has four types of structural and interconnection configurations. The first one, which is shown in Figure 1.3(a), is a mainframe connected to personal computers with certain functions or applications are off-loaded from the mainframe into the PCs.

Another type is PCs connected to a mid-range machine, which, in turn, is connected to a mainframe. As depicted in Figure 1.3(b), all of them are organized in a hierarchical structure with one root and as one moves closer toward the root, have an increasing computing power, function, and possibly control is implied.

Users of these PCs manipulate the mid-range machine to access applications and data backup of one department. The mid-range delivers data to the mainframe which handles enterprise level processing. Figure 1.4(a) illustrates the next type of structural and interconnection configurations.

A distributed system of this type is arranged as a connection of peers which have different details of interconnection and dependency. However, no clear central point of control exists in the system. As shown in Figure 1.4(b), the last type is a collec-

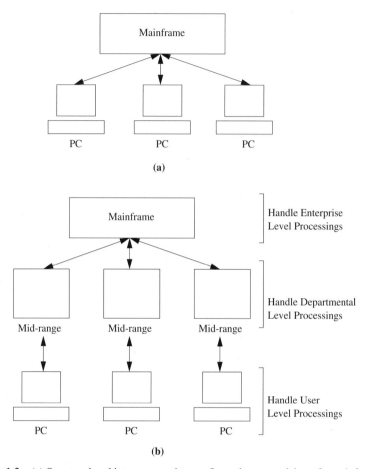

**Figure 1.3** (a) Structural and inter-connection configuration comprising of a mainframe and its connected PCs; (b) hierarchical structure and interconnection configuration.

tion of peer hierarchies. Each of the mainframe or mid-range machines exhibits a hierarchical configuration and is connected to a collection of PCs.

Distributed systems underwent a final evolution around the late 1980s. As shown in Figure 1.5(a), each site in the early distributed systems of this period contained one or multiple individual software providing access to its resources.

Later, the granularity of distribution control became more fine-grained, enabling functions of a single software to be distributed across the network. Thus, as Figure 1.5(b) illustrates, the current distributed system now consists of autonomous computers which are linked by a network. The software used by this system is divided into multiple components, each residing at a different site.

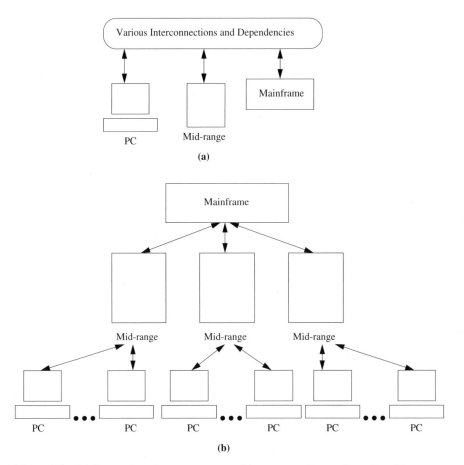

**Figure 1.4**    (a) Connection of peers structure and inter-connection configuration; (b) connection of hierarchical peers structure and inter-connection configuration.

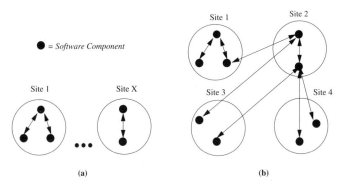

**Figure 1.5**    (a) A distributed system in pre-late 1980s; (b) a distributed system today.

## 1.1.2   Characteristics

A distributed system has six important characteristics [22]: (1) resource sharing, (2) openness, (3) concurrency, (4) scalability, (5) fault tolerance, and (6) transparency. These characteristics are not automatic consequences of distribution. Instead, they are acquired as a result of of a careful design and implementation.

**Resource Sharing**   Resources provided by a computer which is a member of a distributed system can be shared by clients and other members of the system via a network. In order to achieve effective sharing, each resource must be managed by a software that provides interfaces which enables the resource to be manipulated by clients. Resources of a particular type are managed by a software module called *resource manager*, which performs its job based on a set of management policies and methods.

**Openness**   Openness in distributed systems is the characteristic that determines whether the system is extendible in various ways. This characteristic is measured mainly by the degree to which new resource sharing services can be incorporated without disruption or duplication of existing services. The opposite of an open distributed system is a closed distributed system. The set of features and facilities provided by a closed distributed system stay static overtime. New features and facilities cannot be added into the system. This prevents the system from providing any new resources other than those which are already made available. The openness of a distributed system can be viewed from two perspectives: *hardware extensibility* and *software extensibility*. The former is the ability to add hardware from different vendors to a distributed system, while the latter is the ability to add new software or modules from different vendors to a distributed system.

A system is considered being open if its key software interfaces are *published*, that is, the interfaces are specified, documented, and made available publicly to software developers. This process is similar to the process of standardizing these interfaces since both make the interfaces publicly available. However, the former does not require the interfaces to pass official standardization process before they are made available. An example of more open systems are UNIX systems. Resources of these system are used via *system calls*, that is, a set of procedures which are made available to programs and other languages that support conventional procedure facilities. UNIX systems are able to handle a newly added type of hardware by adding new systems calls or new parameters to existing system calls. These systems calls are implemented by one module of the UNIX called *kernel*. However, unless access to the source code is available (like in the case of Linux Operating System (OS)), the kernel is fixed and inextensible. Therefore, the design of the kernel determines the range and the level of supports for different resource types available to UNIX applications. The availability of interprocess communication facilities in UNIX widens the scope for achieving openness. It allows resources that are not accessible through system calls to be manipulated via the interprocess communication facilities instead. It also enables resources on machines with different hardware and software to be used as long as the necessary interprocess communication facilities are available.

**Concurrency**    Concurrency is the ability to process multiple tasks at the same time. A distributed system comprises multiple computers, each having one or multiple processors. The existence of multiple processors in the computer can be exploited to perform multiple tasks at the same time. This ability is crucial to improve the overall performance of the distributed system. For example, a mainframe must handle requests from multiple users, with each user sending multiple requests at the same time. Without concurrency, performance would suffer, since each request must be processed sequentially. The software used must make sure that an access to the same resource does not conflict with others. All concurrent access must be synchonized to avoid problems such as *lost update* (two concurrent access update the same data, but one of the updates is lost), *dirty read* (one access updates the data read by another access, but the former fails and affects the latter), *incorrect summary* (a set of data is updated by an access while the set is being processed by another access), and *unrepeatable read* (an access reads data twice, but the data are changed by another access between the two reads) [29].

**Scalability**    Scalability in distributed systems is the characteristic where a system and application software need not to change when the scale of the system increases. Scalability is important since the amount of requests processed by a distributed system tends to grow, rather than decrease. In order to handle the increase, additional hardware and/or software usually needed. However, this does not mean throwing more hardware and more software into the system would resolve the issue of scalability. In fact, a system which is not scalable does not utilize the additional hardware and software efficiently to process requests. This is because the system is not designed to expand. Such a system will eventually hit its processing capability limits and its performance starts to degrade. On the other hand, a system is said to be scalable if it provides flexibilities to grow in size, but still utilize the extra hardware and software efficiently. The amount of flexibilities the system has determines the level of scalability it provides.

**Fault Tolerance**    Fault Tolerance in distributed systems is a characteristic where a distributed system provides an appropriately handling of errors that occurred in the system. A system with good fault tolerance mechanisms has a high degree of *availability*. A distributed system's availability is a measure of the proportion of time that the system is available for use. A better fault tolerance increases availability. Fault tolerance is achieved by deploying two approaches: *hardware redundancy* and *software recovery*. The former is an approach to prevent hardware failures by means of duplication. Although expensive, this technique improves availability since one or multiple dedicated hardware stand ready to take over the request processing task when a failure occurs. For example, an application might use two interconnected computers where one of them is acting as a backup machine in case the other is unable to process requests. Software recovery is an approach where software is designed to recover from faults when they are detected. Even so, a full recovery may not be achieved in some cases. Some processing could be incomplete and their persistent data may not be in a consistent state.

***Transparency***   Transparency is the concealment of the separation of components in a distributed system from the user and the application programmer such that the system is perceived as a whole rather than as collection of independent components. As a distributed system is separated by nature, transparency is needed to hide all unnecessary details regarding this separation from users. The term *information object* is used to denote the entity to which the transparency can be applied to. There are eight forms of transparency in distributed systems. The first one is *access transparency*, which enables local and remote information objects to be accessed using identical operations. The second one is *location transparency*, which enables information objects to be accessed without the knowledge of their location. These first two forms of transparency are also known as *network transparency*. They provide a similar degree of anonymity for resources found in centralized computer systems. Their existence or inexistence have a strong effect on the utilization of a distributed system's resources. The third transparency is *concurrency transparency*, which enables several processes to operate concurrently using shared information objects without interference between them. *Replication transparency* enables multiple information objects to be used to increase reliability and performance without knowledge of the replicas by users or application programs. *Failure transparency* hides faults and allows users and application programs to complete their tasks even though a hardware or software failure occurs. *Migration transparency* permits information objects to be moved within a system without affecting the operation of users or application programs. *Performance transparency* permits a distributed system to be reconfigured to improve performance as the load fluctuates. Finally, *scaling transparency* permits the system and application to expand in scale without changing the system structure and application algorithms. For example, consider an e-mail address of *amazigh@cs.rmit.edu.au*. Users need not to know about the physical address of machine that must be contacted to deliver an e-mail to this address, nor do they need to know how the e-mail is actually sent. Thus, an e-mail address has both location and access transparency, that is, network transparency.

The presence or absence of the resource sharing, open, and transparent characteristics explained above influences how heterogeneities of a distributed system are addressed. The existence of resource sharing increases the need for the system to be more open. This is because sharable resources of this system are almost certainly made up of hardware and software from different vendors. Without the openness, these resources cannot be used by clients if they are based on technologies from vendors different from those resources. Another problem is that hardware and software of various vendors will not be able to be incorporated into the system, especially in cases where legacy systems exist. Having an openness in the system facilitates the mix-and-match of hardware and software. This allows the system to take advantage of the best features from different products, regardless who their vendors are. The last characteristic that determines a distributed system's approach to its heterogeneities is transparency. If the transparency is not available, clients will be exposed to the complexities of multiple technologies underlying the system. As a result, the system becomes harder to use and requires a lot of training. This could reduce, even eliminate the lure of the distributed systems model completely.

### 1.1.3  Advantages and Disadvantages

The trend of distributed systems is motivated by the potential benefits that they could yield. These benefits are [83][101]:

- *Shareability:* Shareability in distributed systems is the ability that allows the comprising systems to use each other's resources. This sharing takes place on a computer network connected to each system, using a common protocol that governs communications among the systems. Both the network and the protocol are respectively the common communication medium and the common protocol that facilitate sharing. The Internet is a good example of a distributed system. Each computer that wishes to use and/or share resources must be connected to the network and understand TCP/IP.

- *Expandability:* Expandability of a distributed system is the ability that permits new systems to be added as members of the overall system. Foreseeing all resources that will ever be provided is often not feasible. It also influences the ability to determine what level of processing power the host machines must have. A distributed system might end up providing unused resources on machines with under-capacity utilization. Such waste of time and money is resolved by giving the freedom to add shared resources only when they are really needed.

- *Local Autonomy:* A distributed system is responsible to manage its resources. In other words, it gives it's systems a local autonomy of their resources. Each system can apply local policies, settings, or access controls to these resources and services. This makes distributed systems ideal for organizations whose structure consists of independent entities located in different locations. For example, multinational companies might have their systems scattered in different locations, each managing the affairs of a particular branch.

- *Improved Performance:* As the number of clients accessing a resource increases, the response time starts to degrade. The conventional ways of maintaining the response time, for example, upgrading the host machine, can be used to offset this effect. This is further improved with techniques such as replication, which allows the same resources to be copied, and load balancing, which distributes access requests among these copies. The separate nature of distributed systems is also helpful since resources exist in different machines. Requests for these resources are sent to different machines, making the request processing to be naturally distributed. Finally, the number of computers in a distributed system benefits the system, in terms of its processing power. This is because the combined processing power of multiple computers provides much more processing power than a centralized system. The limit of which a single computer can be installed with multiple CPUs prohibit an endless increase of its processing power.

- *Improved Reliability and Availability:* Disruptions to a distributed system do not stop the system as a whole from providing its resources. Some resources may not be available, but others are still accessible. This is because these resources are spread across multiple computers where each resource is managed by one computer. If these resources are replicated, the disruption might cause only minimum impact on the system. This is because requests can be diverted to other copies of the target resources.

- *Potential Cost Reductions:* The first advantage of distributed systems over centralized systems is cost effectiveness. As Grosch's law states, the computing power of a single CPU is proportional to the square of its price. Thus, one CPU X, which has four times the performance of one CPU Y, can be acquired at twice the cost of CPU Y. However, this law became invalid when microprocessors were introduced. Paying double price yields only a slightly higher speed, not four times of the CPU performance. Therefore, rather than paying more for a single CPU, the most cost-effective way of achieving a better price to performance ratio is to harness a large number of CPUs to process requests. Another potential cost reduction occurs when a distributed system is used to handle request processing shared of multiple organizations. All of these organizations could contribute to the setup and maintenance costs. This reduces the per organization costs down compared to setting and maintaining the system independently.

Beside these advantages a distributed system has the following disadvantages:

- *Network Reliance:* Because all computers in a distributed system rely on a network to communicate to each other, problems on the network would disrupt activities in the system as a whole. This is true especially for physical problems such as broken network cables, routers, bridges, etc. The cost of setting up and maintaining the network could eventually outweigh any potential cost savings offered by distributed systems.
- *Complexities:* A distributed system software is not easy to develop. It must be able to deal with errors that could occur from all computers that make up the distributed system. It must also capable to manipulate resources of computers with a wide range of heterogeneities.
- *Security:* A distributed system allows its computers to collaborate and share resources more easily. However, this convenience of access could be a problem if no proper security mechanism are put in place. Private resources would be exposed to a wider range of potential hackers, with unauthorized accesses launched from any computers connected to the system. In fact, a centralized system is usually more secure than a distributed system.

## 1.2  DISTRIBUTED SYSTEM TECHNOLOGIES

*Middleware* in distributed systems is a type of distributed system software which connects different kinds of applications and provides distribution transparency to its connected applications. It is used to bridge heterogeneities that occurred in the

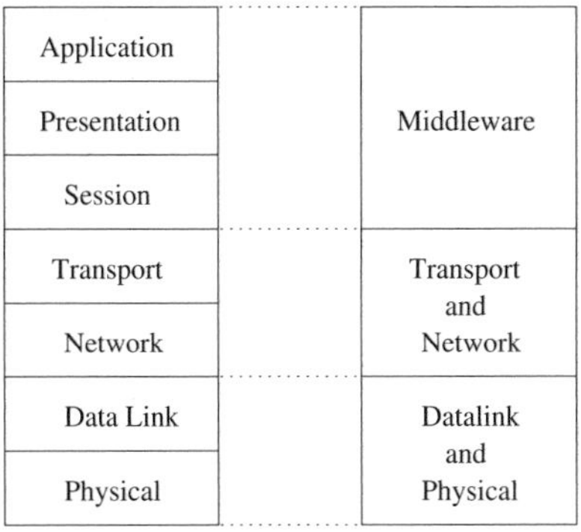

| Application | | |
|---|---|---|
| Presentation | | Middleware |
| Session | | |
| Transport | | Transport and Network |
| Network | | |
| Data Link | | Datalink and Physical |
| Physical | | |

**Figure 1.6**   Middleware and the OSI Model.

systems. As Figure 1.6 illustrates, middleware replaces session, presentation, and application layers of the OSI model.

Based on significant standards or products in the market, middleware can be divided into several categories, such as socket, RPC (Remote Procedure Call), RMI (Remote Method Invocation), DCE (Distributed Computing Environment), DCOM (Distributed Component Object Model) and CORBA (Common Object Request Broker Architecture). Because this book focuses on the CORBA type of middleware, in which details are given in Chapter 2, this section will discuss the remaining middleware approaches. Explanations given in this section provide a quick overview of these approaches, rather than a comprehensive comparison of the middleware.

### 1.2.1   Socket

A socket is a peer-to-peer communication endpoint [82]. The first implementation of sockets is known as *Berkeley sockets*, due to its introduction in 1981 as part of UNIX BSD 4.2 operating system. Sockets are generic interfaces which enable processes that reside in different computers to communicate to each other. They provide the basic infrastructure needed to facilitate communications in distributed systems. As Figure 1.7 depicts, sockets are usually used as interfaces from the upper three layers of the OSI model into the transport layer [98].

From the OSI model point of view, a network application is a combination of its upper three layers. These layers reside in the address space which users have access to. The rest of the OSI layers provide all the necessary basic functionalities which are used by the upper layers. In UNIX, these layers are implemented by the kernel. Access to their address space is forbidden and exclusive only for the system.

Figure 1.8 shows two processes communicating to each other via their sockets. The process that sends data to another process is called *sending process*, while the process that receives this data is a *receiving process*. A socket has a network address which consists of an Internet address and a local port number. Each of the processes that wishes to communicate must create and initialize a socket. Creating a socket returns an I/O descriptor number, whereas the initialization step prepares the socket to

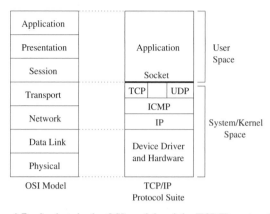

**Figure 1.7**    Sockets in the OSI model and the TCP/IP protocol suite.

send data for sending socket, or accept data for receiving socket. Typically, a sending process creates and initializes its socket before the receiving process performs the same steps. A socket created by the former is called a sending socket, whereas the one created by the latter is a receiving socket. A sending process sends all the necessary data to the server process via its socket. Data to be sent are queued at the sending socket until the underlying protocol has been transmitted. The protocol might require an acknowledgement of the data's successful arrival at the receiving socket. In this case, the data are queued until this acknowledgement is received by the sending process. When these two processes no longer need to communicate, the sending socket must be closed. The receiving socket can also be closed if there are no other processes that wish to communicate with the receiving process. Because socket implementations are based on TCP/IP protocol suite, they are usually used as interfaces to its protocols, for example, TCP, UDP, IP, and ICMP. Depending on the protocols they are interfacing to, sockets can be classified into three types: (1) *datagram*, (2) *stream*, and (3) *raw sockets*.

Datagram sockets are sockets that provide an interface to *UDP (User Datagram Protocol)*. UDP is an unreliable connectionless protocol of TCP/IP protocol suite

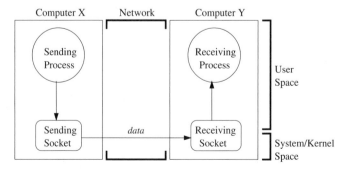

**Figure 1.8**    Interprocess communication using sockets.

which delivers data as limited-size packets called *datagrams*. UDP is unreliable because it gives no guarantee on the successful arrival of its datagrams. UDP always calculates the *checksums* (i.e., a code which is a function of the correct datagram content included in its datagram) of datagrams to determine whether or not they have been received successfully. However, UDP makes no attempt to detect duplicate datagrams nor it has any ordering on the transmission of multiple datagrams. UDP also does not have any built-in acknowledgement and datagram retransmission mechanisms. A datagram might be lost, sent more than once, or arrived in wrong order. The connectionless nature of UDP means that a sending socket is not tied to any particular receiving socket. The same sending socket can be used to send datagrams to multiple receiving sockets without any re-initialization required.

Figure 1.9 describes the code fragments of two communicating sockets. Both processes create their sockets using the `socket` function which returns I/O descriptors. The first argument tells the function to use the Internet as the communication domain, where the latter indicates the socket is a datagram socket. The last argument is used to specify the use of a particular protocol. Setting the argument with value 0 lets the system to choose a suitable protocol. The next step is for both processes to call `bind` to associate their sockets to the process addresses. The sending process sends its data by using `sendto`, while the receiving process receives this data by calling `recvfrom`. Notice that since UDP is connectionless, sending the data to the receiving process requires `sendto` to be specified with the receiving process address, while receiving process with `recvfrom` always receives the sending process address. The advantage of this type of socket over others is its speed. Datagram sockets are fast because they have no overhead of error detection mechanisms. The problem of this approach is that there is a limit to the amount of data that can be sent in a datagram, and its unreliable nature.

Stream sockets are sockets that provide an interface to *TCP (Transmission Control Protocol)*. TCP is a reliable connection-oriented protocol of TCP/IP protocol suite which delivers data in byte streams. Data sent to the receiving process are guaranteed to arrive successfully in the order of which the data are sent without any errors or duplication. Before communication between two processes commences, a connection between their sockets must be established and valid until one of its sockets is closed.

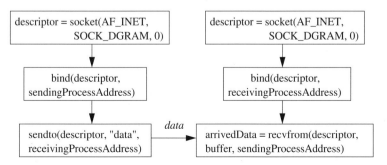

**Figure 1.9**   Code fragments of a sending and receiving datagram socket.

Both the sending and the receiving sockets are bound to each other. This eliminates the possibility of using the sending socket to deliver data to processes other than those of the receiving socket. Data are read immediately by the receiving process in the same order as they are written. However, the data are placed in a queue with a limited size. Thus, the receiver socket blocks if the queue is empty, while the sender blocks when the queue is full.

Figure 1.10 illustrates the code fragment of two communicating sockets. Similar to datagram sockets, both the sending and the receiving processes must create their sockets by calling `socket`. However, the second argument must be specified with `SOCK_STREAM` to indicate the use of streams for delivering the data. The receiving process must `bind` its socket and calls `listen` on the receiving socket. The function indicates that the socket will be a *listening socket*, that is, a passive socket that waits for any incoming request for connections. It also specifies how many waiting connections can be queued by the listening socket. The sending process transfers the request to establish a new connection to the receiving process by calling `connect`. The receiving process calls `accept` to accept the request and create a new connection. The function returns an I/O descriptor, associated with a sending process whose address is passed by this function. This descriptor can be used by `recvfrom` function to receive data sent with `write` function. The total number of bytes of data that need to be received is specified in `dataSize`, while the total number of bytes successfully accepted is returned into `totBytesReceived`. Notice that since the sending socket is bound to a particular receiving socket, the address of the receiving socket is no longer need to be specified every time data are sent. This the reason why the `write` function does not have any parameter for the receiving process's address.

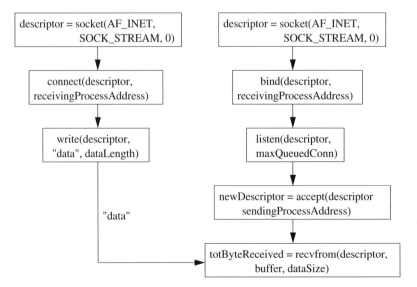

**Figure 1.10**   Code fragments of a sending and receiving stream socket.

The last type of socket, that is, raw sockets, provide an interface to the lower layer protocols such as *IP (Internet Protocol)* and *ICMP (Internet Control Message Protocol)*. Unlike the previous two socket types, raw sockets do not provide the conventional peer-to-peer services. Instead, the use of raw sockets is at a lower level, that is, to read and write the content of datagrams. Such capability enables raw sockets to be used to test new protocols, analyze the content of datagrams, and to manipulate advanced features of existing protocols.

Compared to other middleware, sockets are too primitive to be used in developing a distributed system software. The services they provide are aimed solely at transferring and receiving data successfully. The socket's primitiveness is the main reason of its lack of higher level facilities such those used for marshalling, unmarshalling data, error detection, and error recovery. These facilities must be built from scratch by developers on top of the existing socket primitive facilities. Another problem also arises when the software needs to be used in a platform different from where it was developed and tested. Porting the software to another platform may require the target platform to have the same socket implementation, due to its lack of code portability. Nevertheless, the socket's intimacy with the lower level details is not always a liability. Developers have complete control of a distributed system software built using sockets, down to the lowest software level. This is potentially powerful for optimizing the software or any other tasks that require low-level access to the sent and received data.

### 1.2.2   Remote Procedure Call

RPC or Remote Procedure Call is a type of middleware which allows clients to use services of the servers by calling their procedure calls in a similar manner to those found in normal programs. Both normal and remote procedure calls are usually synchronous and follow the request–reply mechanism, in which a client is blocked until its server responds to the call. Asynchronous implementation of RPC is also available. The control of execution in this RPC is returned immediately to the client after the request has been delivered to the server.

RPC as a concept has been around since the mid-1970s. It was later introduced by *OSF (Open Software Foundation)* as part of *DCE (Distributed Computing Environment)* standard in the mid 1980s. The idea of RPC centers around its view of distributed system software as a set of software components running on different computers, but connected by a common network. Each of the software components is a server which provides its services through a set of procedure calls, analogous to procedure calls in a conventional software. However, unlike a traditional procedure call, which takes place in the same address space, a procedure call in RPC spans two different address spaces (i.e., client's and server's) and is mediated by a common network. The control of execution is passed between these two address spaces according to the flow of execution.

Procedure calls of a server can be made accessible to clients in two ways. The first approach is to extend an existing programming language with all the necessary notations for describing the procedures. The advantage of this approach is that the programming language specific features can be used. The disadvantage is that their code is too closely tied to a particular programming language, making the code not portable. An example of RPC implementation of this approach is Cedar RPC. The second approach is to use a dedicated programming language called *Interface Defini-tion Language* (IDL). A description of the procedure calls is written in this language, which will used to develop *stub* and *skeleton*. A *stub* is a client-side procedure that marshals parameters of procedure calls and unmarshal parameters of their replies. A *skeleton* is a server-side procedure that unmarshalls parameters of procedure calls and marshalls parameters of their replies. The advantage of having IDL is that it is independent of any particular programming language. The only drawback is that no programming language specific features can be used. An example of this type of RPC implementation is the popular *ONC* (Open Network Computing) RPC, developed by Sun Microsystems.

Figure 1.11 illustrates the flow of a procedure call in a RPC software compared to the one in a conventional software. In conventional software the calling procedure plays the role of a client, while the called procedure is the server. The calling procedure might pass some parameters to the called procedures. After the called procedures are executed, it could return some results to the calling procedure. In contrast, a procedure call in an RPC software requires stub and skeleton to perform marshalling and unmarshalling of parameters and results. Request messages and their message replies are sent via a common network, also with the help of the stub and the skeleton.

RPC has three types of message delivery guarantees. The first one is *retry request message*, which guarantees the request to be retransmitted the request until either a

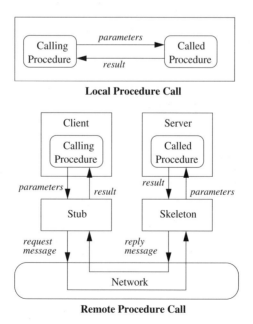

**Figure 1.11**   A procedure call in an RPC and conventional software.

reply is received or the server is assumed to have failed. The second guarantee is *duplicate filtering*, which filters out any duplication, that is, retransmission of previously received request messages. The last guarantee is *retransmission of reply messages*, which retransmits lost message replies without re-executing their procedure calls by keeping a history of those message replies. These guarantees characterize RPC call semantics which determine how request and reply messages are transmitted.

There are three call semantics in RPC. The first one is *"maybe call semantic,"* which has no message delivery guarantee at all. A request message is sent only once and could be lost since there is no retry request message guarantee exists. If the message does reach its destinations and if for some reasons the message is retransmitted, the latter request messages will not be discarded. Furthermore, since this semantic does not guarantee retransmission of message replies, all retransmitted requests will be processed. The next call semantic is *"at-least-once,"* which retransmits a message request when it is lost, has no duplicate filtering, and process all the retransmitted requests. As a result, a request sent with this semantic is guaranteed to be executed at least once, with all retransmitted messages will be processed. The last call semantic is *"at-most-once,"* which guarantees a request to be executed at most once. The request message is retransmitted when it is lost, all duplicates are filtered out, and if the request has been processed previously, its reply message will be taken from the reply message history instead from the result of the target procedure execution.

An RPC program is usually written in C. Below is an example of an RPC program which displays a message on the server side. Its IDL declaration would be:

```
program MESSAGEPROG {
    version PRINTMESSAGEVERS { int PRINTMESSAGE(string) = 1;
    } = 1;
} = 0x20951085;
```

This IDL describes a program called MESSAGEPROG with a version number 1 and program number 0x20951085. Its PRINTMESSAGE remote procedure accepts a string parameter, returns the execution status, and has a procedure number of 1. The client's code fragment below calls the server's remote procedure:

```
int main(int argc,char *argv[]) {
    ...
    CLIENT *clnt;
    int    *result;
    ...
    server  = argv[1];
    message = argv[2];
    ...
    clnt = clnt_create(server, MESSAGEPROG, PRINTMESSAGEVERS, "tcp");
    ...
    result = printmessage_1(&message, clnt);
    ...
```

```
if(*result == 0) {
fprintf(stderr, "%s:could not print your message\n", argv[0]);
exit(1);
}
 ...
}
```

`clnt_create` creates a client handle similar to a socket. The name of the server that the client wants to communicate with is specified in the first parameter. The next two parameters are the name of the program as declared in the IDL file and the program version number. The last parameter indicates what protocol should be used to talk to the server. Once the handle is created, the remote procedure can be invoked by the C function of format `procedureName_versionNo`, for example, `printmessage_1`. Details of the `printmessage_1` function are given below:

```
...
int *printmessage_1(char **msg,struct svc_req *req)
{
static int result;
printf("%s\n", *msg);
result = 1;
return (&result);
}
```

Notice that the function has little differences compared to a normal C function.

The strength of RPC lies in its ease of use, portability, and robustness [88]. Its ease of use is the result of the higher level of abstraction that it provides to the developers and RPC's similarity with normal procedure calls. RPC insulates the lower level details such as marshalling and unmarshalling parameters, freeing developers to concentrate solely on the software logic. Software developed using RPC is easier to be ported compared to sockets. Some RPC implementations even support location transparency. The robustness of RPC-based solutions have been proved in mission-critical applications that require scalability, fault tolerance and reliability. Despite these strengths, RPC has several weaknesses [88][101]. RPC is inflexible to change since it assumes a static relationship between client and server at run-time. This causes client and server codes to be tightly coupled to each other. Another weakness is that RPC is based on the procedural/structured programming model, which is already outdated with the object oriented model. The next weakness is RPC's lack of location transparency. Developers should not be able to determine whether or not the procedure being called is remote or local. For example, developers must themselves be careful not to pass a C reference to a remote procedure. This is because a C reference points to local memory address which has no meaning on the server side. The use of a weakly programming language of C in most RPC implementations could cause problems in marshalling and unmarshalling the passed parameters. The last problem is RPC's inability to handle communication between one client and multiple servers, except when a separate connection is used for each communication. This is because RPC assumes all communications are one-to-one, that is, a client talks to only one server at a time.

### 1.2.3    Remote Method Invocation

RMI or Remote Method Invocation, is a Java-based middleware that allows methods of Java objects located in a *Java Virtual Machine (JVM)* (i.e., a self-contained Java operating environment which simulates a separate computer) to be invoked from another JVM even when this JVM is across a network. RMI was introduced by JavaSoft with JDK 1.1 and is essentially object-oriented Java RPC. Both use IDL to describe the distributed system software interfaces (i.e., methods for RMI and procedures for RPC) involved. The description is later used to produce stub and skeleton. As Figure 1.12 illustrates, the flow of a request is also not much different from its RPC counterpart.

However, RMI does have some differences compared to RPC. The first one is that, IDL in RPC is usually based on procedural C, while IDL is RMI is based on object-oriented Java. Server objects must register themselves with *rmiregistry* to advertise their availability to clients. A RMI client makes use of *rmiregistry* to locate a particular object. Once the object is found, the client will receive a reference to the wanted object. The registry allows developers to manage the availability of all server objects in one place. Java garbage collector handles memory management of these server objects. This garbage collector uses a remote reference counting scheme to determine which server objects can be removed from memory. The scheme counts the total number of connections for each server object in the JVM which is called the *reference count*. Every time a connection is established to an object, its reference count is incremented. The number is decremented when the connection is broken or gracefully terminated. If the former occurs, the client must explicitly re-establish the connection since RMI has no automatic reconnection feature.

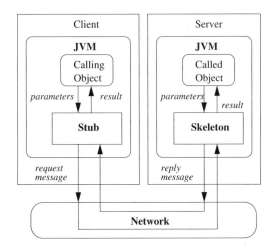

**Figure 1.12**    Simplified view of an object method invocation in RMI.

The following RMI IDL provides an interface description for a server object which prints a person's name on the server, appends the message with "Hello", and returns the message to the client:

```
import java.rmi.*;
public interface SimpleInterface extends Remote {
   String printName(String name) throws RemoteException;
}
```

The above is an interface whose method is printName, accepts a name as a string and throws an exception called RemoteException if the method's execution fails. The implementation of the server object is given below:

```
import java.rmi.*;
import java.rmi.server.*;

public class SimpleServer extends UnicastRemoteObject
     implements SimpleInterface {
  public SimpleServer() throws RemoteException { super(); }
  public String printMessage(String name) throws RemoteException {
     System.out.println(name);
     return("Hello " + name);
  }

  public static void main(String args[]) {
     System.setSecurityManager(new RMISecurityManager());
     try {
          SimpleServer newServer = new SimpleServer();
          System.out.println("SimpleServer attempting to bind
             to the registry");
          Naming.rebind("//numbat.cs.rmit.edu.au:30010/SimpleServer",
             newServer);
          System.out.println("SimpleServer bound in the registry");
     } catch(Exception e) {
          System.out.println("SimpleServer error: "  + e.getMessage());
          e.printStackTrace();
     }
  }
}
```

SimpleServer class must inherit from UniCast class and implement the SimpleInterface before it becomes the implementation class of the RMI interface. The implementation of printMessage method appears like any other Java function. Before an instance of SimpleServer object can be accessed to clients, it must be first registered with rmiregistry. In the above example, main function of SimpleServer is the class responsible to perform this task. *main* registers the object as residing at a host called numbat.cs.rmit.edu.au, with port number 30010 under the name of `SimpleServer`. For the client side, each of the `SimpleClient` class below acts as the client of the `SimpleServer` object:

```
import java.rmi.*;
public class SimpleClient {
   private static SimpleInterface server = null;
   public static void main(String args[]) {
     try {
       server = (SimpleInterface)
       Naming.lookup("//numbat.cs.rmit.edu.au:30010/SimpleServer");
       System.out.println(server.printMessage("Amazigh"));
     } catch(Exception e) {
        System.out.println("SimpleClient error: " +
                           e.getMessage());
        e.printStackTrace();
     }
   }
}
```

SimpleClient first attempts to locate a server object called `SimpleServer` which resides on a hostname of `numbat.cs.rmit.edu.au` and port number of 30010. Upon its successful reference acquisition, the client calls the object's `printMessage` method with its name parameter passed with value of `Amazigh`. Finally, the appended message is returned and displayed on the client's screen as `Hello Amazigh`

Similar to RPC, RMI's main strength lies in its higher level of abstraction it provides compared to sockets. RMI gives a better transparency of low-level details compared to RPC and sockets. RMI software inherits its platform independent and code portability from Java which help to address the problem of heterogeneities in distributed systems. However, its Java-based nature works against RMI when legacy applications exist. Non-Java objects cannot communicate with Java objects via RMI. All legacy applications must be rewritten in Java before they can gain the benefit of RMI. At the end, RMI is suitable only when all Java solutions are used.

### 1.2.4   Distributed Computing Environment

DCE or Distributed Computing Environment, is an OSF middleware standard designed to provide a distributed framework based on a structured/procedural model. DCE 1.0 was released in 1992 with its implementations starting to appear in the following year. Examples of DCE implementations are DCE++ from DEC and HP's OODCE.

Figure 1.13 depicts the DCE architecture which is divided into two parts: *DCE Executive* and *DCE Extended Services*. **DCE executive** consists of several components. The first one is the directory service, which enables the control and management of administrative domains, called *cells*. Services of the directory services are `Cell Directory Services (CDE)`, `Global Directory Services (GDS)`,

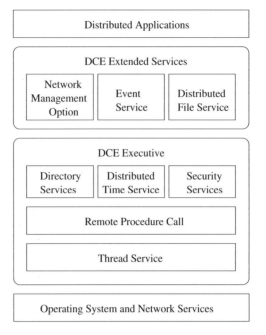

**Figure 1.13**   OSF DCE Architecture.

Domain Name Service (DNS), and Global Directory Agent (GDA). The second one is Distributed Time Service (DTS) is a DCE component which synchonizes time on all hosts in a DCE cell, as well as between cells, using Universal Time Co-ordinated (UTC) standard. *DCE Executive component* is the security service that performs authentication, authorization, integrity, and privacy for all DCE applications. Security service authenticates clients and servers by using Kerberos V5. Authorization in security service allows servers to use access a control list to determine whether a client is permitted to access a given service. Security service maintains the integrity of information in all the received messages by using checksum. The security service protects the privacy of sensitive information during their transmissions from clients to servers with the use of DES encryption. DCE's thread service is based on the POSIX 100.34a draft 4 standard and supports the creation and management of multiple threads of controls within a client or a server.

DCE extended services also consists of several components. The first two components, that is, *network management option* and *event service*, will be offered in the future DCE versions. Network management option provides facilities to access management information using Simple Network Management Protocol (SNMP) and Common Management Information Protocol (CMIP). Event service gives system and user applications a common way to generate, forward, filter, and log events. The last component is Distributed File Service (DFS) which allows files of different cells to be shared in a single logical file system through directory services without the knowledge of location and local access procedures. DFS also supports file replications, fault-tolerance, and log based recovery from hardware failures.

DCE excels over other previously explained middleware because of the level, breadth, and openness of its solutions. The first strength is obvious since DCE offers more than just the ability of clients to call remote procedure of servers, that is, RPC. It also provides a set of services at the level higher than other middleware. These services are developed on top of RPC which are aimed at achieving specific goals. For example, security services are built on top of RPC for goals such as protecting sensitive information from unauthorized access, and so on. DCE is a more complete solution compared to other middleware, due to the breadth of services offered. This is compared to sockets that are only for sending data between clients and servers, RPC, which facilitate procedure calling, and RMI, which is used only for calling methods of remote objects. DCE is open since, compared to RMI, it's a standard, not a proprietary technology. DCE's main weakness is its use of outdated procedural paradigms. Other weaknesses include its limited number of popular implementations and lack of widespread usage.

### 1.2.5 Distributed Component Object Model

DCOM, or Distributed Component Object Model, is a middleware developed by Microsoft that provides a distributed framework based on object-oriented model. It is the distributed extension to the *Component Object Model* (COM), which provides an *Object Remote Procedure Call* (ORPC) on top of DCE RPC [20]. COM itself is a component software architecture that promotes reusability by allowing applications and systems to be built from binary components supplied by different software vendors. DCOM is the latest incarnation of Microsoft's object technology which starts its live from mid-1980s [67] as Dynamic Data Exchange (DDE), that is, an interprocess communication protocol designed by Microsoft that allows applications to exchange messages via shared memory. Later, it evolved to Object Linking and Embedding (OLE) (a compound object model for linking and embedding objects created by different applications), to COM, and finally to DCOM. As illustrated by Figure 1.14, DCOM services are divided into two parts: OLE and COM.

COM provides the underlying object system on which OLE services rely upon. COM services are *uniform data transfer*, *monikers*, and *persistent storage*. Uniform data transfer service is a COM service that provides the basic facilities to exchange data between applications. It extends the windows clipboard to handle OLE objects. Moniker service provides the mechanism to name objects for their identifications. Persistent storage service allows objects to be stored in the disk. It is different from traditional file service, due to its compound model. The model allows the containment relationship of multiple objects within a container to be preserved.

OLE part contains three services: (1) *compound documents*, (2) *drag-and-drop*, and (3) *automation*. Compound documents service provides the ability to link information in a document through three services: *in-place activation*, *linking*, and *embedding*. In-place activation enables container applications to hold component objects, permitting the user to manipulate component application operations. Linking

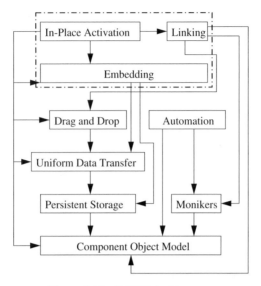

**Figure 1.14**   DCOM Architecture.

enables multiple applications to share common data. Changes to the common data is reflected to all sharing applications whenever the data are changed. Embedding allows container objects to have separate copies of the same data. The next service is drag-and-drop, which permits users to add OLE objects by dragging and dropping them into their containers. Automation service is an OLE service that allows developers to reuse existing components for building a new application by exposing their operations.

Unlike previous middleware, DCOM is an object-oriented based middleware. A DCOM application comprises of a set of objects that provides the application services via methods of these objects. DCOM follows the RPC and RMI approach of using IDL to declare the methods which should be made accessible to clients. DCOM maintains a separation between interfaces and their implementations, that is, DCOM objects. Each of the implementation classes can implement multiple interfaces, but each of them must inherit from *IUnknown* base interface:

```
// Inside unknwn.idl
[ local,
  object,
 ·uuid(00000000-0000-0000-0000-000000000046)
  pointer_default(unique)
]

interface IUnknown {
    typedef [unique] IUnknown *LPUNKNOWN;
    HRESULT QueryInterface([in] REFIID riid,
                           [out, iid_is(riid)] void **ppvObject);
```

```
.  ULONG    AddRef();
   ULONG    Release();
}
```

As depicted above, IUnknown is identified with its unique *Interface Identifier (IID)*. An IID is a 128-bit long *Globally Unique Identifier (GUID)*, which is assigned to each DCOM interface. *IUnknown*'s *QueryInterface* is used to determine if a DCOM object specified in ppvObject parameter supports the interface whose IID given to riid parameter. This function returns HRESULT, which is similar with Java's void. However, it is used to determine whether the function has been successfully executed. The last two functions are used to manage the reference count of the DCOM object implementing this interface. AddRef increases the reference count, while the Release function decreases its value. Both of these return the updated reference count as unsigned long.

Consider the IDL of a DCOM program which allows clients to increase and decrease counter on the server side:

```
import "unknwn.idl";

[ object, uuid(3CFDB283-CCC5-11D0-BA0B-00A0C90DF8BC)]
interface ICounter : IUnknown {
    HRESULT getCount([out] int countVal);
    HRESULT increase([in]  int increment);
    HRESULT decrease([in]  int decrement);
}
```

ICounter interface needs to refer to "unknwn.idl" file for the IUnknown interface declaration. This interface has only three methods: getCount, which sets the variable passed to countVal with the current value of the counter, increase, which adds the value passed to increment parameter to the counter value, and decrease, which subtracts the value passed to decrement from the counter value. The CCounter class below implements the ICounter interface:

```
#include "counter.hh" // IDL generated interface header file

class CCounter : public ICounter {
    public:
        ULONG   __stdcall AddRef();
        ULONG   __stdcall Release();
        HRESULT __stdcall QueryInterface(REFIID riid, void **ppv);
        HRESULT __stdcall getCount(int *countVal);
        HRESULT __stdcall increase(int increment);
        HRESULT __stdcall decrease(int decrement);
    private:
        int    myCountVal;
        ULONG myRefCount; // The reference count attribute
}
```

The actual implementation of this class is shown below:

```
ULONG CCounter::AddRef() { return(++myRefCount)};
ULONG CCounter::Release() {
   if(--myRefCount != 0) { return(myRefCount); }
   delete(this);
   return(0);
}


HRESULT CCounter::QueryInterface(REFIID riid, void **ppv) {
   if(riid == IID_IUnknown) { *ppv = (IUnknown*) this; }
   else if(riid == IID_IDisplayer) { *ppv = (ICounter*) this; }
      else { *ppv = NULL;
         return(E_NOINTERFACE);
   }
   AddRef();
   return(S_OK);
}


HRESULT CCounter::getCount(int *countVal) {
   (*countVal) = myCountVal;
   return(S_OK);
}


HRESULT CCounter::increase(int increment) {
   myCountVal = myCountVal + increment;
   return(S_OK);
}


HRESULT CCounter::decrease(int decrement) {
   myCountVal = myCountVal - decrement;
   return(S_OK);
}
```

AddRef function simply adds myRefCount variable by one. The function Release subtracts one from myRefCount and removes the object from memory if the reference count has reached zero. QueryInterface function sets the ppv parameter with the appropriate implementing object, depending on the IID passed to riid parameter. The rest of the functions are similar to normal C++ functions. The only difference is that, it returns S_OK to the client, which notifies the successful execution of the function called. The client code for the counter application is as follows:

```
#include <stdlib.h>
#include <iostream.h>
#include "counter.hh"

int main(void) {
   // Local declarations
```

```
IUnknown *pUnknown;
ICounter *pCounter;
int      counterVal = 0;

// Initialize server
CoInitialize(NULL);

// Instantiate a DCOM class
CoCreateInstance(CLSID_Counter, NULL,
                 CLSCTX_INPROC_SERVER,
                 IID_IUnknown,
                 (**void) &pUnknown);

// Check if the object supports ICounter interface
pUnknown->QueryInterface(IID_ICounter,
                 (void**) &pCounter);

// Perform and verify getCount function execution
pCounter->getCount(&counterVal);

count << "Current counter value is " << counterVal << endl;

// Perform and verify increase function execution
pCounter->increase(10);

// Perform and verify decrease function execution
pCounter->decrease(5);

// Perform and verify getCount function execution
pCounter->getCount(&counterVal);

cout << "Current counter value is " << counterVal << endl;

// Decrease the object's reference counter
pUnknown->Release();

// Remove server initializations
CoUninitialize();

return(EXIT_SUCCESS);
}
```

All DCOM library functions in the above sample code starts with Co prefix. The first function executed is CoInitialize, which prepares the client for processing. CoCreateInstance is the next DCOM function executed. It creates a new instance of CCounter, which will be cast to the CCounter object by the QueryInterface function. Later, getCount is executed and returns the current count value. increase is then executed to add ten to the count value. This is followed by the execution of decrease to subtract five from the count value. The getCount is re-executed to display the last count value before the client finishes. Release function's execution decreases the reference count to notify server that the client no longer needs this object. Finally, CoUninitialize is called before the client terminates.

Compared to sockets, RMI, and RPC, DCOM provides a higher-level abstraction for developing distributed software. DCOM architecture has a set of services (e.g. automation) built on top of low-level services like persistent storage service, similar to those specified in OSF DCE. DCOM's is built on top of proven desktop system architecture which is ideal for for desktop centric distributed systems. Microsoft's dominance in the personal computer industry gives DCOM a considerable influence in middleware. DCOM's architecture is well defined, with its specification being authoritative [100]. However, despite that, it is now managed by an Open Group affiliate called Active Group, the perception of DCOM as being Microsoft's proprietary technology remains. Microsoft still has the power to define DCOM standards before passing them the Active group for approval. This negative image plays an adverse role to DCOM's wider acceptance in the middleware industry. The DCOM's focus on desktops makes it problematic to extend DCOM to enterprise architecture. Although DCOM has been redefined for the enterprise level, its design does not gracefully reflect this. DCOM architecture is not well-partitioned because the boundaries between its layers are not clearly defined. All programs written in DCOM run best only on Microsoft-based products. Some DCOM implementations are already available on non-Microsoft platforms, but these will inevitably be hindered by inadequate compiler, tool, and run-time support [100].

## 1.3  SUMMARY

A distributed system is a collection of autonomous computers linked by a network and equipped with distributed system software. Distributed systems might have some of the following characteristics, depending on their designs: resource sharing, openness, concurrency, scalability, and transparency. The existence of resource sharing, openness, and transparency plays an important role in addressing heterogeneities of the system. The distributed systems model provides the benefit of shareability, expandability, local autonomy, improved performance, improved reliability and availability, and potential cost reduction. However, the distributed systems model relies heavily on a common network for communications. The complexities of distributed systems make it difficult to develop a software that can exploit multiple computers and hide the system heterogeneities. The higher possibility of security breaches is another disadvantage. The easy access and dispersed nature of distributed systems are causing problems in providing an effective security mechanism for the model.

Distributed systems use middleware to connect different kinds of applications and provide distribution transparency to its connected applications. They are also used to bridge heterogeneities that occurred in the systems. Examples of important middleware are sockets, RPC, RMI, DCOM, and CORBA. Sockets are peer-to-peer communication endpoints. Sockets solution is the most primitive middleware compared to others, making it unsuitable for distributed system software development. RPC and RMI provide a higher level of facilities than sockets. However, RPC is based on the old procedural model, whereas RMI are based on Java. DCOM and CORBA are based on an object-oriented model. DCOM is a desktop-centric middleware developed by Microsoft, whereas CORBA is an enterprise-focused middleware standard maintained by OMG. A more complete coverage of CORBA and its concepts are explained in the next chapter.

## 1.4  REVIEW QUESTIONS

- What is a distributed system? How does a distributed system differ from a centralized system?
- Why is a good distributed system software important to a distributed system?
- What are the characteristics of distributed systems? Explain the relationship between these characteristics and the system heterogeneities.
- Why does the effect of disruptions to a subset of computers in a distributed system influence only some resources it manages rather than all of them?
- Why is a distributed system considered as less secure compared to a centralized system?
- How is the separate nature of distributed systems helpful in improving the overall performance?
- What is middleware? What does it do? What are the OSI layers that middleware replaces in the overall distributed system software?
- Why is developing a distributed system software using sockets much harder than building them using CORBA?
- What is the major difference between RMI and RPC?
- What are the strengths and weaknesses of DCE and DCOM?

## 1.5  EXERCISES

- One of the benefits of distributed systems is the potential cost reduction they provide. What are the factors that could prevent this benefit from being realized?
- If reliable connections are possible with stream sockets, then are unreliable and connectionless datagram sockets still needed?
- A distributed system consists of multiple computers dispersed at different locations which are connected together by a network. Discuss why this becomes the source of problems for distributed applications that rely on time accuracy.
- Discuss cases where distributed systems are not suitable to use as the model for developing a computer system.

# CHAPTER 2

# Introduction to CORBA

This chapter provides an inside view of CORBA with details of its different elements such as the CORBA reference object model and the Object Management Architecture (OMA). It also goes into details on some of the major elements of the CORBA architecture: Object Request Broker (ORB), Interface Definition Language (IDL), Interface and Implementation Repositories, and object adaptors. We show how object binding works in CORBA environments, and this is done by using either transient and persistent object references. At the end of the chapter, the CORBA technologies are compared with related technologies (e.g., DCE, DCOM and RMI).

## 2.1 OVERALL PICTURE

The explosion of growth in the computing industry has developed an increasingly pronounced need for the sharing of computing resources. The days where we had a stand-alone desktop, the use of which depends on the local applications installed are gone, and distributed computing is here. Users want access to information stored in remote systems, and mechanisms which allow this facility are becoming prolific. CORBA, an acronym for Common Object Request Broker Architecture, is a standard adopted by the OMG (Object Management Group) to enable interoperability between applications in heterogeneous distributed environments, without regard for where they are located. Other solutions to the distributed integration problem are Microsoft's DCOM (Distributed Component Object Model), and DCE (Distributed Computing Environment). This book focuses on the technical details of CORBA technology because it provides open communication between different systems and does this in a standard manner. We believe that this standard may help vendors, developers and researchers in providing acceptable solutions to the problems related to software interoperability. This is the main reason for choosing to describe CORBA and explaining in more technical detail the issues and solutions related to this technology.

OMG is a group of vendors who jointly developed a common way to interact with distributed objects. The group was founded in April 1989 by twelve commercial vendors: IBM, BNR Europe Ltd., Expersoft Corp., ICL plc, Iona Technologies Ltd., DEC, Hewlett-Packard, HyperDesk Corp., NCR, Novell USG, Object Design Inc., and SunSoft. Since its formation, the OMG has grown to more than 600 members whose goal is to provide a common architectural framework, across heterogeneous hardware platforms and operating systems, for inter-communication of application objects. For that, they released specifications for the Common Object Request Broker Architecture (CORBA) [70] and other related technologies. The CORBA architecture is to be vendor, platform and language neutral. The Interface Definition Language (IDL), as the specification language for the interfaces of objects, is the "glue."

CORBA is an open distributed object computing infrastructure. Its objective is to automate many common network programming tasks such as object registration, location, and activation; request demultiplexing; framing and error-handling; parameter marshalling and un-marshalling; and operation dispatching. This automation of what are usually networking functions is done with a software intermediary called the Object Request Broker (ORB). It sits on the host between the data and the application layer (i.e., one level lower than the application layer—level 7 in the OSI model) and it handles, in a transparent manner, request messages from clients (which can be user or server objects) and servers (i.e., implementations which provide specific services). The first implementations of the ORBs under the CORBA 1 specifications were not concerned with representing objects in a meaningful way outside of the boundary of the ORB. The CORBA 2 specifications address interoperability at a higher level, that is, object representation across the boundaries of ORBs. By implementing interoperability, the boundaries of a given ORB need not limit the scope of an application.

The CORBA paradigm is based on a combination of two existing methodologies. The first, distributed client–server computing, is based in part on message-passing systems most commonly found in UNIX-based environments. The second methodology is object-oriented programming. An ORB plays the role of an object-oriented remote procedure call (RPC) application program interface. It provides common services, such as basic messaging and an RPC-type communication between clients and servers, directory services, meta-description, and location and host transparency. CORBA is based on a peer-to-peer communication model and supports both asynchronous and a limited version of asynchronous communications. Location transparency refers to the fact that clients do not need to be aware of where the servers are located. ORBs are responsible for finding these servers, based on information contained within client requests (such as references). Host transparency is maintained within CORBA where ORBs can access and make calls to different CORBA objects on various machines. If a client application (process) is running on one host, then that host's ORB is able to locate data in a different place on that host or on a different machine altogether. This is achieved largely through the different repositories (e.g., interface and implementation repositories) and the information contained within object references.

The presence of object-oriented methodology in CORBA is the result of necessity, not of choice. Object-oriented programming is merely a different, convenient way to explain and develop a program, and the adoption of an object-oriented approach is motivated by the desire for software development with reusable components that interact with one another through well-defined interfaces. In CORBA, three basic features of object-oriented programming are used. First, polymorphism among objects is allowed. The ORB makes different (interface of) objects and their associated implementations independent and reusable by different applications. Second, encapsulation is utilized. Each client application knows nothing about the implementation it accesses; it merely makes requests of the respective objects through the ORB, and the object retrieves the data for the application. Third, data inheritance is provided. If one description of an object is designed to interface with an ORB, any object derived from that parent object will preserve its parent's interface.

A CORBA object has an interface and an implementation. The interface is not bound to a specific implementation programming language, but is instead written in a special-purpose Interface Definition Language (IDL), which, in turn, translates to different constructs in the different implementation languages via language mappings. This makes it possible to call an object implementation written in a given language (e.g., Cobol) from a client program written in another language (e.g., Smalltalk). As per the CORBA 2.0 standard, the ORBs from different vendors are able to interoperate, because the CORBA 2.0 specifies the protocols that should be used for ORB-to-ORB communication. The most common CORBA protocol is the IIOP (-Internet Inter ORB Protocol) which is a specialized version of GIOP (-General Inter ORB Protocol).

In summary, CORBA provides several advantages over existing distributed systems. From the software development point of view, developers can use CORBA to distribute applications across client–server networks. Instead of having hundreds of thousands of lines of code running on computers with dumb terminals, smaller, more robust applications that communicate between file servers and workstations are now necessary. CORBA keeps the distribution of applications simple; a plug-and-play architecture is used to distribute the client–server applications. The programmer then can write applications that work independently across platforms and networks. CORBA also enables integration of different software applications without a need to rely on low-level communication facilities. Other benefits of CORBA are:

- It interworks well with different middlewares, including Microsoft distributed system (DCOM).
- The CORBA Services provide a set of optional extensions that address areas that the core itself cannot address: for example, transactions, naming, events, and trading. It is integrated with other technologies, such as databases, reliable messaging systems, threads, and user interface generation systems.
- It applies to many different vertical markets. The core level is applicable to all of these, and specialized implementations can be provided in areas such as real time and embedded systems. The upper layers, both the CORBA services and the CORBA facilities, can be applied differently in the various vertical markets. The OMG has set up a number of active special interest groups to address these special needs.
- It supports both static and dynamic usage. The dynamic parts are more difficult, but they need to be used only by a subset of CORBA programmers.

- IDL is mapped separately to each programming language, so usage of each language is natural; for example, in object-oriented languages the normal steps for implementing and using classes still apply.
- There is an agreed protocol in phase, IIOP, for facilitating communication between ORBs. It is a well-established and widely adopted standard that is written and maintained by an open procedure.

## 2.2    CORBA 1, CORBA 2, AND CORBA 3

CORBA 1.1 was adopted in 1991 by the OMG. CORBA 1.1 introduced the IDL (Interface Definition Language) which is the language through which the interface for all CORBA applications is defined. In the earlier versions of CORBA (e.g., CORBA 1.0., 1.1, etc.), OMG focused on the specification of the core part of CORBA, that is, the ORB, as well as a few basic services (such as Naming, Trading, and Event services). OMG did not provide for interoperability between ORB implementations, that is, a possible way to make invocations, whether they are static or dynamic, across different ORBs, not automatically supporting the same language mapping. In later versions, CORBA implementations provided guaranteed out-of-the-box interoperability by means of UNO GIOP hosted on the TCP/IP networking transport service, called IIOP (Internet Inter-ORB Protocol). CORBA 3.0 specifications add a new dimension of capability and ease-of-use to CORBA, and refer to three major categories: (1) Internet integration, (2) quality of service control, and (3) CORBA's component architecture. The focus of this book is on the specifications of CORBA 1 and 2. The CORBA 3 specifications are not yet totally finalized. We will therefore provide an overview of CORBA 3; and details about CORBA 1 and CORBA 2 can be found in Chapters 2 and 5.

The Internet integration specifications enhance CORBA integration with the increasingly popular Internet: security (firewall specification) and naming (Interoperable Name service). The CORBA 3.0 firewall specification defines transport-level firewalls, application-level firewalls, and a bi-directional GIOP connection that is useful for callbacks and event notifications. The Interoperable Name Service defines one URL-format object reference, iioploc, which can be typed into a program to reach defined services at a remote location, including the Naming Service. A second URL format, iiopname, actually invokes the remote Naming Service using the name that the user appends to the URL, and retrieves the IOR of the named object.

The CORBA 3.0 quality of service control includes specifications for asynchronous messaging and quality of service control, and the specifications for minimum, fault-tolerant, and real-time CORBA. The new messaging specification defines a number of asynchronous and time-independent invocation modes for CORBA, and allows both static and dynamic invocations to use every mode. Asynchronous invocation results may be retrieved by either polling or callback. The choice is made by the form used by the client in the original invocation. Minimum CORBA is primarily intended for embedded systems. Embedded systems, once they are finalized and burned into chips for production, are fixed, and their interactions with the outside network are predictable—they have no need for the dynamic aspects of CORBA, such as the DII or the interface repository that supports it, which are therefore not included in Minimum CORBA. Real-time CORBA standardizes resource control (e.g., threads, protocols, connections, etc.) by using priority models to achieve predictable behavior for both hard and statistical realtime environments. Fault-tolerance for CORBA is being addressed by an RFP, also in process, for a standard based on entity redundancy, and fault management control.

The CORBA's component model refers to CORBA components and CORBA scripting. CORBA components represent a multi-pronged advance with benefits for programmers, users, and consumers of component software. The three major parts of CORBA components are the following: (1) a container environment that packages transactionality, security, and persistence, and provides interface and event resolution; (2) integration with enterprise JavaBeans; and (3) a software distribution format that enables a CORBA component software marketplace. The CORBA components container environment is persistent, transactional, and secure. For the programmer, these functions are pre-packaged and provided at a higher level of abstraction than the CORBA services provide. This leverages the skills of business programmers who are not necessarily skilled at building transactional or secure applications, who can now use their talents to produce business applications that acquire these necessary attributes automatically. Containers keep track of event types emitted and consumed by components, and provide event channels to carry events. The containers also keep track of the interfaces provided and required by the components they contain, and connect one to another where they fit. CORBA components support multiple interfaces, and the architecture supports navigation among them. Enterprise JavaBeans (EJBs) will act as CORBA components, and can be installed in a CORBA components container. Unlike EBJs, of course, CORBA components can be written in multiple languages and support multiple interfaces.

## 2.3   OBJECT MANAGEMENT GROUP

OMG (Object Management Group) has developed a (i) conceptual model, known as the reference object model, and (ii) a reference architecture, called the Object Management Architecture, which was briefly discussed in Section 2.3.2.The reference object model defines how objects distributed across a heterogeneous environment can be described, while the reference architecture characterizes interactions between those objects.

### 2.3.1   Reference Object Model

This section describes the CORBA object model. Because CORBA is solidly grounded in the fundamentals of object-oriented paradigm, we will first describe the main concepts related to this paradigm, and later introduce those specific to CORBA. Because CORBA deals with distributed environments, some of the concepts of the object-oriented paradigm (e.g., type/class inheritance, polymorphism, etc.) are revised in the CORBA reference object model.

**The Object Paradigm**  This paradigm has been known for several decades and is used in different areas, such as programming languages (e.g., C++, Smalltalk), and databases (e.g., object-oriented databases). There are non "clear" concepts attached to this paradigm as its interpretation differs from one area to another. However, most of the research communities agree that an object model should support the following main concepts: class/type, polymorphism (e.g., overriding, overloading, and late binding), object identity, inheritance, encapsulation, and the concept of complex objects.

- The notions of *class* and *type* are generally used to refer to the same concept. However, there are two types of object-oriented systems: those supporting the concept of class and those supporting the concept of type [2]. In the first category, are systems such as Smalltalk and Gemstone. In the second category, we can find systems such as C++ and Simula.

  A *type* summarizes the common features of a set of objects with the same characteristics. It corresponds to the notion of an abstract data type and has two parts: the interface and the implementation (or implementations). Only the interface part is visible to the users of the type. The implementation part of the object is seen only by the type designer. The type interface consists of the list of operations together with their signatures (i.e., the type of the input parameters and the type of the result). The type implementation has a data part and a procedural part. The data part is the representation of the state of the object (that is the values of its attributes), and the procedural part describes the implementation of the operations (that is the programming code).

  In programming languages, types are used as tools to increase programmer productivity, by ensuring program correctness at compile type (i.e., type checking).

  The concept of *class* is different from that of type. Its specification is the same as that of a type, but it is more of a run-time notion. It contains two aspects [2]: an object factory and an object warehouse. The object factory can be used to create new objects, by calling a specific operation (e.g., constructor in C++), or by cloning some prototype object representation of the class. The object warehouse means that which is attached to the class, that is, a list of objects that are instances of the class. Classes are therefore not used for checking correctness of a program but rather to create and manipulate objects.

- An *object* represents an instance of a class. It is defined as a recording of the values of the type representing the class, with additional information allowing it to be identified independently on its values. This is called object identity.

- An *object identity* is like a memory address which allows it to uniquely identify objects independently from their values. There are two major characteristics of the concept of object identity: (a) an object identity is unique; therefore, there are no two objects with the same object identity, even if they have been deleted, (b) the change of the structure/type or values of objects will not change their object identity.

- *Encapsulation* comes from (i) the need to cleanly distinguish between the specification and the implementation of an operation, and (ii) the need for modularity. Modularity is necessary to structure complex applications. Encapsulation acts like a "rule" allowing only the interface of objects to be visible to clients; the implementation is hidden and therefore not accessible. One of the major advantages of encapsulation is the ability to change the implementation of operations without affecting their interface.

- *Inheritance* represents the ability to re-use types, that is, re-using both the interface and the implementation of types to refine them and to define more specific ones, called sub-types. This subtyping relationship—a relationship between a sub-type and its super-type—is called type inheritance. It defines a hierarchy between types. For example, we can define that $T_{Person}$ is a type representing all people. This type has name and age as attributes (i.e., part of the implementation of the type) and two operations $die()$ and $marry()$ (i.e., the signature of these operations represents the interface of the type, and their implementation code is a part of the implementation of the type). We can create another type $T_{Employee}$ as a special kind of person, who inherits attributes and operations of $T_{Person}$, and has a special attribute salary and a special operation $pay()$.

  So inheritance facilitates better structuring (i.e., factorization of specification and implementation) by allowing re-usability.

- *Overriding*, *overloading* and *late binding* relates to the concept of polymorphism, that is—the ability to associate multiple types of the same operation. The type hierarchy allows re-implementation of the same operation for different types (called overriding). For example, a single (abstract) operation $marry()$ can have two different behaviors, one in the the type $T_{Person}$ and another one at the type $T_{Employee}$. At run-time, the system will be able to determine the appropriate implementation to use when the operation $marry()$ is invoked (and this called late binding). Therefore, it is not necessary to check the type of object who called the operation at compile-time. Finally, overloading allows the definition of several implementations of the same operation within the same type.

***CORBA Reference Object Model***   The CORBA object model is similar to the one presented earlier; however, there are a few major differences, in particular, regarding the meaning of the different concepts. For example, because CORBA deals with distribution of processes or/and data, the concept of inheritance defined in object-oriented models needs to be re-defined. The inheritance we defined earlier is not appropriate in heterogeneous distributed environments (like CORBA) because it models the type inheritance, that is, the inheritance of specifications (operations) and the inheritance of implementations (data and code of operations). Because a type in CORBA is defined only as the part related to the clients, the operations, then the inheritance of operations seems to be the logical one to have in CORBA environments. The inheritance of implementation is not considered because the implementation part of types (the data and the code of operations) is implemented in different programming paradigms, such as C++, C, Java. Therefore, inheriting the implementation part of the types is possible, however not often required.

The CORBA object model is abstract in that it is not directly realized by any particular technology. A CORBA object system is a collection of objects that isolates the requesters of services (clients) from the providers of services by a well-defined encapsulating interface. In particular, clients are isolated from the implementations of services as data representations and executable code. The CORBA object model is defined as two models: one model (i.e., client model) which describes the object semantics, that is, the concepts that are meaningful to clients, including concepts such as object creation and identity, requests and operations and types and signatures; the other model (implementation model) describes concepts related to object implementations, including such concepts as methods, execution engines, and activation.

The CORBA object model is an example of a conventional object-oriented model, where a client sends a message to an object. Conceptually, the object interprets the message to decide what service to perform. In the conventional model, a message identifies an object and zero or more actual parameters. As in most conventional object models, a distinguishing first parameter is required, which identifies the operation to be performed; the interpretation of the message by the object involves selecting a method based on the specified operation. Operationally, of course, method selection could be performed either by the object or the ORB.

**Object Semantics**   Object semantics define concepts that are relevant to the clients. Here we introduce such concepts, as proposed in the CORBA document [70].

- As with conventional object-oriented models, objects are entities of an object system. An object is an identifiable, encapsulated entity that provides one or more services that can be requested by a client.
- Clients request services by issuing requests. The term "request" is broadly used to refer to the entire sequence of causally related events that transpire between a client initiating a request and the last event causally associated with that initiation. The information associated with a request consists of an operation, a target object, zero or more (actual) parameters, and an optional request context.

   Parameters in a request are instantiated with values. A value is an instance of an OMG data type. There are non-object values (string), as well as values that reference objects, called object references. An object reference is a value that reliably denotes a particular object. Specifically, an object reference will identify the same object each time the reference is used in a request, subject to certain pragmatic limits of space and time.

- Objects can be created and destroyed. From a client's perspective, there is no special mechanism for creating or destroying an object, as it exists in object-oriented systems (e.g., constructors in C++). Objects are created and destroyed as an outcome of issuing requests. The outcome of object creation is revealed to the client in the form of an object reference that denotes the new object.

- CORBA types are similar to those defined in conventional object models. Types are used in signatures to restrict a possible parameter or to characterize a possible result. The extension of a type is the set of entities that satisfy the type at any particular time. An object type is a type whose members are object references. In other words, an object type is satisfied only by object references.

   There are different types, those defined by CORBA and those defined by clients. A CORBA type can be either a basic type (such as Boolean, characters, etc.) or a constructed type. A constructed type can be either a tuple type (which consists of an ordered set of <name,value> pairs), union type, sequence type (which consists of a variable-length array of a single type), an array type (which consists of a fixed-shape multidimensional array of a single type), an interface type (which specifies the set of operations that an instance of that type must support), or a value type (which specifies state as well as a set of operations which an instance of that type must support).

- Interfaces are probably the key concept of the CORBA object model. They describe a set of possible operations that a client may request of objects, through their interfaces. Compared to conventional object models, CORBA interfaces are the operations part of types (the specification of the types). The implementation of the type (i.e., the data and the implementation of the operations) is "separated" from the type specification. Obviously, an interface may have several implementations, and the particularity of the CORBA object model is that these implementations can be done in different programming languages, such as C, C++, and Java. However, as we will see later on, interfaces must be defined with the OMG standard specification language, called the Interface Definition Language (IDL). Section 2.4.2 describes the main concepts of this language, and Chapter 3 shows how to specify and implement interfaces by using a CORBA complaint system such as OrbixWeb.

   An interface provides a syntactic description of how a service provided by an object that is supporting this interface, is accessed via this set of operations. An object satisfies an interface if it provides its service through the operations of the interface according to the specification of the operations.

   The interface type for a given interface is an object type, such that an object reference will satisfy the type if and only if the referent object also satisfies the interface.

   Interface inheritance provides the composition mechanism for permitting an object to support multiple interfaces. The principal interface is simply the most-specific interface that the object supports, and consists of all operations in the transitive closure of the interface inheritance graph.

- An operation is an identifiable entity that denotes an indivisible primitive of service provision that can be requested. The act of requesting an operation is referred to as invoking the operation. An operation is defined as in conventional object models; it has an identifier (i.e., its name) and has a signature (that describes the legitimate values of request parameters and returned results). The general form for an operation signature is:

```
[oneway] <op_type_spec> <identifier> (param1, ..., paramL)
         [raises(except1,...,exceptN)]
         [context(name1, ..., nameM)]
```

where: oneway is an optional keyword that indicates that best-effort semantics are expected of requests for this operation; the default semantics are exactly-once if the operation successfully returns results or at-most-once if an exception is returned. The <op_type_spec> is the type of the return result. The <identifier> provides a name for the operation in the interface. The parameters are flagged with the modifiers in, out, or inout indicate the direction in which information flows (with respect to the object performing the request): in means that the value of the parameter will be provided by the client when the operation is invoked, out means the opposite of in (i.e., the value of the parameter will be returned after the execution of the operation), inout means that the parameter can be in or out. The optional raises expression indicates which user-defined exceptions can be signalled to terminate an invocation of this operation; if such an expression is not provided, no user-defined exceptions will be signalled. The optional context expression indicates which request context information will be available to the object implementation.

- An interface may have attributes. Because interfaces model the specification part of types, attributes referred in interfaces do not relate to data persistence as in conventional object models. In fact, data persistence relates to the implementation of interfaces.

  An attribute is logically equivalent to declaring a pair of accessor functions: one to retrieve the value of the attribute and one to set the value of the attribute. An attribute may be read-only, in which case only the retrieval accessor function is defined. From a CORBA perspective, the main difference between an attribute and an operation is that for the former no exception can be associated to it.

***Object Implementation***   The object implementation describes the concepts relevant to realizing the behavior of objects in a computational system. The implementation of an object system carries out the computational activities needed to effect the behavior of the requested services. These activities may include computing the results of the request and updating the system state. During this process, additional requests may be issued.

The implementation model consists of two parts [70]: the execution model and the construction model. The former describes how services are performed, and the latter describes how services are defined. A requested service is performed in a computational system by executing code that operates upon some data. The data represent a component of the state of the computational system. The code performs the requested service, which may change the state of the system. Code that is executed to perform a service is called a method. A method is an immutable description of a computation that can be interpreted by an execution engine. A method has an immutable attribute called a method format, that defines the set of execution engines that can interpret the method. An execution engine is an abstract machine (not a program), that can interpret methods of certain formats, causing the described computations to be performed. An execution engine defines a dynamic context for the execution of a method. The execution of a method is called a method activation. When a client issues a request, a method of the target object is called. The input parameters passed by the requestor are passed to the method and the output and input–output parameters and return result value (or exception and its parameters) are passed back to the requestor.

The construction model provides mechanisms for realizing behavior of requests. These mechanisms include definitions of object state, definitions of methods, and definitions of how the object infrastructure is to select the methods to execute and to select the relevant portions of object state to be made accessible to the methods. Mechanisms must also be provided to describe the concrete actions associated with object creation, such as association of the new object with appropriate methods. An object implementation or implementation, for short, is a definition that provides the information needed to create an object and to allow the object to participate in providing an appropriate set of services. An implementation typically includes, among other things, definitions of the methods that operate upon the state of an object. It also typically includes information about the intended types of the object.

Table 2.1 summarizes the main differences between conventional object models and the CORBA object model.

**TABLE 2.1   Conventional Object Models and CORBA Object Model**

| Conventional Object Models | CORBA Object Model |
| --- | --- |
| `class` as object factory and data warehouse | no support of the concept of class. The object factory is a function that is supported by an ordinary interface |
| `type` | `interface` |
| `type inheritance` includes inheritance of operations and inheritance of implementation | supports for `interface inheritance` only |
| `overriding, overload, late binding` | no support for overriding, overloading, and late biding |
| `object identity` | `object reference` as an extension of object identity to include additional information, such the information about location of objects (e.g., host, port number, adaptor name) |
| `encapsulation` | `encapsulation` |

## 2.3.2 Object Management Architecture

OMA (Object Management Architecture) provides a framework which defines the functions supported by the component technology specifications with the OMG. As such it forms the foundation for building applications constructed from distributed objects and for interoperability between applications in homogeneous and heterogeneous environments.

As depicted in Figure 2.1, the OMA reference model consists of the following components: Object Request Broker (ORB), Object Services (COSS), Common Facilities, Application Objects, CORBA Domains. The ORB component is mainly responsible for facilitating communication between clients and objects. It is the central body, a broker provides the basic mechanism for transparent communication between distributed objects, and enables them to transparently make and receive requests and responses in a distributed environment. Object Services are a collection of basic services for using and implementing objects. Services are required to construct distributed applications, and are independent of application domains. An example of Object Services is the Life Cycle Service, which defines conventions for creating deleting, copying and moving objects; however, it is not concerned with the details of the objects implemented in the application. Common Facilities are a collection of services that may be shared by many applications, but are not as fundamental as the Object Services. These facilities provide general purpose capabilities useful in many applications. An electronic mail managing facility might be an example of a Common Facilities object. Application Objects correspond to the traditional notion of applications; they are software that is specifically designed to solve a business problem, and make use of the services facilities and domains as required. There is no

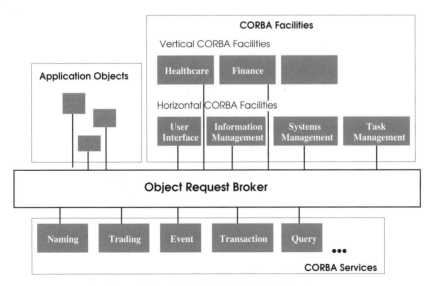

**Figure 2.1**   OMG Object Model Architecture.

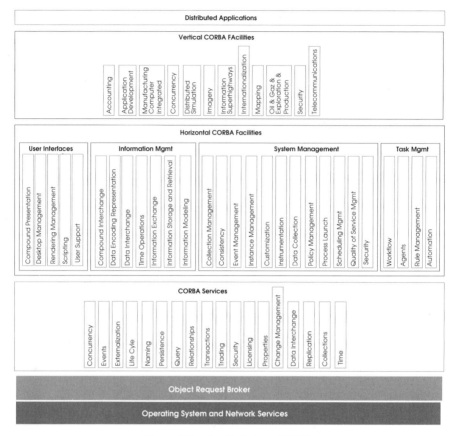

**Figure 2.2** Detailed view of OMA.

standardization for the Application Objects, and they lie in the uppermost layer of the reference model. CORBA domains are services that are generalized, and targeted toward a specific vertical market, such as telecommunications, or finance.

A detailed description of each component of the OMA is depicted by Figure 2.2.

***Object Services*** The value-added services provided by CORBA are collectively known as CORBA Services (COSS). COSS are domain-independent interfaces that are used by many distributed object programs. There are several services, including Naming, Events, Life Cycle, Persistence, Relationship, Externalization, Transaction, Concurrency, Property, Licensing, Time, Trader and Security. Several of these services, such as Naming, Events, Transaction, Trading, and Security services, are supported by most CORBA systems.

The Naming Service allows the retrieval of distributed objects by the names of the distributed objects. Therefore, clients do not need to remember the references to objects they want to use. Names, which are like "semantic identifiers," are assigned to objects and used by clients to easily retrieve them. The Trading Service complements the functionalities of the Naming Service, enabling retrieval of distributed objects based on their properties. Objects are registered with traders, that is, objects which can retrieve other objects that are recorded in their repositories, based on property values. Traders are then used to find objects with certain values for properties. For example, the request to a trader will be to find a room in a hotel which costs 50 and with a bathroom in it. In this context, the objects related to different instances of hotels will have the "cost" and "whether or not it has a bathroom" will be the properties associated to these objects. Obviously, these properties are not automatically those recorded with the state of objects.

The CORBA Object Query and Transaction Services can be classified as "database" services. Often these services deal with "persistent objects." Objects are made persistent either by using the Persistent Service or transparently done by the ORB (through specific components, such as adaptors). The CORBA Object Query Service (OQS) allows declarative access to heterogeneous database systems, including relational databases (e.g., Oracle and Sybase) as well as object-oriented databases (e.g., ObjectStore and $O_2$). The Oject Query Service provides operations to query objects based on several standard languages (such as OQL). Interfaces are proposed to describe different elements involved within the querying of objects, such as various collections (e.g., queryable collection) and query components (e.g., query evaluators). Users can invoke queries on collections of objects and the Object Query Service returns collections of objects that satisfy the given predicate. The Object Transaction Service provides operations to control the scope and duration of transactions. It allows multiple objects potentially residing at different resource managers to participate in a global atomic transaction and allows objects to associate their internal state changes with the transaction. The Object Transaction Service also is responsible for the coordination of the completion of distributed transactions by implementing presumed abort two phase commit (2PC) protocol across heterogeneous, autonomous, and distributed objects based systems.

In this book we have chosen to discuss only a few COS Services, which we believe are important for distributed applications. These include the Naming Service (in Chapter 7), the Trading Service (in Chapter 8), the Event Service (in Chapter 9), the Transaction Service (Chapter 10), and the Query Service (Chapter 11). The first three services are basic ones for distributed systems and useful for locating objects and enabling advanced communication between these objects. The transaction service enables the building of robust and reliable applications. The Query service is important when dealing with persistent objects, and in particular, when databases are used as persistent storage. Because databases represent a large number of existing industrial applications, their integration with CORBA is a step-forward. The Query service provides an important mechanism to retrieve and update objects within several data repositories.

As mentioned earlier, the remaining CORBA services which are not discussed in this book are equally important. We have chosen to describe a few specific services, in particular those related to "databases," because we believe they will be the ones that benefit the most from CORBA.

***Common Facilities*** Where CORBA Services provide services for objects, CORBA facilities provide services for applications. These interfaces are also horizontally oriented, but unlike Object Services they are oriented toward end-user applications. CORBA Facilities standardize all interfaces that are common across all CORBA domains. An example of such a facility is the Distributed Document Component Facility (DDCF), a compound document Common Facility based on OpenDoc. DDCF allows presentation and interchange of objects based on a document model, for example, facilitating the linking of a spreadsheet object into a report document.

***Domain Interfaces*** These interfaces fill roles similar to Object Services and Common Facilities but are oriented toward specific application domains. For example, one of the first OMG RFPs, issued for Domain Interfaces is for Product Data Management (PDM) enablers for the manufacturing domain. Other OMG RFPs will soon be issued in the telecommunications (CORBAAtel), manufacturing (CORBAAman), medical, and financial domains.

***Application Interfaces*** These are interfaces developed specifically for a given application. Because they are application-specific, and because the OMG does not develop applications (only specifications), these interfaces are not standardized. However, if over time it appears that certain broadly used services emerge out of a particular application domain, they might become candidates for future OMG standardization.

## 2.4 COMMON OBJECT REQUEST BROKER ARCHITECTURE

Figure 2.3 illustrates the primary components of CORBA. Object implementations define operations that implement a CORBA IDL interface. They can be written in a variety of languages, including C, C++, Java, Smalltalk, and Ada. A client is the

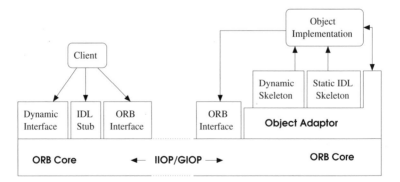

**Figure 2.3** The Common Object Request Broker Architecture.

program entity that invokes an operation on an object implementation. The services of a remote object are accessed in a manner that is transparent to the caller.

An ORB is a logical entity that may be implemented in various ways, such as one or more processes or as a set of libraries. To decouple applications from implementation details, the CORBA specification defines an abstract interface for an ORB. This interface provides various helper functions such as converting object references to strings and vice versa, and creating argument lists for requests made through the dynamic invocation interface described below.

A client application program is written in a language supported by the ORB. Every ORB supports one single language mapping (e.g., C++, Java, etc.) in which appropriate proxies (e.g., client proxy as the stub and server proxy for the skeleton) are generated in this language. The client program will refer to object types that are defined within an IDL application. When the IDL application is compiled, the ORB generates stubs and skeletons which serve as the "glue" between the client and server applications, respectively, and the ORB. They are basically responsible for marshalling (for the stub) and un-marshalling (for the skeleton) client requests. They are written in the language supported by the ORB. When a client invokes an operation of an interface of the IDL application, this operation will be marshalled by the stub and forwarded to the ORB. This type of invocation is called a `static invocation`, because the operations invoked by the client are known at compile time by the stub.

However, there is another alternative where the client wants to call an operation that is not known by the stub. This situation may occur, for example, when the implementation object has been changed within the server (e.g., adding an implementation of an operation) and the IDL application has not been re-compiled to generate a new stub (which will be aware of the new operation and therefore able to marshall it). Another situation will be a client wanting to delegate the execution of an operation to an implementation object without having the IDL interface known by the stub (e.g., a client that receives a remote object reference from the Trading Service and wishes to invoke an operation on the object). For such types of invocation, called `dynamic invocation`, OMG provided the Dynamic Interface Invocation (DII), where clients can directly access the underlying request mechanisms provided by the ORB. Applications use DII to dynamically issue requests to objects without requiring IDL interface-specific stubs to be linked in. Unlike IDL stubs, DII also allows clients to make non-blocking deferred synchronous (separate send and receive operations) and oneway (send-only) calls.

So far we have described the client side. Regarding the server side, as shown in Figure 2.3, there are several components that are used by the ORB to negotiate the execution of the operation issued by the client, either statically or dynamically. If the operation has issued the operation using Static Stub Invocation (SSI) mechanism, then the ORB will forward the request to the `Object Adaptor`, and this is done by using the information contained within the reference of the object in which the operation is invoked by the client.

Object references contain details which help the execution of operations within the servers. They include information, such as the server location, the adaptor identity, and the oid of the object within the server. The Object Adapter assists the ORB with delivering requests to the proper object implementation and with activating appropriate objects within the server. To do that, the adaptor needs to keep track of information, such as the association of oids with their servant classes. In this way, when the ORB delegates the execution of the operation to the adaptor, this will first identify the servant class of the object and then ask the skeleton to un-marshal the operation so it can be invoked on the appropriate object implementation in the server.

The Object Adaptor has other functionalities than just activating and deactivating objects in servers. Object adaptors also are responsible for enforcing security policies specified on the implementation objects. Chapter 4 gives a detailed discussion about the main functions of the Object Adaptor and the different categories of adaptors, such as Basic Object Adaptor and the more recently standardized OMG adaptor, the Portable Object Adaptor.

DSI is the server side's analogue to the client side's DII. The DSI allows an ORB to deliver requests to an object implementation that does not have compile-time knowledge of the type of the object it is implementing. The client making the request has no idea whether the implementation is using the type-specific IDL skeletons or is using the dynamic skeletons.

As explained earlier, OMA is an architecture for distributed objects. At the lower communication level, the object interaction takes the form of Remote Procedure Calls (RPCs), which are synchronous invocations. CORBA also allows, to a certain degree, asynchronous interaction by specifying a oneway operation semantics in which the client continues its computation without waiting for a result from the server after issuing the request. The oneway operation is a request-only operation with best-effort semantics; it does not return any result and the requester never synchronizes with the completion (if any) of the request.

### 2.4.1 ORB Core

The ORB provides a mechanism for transparently communicating client requests to target object implementations. The ORB simplifies distributed programming by decoupling the client from the details of the method invocations. This makes client requests appear to be local procedure calls. When a client invokes an operation, the ORB is responsible for finding the object implementation, transparently activating it if necessary, delivering the request to the object, and returning any response to the caller.

The ORB is the negotiator of this framework. An ORB knows about the interfaces to certain objects. The IDLs for the objects it knows are located in a dynamic listing called the interface repository. An ORB has the ability to know of other objects that reside in different host systems. When queried, the ORB tries to match the requested data object to its interface repository. Then through its implementation repository, the ORB will attempt to send a message to the object. If the data object or its server is not running, the ORB will obtain the reference of how and where to start the object in the implementation repository or an associated database. Once the ORB has the correct reference, it will attempt to start that object and then proceed to send the original message. If this process fails or the ORB does not know of the requested object, the ORB will return an appropriate error message to the calling client application or object.

The ORB removes the complexity of distributed network programming for developers. There is no longer need to worry about how to set up and test low-level RPC routines to carry data from one application to another. Clients simply set up IDL references to the object and response methods within the object, and then, compile and register the object (and possibly its server).

The OMG-specified interface repository is kept within a CORBA host and is maintained by the ORB process (a demon). The interface repository is a listing of all object IDLs the ORB needs to be aware of. The object IDLs are not constrained to the same host that the ORB is running on. They could be on different hosts but must be registered in an interface repository for use. This repository allows for persistent objects. It does not care about the status of an object; it is in essence the ORB's database of interfaces for use at run time. Therefore, applications need not be compiled or linked with the information of other CORBA objects, but they may still issue calls and use the information through DII.

Also maintained by the ORB demon is a specified implementation repository. This repository allows ORBs to locate and activate the various implementations of objects. The CORBA objects are not required to be running processes. Thus, the ORB is required to know how to activate an object, if necessary. Usually activating an object requires a symbol table or other database that has the specified path to the object or server and other necessary information. Such information could be the last time the object or server was accessed. If another CORBA object issues a request to a non-running CORBA object, the implementation repository allows the activation of the requested object and the passing of the original request. At run time, this activity is invisible to the developer.

## 2.4.2   Interface Definition Language

IDL is the language used by clients to specify interfaces for the object in the server. The IDL provides an independent, programming language neutral way of specifying the interface of implementation objects, that is, the operations and attributes of implementation objects. Interfaces are specified in the client side as IDL files. In the server side, servants are provided as abstract specifications for the implementation objects. Such servants can be C++ or Java classes, depending on the mapping language supported by the ORB.

This is different from centralized systems, where both the specification and the implementation are defined within a single system using a single specification and implementation language, like C++ or Java. Because CORBA deals with the distribution of objects (or distributed objects), as illustrated in Figure 2.4, is "split" into two components: one component involves the IDL interface and the other component describes the implementation of the IDL interfaces. There may be several implementations for the same interface, which are located in different servers. The implementations might be in different languages. The ORB, together with the adap-

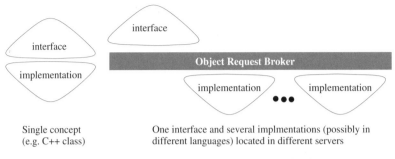

Single concept                    One interface and several implmentations (possibly in
(e.g. C++ class)                  different languages) located in different servers

**Figure 2.4** "Centralized object" vs. "distributed object."

tors, is responsible for selecting the appropriate implementation when a client makes an invocation. As mentioned earlier, the appropriate implementation object is selected by the ORB and the adaptors by analyzing the information contained within object references.

Chapter 3 provides all of the details necessary to implement a CORBA application using either SSI or DSI. This chapter also shows how to define interfaces and compile them to generate appropriate client and server proxies. Here we provide a simple example of an IDL specification to make clear some of the concepts we explained earlier. The keyword "interface" is used to specify interfaces, such as those of Account, CheckingAccount and Bank distributed objects. The specifications of these objects contain attributes (such as name and balance) and operations (such as MakeDeposit()). Because IDL deals only with specifications, for each interface another factory interface needs to be defined in order to specify operations that create objects. In the example below, the interface Bank is an example of the factory interface which is used to create objects of the types Account and CheckingAccount, and this is through the operations newAccount() and newCheckingAccount(). Because the Bank interface behaves like a factory interface, only one object implementation of this interface is generally needed to create any object of type Account or CheckingAccount, and this is generally done when a server is initialized.

```
interface Account {
    readonly attribute float balance;
    readonly attribute string name;
    void makeDeposit(in float f);
    void makeWithdrawal(in float f);
};
interface CheckingAccount: Account {
    readonly attribute float overdraftLimit;
};
// a factory for bank accounts
interface Bank {
    Account newAccount(in string name);
```

```
    void deleteAccount(in Account a);
    CheckingAccount newCheckingAccount(in
            string name, in float limit);
};
```

In the example above, the interface CheckingAccount is defined to inherit from the Account interface. Contrary to object-oriented models, where "inheritance" means "inheritance of specification as well as inheritance of interfaces," the inheritance in IDL only means inheritance of the interface, that is, inheritance of the operations and the attributes defined within the interface Account. Therefore, implementation objects of the interface Account and implementation objects of the interface CheckingAccount, which may or not be in different servers, support the same interfaces, but may have completely different behavior. This means that the implementation of the operations for the interface Account is not atomically inherited from object implementations of CheckingAccount. However, if this behavior is required, the implementation inheritance can be done in the server side.

A final comment regarding the IDL specification above concerns the attribute specification, such as balance and name. Because IDL deals only with specifications, these attributes express operations instead. This is mainly because "persistency" is an implementation issue; therefore, the operations related to these attributes should be linked to the appropriate persistent data of object implementations. These attributes are similar to accessors (when readonly keyword is used) and modifiers of C++. One of the main differences between attributes and operations is that the former cannot have associated exceptions.

Figure 2.5 shows the different types supported by CORBA. To summarize the discussion on IDL, this language is a separate language within the CORBA specification with the same lexical rules as C++. New keywords are introduced to handle distributed computing concepts. IDL semantics should coincide with the ANSI C++ standardization effort, and the IDL has full support for C++ preprocessing. The IDL describes the interfaces that client objects use when they want to reference an object implementation. Each IDL interface is defined completely for the object. The IDL also provides information necessary to develop clients that use an object's interface operations. IDL has been mapped successfully to several languages, including C, C++, Java, and Smalltalk.

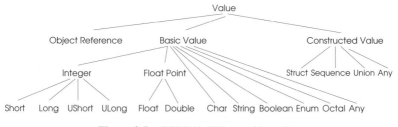

**Figure 2.5** CORBA's IDL type hierarchy.

### 2.4.3    Interface and Implementation Repositories

In the CORBA architecture, there are two repositories, the interface repository (IFR) and the implementation repository (IPR). Each of them acts like a "dictionary" providing meta-descriptions about specific information. IFR provides a meta-description of the IDL types at the client side (e.g., list of operations for a given interface), whereas an implementation repository provides a meta-description about the implementation information at the server side (i.e., list of servers that are active and how they can be activated). Each of these repositories plays an important role during operation invocations.

This section discusses the IFR and its OMG standard. Because the implementation repository is related to the implementation part of an ORB, OMG has provided neither a structure nor an interface of such types of repositories. Each vendor implements such implementation repositories in a specific way by containing any information required by the ORB to perform basic functions in the server side, such as activating/deactivating servers.

*Interface Repository*  IFR is the component of the ORB that provides persistent storage of interface definitions that it manages and provides access to a collection of object definitions specified in OMG IDL. All the information defined within IDL applications is stored as instances of IFR meta-types. For example, InterfaceDef is a meta-type that is used to record all information about every interface, including the list of its operations, the list of attributes, the list of exceptions and the list of inherited interfaces (i.e., base interfaces). When a client compiles the IDL, this meta-type, as well as others, are instantiated to contain appropriate information about the IDL application. For instance, in the example of Section 2.4.2, when the IDL containing the interfaces Account, CheckingAccount, and Bank is compiled, then three instances of the meta-type InterfaceDef are created to store the details of each of these interfaces. For the interface Account, for example, the instance of InterfaceDef will record the following details: balance and name as attributes (instances of the meta-type AttributeDef, makeDeposit() and makeWithdrawal() as operations (instances of the meta-type OperationDef). One of the advantages of storing the details of the interface Account is being able to dynamically browse the details of this interface at run-time. Users can look up the content of the interface repository and later be able to check the new operations that are added to the interface.

Figure 2.6 depicts a partial view of the different meta-types of the IFR, and Chapter 3 shows how they are used to browse the content of the IFR. These meta-types record all the information about IDL applications, and they are used by the IDL compiler for type-checking of request signatures—whether the request was issued through the DII or through a stub. This information is recorded within IFR and can also be used to assist in checking the correctness of interface inheritance graphs and assist in providing interoperability between different ORB implementations.

As the interface to the object definitions maintained in an IFR is public, that is, accessible from clients using the OMG's operations of the IFR, the information maintained in the IFR can also be used by clients and services. For example, the IFR can

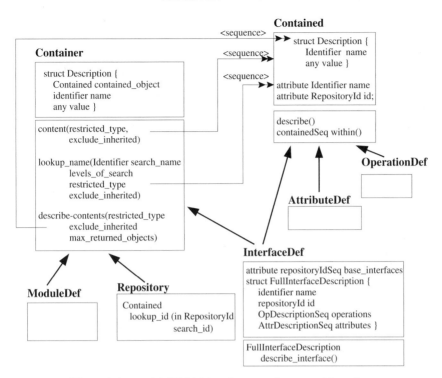

**Figure 2.6**    Partial CORBA interface repository type hierarchy.

be used to manage the installation and distribution of interface definitions, provide components of a CASE environment (e.g., an interface browser), provide interface information to language bindings (such as a compiler), and provide components of end-user environments (e.g., a menu bar constructor).

**Implementation Repository**    OMG has not provided any standard regarding the implementation repository mainly because it relates to the implementation part of the ORB. Information contained within this repository is not available to clients; however, it is used by the ORB to perform object binding. There are two types of bindings in CORBA, direct and indirect. The direct binding is performed by the ORB itself, whereas the indirect binding is based on the use of the implementation repository. This also can provide additional features, such as load balancing, object migration and sever migration. The features of each implementation repository depend on the vendor.

As detailed in Section 2.5, before the client invokes an operation, a reference to an object is retrieved. There are different ways to find such a reference. One way is to use either the Naming Service, when the name of the object is known by the client, or the Trading Service when the object is registered with a trader. The other way is to read the string version of the reference, when this is stored in a file. References are in a compatible form to the standard CORBA reference, called IOR (Interoperable Object Reference). Details about IOR are given in Chapter 5. Briefly, an IOR contains three types of information [47]: (1) type name (which acts like an index into IFR so IDL definitions can be retrieved at runtime), (2) the protocol and address details, which specify addressing information, such as the host name and the TCP port number, and (3) the object key, which consists of the name of the object adaptor and the name of the object. An example of IOR can be as follows:

```
IDL:iServiceApp:1.2 | goanna:2222 | OA7,obj120
```

CORBA distinguishes between two types of IORs: the transient IOR and the persistent IOR. The former is a reference that exists for as long as its associated server process remains available. Once the server shuts down, the reference is not accessible anymore, even if the server is restarted. The latter is persistent by nature; it is accessible even if the server shuts down and is later restarted. The implementation repository is used when persistent IORs are used. Because information about the host name and port number is embedded within IORs, appropriate information should be stored in the implementation repository so any change of a server to a different host or port number will be detected and the ORB can transparently start the server, do the binding, and shut down the server after some period of idle time. In short, to bind persistent IORs, ORBs provide an implementation repository to store all necessary information about servers.

The implementation repository has several functions, among which is its responsiblity for the maintenance of the registry of servers, for the storage of active servers, as well as their appropriate details, such the current host and port number, and for starting servers on demand if they are registered for automatic activation. The implementation repository generally maintains a table that has the following information:

| Adapter Name | Start-up Command | Address |
|---|---|---|
| OA7 | rsh amazigh "/usr/local/bin/jim -x" | goanna:2222 |
| OA1 | | miki:1030 |
| OA4 | /usr/local/bin/robert | |

The first two attributes of the table are instantiated when a server is installed. The last attribute records the host and port number at which the server is currently running. An empty address indicates that the server is stopped.

### 2.4.4 Object Adaptors

The rationale behind the inclusion of an (object) adaptor in the OMG architecture is interface flexibility and management. Without an adaptor, to communicate, both ORB and implementations must either agree on one fixed set of interfaces or support multiple sets of interfaces. The solution with a unique set of interfaces is not desirable because different sets of interfaces might be wanted, depending on the application's goals. For example, implementations are needed to perform a radically new kind of service, new functionalities are added, or better performance is needed. The second alternative, the support of multiple sets of interfaces, is too complex and could result in only a subset of the adaptor's interfaces being used. Confusion might also occur over which set of interfaces should be selected. It is conceded that foreseeing all types of interfaces that the implementations and the ORB will have is impossible.

The ORB and the object adaptor together provide the binding of client operations to appropriate object implementations. When an invocation is made, the client-side ORB is responsible for interpreting the object's profiles, for locating the server in which the object is implemented, and for sending a request to that server. On the server side, the request is received by the ORB, the following steps of dispatching are generally performed:

- The ORB finds the object adapter that the object is implemented in and passes the request on to that adapter.
- The object adapter finds the servant that implements the object.
- If the servant uses a static skeleton, the request is unpacked by IDL-generated code and the desired method is invoked.

But before any of this can happen, the object adapter must first know about the servant (i.e., the abstract class from which an object implementation is created). After registering the servant with the object adapter, an implementation must be able to create and export object references that address the servant. Therefore, in addition to the invocation of operations on object implementations, the object adapter provides an administrative interface as well. Here we summarize the functions of an object adapter: (i) the registration of implementations (with the implementation repository), (ii) the generation and interpretation of object references, (iii) the mapping of object references to their corresponding implementations, (iv) the activation and deactivation of object implementations, (v) the invocation of methods via a skeleton or the DSI, and (vi) involvement in the enforcement of the security policies of object implementations.

An object adaptor provides three interfaces: one to the ORB, which consists of a single method to receive an incoming request, one to the user code to which this request will be passed, by using either the Dynamic or Static Skeleton Interface, and one administrative interface through which an implementation can cause objects to be activated or deactivated, and which can influence the processing of requests.

In the initial OMG's specifications, the object adaptor was known as the Basic Object Adaptor (BOA). It provided basic functionalities, as listed in its IDL specification:

```
interface BOA {
   Object create (in ReferenceData id,
       in InterfaceDef intf, in ImplementationDef impl);
   void dispose (in Object obj);
   ReferenceData get_id (in Object obj);
```

```
  void change_implementation (in Object obj, in ImplementationDef impl);
  void impl_is_ready (in ImplementationDef impl);
  void deactivate_impl (in ImplementationDef impl);
  void obj_is_ready (in Object obj, in ImplementationDef impl);
  void deactivate_obj (in Object obj);
};
```

An object can enter three states during its lifetime: (1) not-existent, (2) inactive, and (3) active. An object is initially in the not-existent state, meaning that the ORB does not know of the object and that invocations are not possible but will be rejected with an appropriate error message. When an object is created (e.g., call of the operation newAccount() on an object of type Bank), object references can be exported. Several pieces of information are embedded within these references, such as the oid of the object, the reference of the adaptor and the reference of the server. By using the Naming or Trading Service, clients can retrieve objects and receive their object references. Initially, these objects are inactive, and method invocations will be withheld on the server side by the BOA and block until the object transitions to the active state. After activation, method invocations received by the ORB core are passed on to the implementation until it is deactivated again. The process of objects activation and deactivation can happen more than once and is transparent to the client. A server might wish to disallow upcalls from the ORB for some time while other tasks are being done, or to replace the implementation. Once an object is not needed anymore, it can be destroyed to returned to the not existent state, causing the BOA to act as if it had never existed. All of the information about the states of object implementations as well as other details (e.g., security) are stored within the implementation repository.

BOA's specifications were simple; however, they were plagued by problems with regard to the issues of BOA portability, clarity, and completeness. As a result, currently available BOAs are vendor-specific and incompatible. OMG has recently released the specification of another adaptor, called Portable Object Adaptor (POA), which is not an improved version of BOA. POA was designed from the ground up with portability in mind. Server codes benefit the most from POA since they can now operate across different CORBA products. POA interfaces are declared in such a way as to give more room and more flexibility for future expansions of POA. Like BOA, POA is also designated to handle objects with the most conventional implementations.

Chapter 4 provides a detailed description of BOA and POA and shows their differences with regards to aspects of architecture and policies.

## 2.4.5  CORBA Interoperability

The CORBA interoperability standard was developed to allow different ORBs to communicate. CORBA interoperability provides a gateway infrastructure that makes different ORB implementations compatible. It sits in the transport layer of the OSI model. The General Inter-ORB Protocol (GIOP) specifies one main constraint: different ORBs must be TCP/IP compliant. This specialized form of the GIOP is referred to as the Internet Inter-ORB Protocol (IIOP).

Through the CORBA specification, the CORBA methods and services allow the object methodology to be carried to a distributed, enterprise network. Through IIOP, CORBA is standardized to a lower network level (of OSI) so it may be used between multiple heterogeneous enterprise networks. Seven specified IIOP message types exist: *Request, Reply, CancelRequest, LocateRequest, LocateReply, CloseConnection*, and *MessageError*. All message types are straightforward, except for the two Locate message types, which are used for network speed optimization routines.

Different implementations of ORBs could either be straight IIOP run over TCP/IP networks or could run over a different type of network infrastructure, such as Novell's NetWare or a Windows NT Transport Driver Interface (TDI). For the latter to occur, the ORB implementation would need an associated "bridge" implementation. This bridge allows its ORBs to communicate with IIOP-based ORBs. When writing a bridge, an implementation can be developed with the Dynamic Skeleton Interface mentioned previously.

## 2.5   CORBA BINDING

As explained in Section 2.4.3, there are two type of object references, transient and persistent IORs. For each of these types, specific binding needs to be used.

### 2.5.1   Binding of Transient IORs

The binding of transient IORs requires that the server is available at the time when the client invokes an operation. Such a type of binding involves several steps, including (a) opening the connection with the server, (b) the location of the servant of the object by the object adaptor, (c) the return of the result of execution. These steps are depicted by Figure 2.7.

**Step (a):** Based on the information contained within the IOR, the client-side ORB runtime opens a communication on the host and port number specified in the IOR and sends a request message to the server process. The message contains information which helps the server and adaptor to invoke the client operation: the size of the message, the object key (i.e., adapter and object names), the name of the operation to be invoked, and parameters of the operation.

**Step (b):** The server uses the information within the message to locate the appropriate adaptor. As it will be detailed in Chapter 4, the adaptor will use a table called the Object Map Table to locate the servant, and this is based on the name of the object. This is one type of lookup, where the table is browsed to find the servant. However, there are other alternatives, such as using a default servant class, which may be useful for specific objects, such as database objects, in which appropriate functions can be used.

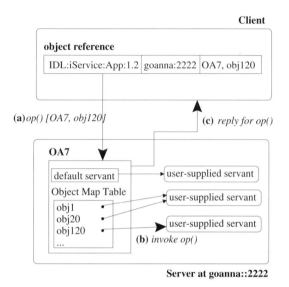

**Figure 2.7**   Binding of transient IORs.

**Step (c):** The server sends a reply message to the client. This message contains the request identifier sent to the corresponding request, and also contains the result of the operation, (when this is successfully invoked in the server). In case of invocation failure, then the message contains exception information stating the reasons for the failure.

## 2.5.2   Binding Persistent IORs

The implementation repository is used to enable the binding of persistent references. Details of the implementation repository are embedded within these persistent IORs. They are created by servers with the following information [47]:

- The interface repository ID of the most derived interface (as for transient IORs),
- The host name and port number of the implementation repository,
- The adaptor and object names (as for the transient IORs).

The server registers each servant with the same adapter and object name that it used for the previous installations of that servant. To bind a persistent IOR, the principle is the same as for transient IORs. With regards to the ORB opening a connection, instead of connecting to the server directly, it connects to the server that runs the implementation repository. This server unpacks the information related to the adaptor name and uses it as an index in the server table to check the details about the server on which the operation will be invoked. As explained earlier in Section 2.4.3, the implementation repository maintains a table that contains details about the servers which are active or non active, as well as the commands to start-up the different servers.

Depending on the way the server has been registered (e.g., automatic or manual), the implementation repository will either return a location-forward reply to the client or an exception. The location-forward reply is a form of another IOR, which is constructed by the implementation repository based on the details available in the table that it maintains. This mainly occurs because the server has probably moved to another host or to another port of the same hosts. Therefore, the client will need to re-send the request with the appropriate IOR (sent by the implementation repository) constructed from up-to-date information about the servers. Once the request arrives at the appropriate server, the binding is identical to that of the transient IORs.

Figure 2.8 summarizes the different steps involved in the binding of a persistent IOR with an automatic server start-up. For the manual start-up server, basically if the server is registered but not running, the implementation repository will return an exception which states that the server needs to be manually re-started. If the server is running, then the binding process is the same as for the automatic-start up.

**Step (a):**  The client invokes an operation, say op(), on an object obj120. Because the server where the object is located may have changed host or port number, the invocation is done on the implementation repository. As shown in Figure 2.8, a reference is created at the client side that contains details about the implementation repository.

**Step (b):**  When the implementation repository receives the request from the ORB, and because the server is registered with automatic start-up option, then the implementation repository starts up the server.

**Step (c):**  The server informs the implementation repository of its current address, that is, the host and the port number.

**Step (d):**  The implementation repository returns to the client the current address of the server, so the client invocation can be performed with the right information.

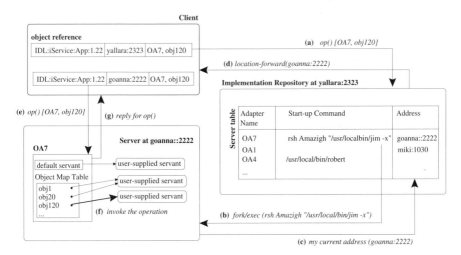

**Figure 2.8**   Binding of persistent IORs.

**Step (e):** The client creates a new IOR with appropriate information about the location of the server included. In the example of Figure 2.8, the newly constructed IOR contains the address of the server, that is goanna:222.

**Steps (f)–(g):** When the operation is invoked with the new IOR, the remaining steps are similar to those of transient IORs; the server looks in the Object Map table to select the appropriate servant and invokes the operation.


## 2.6   CORBA AND EXISTING TECHNOLOGIES

This section discusses the differences between CORBA and related technologies, in particular, DCE, DCOM, and RMI.


### 2.6.1   DCE vs. CORBA

Both DCE and CORBA are middleware technologies that support the construction and integration of client–server applications in heterogeneous distributed environments. As they are similar technologies, it is highly desirable that they are able to interwork with one other. However, they are not equivalent technologies. As explained in Section 1.2.4 of Chapter 1, DCE is designed around a procedural programming model, while CORBA has been designed with an object-oriented programming model. The advantages of the use of an object-oriented model such as the CORBA model include support for the following features: encapsulation and data hiding, abstraction of common features into classes, inheritance of interface, and implementation. Other differences in capabilities are:

- DCE has support for mechanisms that maintain the server state during a particular transaction. This mechanism is known as contexts. CORBA has no such mechanism and it falls on the programmer to manage this.

- DCE supports pointers both within operation parameters, and as operation parameters. The DCE run-time system will serialize (or marshal) values comprising a data-structure, including values addressed by pointers, in preparing for transmission to the server. DCE then un-marshals them on the server side. The CORBA constructs for building complex data types do not include the idea of pointers. This means that either extra code must be written by the programmer to pass complex structures containing pointers as parameters, or the programmer may redefine the data structure to be a collection of one or more objects, which of course, CORBA does support.

- CORBA, unlike DCE, supports the types "Any" (for fixed type length) and "DynAny" (for variable type length), which allows a value of an arbitrary type to be passed.

- CORBA IDL, unlike DCE IDL, supports interface inheritance, and defines a hierarchical namespace. DCE IDL defines a flat namespace.

- CORBA includes the definition of an interface repository to facilitate dynamic querying of data type information. DCE has no such equivalent.

- CORBA defines a DII (Dynamic Invocation Interface) to allow the invocation of objects without static knowledge of them. This allows arbitrary operation invocation on arbitrary object types at runtime. DCE only goes as far as the CORBA static invocation interface.

- CORBA supports automatic server activation, whereas DCE servers must be activated by other means, such as human intervention.

- CORBA services cover a far broader spectrum of application support than DCE.

### 2.6.2 DCOM vs. CORBA

DCOM and CORBA are two popular distributed object models. As explained in Section 1.2.5 of Chapter 1, DCOM is a distributed extension to COM which builds an object remote procedure call (ORPC) layer on top of DCE RPC to support remote objects–at the top layer, or the basic programming architecture. Exactly how the client is connected to the server is totally hidden from the programmers. The client and the server programs interact as if they reside in the same address space on the same machine. In terms of the infrastructure which provides the client and the server with the illusion that they are both located in the same address space, the main difference between DCOM and CORBA is how server objects are registered and when proxy/stub/skeleton instances are created.

COM and CORBA both provide a framework for creating and using components that can interface with each other, as well as with other applications, libraries, system software and networks in a standard, well-defined manner. CORBA was designed from the ground up to support components that could exist anywhere on a network; COM originally ran on a single system. Distributed COM (DCOM) is the distributed extension to COM that builds an object remote procedure call layer on top of DCE RPC to support remote objects. Distributed COM added the ability for COM components to interface across the network. An essential part of both frameworks are the value-added services. DCOM is a Microsoft technology that exists as a single implementation; CORBA was defined by a consortium of vendors, the OMG, value-added services. Some of the value-added services associated with DCOM include Microsoft Transaction Service (MTS), Microsoft Message Queue Server (MMQS), Microsoft Cluster Server (MCS) and Microsoft Management Console (MMC). DCOM does not provide a centralized naming service. This essential part of a scalable architecture allows users locate a particular application or component no matter where it resides in the enterprise. While DCOM provides a rich set of tools and technologies for implementing distributed object systems, its most significant drawback is that it is a Windows-only solution and many of the tools are new and still maturing.

Another difference to note between DCOM and CORBA, at the programming Layer, is the way they perform exception handling. CORBA provides support for standard C++ exceptions and some CORBA specific exceptions. In addition, user-defined exceptions are also allowed and are declared in the IDL. The IDL compiler maps a user-defined exception to a C++ class. In contrast, DCOM requires that all methods return a 32-bit error code called an HRESULT at this layer.

DCOM supports objects with multiple interfaces, while CORBA allows an interface to inherit from multiple interfaces.

### 2.6.3 RMI vs. CORBA

The differences between RMI and CORBA as summarized in the following table.

| Feature | CORBA/IIOP | RMI |
|---|---|---|
| Parameter Marshaling | Yes | Yes |
| Parameter Passing | in, out, in/out | in |
| Dynamic Stub Downloads | Yes | Yes |
| Dynamic Class Downloads | Maybe | Yes |
| Objects Passed by Value | Yes (with RMI over IIOP) | Yes |
| Garbage Collection | Yes (via ORB and POA) | Yes (via language) |
| Interface Descriptions | Yes | Yes |
| Distributed Dynamic Discovery | Yes (via the IR) | No |
| Distribute Dynamic Invocations | Yes (via DII) | No |
| Wire-level Security context | Yes (via CORBA security) | No |
| Persistent Naming | Yes | No |

### 2.7 SUMMARY

In this chapter we have provided details about OMG's Common Object Request Broker Architecture. We began this chapter by explaining the significance of the use CORBA environments. We have also explained the different versions of CORBA, including CORBA 1, CORBA 2 and CORBA, in which details for every version are given.

Unlike other architectures, such as DCOM, CORBA is an architecture for open distributed systems. We explained the different parts of this architecture, including the ORB core, the IDL, the interface and implementation repositories, the object adaptor, and the communication protocol (i.e., IIOP/GIOP). In addition to this architecture, we have shown how object binding works in two cases: one relating to transient object references, and the other persistent object references, where the implementation repository is used to activate and deactivate servers. Finally, we described the main differences between the CORBA technology and the existing middleware technologies, such as DCOM, DCE and RMI.

## 2.8 REVIEW QUESTIONS

- How are polymorphism, encapsulation, and inheritance applied in CORBA?
- What are the advantages of CORBA over existing distributed systems?
- What are the fundamental differences between conventional object models and the CORBA reference object model? Explain the factor that motivates these differences. What is the similarity between these two kinds of models?
- How can a CORBA object be made to support multiple interfaces?
- Explain briefly the functions of naming service, trading service, persistent service, object query service, and object transaction service.
- What are the functions of DII, DSI, object adaptor, and ORB core?
- Explain the motivation behind the inclusion of an object adaptor in the OMG architecture. What motivated OMG to replace BOA with POA?
- Can a CORBA object with a certain interface have multiple implementations? Justify your answer.
- Explains briefly the indirection that occurs when establishing a connection for persistent IORs.
- Give three differences for each comparison of CORBA with DCE, DCOM, and RMI.

## 2.9 EXERCISES

- A client receives a transient object reference from its server. The reference is later used to invoke the referenced object. However, the server was already shutdown; thus an exception is returned. After waiting for a couple of minutes, the client again sends the same request to the referenced object and succeeds. Discuss why the client's first attempt fails, while the second succeeds.
- OMG introduces POA to provide server code portability. When does this feature become important to a CORBA application?

# CHAPTER 3

# CORBA Programming

This chapter provides step-by-step tutorials on CORBA programming. The explanations given are not meant to be complete, but rather sufficient. However, it is necessary to know about object object-oriented concepts and Java programming, and have a basic understanding of the the overall ORB architecture. An important part of the existing literature has been published on object-oriented concepts (e.g., [14]) and Java programming (e.g., [21, 89]). Chapter 2 presented appropriate details of the CORBA architecture and the different elements of the OMG's Object Management Architecture.

Topics discussed in this book are about the CORBA standard, not about any of its ORB products. Propietary features and mechanisms are irrelevant and are not discussed. However, product-specific mechanisms like compilation and server registration commands are unavoidable in developing CORBA applications. Whenever a specific mechanism is used, this will be noted. All sample programs in this chapter have been developed and tested under OrbixWeb version 3.0, IONA's ORB product based on Java.

This chapter is organized as follows: The next section proposes an overall picture on how to program in CORBA and the required concepts; it also describes a sample application which will be used to explain the different CORBA programming steps. The rest of the chapter is composed of three main parts: (1) basic CORBA programming in Section 3.2, (2) dynamic types in Section 3.3, and (3) advanced CORBA programming in Section 3.4. Basic CORBA programming involves details about the Interface Definition Language (IDL), Static Interface Invocation (SSI), and Static Skeleton Interface (SSI). CORBA dynamic types relate to TypeCode and type Any. Finally, in the section about CORBA advanced programming, we will be covering the Dynamic Interface Invocation (DII), the Dynamic Skeleton Interface (DSI), and the Interface Repository (IFR).

## 3.1 OVERALL PICTURE

Unlike conventional programming, CORBA applications maintain a distinction between the interfaces of its objects and their implementations. The reason behind this division originates from the distributed application characteristics inherited by CORBA applications. A distributed application is usually heterogeneous and relies on others for the resources it requires but does not have. The heterogeneity of distributed applications eliminates the possibility of having a universal environment when no appropriate facilities are available on at least one platform. The distributed applications' reliance on resources of other distributed applications could cause changes to propagate to applications that use those resources. Interface-implementation separation addresses these problems by dictating interactions between applications to be purely based on their interfaces. In other words, the interfaces and their access information are the only things that must be agreed upon by both sides. This allows the server, which handles these interfaces, and the client, which manipulates them, to be developed in different programming environments so long as the same interfaces are used by both parties. Changes to the implementations have no or lesser impact on the client, except if they involve changes to the interfaces and/or to their access information.

In order to develop a CORBA application, programmers have to choose which ORB product and programming language to use. If they are the same for both client and server, it is said that the client and the server are developed in a single and (common) programming environment. Otherwise, there are multiple programming environments, one for each communication side. Figure 3.1 depicts the different CORBA application development steps, both in single and multiple programming environments.

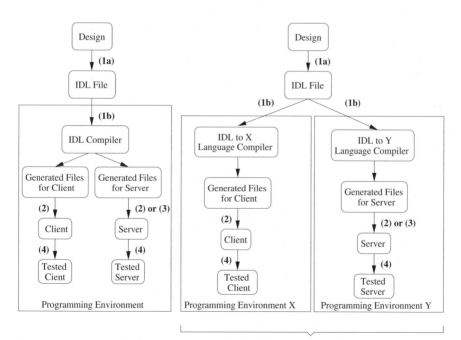

**Single Programming Environment**　　**Multiple Programming Environments**

**Figure 3.1**　Programming steps in different programming environments.

**Steps (1a) and (1b).** These steps consist of developing the required interfaces for an application by (i) writing the IDL (Interface Definition Language) file(s) and later on compiling them. These files contain interface declarations and their compilation generates additional files required by developers, to develop the client and the server, as well as files facilitating the communication between the client and the servers (e.g., stubs and skeletons).

**Step 2.** This step is concerned with the development of the client application and uses the interfaces specified in the IDL file(s). If the interfaces are known to the client at compilation time, then the client would be able to use SII (Static Invocation Interface) to invoke methods available in the object's interfaces. Otherwise, the client will need to use DII (Dynamic Invocation Interface). SII can also be used in conjunction with dynamic types (e.g., TypeCode and type Any) to be able to dynamically check the types of objects and the IFR (Interface Repository) can be used to obtain certain information (e.g., modules, interfaces, operations).

**Step 3.** This step is concerned with implementing the server. If the interfaces are known to the server during its compilation, the server can use SSI (Static Skeleton Interface) to service incoming requests. Programmers must later choose between two implementation styles, that is, BOA (Basic Object Adapter) or TIE, before proceeding to write the implementations. On the other hand, if the interfaces are unknown, DSI (Dynamic Skeleton Interface) is used. Like DII, an SSI implementation can use TypeCode, type Any, and the IFR.

**Step 4.** This step is concerned with the testing of the implemented application. Programmers need to compile the application, register the server, and run the application. Unique to the server registration step is the creation of a new entry in the IR (Implementation Repository). This entry is used to start a server process when requests arrive.

Both the client application and the server can be developed simultaneously or one after another. The numbering in both graphs in Figure 3.1 reflects this fact. Another point worth noting is that client and server style (SSI or DSI) is transparent to both sides. Such details are implementation-dependent and do not concern application interfaces. Programmers are free to mix and match these approaches, for example, SII clients can talk to a DSI server, and DII clients can communicate with an SSI server and so on.

To make the different steps in implementing CORBA applications clear, we have chosen to illustrate then on a sample application, the iService application. A company called iService (Internet Service) has hired Twinlab Co. to develop a prototype of its application. This application provides three kinds of services: free, paid, and tryable services. All transactions made on these services are quoted in U.S. dollars. Users must register their personal details using the application's client software before using these services. Newly registered users are given US$100 of initial credit. Users are able to increase their credits by transferring money directly to iService's bank account. Payments can be made in any currencies and will be exchanged into U.S. dollars at the current rate. All payments are verified by iService employees using the application. After payments have been approved, an iService's employee will

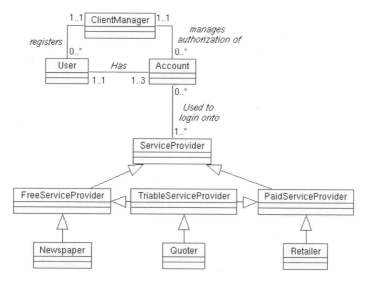

**Figure 3.2** UML diagram of the iService application.

use the application to increase the user's credits. Each user is allowed to have at most three accounts. An account has a unique login name and is protected by a password. Access to both a user's personal details and accounts are protected by a different password. iService currently operates three services: (1) news, (2) retail, and (3) a price-quoting service. As the company expands its offerings, the number of services is expected to grow. iService has also given Twinlab Co. a UML diagram to speed up its development process. The diagram is shown in Figure 3.2.

## 3.2 BASIC CORBA PROGRAMMING

This section discusses the basic features of CORBA programming. These features are enough for programmers to start developing a complete CORBA application. The type of applications that will be built here are static CORBA applications. Stubs and skeletons are bound to their interfaces as they have been declared at compilation time.

### 3.2.1 Interface Definition Language

IDL (Interface Definition Language) is OMG's specification language, used to describe the interfaces that clients use and servers handle. IDL cannot be used to develop the implementations of these interfaces; it is used solely to define interfaces. IDL declarations are stored in an ASCII file whose name ends with an .idl extension. This file is easily transferable by e-mail, ftp or by other ways of acquiring an ASCII file.

From a programming point of view, IDL is a subset of the proposed ANSI C++ standard, with additional constructs to support the operation invocation mechanism. It has similarities with other major object-oriented languages: it is case sensitive (like C++ and Java), has a preprocessor (C++), and uses the same comment characters (as C++ and Java). However, IDL does not understand any implementation-related constructs, such as access controls. IDL declarations are always public since the notions of private and protected are pertinent to the implementation and irrelevant to the interface. The same reasoning applies to constructor, destructor, overloaded methods, and procedural components. Additionally, some constructs are unique to IDL. Examples include parameter passing modes and readonly attributes. Others, like the integer datatype, simply do not exist.

IDL reconciles diverse object-models and programming languages by applying its own object model, the CORBA object model, and by being a neutral language. CORBA application designs must comply with this object model and have their interfaces defined in IDL. IDL neutralitity is motivated by the principle of interface-implementation separation. This establishes IDL as a purely declarative language, concentrating on interface descriptions, instead of on implementation details. Its neutrality means that these interface descriptions are programming language independent. The contents of these descriptions are not executable, even though they are abstracted from the implementations.

IDL does not replace the role of conventional programming languages, like Java, as the programming language used to develop the implementations. In fact, IDL complements them by providing programming language independent constructs for describing interfaces. Interface descriptions defined by these constructs are compiled by an IDL compiler. The compiler verifies the syntax and translates each of the constructs into conventional programming language native construct(s), in a process called mapping. The result of this compilation is a set of programming language-specific files containing the translated native constructs. These generated files are used by programmers to develop the implementations. The conventional programming language selected to implement interfaces is known as the language binding. OMG publishes IDL mapping specifications, each for a language binding. An IDL mapping specification describes the rules on how IDL constructs are mapped to a language binding. IDL mapping specifications are available for most of the popular programming languages: Java, C++, C, Smalltalk, COBOL, Ada. Programmers can select a conventional programming language as their language binding, so long as an IDL mapping specification and a CORBA compliant ORB product supporting this specification are available.

There are two steps to developing interfaces: (1) write the IDL file(s) and (2) compile them. The first step declares all of the necessary definitions using IDL constructs, based on the application's design. The second step executes the IDL compiler for syntax verification and mapping. Examples of files generated from this step are stubs and skeletons. Further details on commonly used IDL constructs and their application to the sample program are explained in the rest of this IDL section. Readers can refer to the documentation of the ORB product used (e.g., OrbixWeb's manual) or OMG's "IDL to Java Mapping specification" for the complete IDL syntax and mapping.

***Basics***    An IDL identifier is an arbitrarily long sequence of ASCII alphabetic, digit, and underscore characters. It is case sensitive and always begins with an alphabetic character. It must not have the same name as any IDL keyword, and must be declared in lower-cases.

As shown below, comment characters are identical to C++ and Java.

```
// This is a comment.
/* This is also
   a comment */
```

IDL also recognizes full standard C++ pre-processing features. The first one is macro substitution, which is used to improve code readability.

```
#define ACCOUNT_NO 5736912
```

The above macro tells the compiler to replace every occurrence of ACCOUNT_NO with 5736912. The next one is source file inclusion, for example:

```
#include "orb.idl"
#include <orb.idl>
```

In both #define statements the IDL compiler will include an IDL file. called orb.idl, in the compilation process. However, the included file in the first one is taken from the current working directory. The IDL file in the latter inclusion is part of the ORB product whose location is known to the compiler. Source file inclusion is required when at least one IDL construct, declared in the included file, is used by other constructs in included file. The last feature is conditional compilation and can be expressed as follows:

```
#ifdef iServiceApp_IDL
#define iServiceApp_IDL
// Not shown
...
#endif
```

The above preprocessor prevents all declarations between #define and #endif from being included more than once. The inclusion occurs only when the symbol iServiceApp_IDL has not been defined anywhere else. This preprocessor is usually used when one IDL file is included in multiple IDL files, to prevent inadvertant redeclaration.

***Module***    A module is a group of related constructs; it is used to provide a name space to the constructs and to avoid naming clashes. It is particularly useful for organizing an IDL file with a large number of constructs or to differentiate between constructs which have the same name. Declaring constructs inside a module is a good programming practice as it makes the IDL file more maintainable.

An IDL module is mapped to a Java package with the same name. For example, a module declaration from our sample application is shown below.

```
module iServiceApp {
// Not shown
...
};
```

This module, after IDL compilation, is mapped to

```
package iServiceApp;
....
```

A module can also be declared inside of another module. An example of this nested declaration is found in the module CORBA which contains pre-defined IDL constructs.

```
module org {
   module omg {
      module CORBA {
         // Not shown
         ...
      };
   };
};
```

This module is mapped to a Java package `org.omg.CORBA`. All IDL constructs declared inside of a module are mapped to the corresponding Java construct(s) within the scope of the generated package. IDL constructs whose declarations are not enclosed in a module are mapped into Java global scope. Consider if there was an IDL construct named Construct which is mapped to a Java class of Construct and encapsulated in a module called Package, the result of mapping this construct is a Java class with the full scope name of Package.Construct.

**Interface**   An IDL interface is a description of the services provided by one type of object. This service is made available to clients through interface attributes and operations. Without this interface, clients would not know how to access the service. An interface is similar to a class in Java, but free of any implementation related constructs. In fact, an IDL interface might be implemented by one or multiple Java classes. An interface is declared with the keyword interface, as illustrated below:

```
module iServiceApp {
   interface User {...};
   ...
};
```

Like any other object, a CORBA object can have attributes and operations:

```
module iServiceApp {
  interface User {
    // Attributes
    readonly attribute long id;
    attribute User spouse;
    ...
    attribute string phoneNo;
    readonly attribute float credits;
    ...
    // Operations
    void addCredits(in float creditAmount,
        in string currencyCode);
    void decreaseCredits(in float chargedAmount);
  };
  ...
  interface Retailer ... {
    // Operations
    string getItemList(in Account account);
    void order(in Account account, in string itemId,
        in short quantity);
    void bargain(in Account account, in string itemId,
        inout float price);
    void getItemDetail(in Account account, in string itemId,
        out string name, out float price ,
        out string  description);
  };
  ...
};
```

Four attributes are defined in the above code fragment of the User interface declaration: id, spouse, credits and phoneNo. The presence of the readonly keyword at the start of an attribute declaration determines whether or not the value of this attribute is editable. For example, the values of spouse and phoneNo are changeable by all clients, while values of id and credits are only readable. An attribute must be declared as having a certain datatype. This datatype is usually selected from one of the basic, constructed, template, or interface datatypes. Datatypes of the attributes in the example are all from basic datatypes, except for spouse which is of type interface. Attribute id is of type long, phoneNo is a string attribute, and credits is a float attribute. The spouse declaration is different from other attribute declarations since it is a self-referential declaration. This is because the attribute uses the IDL construct in which it is declared. Account, used by the Retailer interface, is an example of constructed types. Details of this datatype are given in the constructed datatypes section.

As explained in Chapter 2, IDL attributes are not like conventional class attributes, which record persistent data. Declaring an attribute in the interface is not the same as a Java attribute being declared in the implementation. In fact, as we will see later, attributes are actually mapped to Java functions. This mapping strategy allows programmers to assign the value of the result of processing in the Java function to the id attribute, rather than being merely a contained value.

Besides attributes, a CORBA object, which is an instance of a CORBA interface, may have a number of operations. Operations are analogous to functions in Java. They both typically have return values and parameters. One noticeable difference is the existence of parameter passing modes—in, out, and inout inout—in the operation declarations. These keywords specify the direction in which the parameter is being passed. For example, the parameter chargedAmount from the addCredits operation is passed from the caller, the client, to the called object. The out mode of getItemDetail's name, price, and description means that these parameters are passed from the called object to the caller. Parameters with inout mode, such as the price of a bargain operation, are passed in both directions.

An interface is mapped to a signature and an operations Java interface. A signature interface is the datatype used when the IDL interface is referred to by other mapped constructs, while an operations interface contains the mapped operation's signatures. The name of the former is the exact name of the mapped IDL interface. The latter interface is of type: _InterfaceNameOperations. Stub and skeleton classes are also generated. They are of types: _InterfaceNameStub and _InterfaceNameSkeleton, respectively. Three files are also generated, allowing programmers to use one of two implementation styles. The first is for BOA's skeleton class with the name of _InterfaceNameImplBase. The skeleton class or implementation base class in OrbixWeb should not be confused with OrbixWeb's _InterfaceNameSkeleton class. The second file is for TIE's TIE class which has the name of _tie_InterfaceName, and the operations interface mentioned earlier. The usage explanation of these files is given in the SSI section. (Readers should note that the last two files are specific to OrbixWeb.) IDL constructs declared inside an interface are mapped to the corresponding Java constructs in a package InterfaceNamePackage. An interface declared inside of a module will have a full class name of ModuleName.InterfaceNamePackage.

Each interface attribute is mapped to two public Java functions: one to set the attribute and another to return its value, except for the readonly attributes, which have only return functions. For example, the User's id and phoneNo attributes are mapped to:

```
public int id() {...}
public String phoneNo() {...}
public void phoneNo(String value) {...}
...
```

IDL operations are also mapped to public Java functions. Their return types are mapped to the corresponding Java datatypes, while their parameters are mapped to parameters of the Java functions. These parameters have the same names as their operation parameter counterparts, with their datatypes mapped to the appropriate Java datatypes. Mapping out and inout parameters also generates holder classes for the parameters' datatypes. Holder classes are explained later in the Holder and Helper section. For example, the Retailer's operations are mapped to:

```
public String getItemList(Account account) {...}
public void order(Account account, String itemId, short quantity) {...}
public void bargain(Account account, String itemId,
  FloatHolder price){...}
public void getItemDetail(Account account, String itemId,
  StringHolder name, FloatHolder price, StringHolder description) {...}
...
```

***Interface Inheritance*** Interface inheritance is similar to the inheritance used in other object-oriented programming languages; however, it is restricted to the inheritance of specification only. An IDL interface can inherit from one or multiple interfaces. An inheriting interface is known as a derived interface, while the inherited interface is called the base interface. If a derived interface inherits from a base interface, this inheritance is a single interface inheritance. However, if the derived interface inherits from more than one base interface, the derived interface is said to have a multiple interface inheritance. Declaring an inheritance is achieved by adding " : " after the name of derived interface, and following this with the name of the base interface(s). Examples of inheritance declarations from our sample application are depicted below:

```
interface ServiceProvider {...};
interface FreeServiceProvider : ServiceProvider {...};
interface PaidServiceProvider : ServiceProvider {...};
interface TriableServiceProvider : FreeServiceProvider,
  PaidServiceProvider {...};
...
```

A single interface inheritance is translated to the inheritance of the derived interface's operations. In other words, a single inheritance is when then derived interface inherits all operation all operations of its base interface. Both the TIE and the skeleton class implement the derived interface's operation interface, as depicted in Figure 3.3.

For example, mapping FreeServiceProvider creates the following Java code:

```
package iServiceApp;
public interface FreeServiceProvider extends ServiceProvider {...}
```

Also, FreeServiceProvider's skeleton and TIE class are created:

```
// Skeleton class
package iServiceApp;
public abstract class _FreeServiceProviderImplBase ...
  implements FreeServiceProvider {...}

// TIE class
package iServiceApp;
public class _tie_FreeServiceProvider ...
  implements FreeServiceProvider {...}
```

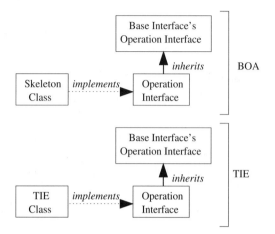

**Figure 3.3** Mapped single inheritance.

A multiple interface inheritance maps to the derived interface inheriting all operation interfaces of all its base interfaces. This is possible since Java supports multiple inheritance of Java interfaces, instead of class. Both TIE and the skeleton class implement the derived interface's operation interface, as illustrated in Figure 3.4.

For example, mapping TriableServiceProvider generates the following Java code:

```
package iServiceApp;
public interface TriableServiceProvider
   extends FreeServiceProvider, PaidServiceProvider {...}
```

Also, the following classes are generated:

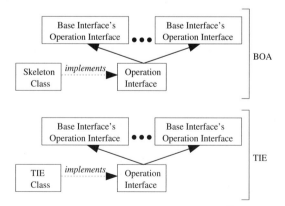

**Figure 3.4** Mapped multiple inheritance.

```
// Skeleton class
package iServiceApp;
...
public abstract class _TriableServiceProviderImplBase ...
  implements TriableServiceProvider {...}

// TIE class
package iServiceApp;
public class _tie_TriableServiceProvider ...
  implements TriableServiceProvider {...}
```

An interface's inheritance relationships do not guarantee that its implementation class has the same inheritance tree. In other words, the number of base interfaces inherited by a derived interface is not always the same as the number of implementation classes used to implement the derived interface. For example, the FreeServiceProvider interface might be implemented by one Java class which inherits from the ServiceProvide's implementation class. Another possibility is having one implementation class which does not inherit from any other implementation class at all, but implements all interface inheritance relationships, starting from ServiceProvider until FreeServiceProvider itself. Exactly how these interface relationships are implemented is explained in Section 3.2.3.

***Holder and Helper Class*** A parameter's value in Java is always passed by value and never by reference. Due to this restriction, values passed to the mapped out and inout parameters must be contained in an instance of a class called the holder class. For basic IDL types, a holder class name is the name of the corresponding Java datatype name with its first character capitalized and the word "Holder" appended at the end. For example, the holder class name of IDL's long is IntHolder. A holder class name for a programmer or an OMG defined datatype is the name as the corresponding Java datatype name of the mapped datatype with the word "Holder" appended at the end. For example, the User interface has a holder class named UserHolder with the following details:

```
package iServiceApp;
public final class UserHolder implements
  org.omg.CORBA.portable.Streamable {
    // The contained value
    public iServiceApp.User value;
    public UserHolder() {}
    public UserHolder(iServiceApp.User value) { this.value = value; }
    ...
}
```

A helper class assists programmers in manipulating an IDL datatype. It provides them with static functions to pass the datatype's value in Any (i.e., insert and extract to/from Any), return the datatype's TypeCode (type), IDL's Id (id) of this datatype, and to read and write the type from a stream (read and write). For an interface, this also includes two additional static functions: *bind*() and *narrow*(). *bind*() is an OrbixWeb-specific function used to bind to a CORBA object and *narrow*() is a CORBA-compliant function used to cast down an object reference to a more specific interface. Programmers must use *narrow*() to cast a CORBA object, instead of using the normal Java casting. This is necessary because such casting would only convert the reference to a Java interface, rather than to the desired CORBA interface. For example, the following code converts an object reference with the interface org.omg.CORBA.Object to a reference of a User interface:

```
// Assuming object has already contained a
// valid User's object reference
User user = UserHelper.narrow(object);

// The following is not the correct way
User user = (User) object;
```

The rules for naming a helper class are similar to those of naming a holder class. The only difference is that the appended word is Helper instead of Holder. An example of a helper class for the interface User is described below:

```
package iServiceApp;
public class UserHelper {
 public static void insert(org.omg.CORBA.Any any,
     iServiceApp.User value) {...}
 public static iServiceApp.User  extract(org.omg.CORBA.Any any) {...}
 private static org.omg.CORBA.TypeCode _type;
 public static org.omg.CORBA.TypeCode type() {...}
 ...
 public static String id() {...}
 public static iServiceApp.User
     read(org.omg.CORBA.portable.InputStream _stream) {...}
 public static void
     write(org.omg.CORBA.portable.OutputStream _stream,
         iServiceApp.User value) {...}
 public static final iServiceApp.User bind() {...}
 public static final iServiceApp.User bind(String markerServer) {...}
 public static final iServiceApp.User  bind(String markerServer,
     String host) {...}
 public static iServiceApp.User narrow(org.omg.CORBA.Object _obj)
     throws org.omg.CORBA.BAD_PARAM {...}
}
```

All IDL datatypes have a holder and a helper class, except for data types declared with a typedef statement, which have only helper classes. Programmer defined datatypes have their holder and helper classes, generated by the IDL compiler. On the other hand, holder and helper classes for OMG defined datatypes are pre-generated and are an integral part of the ORB product.

***Constructed Types*** Constructed types are IDL datatypes created by programmers from other IDL datatypes. An example of a constructed type is structure. An IDL structure is an aggregate collection of variables. It might consist of variables with the same types or different types. Structs should be used when a set of variables is manipulated as an unit but grouping them as an object is unnecessary. Structs should also be used when sending a large number of related values.

Let us consider the following example related to a user's accounts which is extracted from the sample application:

```
struct Account {
  User owner;
  string password;
  string loginName;
};
...
```

An account has three attributes: owner, password, and login name. One could create the account as a CORBA object, with each of the attributes being editable. However, it is almost certainly the case that the cost of maintaining a CORBA object is more expensive than the cost of maintaining a simple structure. Another reason is that having these variables as a structure does not affect the quality of the design. Thus, it is desirable to create them as a structure instead. Another example is found when all accounts of all users must be sent for purposes such as replication or caching.

An IDL structure is mapped to a final Java class which has the same Name. It has a public attribute for each of the structure members, one non-parameterized constructor which initializes all fields to zero or null, and another constructor which takes all of the structure members as its parameters, for initializing the structure. For example, the IDL structure Account is translated to:

```
package iServiceApp;
public final class Account
  implements java.lang.Cloneable {
  public User owner;
  public String password;
  public String loginName;
  public Account() {}
  public Account(User owner, String password, String loginName) {
    this.owner = owner;
    this.password = password;
    this.loginName = loginName;
  }
...
}
```

Enumerated types are another example of constructed types. Enumerated types are custom-made IDL types which enable programmers to represent their values as identifiers. Similar to macro substitution, enumerated types improve code readability. However, enumerated types are not just aliases as in macro substitution, they are IDL datatypes. The keyword enum declares an enumerated type, followed by its name and identifiers that represent the datatype's values. For example, an IDL declaration to declare an enumerated type called ParamMode with values of IN, OUT, and INOUT is:

```
enum ParamMode { IN, OUT, INOUT };
```

An enumerated type is mapped to a final Java class of the same name. Each of the datatype values is mapped to two Java constructs. The first one is a static final attribute (a Java constant) whose name is prefixed by an underscore. This constant holds the actual Java integer value which is symbolized by an identifier of the enumerated type. The next one is also a static final attribute, but without the prefix. It is the Java object representation of the integer value. Two functions are also created: value which returns the integer, that is, the current Java constant value, and *from_int*() that returns the Java object representation of a specified integer value. For example, the ParamMode enumerated datatype above is mapped to:

```
package iServiceApp;
public final class ParamMode
   implements java.lang.Cloneable {
   public static final int _IN = 0;
   public static final ParamMode IN = new ParamMode(_IN);
   public static final int _OUT = 1;
   public static final ParamMode OUT = new ParamMode(_OUT);
   public static final int _INOUT = 2;
   public static final ParamMode INOUT = new ParamMode(_INOUT);
   public static final ParamMode IT_ENUM_MAX =
      new ParamMode(Integer.MAX_VALUE);
   private int ___value;

   public int value () { return ___value; }
   public static ParamMode from_int (int value) {
     switch (value) {
        case _IN : return IN;
        case _OUT : return OUT;
        case _INOUT : return INOUT;
        default :
            throw new org.omg.CORBA.BAD_PARAM("Enum out of range");
     }
   }
   private ParamMode (int value) { ___value = value; }
   ...
}
```

***Named Types***    A named type is essentially an alias to an existing IDL type. It improves the readability of the code by introducing a datatype which is conceptually different, but programmatically the same, as the aliased datatype. Recall from our sample application that all transactions are quoted in US dollars except when increasing user credits, which could be done in any currency. Rather than using a float datatype for money, it would be more meaningful if a named type USDollars is used, with the exception of addCredits which accepts all international currencies. Therefore, the sample IDL has now become:

```
module iServiceApp {
    // Simple typedef declarations
    typedef float Money;
    typedef Money USDollars;

    interface User {
        ...
        readonly attribute USDollars credits;
        ...
        // Operations
        void addCredits(in Money creditAmount,
            in string currencyCode);
        void decreaseCredits(in USDollars chargedAmount);
    };

    interface Retailer ... {
        ...
        void bargain(in Account account, in string itemId,
            inout USDollars price);
        void getItemDetail(in Account account, in string itemId,
            out string name, out USDollars price ,
            out string description);
    };
    ...
```

Money is an alias of float, while USDollars is the alias for Money. All float declarations, except for addCredits's creditAmount parameter have been replaced with USDollars. creditAmount is declared as having a named type of Money since the parameter can carry all currency values whose currency code is determined by currencyCode. The result of mapping the above declarations is the same, with the additional helper class created for each of these named types.

***Template Types***    A template type is a parameterized IDL type used to declare a new datatype. Additional information must be passed to its parameter(s) in order to complete the declaration of the new type. An example of a template type is sequence, which is a variable length list of elements of the same type. It should be used when there is a need to send a collection of elements, but the exact number of elements can not be determined statically. There are two kinds of sequences available: bounded and unbounded. Both may have a varying number of elements every time they are transferred; the former has a maximum number of elements that can be held by the sequence. Sequences used in our sample application are unbounded sequences. An example of these sequences is described below.

```
struct Account {
   ...
   string password;
   string loginName;
};
typedef sequence<Account> Accounts;
interface User {
   readonly attribute Accounts accounts;
   ...
};
...
```

A sequence is mapped to a Java array of the same name. For example, the declaration of the accounts attribute above is mapped to:

```
public Account[] accounts() {...}
...
```

A bounded sequence will go through bound checking before being sent. This ensures the array length will always be less than the maximum number of elements specified in the IDL declaration of the sequence.

Forward Declaration

A forward declaration is an incomplete definition of an IDL type declared before the declaration of its dependents. It is used to solve cyclic dependencies or to make the code more elegant. An example of forward declaration is illustrated below:

```
// Forward declaration
interface User;
struct Account {
   User owner;
   ...
};

// Normal, i.e. the complete IDL declaration
interface User {
   void addAccount(in Account newAccount);
   ...
};
...
```

Account requires that the User be declared earlier, while User requires the opposite. Such cyclic dependencies can only be broken by declaring the interface User twice. The first one is the forward declaration, while the latter declaration is a normal interface declaration.

Forward declarations enhance code elegance by freeing programmers to place the complete IDL declarations in any order. Usually, the order of these forward declarations must follow the order of dependence of the datatypes declarared in these declarations. Consider the following example.

```
interface User {...};
interface ClientManager {
   ...
   User register(in string firstName , in string   lastName,
         in string password  , in Address  address ,
         in string phoneNo    , in Accounts accounts);
};
...
```

If relocating the ClientManager declaration to a place below the User declaration increases code elegance, then the above IDL declaration must be modified to:

```
// Forward declaration
interface User;

interface ClientManager {
   ...
   User register(in string firstName , in string   lastName,
                 in string password  , in Address  address ,
                 in string phoneNo    , in Accounts accounts);
};

// Normal, i.e the complete
// User declaration
interface User {...};
...
```

**Exception**   An exception is an IDL construct which signals the occurrence of an error. It should be used when certain conditions cannot be handled. There are two kind of exceptions: *system exceptions*, which are pre-defined and usually raised at runtime by the ORB; and *user-defined exceptions* which are declared by programmers and raised by implementations. The latter cannot be raised by interface attributes, only by interface operations. An exception is similar to a structure, because it can have multiple members. These members are accessible when it is caught by the code. For example, consider the following IDL declarations:

```
exception InvalidAccount { string reason;};
interface User {
   ...
```

```
  readonly attribute Accounts accounts;
  void addAccount(in Account newAccount)
    raises(InvalidAccount);
    ...
};

exception InsufficientCredits {
  float creditsRequired;
  float currentTotCredits;
};
interface Retailer : PaidServiceProvider {
  void order(in Account account, in long itemId, in short quantity)
    raises(InvalidAccount, NotExist, InsufficientCredits);
    ...
};

  ...
```

*InvalidAccount* exception is raised by the operation *addAccount()* whenever a new account cannot be added to the user's list of accounts. The exact cause of the failure is described by an error message in reason. This error message can be used by the client's code, which displays the message whenever the exception is raised. Another exception, *InsuficientCredits*, is raised whenever an user does not have enough credits to create an order. The exception contains the number of credits that are required (*creditsRequired*) and amount of credits the user currently has (*currentTotCredits*). This information can be used to notify the user about the error.

At first, exceptions may seem more complex than required for the simple task of signalling errors. One could remove all exceptions altogether and use a Boolean or a structure instead. However, there are some drawbacks to using these datatypes. For a Boolean value, no additional information is returned other than the fact that an exception has been raised. For structures, they could be confused with normal return types. Thus, having exceptions is appropriate since it provides programmers with a dedicated IDL construct that encapsulates the necessary information about the error.

An exception is mapped to a final Java class with the same name. System exceptions inherit from org.omg.CORBA.SystemException, while user-defined exceptions extend org.omg.CORBA.UserException. Operations that raise CORBA exceptions are mapped as before, but with an additional Java throws statement appended. Raising a CORBA exception is performed by using throw. For instance, the exception *LoginFailed* is mapped to:

```
package iServiceApp;

public final class LoginFailed  extends org.omg.CORBA.UserException
  implements java.lang.Cloneable {
    public String reason;
    public LoginFailed() { super(); }
```

```
    public LoginFailed(String reason) {
       super();
       this.reason = reason;
    }
  ...
}
```

**Compiling**   The complete IDL declarations of our sample application, so far, is shown below.

```
#ifndef iServiceApp_IDL
#define iServiceApp_IDL
module iServiceApp {
  // Simple typedef declarations
  typedef float Money;
  typedef Money USDollars;

  // Forward declaration
  interface User;
  struct Account {
     User    owner;
     string password;
     string loginName;
  };
typedef sequence<User>    Users;
typedef sequence<Account> Accounts;
struct Address {
   string state;
   string street;
   string country;
};
exception InvalidAmount { string reason; };
exception InvalidAccount { string reason; };
interface User {
  // Attributes
  readonly  attribute long      id;
  attribute            User      spouse;
  attribute            Address   address;
  attribute            string    phoneNo;
  readonly attribute   USDollars credits;
  attribute            Users     children;
  readonly attribute   Accounts  accounts;
  attribute            string    lastName;
  attribute            string    firstName;

  // Operations
  void addAccount(in Account newAccount) raises(InvalidAccount);
  void addCredits(in Money creditAmount,
         in string currencyCode) raises(InvalidAmount);
```

```
    void decreaseCredits(in USDollars chargedAmount);
};
exception InvalidDetail { string reason; };
  exception LoginFailed { string reason; };
interface ClientManager {
  // Operations
  Account login(in string loginName, in string password)
      raises(LoginFailed);
  User register(in string firstName,
        in string  lastName,
        in string  password,
        in Address address ,
        in string  phoneNo ,
        in Accounts accounts);
         raises(InvalidDetail, InvalidAccount);
};
interface ServiceProvider {
  // Attributes
  readonly attribute string manual;
  readonly attribute string announcement;
};
interface FreeServiceProvider : ServiceProvider {
  // Operation
  string getAd(in Account account) raises(InvalidAccount);
};
interface PaidServiceProvider : ServiceProvider {
  // Operation
  string getPaymentInfo(in Account account) raises(InvalidAccount);
};

interface TriableServiceProvider : FreeServiceProvider,
          PaidServiceProvider {
   // Attribute
   readonly attribute USDollars initCredits;
};
interface Newspaper : FreeServiceProvider {
  // Operations
  string getHeadline(in Account account) raises(InvalidAccount);
  string getLocalNews(in Account account) raises(InvalidAccount);
  string getWorldNews(in Account account) raises(InvalidAccount);
  string getSportsNews(in Account account) raises(InvalidAccount);
  string getWeatherNews(in Account account) raises(InvalidAccount);
  string getBusinessNews(in Account account) raises(InvalidAccount);
};
 exception NotExist { string reason; };
 exception InsufficientCredits {
    float creditsRequired;
    float currentTotCredits;
};
```

```
interface Retailer : PaidServiceProvider {
  // Operations
  string getItemList(in Account account) raises(InvalidAccount);
  void   order(in Account account, in long itemId, in short quantity)
           raises(InvalidAccount, NotExist, InsufficientCredits);
  void   bargain(in Account account, in long itemId,
           inout USDollars price) raises(InvalidAccount, NotExist);
  void   getItemDetail(in Account account,
           in long itemId,
           out string name,
           out USDollars price,
           out string  description)
           raises(InvalidAccount, NotExist);
};
interface Quoter : TriableServiceProvide {
  // Operations
  string   getQuotableList(in Account account) raises(InvalidAccount);
  USDollars getQuote(in Account account,
             in long quotableId)
             raises(InvalidAccount, NotExist,
             InsufficientCredits);
};
};
#endif
```

The above IDL is compiled in OrbixWeb by executing the following command:
idl iServiceApp.idl. Programmers can also utilize Makefile, which contains a
similar command, by typing make idl at the command prompt. Compilation generates a directory, called java_output, in the current directory. This directory contains
all of the files which result from the mapping process. In the remaining sections we
will show how these files are used.

### 3.2.2   Static Invocation Interface

SII or the Static Invocation Interface is a set of APIs commonly used by clients to
invoke objects. This is because the interfaces of most CORBA applications are resolvable at compile-time. In turn, these interfaces allow the IDL compiler to generate
the SII, based on the interfaces. SII is usually referred to by CORBA programmers as
the stub. It is generated in the chosen language binding as a result of mapping interfaces. Clients that use SII assert that the interfaces will not change, and that changes
to interfaces require SII regeneration by means of re-mapping. As a result, clients
that use this modified SII must be recompiled.

In Java binding, the role of client is usually played by a client executable class.
A client executable class is a Java class with a static main function. It is similar to
other executable Java classes, but differs because of its use of SII. From example, the
client executable class from our application is:

```
package iServiceApp;

// All import statements
// are declared here
...
public class Client {
  ...
  public static void main(String args[]) {...}
  ...
}
```

Readers should note that the class name Client is not compulsory. Having client executable classes does not imply that these classes are the only kind of classes that can assume the client role. In fact, all classes which use SII to invoke objects have the role of client.

Developing a client-executable class consists of several programming steps: (i) initialization of the ORB, (ii) obtaining an object reference, and (iii) invocating operations on object references. Below are the details of each steps.

### Step 1 (Initialization of the ORB)

ORB is accessed through a singleton Java class org.omg.CORBA.ORB. The client's connection to the ORB needs to be initialized before being used. The ORB initialization is accomplished by calling its init static function, i.e., $ORB.init()$. This function returns an instance of the initialized ORB and should be called before any other CORBA statements in the code.

### Step 2 (Getting hold of an object reference)

Prior to CORBA object manipulation, a client must acquire a reference to the object. This step is repeated for each of the objects accessed by the client. Acquisition is accomplished by one of the following methods: performing the object binding; stringifying the object reference; or invoking a method on another object.

***Object Binding***   An object binding is a reference acquisition method in which a reference is obtained by searching for the desired object in the server. An object binding in OrbixWeb relies on the use of the proprietary function $bind()$ which is owned by the target object's interface helper. A code fragment, which performs a binding process follows.

```
private ClientManager connectToClientManager(String args[]) {
  // Local declaration
  ClientManager clientManager = null;
  ...
  if(args.length == 1) {
    ...
```

```
    clientManager = ClientManagerHelper.bind(":iService", args[0]);
}
else { System.out.println("usage : client <host> ");}
...
return(clientManager);
}
```

...

The *bind*() function used in the example accepts two parameters: the object's marker with its server name, and the host machine's name. An object marker is OrbixWeb's term for an object id or object name. It is unique within the scope of a server and used to identify an object. A string passed as the *bind*() function's first parameter must be in the format Marker:ServerName. A server name is a unique name given to identify an application server. It might not be specified at all, as in the above example. This allows bind() to return a reference to the first object found having the same IDL interface. The host name parameter must be the Internet host name or Internet IP address. A host name is different from a server name. A host name is the name of the machine where the server process resides, whereas a server name is the name registered by the programmer to identify a CORBA application's server.

**Stringification of Object Reference**    A reference to an object can be converted to a string. This feature is useful for storing the reference persistently on the disk. ORB's *object_to_string*() function converts an object reference to a string, with *string_to_object*() doing the opposite. Once a stringified string has been converted to an object reference, the reference can be cast to the appropriate interface type, by using the interface helper's *narrow*() function. The following code fragment stringfies a user object to string and vice versa.

```
ORB orb = ORB.init()
...
User user = null;
...
// Assuming object has been bound earlier
String stringifiedObjRef = orb.object_to_string(user);
...
Object objRef = orb.string_to_object(stringifiedObjRef);
user = UserHelper.narrow(objRef);
```

**Object Invocation**    In this method, an operation or an attribute of an object whose reference was acquired earlier is accessed. The operation or attribute returns another object reference for the client. An example of such operation is provided in the next programming step.

In OrbixWeb, whenever an object reference enters a client address space a proxy is created; this is a local representative for the remote object. All requests made to the object reference are forwarded to the proxy, which in turn passes them to the remote object via the ORB. This process is shown in Figure 3.5.

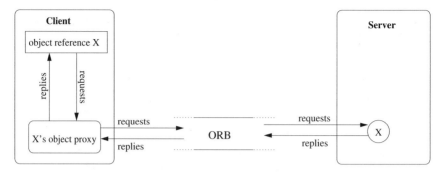

**Figure 3.5**   A request delivery by a proxy.

## Step 3 (Invocation of operations on CORBA objects)

The last step is to invoke attributes and/or operations on the objects. This step can be repeated several times by the client when an object's information is needed. The invocation of an object's attributes and operations are similar because, as explained earlier, attributes are mapped to functions of the stub.

Let us consider the following fragment of application code.

```
private User registerIndividual(ClientManager clientManager) {
 ...
 User newUser = null;
 ...
 newUser = clientManager.register(firstName, lastName, password,
            address, phoneNo, accounts, INIT_CREDITS, USD_CODE);
  ...
  return(newUser);
}
 ...
```

Compare the above code fragment, which invokes an operation, with the following code fragment, which obtains an attribute value by calling the mapped function of a quoter interface's announcement attribute.

```
private void handleQuotingService(String[] args, Account account) {
  ...
  System.out.println(quoter.announcement());
  ...
}
 ...
```

For non-CORBA programmers, both register and announcement appear to be just two normal Java functions. Invoking operations with out or inout parameters require the use of their holder classes. For example, a code fragment that invokes Retailer's getItemDetail which has three out parameters (name, price, and description) is provided below. The operation gets details of an item that will the be displayed by the client executable to the screen.

```
// Local declarations
StringHolder name        = new StringHolder();
FloatHolder  price       = new FloatHolder();
StringHolder description = new StringHolder();
...
retailer.getItemDetail(account, itemId, name, price, description);

System.out.println("Details");
System.out.println("-------");
System.out.println("Name        : " + name.value);
System.out.println("Price       : " + price.value);
System.out.println("Description : " + description.value);
System.out.println("");
...
```

An example of an IDL operation invocation with an inout parameter is Retailer's operation of bargain. Note that readFloat reads a floating point number from the user's keyboard input:

```
// Local declaration
FloatHolder floatHolder = new FloatHolder();
...
System.out.print("Price           : ");
floatHolder.value = readFloat();
retailer.bargain(account, itemId, floatHolder);
...
```

Operations that raise exceptions must have all of their Java exceptions caught when executing their Java functions:

```
private User registerIndividual(ClientManager clientManager) {
   ...
  User newUser = null;
  try { newUser = clientManager.
       register(firstName, lastName, password,address, phoneNo,
                accounts);
     } catch(InvalidDetail invDetailEx) {
         System.out.println(invDetailEx.reason);
       } catch(InvalidAccount invAccountEx) {
           System.out.println(invAccountEx.reason);
         }
  return(newUser);
   ...
}
...
```

The rest of the client's executable statements is similar to any other Java programs.

### 3.2.3   Static Skeleton Interface

SSI or Static Skeleton Interface is the server side equivalent of SII. It is referred to by CORBA programmers simply as the skeleton. Like its client counterpart, SSI is the common way of servicing incoming requests; this is because interfaces of most CORBA applications can be resolved at compile-time. The IDL compiler generates SSI based on the interfaces. Servers that use SSI assume that the interfaces stay static over time. Changes to application interfaces require that the SII to be regenerated by re-mapping the IDL file(s). SSI servers must be amended to reflect these changes and be recompiled.

The role of a server in a Java binding is divided among two types of classes: the server executable class and the implementation class. A server executable class is similar to the client executable. Both are Java classes with a static main function and are not the only kind of classes that can assume the role of a server. However, a server executable class uses SSI instead of SII. It is responsible for performing server initialization tasks, for example, notifying BOA about the server's readiness to accept requests. Implementation classes are Java classes that implement the interfaces. A typical CORBA application has one server executable class and multiple implementation classes.

Developing a server consists of several development steps: (a) developing the implementation classes, (b) developing a server executable file, and (c) testing the application.

### Step 1 (Develop implementation class(es))

The following programming steps are repeated for each interface that needs to be implemented: (a) select an implementation style, and (b) write the implementation classes.

***Step 1.1 (Select an implementation style)***   There are two styles in which an implementation can be written: BOA and TIE. BOA is a SSI implementation style which requires that the implementation class inherit from the skeleton class of the IDL interface that needs to be implemented. Figure 3.6 illustrates the inheritance relationship graphically.

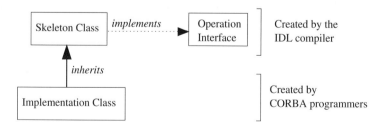

**Figure 3.6**   Inheritance in BOA implementation style.

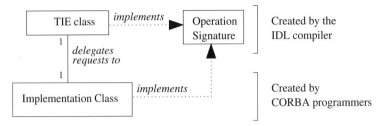

**Figure 3.7** Inheritance in TIE implementation style.

Another alternative is to use the TIE style which requires that the instance of the implementation class be associated with the TIE class of the IDL interface that needs to be implemented. The class implemented in TIE style is also called TIEd class. The implementation class with TIE style must implement the operation Java interface of the IDL interface, instead of BOA's inheritance approach. Figure 3.7 depicts the TIE's delegation relationship pictorially.

BOA's inheritance enables the implementation class to receive requests, process them and send their replies back to clients. In comparison, TIE's delegation achieves the same result by having a TIE class that passes all incoming requests for the implemented CORBA object to its implementation class. Thus, as Figure 3.8 and 3.9 depict, a request to a BOA styled implementation object is received directly, whereas a request to a TIEd object must pass its TIE object. Nevertheless, the performance difference is barely noticeable since a TIE object communicates with its TIEd object via function calls.

Selecting the appropriate style requires consideration of three factors. The first one is whether or not there is a need to separate CORBA functionalities and processing logic. For example, programmers might decide to have the implementation class concerned with processing requests, since this is considered to be more elegant and cleaner. The next one is code reusability. The BOA style has poor reusability since

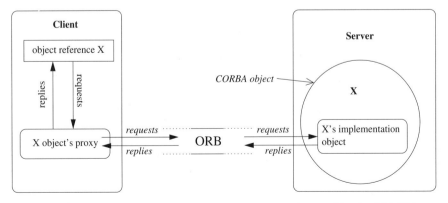

**Figure 3.8** Request flow of a BOA style implemented CORBA object in OrbixWeb.

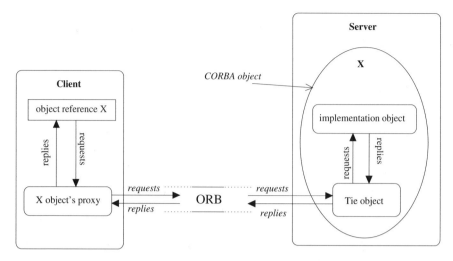

**Figure 3.9** Request flow of a TIE style implemented CORBA object in OrbixWeb.

the implementation class must implement all interface operations and attributes, regardless of whether they are inherited or not. On the opposite side, the TIE style promotes reusability because it permits the implementation class to inherit Java functions and attributes from another implementation class. For example, consider the implementation class NewspaperImpl written using BOA style. NewspaperImpl has inherited from _NewspaperImplBase and must implement all operations and attributes declared by their interface, including those inherited from ServiceProvider and FreeServiceProvider. Figure 3.10 shows this inheritance more clearly.

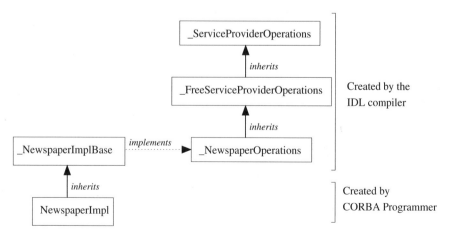

**Figure 3.10** NewspaperImpl in BOA style.

In contrast, if the Newspaper interface were implemented in TIE style, interface ServiceProvider, FreeServiceProvider, and Newspaper can be Implemented, respectively, by ServiceProviderImpl, FreeServiceProviderImpl and NewspaperImpl class. FreeServiceProviderImpl can reuse the code of ServiceProviderImpl and NewspaperImpl can reuse FreeServiceProviderImpl's code, all by inheritance. Figure 3.11 describes these inheritance relationships in more detail.

Besides inheritance, reusability in TIE style can also be achieved if there is an existing class that can be used as the implementation class. This is often the case in legacy applications; the catch is that the existing class must have the same Java function signatures as the operation interface [48]. The existing class might have to be changed to conform to this restriction. The last factor is the amount of memory available. TIE style should not be used if there is insufficient memory to accommodate two Java objects (i.e., TIE and TIEd objects) implementing a CORBA object. Using both styles of implementing a CORBA application is permitted.

***Step 1.2 (Write the implementation class)***    This step is composed of several programming steps, such as (a) the use of appropriately generated class, and (b) the implementation of all mapped interface attributes and operations.

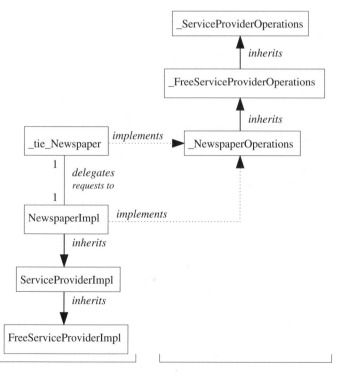

**Figure 3.11**    NewspaperImpl in TIE style.

*Step 1.2.1 (Use of appropriately generated class).*   Initially, the programmer needs to use a generated class of the selected implementation style. An implementation class in BOA must inherit from its skeleton class. For example, the implementation class of the User interface is shown below:

```
package iServiceApp;
public class UserImpl extends _UserImplBase {...}
```

An implementation class in TIE style is associated with the TIE class in two programming steps. The first is to have a class implementing the operation interface of the IDL interface. The implementation class of the User interface would be:

```
package iServiceApp;
public class UserImpl implements _UserOperations {...}
```

The second step is to establish the delegation relationship between the implementation object and its TIE object. It occurs when the implementation or TIEd class is being instantiated. A TIEd class instantiation corresponds to its TIE class instantiation. The TIE class constructor has the TIEd class's instance as a parameter. For example, the delegation relationship for the implementation class in the previous example would be established by the following:

```
User newUser = new _tie_User(new UserImpl());
```

So far, we have considered only single inheritance. If the IDL interface inherits from multiple interfaces, it seems natural for the implementation class to also inherit from multiple implementation classes. Each of the inherited implementation classes is the implementation class of an inherited IDL interface. However, Java does not recognize the notion of multiple inheritance of classes. The closest idea to multiple inheritance is multiple Java interface inheritance; therefore, different approaches are chosen instead. For BOA, the implementation class still inherits from the skeleton

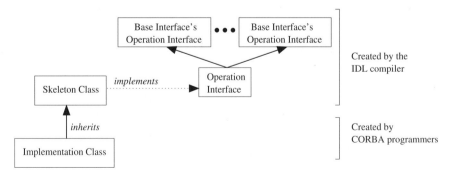

**Figure 3.12**   Multiple inheritance in BOA style.

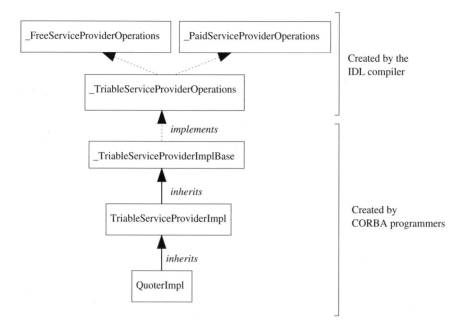

**Figure 3.13**    Quoter's multiple inheritance in BOA style.

class; however, its skeleton class implements all the operation Java interfaces of the inherited IDL interfaces. This is described in Figure 3.12.

For example, implementing the Quoter interface requires that the implementation class to inherit from _QuoterImplBase; Figure 3.13 depicts this multiple inheritance.

For TIE, the implementation class must implement all of these operation Java interfaces. This type of implementation is illustrated in Figure 3.14. Some code from

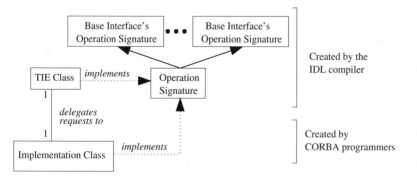

**Figure 3.14**    Multiple interface inheritance in TIE style.

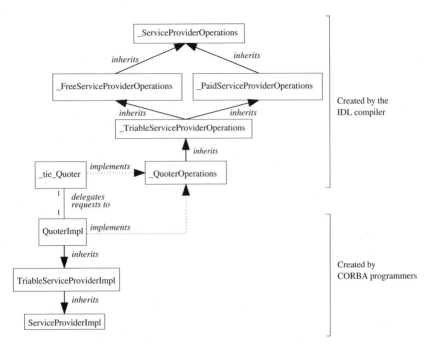

**Figure 3.15**   Quoter's multiple inheritance in TIE style.

the implementation classes of the inherited IDL interfaces might have to be repeated in the implementation class of the inheriting code. Figure 3.15 shows an example of such a case. TriableServiceProviderImpl cannot inherit from both FreeService-ProviderImpl and PaidServiceProviderImpl due to the inexistence of multiple class inheritance in Java. Therefore, there are two possibilities: either inherit from one of the three previously mentioned classes or from ServiceProviderImpl. In the above example, the choice was to inherit from the TriableServiceProviderImpl. This means code that implements operations and attributes of FreeServiceProviderImpl and Paid-ServiceProviderImpl must be repeated in TriableServiceProviderImpl.

*Step 1.2.2 (Implementation of all mapped interface attributes and opera-tions).*   Implementing a mapped interface attribute and operation is similar to writing any other Java functions, regardless of what implementation style is used. For example, the code fragment below implements a ServiceProvider's id attribute and the decreaseCredits operation.

```
// Implementation attributes
private int myId = 0;
private float myUSDCredits = 0;
...
```

```
public int id() {
   return(myId);
}
...
public void
   decreaseCredits(float chargedAmount) {
       myUSDCredits = myUSDCredits - chargedAmount;
   }
...
```

Handling a mapped out or inout IDL parameter operation is similar to the client executable. For example, consider the code fragment of bargain operation which handles an inout parameter of price:

```
public void  bargain(Account account, int itemId, FloatHolder price)
   throws InvalidAccount, NotExist {
     // Local declaration
     float bargainedPrice =
         price.value - (price.value * (float) 0.10);
     System.out.println(account.owner.id() +
         " has bargained US$ " +
         price.value + " for item no " + itemId);
         price.value = bargainedPrice;
}
...
```

Raising a mapped CORBA exception is the same as throwing a Java exception:

```
public Account  login(String loginName, String password)
   throws LoginFailed {

     // Local declaration
     Account account = null;
     account = (Account) myAccounts.get(loginName);
     if(account == null) {
        throw(new LoginFailed(LOGIN_FAILED_MSG));
     }
     if(account.password.equals(password)) {
        throw(new LoginFailed(LOGIN_FAILED_MSG));
     }
  return(account);
}
...
```

When developing a CORBA application, programmers might encounter objects called factory objects. A factory object is an ordinary CORBA object whose function is to create and return other CORBA objects. An example of a factory object is a ClientManager object. Its register operation creates a CORBA object for each newly registered user. A factory object might also give an object marker to new objects during creation. An object marker is then used to identify the object; it must not be null or contain " : " character. The latter applies since that character is used to provide scoping when the object is being located among different objects of different servers. An example of this scoping can be found during the client executable's attempt to bind to a Newspaper object:

```
private Newspaper connectToNewspaper(String args[]) {
  // Local declaration
  Newspaper newspaper = null;
  ...
  newspaper = NewspaperHelper.bind("iNewspaper:iService", args[0]);
  ...
}
...
```

Creating a marked object for an implementation class written using the BOA style is accomplished by passing the object marker to its skeleton class's constructor, for example,

```
// From ClientManagerImpl class:
public User register(String firstName, String lastName,
   String password, Address address, String phoneNo,
   Account[] accounts) throws InvalidDetail, InvalidAccount {
     ...
   myTotUsers++;
   newUser = new UserImpl(myTotUsers, firstName, lastName,
               password, address, phoneNo, accounts, USDCredits);
     ...
   return(newUser);
}
...

// From UserImpl class:
...
private static final
       String USER_ID  = "User";
...
public UserImpl(int id, String firstName, String lastName,
   String password, Address address, String phoneNo,
   Account[] accounts, float USDCredits) {
     super(USER_ID + id);
     ...
}
...
```

In the TIE style, the object marker is passed as the second parameter of the TIE class constructor. Nothing special needs to be done in the implementation class. If the UserImpl from the above example were implemented in the TIE style, it would be:

```
// From ClientManagerImpl class:
...
private static final String USER_ID  = "User";
...
public User register(String firstName, String lastName,
    String password, Address address, String phoneNo,
    Account[] accounts) throws InvalidDetail, InvalidAccount {
    ...
    myTotUsers++;
    String objectMarker = USER_ID + myTotUsers;
    newUser = new _tie_User(new UserImpl(objectMarker, firstName,
                    lastName, password, address, phoneNo,
                    accounts, USDCredits), objectMarker);
    ...
    return(newUser);
}

...
// From UserImpl class:
...
public UserImpl(Sting id, String firstName, String lastName,
    String password, Address address, String phoneNo,
    Account[] accounts, float USDCredits) {
    id = objectMarker;
    ...
}
...
```

## Step 2 (Develop server executable class(es))

Developing a server executable consists of the following programming steps: (a) initialize the server, and (b) notify the ORB.

***Step 2.1 (Initialize the server)***   Server initialization involves at least the initialization of its connection to the ORB. This is usually followed by the creation of boot objects and other initialization steps. Details on boot objects and additional initialization steps are explained below:

*Step 2.1.1 (Initialize the ORB).*   This step is similar to the step of initializing the ORB when developing a client. Both use the ORB's init function, must be performed at least once, and should be executed before any other CORBA statements in the code. However, this step does not initialize the server's connection to the ORB. It initializes the client's connection to the ORB instead.

*Step 2.1.2 (Create boot objects).*   Boot objects are objects that are created when the server starts up. They provide initial points of application access. The server startup provides an opportunity to create these boot objects before clients attempt to access them. For example, the ClientManager, Newspaper, Retailer and Quoter objects are all boot objects. The ClientManager object must be active when clients are trying to logon to their accounts, while the rest of the boot objects must also be active before clients can use services that they provide. Creating these objects earlier during server startup avoids the problem of clients being unable to use those objects because they are inactive. Boot objects are created like any other CORBA object. A code fragment from a server which creates boot objects implemented in BOA is shown below:

```
public static void main(String args[]) {
  // Constants
  private static final String QUOTER_MARKER    = "iQuoter";
  private static final String RETAILER_MARKER  = "iRetailer";
  private static final String NEWSPAPER_MARKER = "iNewspaper";
  ...
  Quoter quoter = new QuoterImpl(QUOTER_MARKER);
  Retailer retailer = new RetailerImpl(RETAILER_MARKER);
  Newspaper newspaper = new NewspaperImpl(NEWSPAPER_MARKER);
  ClientManager clientManager = new ClientManagerImpl();
  ...
}
```

For the server implemented in TIE, the code fragment is as follows:

```
public static void main(String args[]) {
  ...
  Quoter quoter = new _tie_Quoter(new QuoterImpl(), QUOTER_MARKER);
  Retailer retailer =
     new _tie_Retailer(new RetailerImpl(), RETAILER_MARKER);
  Newspaper newspaper =
     new _tie_Newspaper(new NewspaperImpl(), NEWSPAPER_MARKER);
  ClientManager clientManager = new ClientManagerImpl();
  ...
}
...
```

*Step 2.1.3 (Perform other initialization steps).*   Other initialization steps could be opening database connections, preparing a log file, etc. These steps vary from one application to another.

**Step 2.2 (Notify the ORB)**   After its initialization steps are completed, a server must indicate to BOA that it is now ready to accept requests. In OrbixWeb, this consists of converting the org.omg.CORBA.ORB object returned by its init function into a IE.Iona.OrbixWeb.CORBA.ORB and calling its OrbixWeb specific *impl_is_ready*() function with the name of the server specified:

```
package iServiceApp;

// All import statements
// are declared here.
...        `
public class Server {
  ...
  public static void main(String args[]) {
    ...
    // Local declarations
    ORB orb = ORB.init();
    ...
    System.out.println("Server is ready to accept requests");
    _OrbixWeb.ORB(orb).impl_is_ready("iService");
     System.out.println("Server is exiting...");
      ...
}
```

The *impl_is_ready*() function blocks the server until an event occurs, handles that event, and reblocks to wait for another event. It does not return until one of the following occurs: a timeout; an exception is raised while waiting for an event; or IE.Iona.OrbixWeb.CORBA.BOA's *deactivate_impl*() function is executed.

## Step 3 (Test the application)

Once the above programming steps are completed, programmers must proceed with the application testing steps. The command lines used in the following steps are OrbixWeb specific:

- *Compile the client and server classes.* Command lines needed to compile the server are already provided in the Makefile and are automatically performed when make is executed.
- *Start the OrbixWeb demon.* The OrbixWeb demon must be active before the server can be registered. It intervenes when a request arrives for an inactive server by activating the server. In UNIX this is done by executing orbixdj&.
- *Register the server.* Before clients can start using the server, the programmer must register the server with the implementation repository. Server registration creates a new entry in the implementation repository. It needs to be performed only once, or when only registered information (i.e., HostName, ServerName, and ServerAbsoluteClassName) changes. The command line used to register the server is:

  ```
  putit -hHostName ServerName -j ServerAbsoluteClassName.
  ```

  For example, the command line to register a server named iService to run a server executable called iServiceApp.Server on a host machine called numbat is:

```
putit -hnumbat iService -j iServiceApp.Server.
```

## 3.3  DYNAMIC TYPES

This section discusses the CORBA dynamic types used when developing applications. These are like meta-types and they are useful when dealing with type resolution at runtime. Two dynamic datatypes are explained in this section: TypeCode and Any. The former is an IDL datatype which provides information about IDL datatypes, including itself. The latter acts as a universal container for arbitrary datatypes. Using both datatypes enables CORBA applications to handle datatypes which are unforeseen at compile-time and resolvable only at run-time.

### 3.3.1  TypeCode

TypeCode is an IDL datatype that can be used for providing a run-time description of IDL datatypes, including itself; providing a run-time description of the contents of IDL values, for example, the content of an Any value; querying the interface repository (IR) for information about the datatypes it stores; and finally, resolving a value's datatype or other usages that require a datatype's information.

Programmers can use TypeCode as an interface attribute type, a parameter, or as the return value of the operation. When TypeCode is used in an IDL file, programmers must include orb.idl. The following example of its use in an IDL file is taken from Section 3.4.1.

```
#include<orb.idl>
struct ParameterDef {
   string    name;
   TypeCode type;
};
...
```

The next code fragment provides a partial declaration of the TypeCode interface as specified by OMG. Only important operations are shown.

```
module CORBA {
   enum TCKind { tk_null, tk_void, tk_short, tk_long,
      tk_ushort, tk_ulong, tk_float, tk_double, tk_boolean,
      tk_char, tk_octet, tk_any, tk_TypeCode, tk_Principal,
      tk_objref, tk_struct, tk_union, tk_enum, tk_string,
      tk_sequence, tk_array, tk_alias, tk_except
   };
```

```
interface TypeCode {
  TCKind  kind();
  boolean equal(in TypeCode tc);
  ...
};
...
```

The *kind()* function returns the overall classification of the type that TypeCode describes, from the TCKind enumerated values. For example, calling kind on Type-Code of the short datatype returns tk_short. TCKind enumerated values also allow TypeCode to be self-describing.

The operation equal is useful for testing the equality of two TypeCodes. However, the use of this operation should be avoided since the operation is not clearly detailed in the CORBA specification [48]. This causes equal to have an ORB product dependent behavior. Instead, we decided to base datatype comparison, in our sample application, on the overall classification, i.e., using the kind operation.

TypeCode interface is mapped to a Java interface of the same name, while kind operation is mapped to a Java function of TCKind kind(). Each mapped IDL type will have a TypeCode constant of name format _tc_TypeName generated by the IDL compiler. This constant might be used by equal to test whether or not two TypeCodes are the same.

### 3.3.2  Type Any

Any is an IDL type which holds the value of an arbitrary datatype. It is similar to Java's java.lang.Object and should be used to contain values whose datatypes are unresolvable at compile time. Its use also helps to compensate for the loss of operator overloading in IDL. For example, consider all of the operations of the Retailer and Quoter interfaces that have itemId and quotableId parameters, respectively:

```
interface Retailer : PaidServiceProvider {
  void order(in Account account, in long itemId, in short quantity)
      raises(InvalidAccount, NotExist, InsufficientCredits);
  void bargain(in Account account, in long itemId, inout USDollars price)
      raises(InvalidAccount, NotExist);
  void getItemDetail(in Account account, in long itemId, out string name,
      out USDollars price, out string  description)
     raises(InvalidAccount, NotExist);
  ...
};

interface Quoter : TriableServiceProvider {
  USDollars getQuote(in Account account, in long quotableId)
     raises(InvalidAccount, NotExist, InsufficientCredits);
  ...
};
```

Some retail items and quotables might require datatypes other than long. Retail item ids might need to be declared as string should they contain non-numerical values. For quotable ids, they might have to be declared as a string, as it is the case for stock quotes. There are three choices that can be used to solve this problem. One could declare the itemId as string, but this would restrict Retailer from holding ids of more complex datatypes such as IDL struct. Another choice is to overload all operations by declaring the same set of operations more than once, each having the itemId parameter of different IDL datatype. However, this approach is not supported in IDL. The last option is to declare these ids as any. This is the best choice since it accepts all IDL datatypes, including those which are unknown at compile-time. Such flexibility allows the same set of operations to be used with whatever datatypes are passed to them. Thus, the operations have now become:

```
interface Retailer : PaidServiceProvider {
  void order(in Account account, in any itemId, in short quantity)
    raises(InvalidAccount, NotExist, InsufficientCredits);
  void bargain(in Account account, in any itemId,
    inout USDollars price) raises(InvalidAccount, NotExist);
  void getItemDetail(in Account account, in  any itemId,
    out string name, out USDollars price, out string description)
    raises(InvalidAccount, NotExist);
  ...
};

interface Quoter : TriableServiceProvider {
  USDollars getQuote(in Account account, in any quotableId)
    raises(InvalidAccount, NotExist, InsufficientCredits);
  ...
};
```

any is mapped to a Java class of `org.omg.CORBA.Any`. Programmers are required to use `org.omg.CORBA.ORB`'s *create_any*() function to create an instance of `org.omg.CORBA.Any`, for example:

```
Any newAny = ORB.init().create_any();
...
```

In order for an Any variable to hold a value, an insertion function must be used. An insertion typically occurs on the client side, before an Any variable that contains the inserted value is sent to the server for processing. The insertion function required to insert values of a particular datatype is *insert_DataTypeName*. Examples of commonly used insertion function are: *insert_short*(), *insert_long*(), *insert_float*(), *insert_double*(), *insert_Boolean*(), *insert_char*(), *insert_any*(), *insert_Object*(), *insert_string*(). An example of their usage is illustrated by the code fragment below:

```
// From Client executable class
private Any readAny() {
  Any any = null;
  String stringInput = null;
  ...
  try {
    // Read a string from user's
    // keyboard input. (Not shown)
    ...
    any = ORB.init().create_any();
    ...
    any.insert_string(stringInput);
    ...
  }
  ...
  return(any);
}
```

A value of a user defined type (e.g., User) is inserted by using the insert static function of the type's helper class. For example, if the sample application were to insert a User object into an Any variable, the code fragment would be:

```
Any any = ORB.init().create_any();
// Create a new User (Not Shown)
...
UserHelper.insert(any, newUser);
...
```

Extracting a value from an Any usually happens on the server side, particularly in the implementation class. An implementation class must first check what type of data the Any contains by calling its type and executing the kind function of the returned TypeCode. Later, the implementation class calls the appropriate *extract_DataTypeName*() function for the Any value. An example of this extraction is shown in the *convertItemIdToString*() function below:

```
private String  convertItemIdToString(Any itemId)
    throws NotExist {
      // Local declaration
      String convertedItemId = null;

      if(itemId.type().kind() == TCKind.tk_long) {
        convertedItemId =
          Integer.toString(itemId.extract_long());
      }
      ...
      return(convertedItemId);
}
```

## 3.4 ADVANCED CORBA PROGRAMMING

This section discusses advanced features of CORBA programming. These features enable clients to manipulate services without prior knowledge of the interfaces that provide these services. Clients implemented using these features can create requests to interfaces of which they know nothing when they are compiled. Such clients are also capable of traversing through unknown IDL declarations and invoking them. These features also give servers the ability to accept and process any operation call. This is regardless of whether or not the targeted interfaces are already defined in the application IDL. It is important to note that these features capture only the syntactic knowledge of the interfaces, not their semantical understanding. The type of applications that can be built using these features are known as dynamic CORBA applications. Such applications may not be entirely dynamic. Clients could be static, while servers might be dynamic and so on. As this type of application is quite rare, the explanations provided in this section may not be required by most programmers.

### 3.4.1 Dynamic Invocation Interface

The DII or Dynamic Invocation Interface is a generic pre-defined API used to invoke interfaces which are resolved only at run-time. It allows clients to discover interfaces at run-time and create requests for them. DII is rarely used and is limited to a small set of applications. Examples include IDL browsers which explore through interfaces and other IDL constructs, gateway applications which forward requests to non CORBA objects in their appropriate format and vice versa, management support tools, and distributed debuggers. In programming terms, DII does not depend on stubs for request invocation. Thus, these applications are immune to changes or additions to the applications interfaces.

We will consider again the application iService to illustrate the use of DII in developing applications. Here we expand some of the requirements of the iService application to deal with new requirements and expand existing services. TwinLab programmers realize that the current prototype has not taken this into account. If the final product were to follow the current prototype, a software upgrade would be needed for every new type of service added into the interfaces, before clients would access these services. iService immediately rejected this idea since a continuous upgrade could discourage consumers from using the new services. However, the ever-growing nature of the interfaces prevents Twinlab programmers from developing a prototype based on those interfaces. After consulting with iService, they agreed to build the prototype using DII. They also agreed on several programming conventions which govern the way the application interface of a service is manipulated. First, all ServiceProviders are registered with the ServiceManager. Clients will use Service-Provider's serviceList attribute to retrieve a list of available services. A new attribute called opDefList is added to ServiceProvider which returns information required to invoke the interface's operations using DII. This information is contained in type OperationDef structure which has the following IDL declarations:

```
enum ParamMode { IN, OUT, INOUT };
struct ParameterDef {
  ParamMode mode;
  TypeCode  type;
  string    name;
};


typedef sequence<TypeCode> ExceptionDefs;
typedef sequence<ParameterDef> ParameterDefs;

struct OperationDef {
  string        name;
  ExceptionDefs exDefList;
  ParameterDefs paramDefList;
  TypeCode      returnValueType;
};


typedef sequence<OperationDef> OperationDefs;
interface ServiceProvider {
  readonly attribute OperationDefs opDefList;
  ...
}
...
```

Each operation in the interface is essentially a service option whose name is the operation's name. Selecting the option triggers the invocation of the operation. Values passed to its in or inout parameters would be requested from the user. The return value, all out and inout parameters are displayed after the invocation is completed. Proceeding with the development of the prototype, programmers use DII to perform an invocation by following these programming steps: (i) acquire the target object's reference, (ii) create a request object, (iii) populate the request object, (iv) invoke the request object, and finally (v) retrieve the invocation results.

### Step 1 (Acquire the target object reference)

Reference acqusition methods have been explained earlier in the programming steps of client executable development of SII. The reference to the target object need not be obtained in any specific interface. The object may be acquired with an interface ranging from the widest org.omg.CORBA.Object to the object's narrowest interface, as declared in the IDL file.

### Step 2 (Create a request object)

A CORBA request is mapped to a Java abstract class org.omg.CORBA.Request and can be created by using the following org.omg.CORBA.Object's function:

```
public Request _request(String operation);
```

The parameter operation is the name the operation to be invoked. For example, code that creates a request object for a ServiceProvider is:

```
private void handleServiceOption(ServiceProvider serviceProvider,
    OperationDefoperationDef, Account account) {
    ...
    Request request = null;
    ...
    // Create a new request
    request = serviceProvider._request(operationDef.name);
    ...
}
...
```

If an attribute is being called instead, the parameter should be passed with a string in the format of $\_get_{A}ttributeName$, for example, $\_get\_serviceList$ to access serviceList atribute. If an attribute is called to have its value changed, the parameter should be passed with a string in the format of $\_set\_AttributeName$, (e.g., for setting the firstName attribute the string would be: $\_set\_firstName$).

### Step 3 (Populate the request object)

This step consists of several other steps, as detailed below.

### Step 3.1 (Specify the return value's TypeCode).   It is accomplished by using Request's $set\_return\_type()$ function:

```
public void set_return_type(TypeCode tc);
```

An example of its usage, in our application, is:

```
private void handleServiceOption(ServiceProvider serviceProvider,
    OperationDef operationDef, Account account) {
    ...
    Request request = null;
    ...
    // Set the return value type  request.
    set_return_type(operationDef.returnValueType);
    ...
}
...
```

### Step 3.2 (Specify the exception TypeCodes).   If an operation throws exceptions, their TypeCode must be specified to the Request in two steps. The first step is to retrieve an org.omg.CORBA.ExceptionList object which will contain the specified exception TypeCodes. This is accomplished by calling Request's exceptions attribute. Each of the exceptions that could be raised by the operation will have

its TypeCode inserted into the Request. This is achieved by executing the ExceptionList's public void add(TypeCode tc). For example, our sample application has a function called *set Exceptions*() to add all exception TypeCodes into the exception list. The content of this function is:

```
private void setExceptions(Request request, TypeCode[] exDefList) {
    // Local declaration
    int counter = 0;

    for(;counter < exDefList.length;counter++) {
        request.exceptions().add(exDefList[counter]);
    }
}
...
```

***Step 3.3 (Specify All Operation Parameters).*** This step provides Request with all necessary inputs regarding the operation parameters. Which functions should be used to set the input and what exactly this input is depends on the parameter passing mode. First, an appropriate function is executed to return an Any variable which will contain the input. If the parameter passing mode is in, then Request's *add_in_arg*() is called to return the variable, which will be inserted with a parameter value that needs to be passed to the operation. An out parameter requires the execution of *add_out_arg*() function to return the Any variable. This variable must be set to a holder object designated to hold a parameter value set by the operation after its execution. For an inout parameter, *add_inout_arg*() function is used to return the Any variable. This variable must be set with a holder object which holds the value that will be passed to the operation. After the operation invocation, the holder will be set with a new value by the operation.

The last step is to insert the appropriate input into the Any variable. Inserting a parameter value to be passed into the Any variable is accomplished by calling its *insert_DataTypeName*() function. For example, the function used to insert a short is *insert_short*(). Inserting a holder object into the variable requires the use of *insert_Streamable*() function. If there is a basic datatype value to be passed (i.e., the parameter passing mode is in or inout), the value must be passed to the datatype's holder class constructor during instantiation. The newly instantiated holder object is in turn passed to the constructor of another kind of holder class, that is, org.omg.CORBA.DataTypeNameHolderHolder during its instantiation. This is a holder class for the datatype's holder class whose instance is inserted by the *insert_Streamable*() into the Any variable. If the value has a more complex datatype, the value to be passed is specified to its holder class's constructor when it is being instantiated. The holder class to be used has the name of org.omg.CORBA.DataTypeNameHolder, e.g., for Account structure, the holder class is org.omg.CORBA.AccountHolder.

The code fragment below shows the content of the *insert Short*() function in the Client class. The function is used to specify a short operation parameter to the request object. Two new datatypes are introduced in order to facilitate the operation invocation of an unknown interface: ParameterDef and ReturnedParam. ParameterDef contains the parameter's definition which is used to specify the input to the request object. The ReturnedParam class is instantiated for each out and inout parameter. It contains the parameter's name, the parameter's datatype, and its holder object. The holder object contains the value that will be displayed after The operation is executed.

```
private ReturnedParam insertShort(Request request,
    ParameterDef paramDef) {
  // Local declaration
  ReturnedParam returnedParam = null;

  if(paramDef.mode.equals(ParamMode.IN)) {
    System.out.print(paramDef.name + " : ");
    request.add_in_arg().insert_short(readShort());
  }
  else if(paramDef.mode.equals(ParamMode.OUT)) {
    Streamable valueHolderHolder =
      new ShortHolderHolder(new ShortHolder());

  request.add_out_arg().insert_Streamable(valueHolderHolder);
  returnedParam = new ReturnedParam(paramDef.name,
    paramDef.type, valueHolderHolder);
  }
  else if(paramDef.mode.equals(ParamMode.INOUT)) {
    System.out.print(paramDef.name + ": ");
    Streamable valueHolderHolder =
      new ShortHolderHolder(new ShortHolder(readShort()));
    request.add_inout_arg().
      insert_Streamable(valueHolderHolder);
    returnedParam = new ReturnedParam(paramDef.name,
      paramDef.type, valueHolderHolder);
  }
  return(returnedParam);
}
...
```

## Step 4 (Invoke the Request Object)

Request's *invoke*() function triggers the invocation of a request object and causes the request to be sent to the target object, for example:

```
// Invoke the request, i.e., request is sent to the Server
request.invoke();
...
```

## Step 5 (Retrieve the invocation results)

After an operation has been invoked, the return value can be obtained from the request object by first retrieving the contained Any value by using the request's *return_value*() function. The actual return value must later be extracted from the containing Any by calling the appropriate extract function as explained previously in the Any section. For example, the function *displayReturnValue*() from our example retrieves, extracts and displays the return value. If the operation returns no value, i.e., it is declared as a void operation, nothing will be done.

```
private void displayReturnValue(Any returnValue) {

// If the operation returns a value, display the result
if(returnValue.type().kind() == TCKind.tk_void) {
   // No return value, so does not do anything
}
else if(returnValue.type().kind() == TCKind.tk_short) {
   short returnedShort = returnValue.extract_short();
   System.out.println(returnedShort);
}
...
// Similar ifs for the rest of the datatypes
// .....
// .....
}
...
```

Retrieving out and inout parameter values is as simple as accessing the value attribute of the parameter's datatytype holderholder class for basic datatypes or holder class for more complex datatypes. For example, the function *displayReturned Param*() displays an out or inout parameter values returned by the operation. Recall that, a reference to the parameter value's holder or holderholder object is contained within its ReturnedParam object:

```
private void displayReturnedParam(ReturnedParam returnedParam) {
   System.out.print(returnedParam.getName() + " : ");

   if(returnedParam.getType().kind() == TCKind.tk_short) {
      ShortHolderHolder shortHolderHolder =
         (ShortHolderHolder) returnedParam.getHolder();

      System.out.println(shortHolderHolder.value.value);
   }
   ...
   // Similar ifs for the rest of the datatypes
   // .....
   // .....
}
...
```

## 3.4.2 Dynamic Skeleton Interface

The DSI or Dynamic Skeleton Interface is a generic and pre-defined API that enables implementations to receive requests for application interfaces which are known only at run-time. It enables implementations to accept requests, extract details contained in the requests (e.g., operation name, operation parameter values, etc.), and return results. Compared to SSI, DSI is not often used. It may be used to write gateways interfacing between CORBA and non-CORBA applications. Such gateways would appear as normal CORBA servers, containing a number of CORBA objects. In reality, the gateways use DSI to intercept the incoming requests and translate them into calls to the non-CORBA applications. Combined with DII, these gateway objects would be able to translate requests from non-CORBA applications to CORBA requests, that is, bi-directional gateway objects. DSI can also be used to create a CORBA object which acts as a front-end to one or more non-CORBA objects. Having a CORBA object to represent each non-CORBA object usually consumes excessive server resources. In order to reduce consumption, a front-end object could act as a proxy to multiple non-CORBA objects. One way to implement this is to have a parameter specifying which of the non-CORBA objects the operation invocation should be performed on. In terms of programming, DSI does not use the generated skeletons to receive requests. Clients of a DSI application are unable to determine whether DSI or SSI is being used on the server side. The decision to choose DSI or SSI is made on a per-interface basis. The same server might use both DSI and SSI in its implementations, but an implementation is developed only using one of them. The server must indicate that it wishes to use DSI for a specified IDL interface.

An example of DSI usage is given in the iService sample application. In order to promote reusability of its code, iService insists that Twinlab programmers must use an existing ServiceManager implementation. However, although this implementation is derived from a CORBA standard, it is not CORBA compliant. Additional propietary features and information have been incorporated into the implementation. At the end, a translation process is required before an incoming CORBA compliant request can be processed by the ServiceManager implementation. It is decided that a CORBA compliant ServiceManager class will be written, and its object will act as a front-end for existing ServiceManager implementation. The new ServiceManager will have the task of translating incoming requests and their replies, while the existing ServiceManager provides the actual processing for those requests. DSI programming steps that must be taken by the programmers for each implementation class are: (i) write a DSI-based implementation class and (ii) implement _ids() and invoke() functions.

### Step 1 (Write a DSI-based Implementation Class)

This is performed with the following steps: (i) create an implementation class that inherits from the CORBA dynamic implementation, and (ii) implement the _ids() and invoke() functions.

### Step 1.1 (Create an implementation class that inherits from org.omg.CORBA.DynamicImplementation)

```
package iServiceApp;
...
import org.omg.CORBA.DynamicImplementation;
...
public class ServiceManagerImpl
    extends DynamicImplementation {...}
```

### Step 1.2 (Implement _ids() and invoke() functions)    _ids() function is an OrbixWeb specific function that is used to determine what interface(s) the implementation class is implementing, including all inherited interfaces. It returns a Java array of strings; each is the interface repository id of an implemented interface. Details regarding the interface repository are provided later.

```
private static final String IDS[] =
    {"IDL:iServiceApp/ServiceManager:1.0"};
...
public String[] _ids() {
    return(IDS);
}
...
```

The *invoke()* function is called every time a new request needs to be processed. An org.omg.CORBA.ServerRequest object is also passed to this function which encapsulates details regarding the request, e.g., the name of operation or attribute being invoked (*op_name* attribute), parameter details (*params* operation), exception details (*except*). For example, the *invoke()* function from the sample application is shown below:

```
public ServerRequest translate(ServerRequest request) {
    // Local declaration
    ServerRequest nonCORBARequest = request;

    // Perform all the necessary steps to
    // convert the CORBA request to its
    // corresponding Non CORBA request
    // ...
    // ...
    System.out.println("Translating " + request.op_name());
    return(nonCORBARequest);
}

public void invoke(ServerRequest request) {
    // Local declaration
```

```
ServerRequest nonCORBARequest =
    translate(request);
process(nonCORBARequest);
}
...
```

In the example, an incoming request is first translated to a form that can be handled by the non-CORBA implementation class. The result is analyzed by process function and an appropriate NonCORBAServiceManager's function will be called. A return value and/or parameter values must be inserted by the process before the reply is sent. Manipulating ServerRequest to execute the correct NonCORBAServiceManager's function starts with determining the name of operation or attribute being called, for example,

```
...
if(operationName. equals("_get_serviceList")) {...}
else if(operationName.equals("registerService")) {...}
return;
}
...
```

Once the name is known, the parameter details must be extracted from ServerRequest in several steps. These extraction steps are skipped if no parameters are passed. The steps begin with the creation of onr or more Any variables. Each of them will be used to contain the holder object of a passed parameter:

```
process(ServerRequest request) {
    ...
    else if(operationName.equals("registerService")) {
        ...
        Any serviceProvider = orb.create_any();
        ...
    }
}
...
```

It is followed by the instantiation of all of the holder variables which will be used to contain the holder object of each passed parameter:

```
...
else if(operationName.equals("registerService")) {
    ...
    ServiceProviderHolder serviceProviderHolder =
        new ServiceProviderHolder();
    ...
    }
}
...
```

For complex datatypes such as the ServiceProvider interface, use the normal holder class. However, a parameter of simpler IDL datatypes requires the use of two holder classes: one normal holder class and holderholder class. The holder class is used to carry the value of the IDL type, while the holderholder class contains an instance of the holder class. The latter is necessary in order to allow the instance to be passed to a client or server. For example, the DSI code fragment for the User's phoneNo attribute would be:

```
import org.omg.CORBA.StringHolderHolder;
...
ORB orb = ORB.init();
...
if(operationName.equals("_get_phoneNo")) {
   Any returnValue = orb.create_any();
   StringHolder valueHolder = new StringHolder();
   StringHolderHolder valueHolderHolder =
      new StringHolderHolder(valueHolder);
   ...
}
...
```

For in parameters, each of the instantiated holder objects will be filled with the passed parameter value, while for an out it will be used to return a parameter value w resulting from the invocation. In the case of inout, the holder object is used to do both. The next step is to insert each of the instantiated holder objects into its Any variable:

```
...
ORB orb = ORB.init();
...
else if(operationName.equals("registerService")) {
      ...
      Any serviceProvider = orb.create_any();
      serviceProvider.insert_Streamable(serviceProviderHolder);
      ...
   }
   ...
}
```

This step continues with the creation of a named value list using org.omg.CORBA. ORB's *create_list*() with the total number of operation parameters passed as its argument:

```
...
public void process(ServerRequest request) {
   ...
   NVList passedParamValues = null;
   ...
```

```
else if(operationName.equals("registerService")) {
    ...
    passedParamValues = orb.create_list(1);
    ...
}
...
```

A named value list is an instance of org.omg.CORBA.NVList class. It is a list of org.omg.CORBA.NamedValue objects, one for each passed parameter. A named value itself is an IDL datatype with name and value attributes. The former holds the name of the parameter, while the latter is an Any attribute that encapsulates the parameter's value. Now, a named value is added to the named list for each parameter using the named list's *add_value*() function:

```
...
public void process(ServerRequest request) {
    ...
    else if(operationName.equals("registerService")) {
        ...
        passedParamValues.add_value(null, serviceProvider,
            ARG_IN.value);
        ...
    }
    ...
```

*add_value*() parameters are as follows: *item_name* which should be passed with null, *val* for the holder object, and *Flags* for the parameter passing mode. Finally, *params*() of ServerRequest is executed, which fills the named list with the passed parameter values:

```
...
    else if(operationName.equals("registerService")) {
        ...
        request.params(passedParamValues);
        ...
    }
...
```

After *params*() is executed, the holder objects will contain the passed parameter values for the in and inout parameters. These parameter values can be passed to the non-CORBA implementation function. If an exception is raised, it must be caught and sent back to the client. Sending the exception back to the client is achieved by calling ServerRequest's except function with the raised exception passed as its parameter.

```
...
    else if(operationName.equals("registerService")) {
```

```
    ...
    try { myNonCORBAServiceManager.
        registerService(serviceProviderHolder.value);
    } catch (InvalidService invServEx) {
        InvalidServiceHelper.insert(returnedException,invServEx);
    request.except(returnedException);
    }
...
```

If the operation returns some parameter values, then their holder objects must be set appropriately. For example, if there is a NonCORBARetailerImpl that must be reused, the DSI code fragment for the Retailer interface's getItemDetail would be:

```
import org.omg.CORBA.AnyHolderHolder;
import org.omg.CORBA.FloatHolderHolder;
import org.omg.CORBA.StringHolderHolder;
...
else if(operationName.equals("getItemDetail")) {
        ...
        AccountHolder accountHolder = new AccountHolder();
        AnyHolderHolder itemIdHolderHolder =
          new AnyHolderHolder(new AnyHolder());
        StringHolderHolder nameHolderHolder =
          new StringHolderHolder(new StringHolder());
        FloatHolderHolder priceHolderHolder =
          new FloatHolderHolder(new FloatHolder());
        StringHolderHolder descriptionHolderHolder =
          new StringHolderHolder(new StringHolder());
        ...
        // Prepare holder objects
        ...
        myNonCORBARetailer.getItemDetail(accountHolder.value,
          itemIdHolderHolder.value.value, nameHolderHolder.value,
          priceHolderHolder.value, descriptionHolderHolder.value);
        ...
    }
...
// In the NonCORBARetailer class
public void getItemDetail(Account account, Any itemId,
   StringHolder name, FloatHolder price, StringHolder description)
   throws InvalidAccount, NotExist {
    ...
    name.value = "the name of item no " + convertItemIdToString(itemId);
    price.value = TEST_PRICE;
    description.value = "the description of item no " +
       convertItemIdToString(itemId);
    ...
}
...
```

If the operation returns a value, it must be specified to ServerRequest using its result function:

```
...
returnValueHolder.value =
   myNonCORBAServiceManager.serviceList();
returnValue.insert_Streamable(returnValueHolder);
   request.result(returnValue);
```

## Step 2 (Create and Register DSI Objects)

The last programming step is to instantiate the gateway object, that is, Service-ManagerImpl and register it with the server. The registration is performed by using ORB's connect, which also establishes communication between the ORB and the DSI object.

```
Object serviceManager = new ServiceManagerImpl(nonCORBAServiceManager);

// Connect the non CORBA service manager to the ORB
_OrbixWeb.ORB(orb).connect(serviceManager, SERVICE_MANAGER_MARKER);
...
```

### 3.4.3   Interface and Implementation Repositories

Chapter 2 provided details regarding the different CORBA repositories. This section shows how to use the information contained in these repositories to program applications.

***Interface Repository***   The IFR or InterFace Repository is the component of ORB that provides for the storage, distribution, and management of a collection of related objects' IDL definitions. Examples of its application can be found in the CASE tools which aid CORBA application developers; interface browsers which explore IDL definitions and list them to the programmers; CORBA compilers which check for syntax errors; CORBA applications that use DII to invoke objects whose types are not known at compile time, and gateways which might perform request conversion.

IDL definitions are made available by incorporating the information procedurally into stub routines or as repository objects which can be accessed at ORB run-time. They are used by the ORB to interpret and handle values encapsulated by requests; to perform type checking of request signatures to determine whether the request was issued through the DII or through a stub; to assist in checking the correctness of the interface inheritance graph; and to promote interoperability between different ORBs by providing interface information for the objects other ORBs pass. IDL definitions are entered into and retrieved from IFR by manipulating its operations. Usually, there are alternative ways to insert information into the repository e.g., using tools, copying

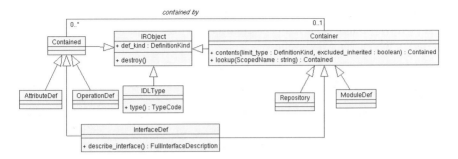

**Figure 3.16**    UML diagram for commonly used IFR definitions.

objects from one repository to another, compiling IDL definitions, etc. In OrbixWeb, putidl and rmidl command line tools are used to enter and remove the IDL definitions. Examples of IDL definitions are definitions for module, interface, exception, etc.

Figure 3.16 shows the UML diagram for commonly used IDL definitions: org.omg.CORBA.IRObject is the base interface for all repository objects. Its def_kind attribute determines the overall classification of the IFR object, while its destroy operation removes the IFR object from the repository. IFR objects that represent the IDL definitions of datatypes such as primitives, interfaces, structures, sequences, and typedef implement org.omg.CORBA.IDLType interface. The interface's type attribute returns the object's datatype as a TypeCode. IDL definitions that can contain other IDL definitions have their IFR objects implementing the org.omg.CORBA.Container interface. For example, module and interface will have their IFR objects stored as org.omg.CORBA.ModuleDef and org.omg.CORBA.InterfaceDef respectively. The contained IFR objects themselves implement org.omg.CORBA.Contained interface. For example, operation and attribute definitions are saved as org.omg.CORBA.OperationDef and org.omg.CORBA.AttributeDef object. Notice that InterfaceDef is both Container and Contained since it can contain IFR objects such as OperationDef and be contained in a ModuleDef. The repository is represented by org.omg.CORBA. Repository object, whose operations can be used to search for IFR objects that match specific criteria, for example, specific TCKind, and so forth.

Recall from the DII section that each ServiceProvider returns information, which is used to perform DII operation invocation, from its opDefList attribute. The problem is that programmers themselves must manually create this information for all operations and ensure that this information correctly reflects the operation. This approach is error prone and potentially returns outdated information. A better way would be to interrogate and retrieve all required information from IFR. This simplifies the application's IDL declarations and implementations since all IDL declarations and the code related to opDefList can be removed. TwinLab Programmers only need to provide the scopedName attribute which returns an absolute name in the format of ModuleName::InterfaceName. The scoped name is used by the client executable to retrieve the appropriate interface definition object.

The different programming steps for manipulating IFR to invoke an interface operation are: (i) acquire the IFR object reference, (ii) retrieve the interface description, (iii) use of the interface description.

### Step 1 (Acquire the IFR reference)

This step is accomplished by using ORB's *resolve_initial_reference*() with its parameter being the "InterfaceRepository" string, which tells the ORB to return an IFR reference. This reference is later narrowed to Repository interface:

```
import org.omg.CORBA.ORBPackage.InvalidName;
...
private Repository connectToIFR() {
    // Local declarations
    Repository IFR = null;
    Object IFRObject = null;
    try { IFRObject = ORB.init().
        resolve_initial_references("InterfaceRepository");
        IFR = RepositoryHelper.narrow(IFRObject);
    } catch(InvalidName invNameEx) {
        System.out.println("Exception during narrow of IFR " +
            "reference : ");
        System.out.println(invNameEx);
    } catch(SystemException sysEx) {
        System.out.println(UNABLE_TO_BIND_TO_IFR_MSG + sysEx);
        }
    return(IFR);
    }
```

### Step 2 (Retrieve interface description)

Programmers might want to first check if the IFR contains anything at all:

```
...
private FullInterfaceDescription
    getFullInterfaceDescription(Repository IFR,
        ServiceProvider serviceProvider) {
        ...
        Contained[] ifrContent = null;
        ...
        // Test if the repository contains anything at all
        ifrContent = IFR.contents(DefinitionKind.dk_all, true);
        if(ifrContent.length < 1) {
            System.out.println("Interface Repository is currently "
                            + "empty");
        }
        ...
```

content operation returns all IFR objects regardless their kinds, that is, dk_all. Boolean value true indicates IFR to exclude IFR objects of inherited interfaces from consideration. Container's lookup function retrieves the interface definition object as Contained object. The name given by the ServiceProvider's scopedName attribute is used as the lookup search criterion. The Contained object returned is narrowed to an InterfaceDef before calling its *describe_interface()*, which returns the interface's full description:

```
...
// Local declarations
Contained contained = null;
InterfaceDef interfaceDef = null;
FullInterfaceDescription fullInterfaceDescription = null;
..
// Retrieve the interface definition from IFR
contained = IFR.lookup(serviceProvider.scopedName());
interfaceDef = InterfaceDefHelper.narrow(contained);
fullInterfaceDescription = interfaceDef.describe_interface();
...
```

This interface description is an IDL structure of type org.omg.CORBA.Interface DefPackage.FullInterfaceDescription whose members provide a complete description of an IDL interface. The structure's member relevant to the example is operations. This member contains a sequence of org.omg.CORBA. OperationDescription, each containing a description about an interface operation. Frequently used members of OperationDescription structure are: the name which contains the operation name, parameters that contain descriptions about the operation parameters, the result which contain the operation return value's type, and exceptions which contains descriptions about all raisable exceptions. Each of the descriptions contained in the parameters is a org.omg.CORBA.ParameterDescription structure. Members of this structure used in the example are name (contains the name of the parameter), type (holds the parameter's type), and mode (has the parameter's passing mode). Each of the exception descriptions contained in the exceptions member is a org.omg.CORBA.ExceptionDescription structure. Its type is used in the example and contains the exception type.

```
typedef sequence <ParameterDescription> ParDescriptionSeq;
typedef sequence <ExceptionDescription> ExcDescriptionSeq;
...
struct ExceptionDescription { TypeCode type;} ;
...
enum ParameterMode {PARAM_IN, PARAM_OUT, PARAM_INOUT};
...
struct ParameterDescription {
        Identifier name;
        TypeCode type;
```

```
            ParameterMode mode;
};
...
struct OperationDescription {
        Identifier name;
        ParDescriptionSeq parameters;
        TypeCode result;
        ExcDescriptionSeq exceptions;
};
...
struct FullInterfaceDescription {
  OpDescriptionSeq operations;
  ...
};
...
```

## Step 3 (Use of interface description)

The information contained in the interface description can be used to create a request using DII. The OperationDescription's name is used as the parameter of Request's _request() function, replacing our own OperationDef's name member. For the set_return()_type() function, the result structure member is used instead of our custom-made OperationDef. The case is similar for exceptions and parameters. Thus, handleServiceOption has now become:

```
    ServiceProvider serviceProvider, Account account) {
      ...
    ParameterDescription[] paramDescList = operationDesc.parameters;
      ...
    request = serviceProvider._request(operationDesc.name);
      ...
    request.set_return_type(operationDesc.result);
      ...
    setExceptions(request, operationDesc.exceptions);
      ...
    returnedParam = setParam(request, paramDescList[counter], account);
      ...
```

The content of setException() function now is:

```
  // Local declaration
  int counter = 0;

  for(;counter < exDescList.length;counter++) {
      request.exceptions().add(exDescList[counter].type);
  }
}
...
```

```
ParameterDescription paramDesc, Account account) {
// Local declaration
ReturnedParam returnedParam = null;
...
if(paramDesc.type.kind() == AccountHelper.type().kind() &&
    paramDesc.type.name() != null &&
    paramDesc.type.name().equals(AccountHelper.type().name())) {
        returnedParam = insertAccount(request, paramDesc, account);
}
else if(paramDesc.type.kind() == TCKind.tk_short) {
        returnedParam = insertShort(request, paramDesc);
    }
...
```

The code that checks the parameter passing mode is now slightly different. For example, a set of if's in the insertAccount has become:

```
ParameterDescription paramDesc, Account account) {
...
if(paramDesc.mode.equals(ParameterMode.PARAM_IN)) {
    ...
}
else if(paramDesc.mode.equals(ParameterMode.PARAM_OUT)) {
        ...
        returnedParam =
        new ReturnedParam(paramDesc.name.paramDesc.type, valueHolder);
    }
    else if(paramDesc.mode.equals(ParameterMode.PARAM_INOUT)) {
            ...
            returnedParam = new ReturnedParam(paramDesc.name,
                paramDesc.type, valueHolder);
        }
...
```

Similar changes also apply to other insert functions.

**Implementation Repository**  As detailed in Chapter 2, IR or Implementation Repository is the component of the ORB which Contains information that allows the ORB to locate and activate implementations of objects. Since most of this information is vendor- or operating system-specific, OMG does not provide a detailed specification of IR. It is commonly used as a place to store additional information associated with implementations. For example, it may provide debugging information, administrative control, resource allocation, security, etc. An implementation repository is usually responsible for maintaining a registry of known servers, recording which servers are currently running on which host and port number, and starting inactive servers which are registered for automatic start-up when their requests arrive.

In OrbixWeb, putit, lsit, rmit, psit, and killit are the command line tools used to manipulate the IR. putit has been explained previously in the SSI section. lsit is used to list all registered servers, for example:

```
Someone@cs lsit
[ IT_daemon: New Connection (numbat.cs.rmit.edu.au:60951) ]
[New Connection (numbat.cs.rmit.edu.au,IT_daemon, *,surset,
 pid=-889250955) ]
Root Directory
    iService
[ IT_daemon: End of Connection (numbat.cs.rmit.edu.au,IT_daemon,
surset,pid=-889245829) ]
```

rmit is used to unregister a server in the following format: rmit ServerName. For example, to remove a server called iService the command is: rmit iService. psit is used to displays details on the active servers, for example:

```
Someone@cs psit
[ IT_daemon: New Connection (numbat.cs.rmit.edu.au:61370) ]
[7611: New Connection (numbat.cs.rmit.edu.au,IT_daemon,*,
surset,pid=3405730599)]
Active servers at node numbat.cs.rmit.edu.au are :
Name       Marker  Code    Comms   Port    Launch  PerClient?
------------------------------------------------------------
iService   *       xdr     tcp     2000    auto    ---
[ IT_daemon: End of Connection (numbat.cs.rmit.edu.au,IT_daemon,
surset,pid=7611)]
```

killit deactivates servers using the following format: killit ServerName. For example, the command to deactivate the iService server is killit iService.

## 3.5  SUMMARY

In this chapter, we have explained the CORBA programming features that are utilized to develop distributed applications. IDL supplies such applications with the ability to interact beyond their confining heterogeneities. The separation between interfaces and their implementations is the enabling factor. This is further enhanced by the freedom to choose between static and dynamic processing. Clients that use static interfaces can choose SII, while those that are unable to determine the interfaces at compile time should select DII instead. For servers that rely on static interfaces, SSI can be used, while servers that receive requests for interfaces that cannot be resolved during compilation ought to use DSI instead. When using SSI, the TIE and BOA implementation styles accommodate existing code reuse and ground-up development, respectively. Dynamic types are used to improve the processing flexibility with their meta information about types (TypeCode) and a universal container (Any). Management, storage, and distribution of an application's IDL definitions are handled by the IFR, while the IR tackles server activations and other implementation-management related responsibilities.

## 3.6 REVIEW QUESTIONS

- What is the difference between conventional programming and CORBA programming?
- How does IDL reconcile heterogeneities in a distributed system?
- Why doesn't IDL recognize private and protected access mode?
- Explain the term "object reference stringification."
- What is the difference between attribute in an IDL interface attribute and a normal object attribute?
- Why do we need helper and holder classes?
- What is the function of Any? When should it be used?
- What is DII? What does it do? When should DII be used? What kind of applications use DII?
- What is DSI? What does it do? When should DSI should be used? What kind of applications that use DSI?
- Explain the two implementation styles in SSI.
- What is the function of IFR? Give examples of applications that must use IFR.
- What is IR? Is IR specified in the CORBA standard? Justify your answer. What is IR usually responsible for?
- Compare how these two implementation styles enable an implementation class to process requests.
- Explain the factors a programmer must consider when choosing the appropriate SSI implementation style.

## 3.7 EXERCISES

- If clients are implemented using DII, what implementation approaches must their servers use: SSI or DSI? Justify your answer.
- Consider an operation with the following IDL declaration:

```
void X();
```

If the code to invoke this operation is provided, what changes need to be made to the code which creates a Request object in order for the same code to be used to invoke the following attribute:

```
readonly attribute long X;
```

- Provide the implementation of the following Student interface in the BOA and TIE approach:

```
interface Person {
   readonly attribute string name;
   attribute            string address;
};

interface Student : Person {
   readonly attribute string no;

   void enrol(in string subjectCode);
};
```

Make all of the necessary assumptions.

- Provide the DII code fragment to invoke the operation invokedOp of the following IDL interface:

```
exception InvokedOpException {};
interface InvokedObject {
   boolean invokedOp(in string param)
          raises(InvokedOpException);
};
```

Pass param parameter with the value of "invokedOpParam".

- Provide the DSI code fragment for the above question. Assume the Java function that implements invokedOp operation is already provided.

# PART II

# ADVANCED CORBA

# CHAPTER 4

# Object Adaptors

OMG provided the specification of two adaptors, the *Basic Object Adaptor* (BOA) and the *Portable Object Adaptor* (POA). BOA was released in an earlier version of the OMG specification. Because of several problems related to this adaptor, such as portability and flexible activation policies, OMG recently released the POA specification.

Even though most of the existing CORBA systems are supporting POA or being updated to support it, we have decided to provide details of BOA (e.g., architecture and object/servant/server activation and deactivation). We believe that this will provide a clear idea about the BOA limitations and therefore make it easier to understand the OMG adoption of POA. This chapter also provides a comparison between BOA and POA with regard to the issues relating to object adaptors. The chapter starts with an overview of CORBA and its adaptors, and in Section 4.2, the architectures of BOA and POA are described. Section 4.3 provides an evaluation of both BOA and POA with regard to a set of criteria. Finally, in Section 4.4, we show how POA can be extended to construct database adaptors that enable making object references persistent.

## 4.1 OVERALL PICTURE

The rationale behind the inclusion of an object adaptor in the OMG architecture is interface flexibility and management. To communicate without an adaptor, both the ORB and the implementations must agree on one fixed set of interfaces or they must support multiple sets of interfaces. Providing a unique set of interfaces is not desirable because different sets of interfaces might be needed, depending on the application's aims. For example, an implementation might perform a radically new kind of service, include new functionalities, or better performance may be needed. The second alternative, that is, to support multiple sets of interfaces, is complex and could result in only a subset of the adaptor's interfaces being used. Confusion might also occur over which set of interfaces should be selected. It is conceded that foreseeing all the types of interface is impossible.

To be efficient, the interface of an adaptor would have to be tailored according to the interface of the ORB and the interfaces of the implementations. This does not mean that adaptors can be introduced sparingly; however, it happens only in special cases and OMG expects to have a small number of adaptors existing. The advantage of placing an object adaptor between an ORB and implementations is to make them independent of each other. In this way, an ORB relies on its adaptor's interface to communicate indirectly with the implementation objects and vice versa. An adaptor will be responsible for adapting the interfaces of its implementation objects for the ORB. It will also allow the implementation object to gain access to the ORB service via the adaptor's public interface.

The adaptor will be then dependent on the interface of its implementation objects and the interface of its ORB. Changes in the interfaces will affect the adaptor's interface.

In addition to the role of linking an ORB with object implementations, object adaptors have other functionalities, including generation and interpretation of object references, method invocation, security of interaction, activation and deactivation of object implementations, mapping object references to their implementation objects, and registration of implementation. In earlier versions of CORBA, BOA (*Basic Object Adaptor*) [70] was proposed as a basic adaptor that provides these functionalities. However, BOA's specification is plagued by problems in its portability, clarity and completeness. As a result, currently available BOAs are vendor specific and incompatible. An RFP (Request For Proposal) for ORB Portability was published to address these problems [71]. This document reveals that OMG had several choices: (i) improve the BOA specification to eliminate multiple interpretations; (ii) allow multiple versions of BOA to exist, each for a major operating environment (e.g., POSIX, Windows, Macintosh) and standardize each of those versions; (iii) publish a new "universal" object adaptor which is not necessarily derived from BOA; or (iv) abandon the BOA standardization effort. The first choice seems too hard, if not impossible. Because of too many incompatible versions of BOA, producing a specification that considers all of them seems like a futile attempt. The second will cause the proliferation of multiple versions of BOA. The next choice promises a clean break from the past but invalidates existing applications. The last one is a "hands-off" approach and should not be selected. Ultimately, OMG decided to start fresh by taking the third choice as their solution [74]. They agreed to let the vendors keep their BOAs, but no new BOA specification will be published. Applications that use BOAs will continue to function and be supported by the ORB vendors.

POA (*Portable Object Adaptor*) is the OMG's new adaptor. It is not an improved version of BOA and is specified in [78]. POA was designed from the ground-up with portability in mind. Server code benefits most from POA, since they can now operate across different CORBA products. POA interfaces are declared in their own PortableServer module. This gives more room and more flexibility for future expansions of POA. Like BOA, POA is designed to handle objects with conventional implementation.

## 4.2 ARCHITECTURES

When an invocation is made, the client-side ORB is responsible for interpreting the object's roles, for locating the server in which the object is implemented and for sending a request to that server. On the server side, the request is received by the ORB, where three steps of dispatching are necessary: (i) the ORB must find the object adaptor that the object is implemented in and pass the request on to that object adaptor; (2) the object adaptor must find the servant that implements the object; and (3) if the servant uses a static skeleton, the request is unpacked by the IDL-generated code and the desired method is invoked. Before any of this can happen, the object adaptor must first know about the servant. After registering the servant with the object adaptor, an implementation must be able to create and export object references that address the servant. So besides merely performing invocations, the object adaptor must provide an administrative interface as well. The object adaptor will be responsible for: (i) registration of implementations; (ii) mapping object references to the corresponding object implementations; (iii) activating and deactivating objects and implementations; (iv) generating and interpreting object references; (v) method invocation; and (vi) security of interactions.

Figure 4.1 shows the object adaptor in relation to the other server-side parts of an ORB. The object adaptor is trapped between the ORB core and the object implementation and provides three interfaces: one to the ORB, consisting of a single method to receive an incoming request; one to the user code, for forwarding requests, using either DSI or DII; and one interface through which an implementation can cause objects to be activated or deactivated and can influence the processing of requests.

The most simple object adaptor would be no more than a table that maps object keys (the server-side part of an object reference) to servants. Upon invocation, only

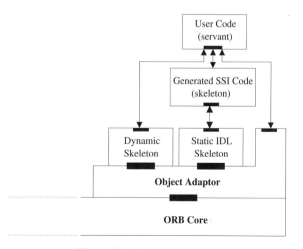

**Figure 4.1** ORB server side.

a single table lookup would be necessary; activation and deactivation of servants would cause insertions and deletions into that table.

### 4.2.1 Basic Object Adaptor

The BOA's purpose was to be a simple and generic type of object adaptor that could be used, as the name suggests, for basic purposes. As such, its interface is intentionally minimalistic, providing several methods, conveniently specified in IDL as shown below:

```
module CORBA {
    // from Interface Repository interface
    interface interfaceDef;

    // from Implementation Repository
    interface ImplementationDef;

    interface Object;

    // an object for the authentication service
    pseudo interface Principal;

    typedef sequence<octet,1024> ReferenceData;


    ...


    pseudo interface BOA {

        // implementation activation and deactivation
        void impl_is_ready (in ImplementationDef impl);
        void deactivate_impl (in ImplementationDef impl);
        void obj_is_ready (in Object obj,
                           in ImplementationDef impl);
        void deactivate_obj (in Object obj);

        // generation and interpretation of object references
        Object create (in ReferenceData id,
                   in InterfaceDef intf,
                   in ImplementationDef impl);

        void dispose (in Object obj);
        ReferenceData get_id (in Object obj);
        void change_impelemtation (in Object obj,
                                   in ImplementationDef impl);

        // identification of the principal making a
        // request Principal
        get_principal (in Object obj, in environment ev);
```

```
};
  ...
};
```

Figure 4.2 depicts a global picture of BOA. It shows the translation of a user's (IDL) operation to a set of BOA operations. The first step is to start a server process when the first request to its object arrives. The implementation registers as being ready to receive requests, by calling $BOA :: impl\_is\_ready()$. Next, BOA performs an up-call to the object activation routine. Later, BOA delivers the requests to the object using the appropriate skeleton method. The implementation might or might not use BOA's services, through its interface for operations such as object deactivation using $BOA :: deactivate\_obj()$.

### 4.2.2 Portable Object Adaptor

POA is an object that is visible to the server. Object implementations are registered with the POA. As for BOA, the ORB, POA, and object implementations cooperate to determine on which servant the operation should be invoked, and to perform the invocation. As shown in Figure 4.3, there are several elements within the POA architecture that are involved in the process of activation and invocation: servant, object reference, POA, policy, POA manager, servant manager, and adaptor activator. In this section we will provide definitions of these elements of the POA architecture based on [79] and will explain how their roles fit within the overall picture of the POA functions.

- Basically, a servant class is a programming language object (e.g., C++ class) that implements operations on one or more objects (e.g., C++ objects). Servants generally exist with the context of a server process.
- A user has a reference to an object, called an object reference, and invokes an (IDL) operation on that object. The request is mediated by the ORB and transformed into invocations on a particular servant. An object reference in the POA model is the same as in the CORBA object model. This reference contains an

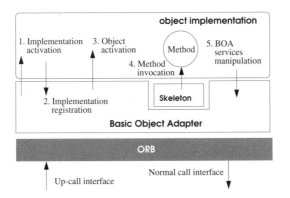

**Figure 4.2**  BOA operations in a shared server.

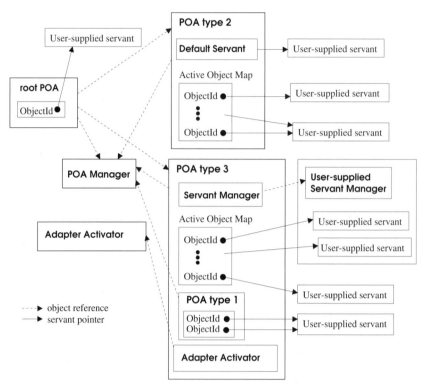

**Figure 4.3**    POA architecture.

object Id and a POA identity. In a few ORB implementations, object references contain additional information that helps increase efficiency of the binding process (e.g., location of the server).

- A POA is an identifiable entity within the context of a server. Each POA provides a name space for object ids and name space for other (nested or child) POAs. Policies, as shown in Figure 4.4, associated with a POA, describe the characteristics of the objects implemented within that POA. Nested POAs form a hierarchical name space for objects within a server.

- A Policy is an object, associated with a POA by an application, in order to specify a characteristic shared by the objects implemented under that POA. The specification defines policies controlling the POA's threading model as well as other options related to the management of objects. Other specifications may define other policies that affect how an ORB processes requests on objects implemented in the POA.

- The servant manager activates and deactivates servants when requested by the ORB (through specific operations). The servant manager is responsible for managing the association of an object (as characterized by its object id value) with

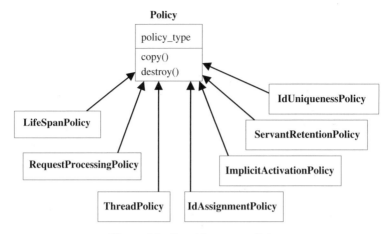

**Figure 4.4**   Portable server policies.

a particular servant, and for determining whether an object exists or not. There are two types of servant managers, namely *Servant Activator* and *Servant Locator*. The type used in a particular situation depends on policies in the POA.

- An adaptor activator is an object that the application developer can associate with a POA. The ORB invokes operations on an adaptor activator when a request is received for a child POA that does not currently exist. The adaptor activator can then create the required POA on demand.

Clients hold references upon which they can make requests. These references can be obtained by using CORBA services (e.g., Naming Service, Trading Service). When a request is invoked by using the information within the reference, as explained in Section 2.5 of Chapter 2, the first thing that the ORB does is to locate the appropriate POA object, which in turn has enough information to locate the responsible servant for the object for which the request is invoked. As we will see later on, POAs are identified by name within the namespace of their parent POA. The location POA starts from the root POA hierarchy (called `rootPOA`) and proceeds until the correct POA is found. The full path name is extracted from the reference to locate the position of the POA within the hierarchy.

There are several ways to locate a POA within a hierarchy, and obviously these are implementation considerations (and therefore OMG will not provide any detail). One option is that the request is delivered to `rootPOA`, which then scans the first part of the path name and then delegates the request to one of its child POAs. The request is handed down the line until the right POA is reached. This way follows a linear access to the POAs along the inheritance hierarchy, which is generally appropriate when the hierarchy is small. When there is a large number of adaptors, a better option is needed. For example, an access method (index or hash table) can be used to increase the performance of the lookup of the appropriate POA within the hierarchy.

If the lookup of the POA hierarchy fails, that is, the appropriate POA is not found, then the application (programmer) has the opportunity to create and register the required POA by using an adaptor activator. As shown in Figure 4.3, an adaptor activator is a user-implemented object that can be associated with an existing POA within the POA hierarchy. It is given an opportunity to create the required POA. If it cannot, the client receives an exception.

The creation of POA's children requires user intervention because programmers usually wish to assign a custom set of policies by writing the code that does this. An example of policy can be as follows: if a new POA is to be created but no adaptor activator has been registered with its parent, then the request will fail. Within the adaptor activator, the user cannot only create further child POAs, but also activate objects managed by these child POAs, possibly by reading state information from the disk.

Once an object's POA has been found, further processing depends on the POA's servant retention policy and its request processing policy; Figure 4.4 shows the different types of policies. The POA uses the oid of the object reference to locate the servant. Figure 4.3 shows the three possible ways to find the responsible servant, and these are based on the different policies: RETAIN, use_default_servant, and use_servant_manager. In the former, that is, POA has a servant retention policy of RETAIN, then POA performs a lookup in the *Active Object Map* to find if there is a servant associated with the oid value from the request. If found, the POA invokes the operation on the servant. This case relates to "POA type 1" in Figure 4.3. The lookup method can have a big impact on the POA's overall performance. As mentioned above, appropriate access methods are useful when large numbers of objects are registered.

If the servant retention policy is non-RETAIN, or has the RETAIN policy but no matching entry is found in the Active Object Map, the request processing policy is considered. If its value is a use default servant, the user can provide a single default servant that will be used regardless of the request's oid. The POA invokes the operation on the default servant associated to it. If a default servant is not found, then the POA raises an OBJ_ADAPTOR system exception. This case relates to "POA type 2" of Figure 4.3.

A default servant is useful when handling a group of usually identical objects through a single servant. A default servant can use the POA's context-sensitive introspection methods to query the oid of the current request and behave accordingly. Default servants provide scalability using the flyweight patterns: the server does not grow with the number of objects. Rather, the server can produce arbitrary numbers of object references while the number of active servants is constant. A database server is an example of the usage of a default servant. Each table would be represented by using a different POA and the key value is used as oid. In this way, all table rows are objects with their own object reference. Only a single default servant is needed per table; in an invocation, this default servant would query the request's oid and use it as a table index. By using the DSI, the default servant could even be identical for all database tables, examining the table structure to select its parameter's types.

The request processing policy can be set to use the servant manager, providing even more flexibility than in the previous policies. This case relates to "POA type 3" of Figure 4.3. Because the POA has a reference to a user-provided servant manager (see Figure 4.5), it delegates the search to this manager which will invoke specific operations (such as incarnate or preinvoke), depending on the type of the manager. There are two types of server managers, servant locator and servant activator, which can be used depending on the servant retention policy. If this policy's value is RETAIN, the servant activator will incarnate a new servant which will, after the invocation, be entered into the Active Object Map itself to reflect the new update. If the servant retention policy is non-RETAIN, the servant manager would have to be a servant locator; its task is to locate a servant suitable only for a single invocation. The servant locator supplements the default servant mechanism by providing a set of default servants. This is generally important for critical applications, when load balancing is required; the server locator selects the servants with the less load.

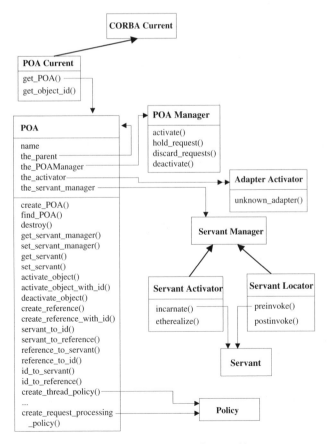

**Figure 4.5**   Different elements of a portable server.

Both servant activator and servant locator can also throw a special forward exception instead of returning a servant [79]. This exception contains a new object reference to forward the request to, possibly to an object realized in a different server on another system, employing the GIOP location forwarding mechanism. Forwarding allows, for example, the implementation of load balancing or redundant services: the servant manager would check its replicated servers and forward the request to an available one.

Figure 4.6 summarizes all the steps described above. A overall picture of the different elements related to the OMG's POA is given in Figure 4.5. Details of their IDL interfaces can be found in [79].

## 4.3   TECHNICAL ISSUES

This section provides a detailed description of BOA and POA, concentrating on different issues involved in processing object requests.

### 4.3.1   Overview

It is important to put both adaptors side by side to give a better understanding of their strengths and weaknesses. In order to do this, there are several aspects of an adaptor that need to be evaluated: server, object, servant, object grouping, request redirection, and multithreading and concurrency control.

**Server**   A server must be registered before the adaptor can activate it. Activation happens when the first request arrives for the implementation. During its up-time, a server allocates and deallocates memory used by its active objects. When no longer needed, the server and its objects will be deactivated. Although this scenario is typical of a server lifetime, there are a few issues to be considered. One of them is related to the way servers are registered and how they manage their memories. Another issue is about the way servers are gracefully deactivated and the way objects and their servants participate in this process.

**Object**   Several issues are related to objects. These include object identity (oid), lifespan, activation, deactivation, binding and lifetime relationship with their servants. Here we describe these concepts.

Each object has an oid, differentiating itself from others. The way an oid is defined and the information it supports (operations, etc.) are to be considered. An object's lifespan is the time period during which the object exists. Classified by their lifespan, there are two kinds of objects: persistent and transient. A persistent object is an object that can survive beyond the process that created it. Persistent objects continue to exist until they are explicitly deleted, while a transient object's lifespan is constrained by its creating process. Whether or not the object lifespan is contemplated in an adaptor should be considered. Object activation prepares an object to accept and process its requests, whereas object deactivation shutdowns an active ob-

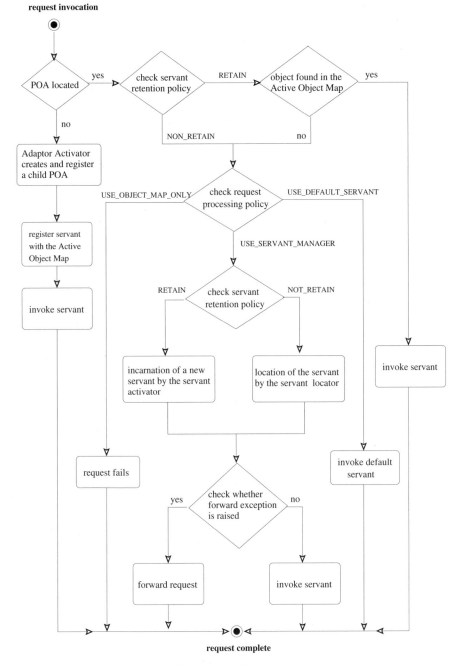

**request invocation**

**Figure 4.6**    POA-based request processing.

ject. Issues about object activation and deactivation relate to the way objects of an adaptor are activated and deactivated, the styles of activating objects, and whether or not objects can be activated on demand (activated when the first request arrives) and if so. Finally, regarding the relationship with servants, the issues to be considered are the types of relationships that exist between objects and their servant lifetime and the way this affects object implementations.

**Servant**    An important aspect of servants is the registration process. A servant is registered to record the association with its implemented object. There are two ways of registering a servant: explicit and implicit registration. An example of implicit registration is when a servant class's instantiation triggers its constructor to performs registration. In contrast, an explicit registration is usually obtained by explicitly calling a method. The types of registrations supported and how a servant is registered are important considerations for an adaptor.

Another important aspect of servants is the relationship between servant, skeleton and stub. One feature of this relationship that deserves special attention is collocation, an optimization technique which avoids request/reply overheads (marshaling, unmarshaling, etc.) when the target object is in the same process as the requesting object. This is achieved by having a separate inheritance hierarchy for the client-side and the server-side classes, allowing a request to be passed to the appropriate local servant when its target object is local or to the stub if the object is remote. The level of control which an adaptor has on the servant-skeleton-stub relationship is crucial for the server code's portability and performance.

**Object Grouping**    Objects with the same characteristics are grouped together to simplify their manipulation. Object grouping enables programmers to apply the same set of operations to the members of a group, which is important when objects in the group need to be processed in a uniform manner. The issues to be considered are whether or not the adaptor supports object grouping and how a group is structured.

Assuming object grouping exists, object group activation and deactivation are also important issues. Object group activation activates an entire group of related objects when any single object in this group is accessed, similarly for object group deactivation. The purpose is to avoid overheads that might on a per-object invocation. What sort of strategy is devised by the adaptor should be carefully weighed.

**Request Redirection**    Request redirection is the act of forwarding requests to another object. It is applied in cases where the destination object is unable to or refuses to process the request.

**Multithreading and Concurrency Control**    Single threaded servers are not scalable and maybe unable to handle a large number of requests, because requests are processed sequentially rather than concurrently. Employing multithreading increases a server's scalability, but raises the issues of thread allocation, critical section, and multithreaded requests.

Thread allocation is an act of assigning a request to a thread for its concurrent processing. How requests are distributed to their threads is reflected in the selection of thread policy. There are several thread allocation policies [34] to choose from: thread pool, thread per request, thread per client, thread per connection, thread per servant and thread per object. Servers with a thread pool pre-create their threads during startup; each incoming request is assigned to a thread. In the rest of the policies, operations are assigned a new thread. This thread is spawned for a request, client, client's connection, servant, and object, respectively. The issues related to thread allocation are the time when thread assignment take place, who should perform this and how it is done.

Critical sections are parts of a program where only one active thread should exist at any given time; if this not enforced, wrong results can occur. Ensuring this requires mechanisms such as locking and thread synchronization. Some means should be provided to specify and protect an object's critical sections.

A multithreaded request is a request which is handled by multiple threads. The request is broken down to smaller tasks and each of them is assigned to a thread. These tasks should be computationally complex enough to justify their thread creation. The approach taken by an adaptor to accomplish efficient request multithreading needs to be investigated.

### 4.3.2    Basic Object Adaptor

This section provides details about BOA, elaborating on issues described in Section 4.3. As mentioned earlier in this chapter, BOA has problems with its specifications. Some of these problems, such as object activation and oid assignment, are caused by their operations having an `ImplementationDef` interface as its parameter. This interface contains information that describes an implementation object. Since OMG saw this information as system specific, it decided not to standardize `ImplementationDef`. As a result, operations that have this interface as their parameters are not portable. Other sources of problems are: BOA's basic nature (for problems in multithreading and concurrency control, relationship between object and servant lifetime, object grouping, object group activation and deactivation), considered as being environment specific (for the problems in server's memory management and registration) and inadequate specification of other problems.

***Server***    Information related to the server registration process is left undefined because its characteristics are environment specific. Regarding the server activation issue, BOA specifies four policies to activate its servers: shared server, unshared server, server per-method and persistent server. These policies are illustrated in Figure 4.7. Under the shared server policy, multiple active objects of a given implementation share the same server. Figure 4.2 depicts a shared server policy. For the unshared server policy, there is only one object of a given implementation active. Object activation is not necessary in this policy. Servers based on this policy are launched for each method invocation, whereas servers in the persistent server policy are activated by means external to BOA. Note that concept of "persistency" used in this context

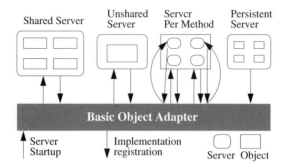

**Figure 4.7**   Steps in activating server in all policies.

is different from the same concept used in database systems. A more appropriate meaning is "externally activated server" [87] .

When a server with an unshared activation policy is ready to accept a request, it will notify BOA by calling $BOA :: obj\_is\_ready()$. This also activates its sole object, eliminating any need to perform a separate object activation. Servers with other activation policies should use $BOA :: impl\_is\_ready()$ instead and carry out their object activations in another step.

During the server's up-time, its implementation might receive a request that returns a value. When this happens a memory space will be allocated to hold this value. Similarly, a memory space is also allocated for the implementation when its object is activated. When the server needs to be shut down, an appropriate deactivation's operation will be called. Depending on the server's activation policy, a server can be deactivated by calling $BOA :: deactivate\_impl()$ (if the server is a shared or persistent server) or $BOA :: deactivate\_obj()$ (if the server is an unshared server), or automatically after processing a request (if the server is a per-method server).

Although the above process seems clear, there are several details missing. First, there is no mention on how BOA and implementation objects are synchronized after their server is activated. Without synchronization, BOA might start to deliver the request even when the target object's implementation is not ready with its event handling process. In some ORB products (e.g., Orbix [52, 53]), their server calls $BOA :: impl\_is\_ready()$ and blocks. Others make multiple $BOA :: impl\_is\_ready()$ calls, with another operation is used for synchronization. This causes $BOA :: impl\_is\_ready()$ to behave differently from one ORB product to another. No specification regarding server memory management is given. Some rules for each BOA's operating environment (e.g., POSIX) should have been defined, but they were considered to be system dependent [71]. Also, how the objects and their servants can partake in the server's deactivation process is not mentioned.

**Object**   An oid in BOA is usually embedded in the object reference and unique within the scope of a server. It is of the type ReferenceData and mapped to a sequence of 1024 octets. An oid's value needs to be converted to ReferenceData before it can be used to assign an object. Oid assignment can be done by calling

$BOA :: create()$ which creates an object reference as a side effect. Other arguments of $BOA :: create()$ are: `ImplementationDef` and `InterfaceDef`. The first argument was explained earlier, while the function of the second one is to define the object's interface. No ambiguities appeared from $BOA :: create()$ itself; however, the creation of an `ImplementationDef` has never been completely specificatied. For this reason, assigning an oid in BOA cannot be performed in a standardized manner. No other support on oids is available.

All BOA objects are persistent; however, BOA does not provide any specifications on transient objects. Proprietary mechanisms are used instead to carry out their creations. When the first request for an object arrives, BOA will perform an up-call to its object activation routine. The object's Id is made available for activating the appropriate object. After the object is activated, it will indicate its readiness to BOA by calling $BOA :: obj\_is\_ready()$.

Previously we showed all that BOA specifications give concerning object activation. No additional details on the routine's characteristics are given; this affects the availability of activation on demand. There are several points not addressed in the specification, including: (i) the parameters of the routine, (ii) the way BOA starts the activation, (iii) the way appropriate code is loaded and passed to BOA, (iv) the initialization of the state of the target object's state, and (v) the assignment of objects to the server. The point (v) is determined by the object implementor's defined policy. How this policy is defined in the `ImplementationDef` is again, unspecified. Vendors attempt to resolve these questions with their own solutions (e.g., Orbix with its `Loader` class [52, 53]), but these are proprietary. Furthermore, BOA does not explicitly mention the object activation styles available. Although, in practice it is clear that most, if not all, ORB products use the servant per-object activation style: one servant is instantiated and registered for every activated object.

Deactivating BOA objects is the job of their implementations and is accomplished by calling $BOA :: deactivate\_obj()$. When there are too many objects active in the server, some might have to be deactivated to free up the server's memory. However, there is no call-back function that can be used by BOA to deactivate them. In some CORBA products, an object's deactivation is triggered by its servant's destructor, while others use a third call-back function.

Figure 4.8 shows the relationship between object and servant lifecycles. As depicted, the BOA specification does not attempt to isolate an object's lifetime from

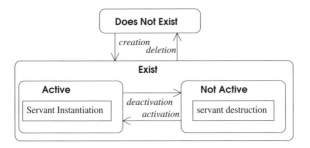

**Figure 4.8**  Object and servant lifecycles in BOA.

its servant's. Thus BOA's object activation is analogous to its servant instantiation. Similarly, an object deactivation in BOA will cause its servant to be destroyed. This coupling prevents servants from being reused to implement more than one object. Nevertheless, BOA offers a simple, but reasonably solid concept of object and servant lifetimes.

**Servant**   There is no mention in the BOA specification about any mechanism for registering servants; instead, vendor-specific mechanisms are used, and the mechanisms are based on implicit registration using the servant's constructor. The specification does not provide details on skeletons and their relationship with servants. Servant methods and their signatures are described, but not the names of base classes that the servants have to inherit from. Eventually, servants code are not portable.

Other than allowing a separate inheritance hierarchy, little or no information related to collocation can be found in BOA specification because collocation is an implementation-specific issue rather than an independent one. Support for collocation varies from one ORB product to another. Most products have their ORBs checking the location of a target object. If it is local, the ORB will use the target object's stub to contact its remote implementation. Otherwise, ORB will call BOA to return the implementing servant. Location transparency is preserved since the client has no indication of where the target object actually resides. Clients cannot distinguish the target object's stub from its servant, and this because both have the same interface name and method signatures. However, if an interceptor [78] is used, (i.e., an additional component of an ORB which can provide additional processing steps before a request/reply continues with its normal invocation path,) it might not be able to detect local invocations [34]. Therefore, not all requests and replies will go through the interceptor. This could cause problems, especially if the interceptor is used to provide security and access control.

**Object Grouping**   Details on object grouping are unavailable in BOA. Usually, programmers have to develop their own solution. No strategy has also been put in place to address object group activation and deactivation.

**Request Redirection**   CORBA 2.0 's GIOP specification states that the use of a reply message with LOCATION_FORWARD status diverts requests to another object. This message contains a reference to an object where the request should be re-sent. Clients will transparently send the current and subsequent requests to the other object. However, BOA does not specify how to exploit this feature in a standardized manner. Even if it did, no operations for manipulating this message are declared in the GIOP specification. That message is used only by the ORB internally.

**Multithreading and Concurrency Control**   No details on multithreading and concurrency control can be extracted from the BOA specification. In Orbix for example, the ThreadFilter class is used to deal with thread allocation. Some levels of support for other issues are also available, but these are proprietary.

### 4.3.3  Portable Object Adaptor

This section shows how POA addresses the issues presented in Section 4.3. Even though some of these issues, such as server management, were briefly described in Section 4.2.2 we prefer to re-discuss them in a more detailed way to make sure that the concepts related to POA are well understood.

Unlike BOA, multiple instances of POA can exist in a server; each is identified by its name. As depicted in Figure 4.9, these instances are organized in a hierarchical structure with rootPOA as its root. A root POA is managed by the ORB and its references can be obtained by calling $ORB :: resolve\_initial\_references()$. POA provides a namespace for its object's oid and another namespace for other POAs. Each POA manages a group of objects that share the same characteristics. An object is considered to be managed by a POA if its creation happened in that POA. Once an object has been created in one POA, its management responsibility cannot be transferred to another POA. Characteristics of the managed object are reflected in its policies. The value of a policy is set during the POA's creation or the policy's default value is used. A POA's policy is not inherited from its parent, nor it can be changed.

***Server***   The POA specification did not have enough details regarding server registration, memory management rules, and process activation. Even so, the details of the synchronization process between the POA and its implementations are provided. Each POA is synchronized by its POAManager. This can be achieved because the POA manager controls the processing state of its POAs. There are four processing states of the POA manager: Active, Holding, Discarding, and Inactive. Its state transition diagram is shown in Figure 4.10. When a POA manager is in the active state, its POAs receive and process incoming requests. When a POA manager is in holding state, all incoming requests are queued. If a POA manager is in the discarding state, all incoming requests will not be queued or delivered. POAs whose POA manager are in the inactive state are ready to be destroyed; once a a POA manager enters this state it cannot proceed to any other state. Its POAs will stop working and all of their requests will be rejected.

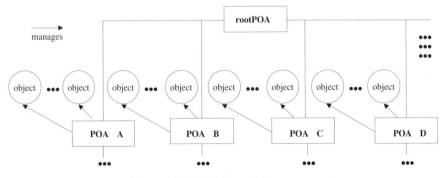

**Figure 4.9**   POA hierarchical structure.

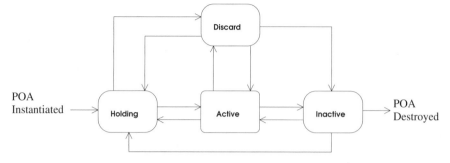

**Figure 4.10**   POA manager states.

A POA server is shut down by calling $ORB :: shutdown()$. This operation includes the option of immediately shutting the server down or waiting until all ORB processing tasks (object deactivation and requests processing) have been completed. When a server is being shutdown, all of its adaptors are deactivated and each of them triggers deactivation of their objects. This object deactivation allows objects and their servants to participate in the overall server deactivation process.

***Object***   An oid is unique within the scope of a POA instance. It is opaque, has the type of `ObjectId` and is mapped to a standardized sequence of octets. An object's oid is usually embedded inside object references along with the object's POA name. An oid's value must be translated to octets before being assigned to an object. Two POA policies related to object identity are: id assignment and object id uniqueness policies. The id assignment policy provides two oid assignment methods: assigned by the server (has the policy value of USER_ID) or assigned by the POA (with the policy value of SYSTEM_ID). If no policy value is given at the POA creation, the default value SYSTEM_ID is used. The operation $POA :: create\_reference()$ is used for the first method, while the latter should call $POA :: create\_reference\_with\_id()$. Both operations return a new reference, pointing to an object of the assigned oid. Their usage is CORBA compliant.

Before describing the object id uniqueness policy, we first introduce the concept of object lifetime. Different from the BOA approach, the lifetime of an object and its servants in POA are separated. An object activation does not always correspond to a servant instantiation, similarly for object deactivation. Thus, the concepts of incarnation and etherealization are introduced to emphasize this point. Incarnation is a process of giving bodily form (i.e., servant) to a virtual CORBA object. Incarnation establishes an association between a servant and an object to serve the object's requests; in other words, it creates an implementation relationship between an object and its implementing servant. On the other hand, an etherealization is a process of taking away an object's bodily form/servant from it. This breaks the association between a servant and its implemented object and causes the object to be "unimplemented." As pictured in Figure 4.11, incarnations always occur when objects are activated. However, as we will see later for object deactivation, etherealization might not even be performed in an object lifecycle. Figure 4.11 also shows that a servant's

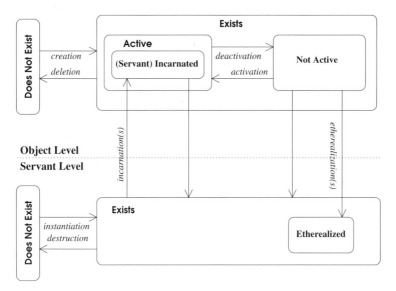

**Figure 4.11**   Objects and servants lifecycles in POA.

instantiation can happen before its object incarnation. The servant's destruction can occur later, possibly long after its object etherealization. This raises the possibility of one servant implementing multiple objects. The advantage of this separation is better memory and performance optimization techniques, although this could make the actual programming work confusing for people who are already used to BOA's lifetime concept.

As explained in Section 4.2.2, POA has several activation styles that can be chosen from. A choice can be made between various combinations of request processing and servant retention policy values. The request processing policy specifies how requests are processed by the POA, whereas the servant retention policy determines if a POA should RETAIN servants of active objects in its Active Object Map. This is owned by the POA and contains entries indexed by oids, each recording the association between an active object's oid and its implementing servant. When a request arrives for an object, this table will be referred to, for retrieieving the implementing servant.

When the ORB receives a request for an object, it will look for the target object's POA. Depending on the ORB product being used, the ORB might use the name of the POA, embedded in the target object's reference for this purpose. If this POA does not exist, its parent's `AdaptorActivator` will perform its creation process. An adaptor activator is developed by the programmer, but not needed for pre-created POAs. In order to create a particular POA in the POA hierarchy, all POAs that lead to it will also have to be created. Each of them will be created by their parent's `AdaptorActivator`. If we consider the example of POA A5 of Figure 4.12 when it is about to be created, if POA A1, A2, A3, A4 do not exist, then A4 will cause all of them to be created. POA A1 and A2 will be created by

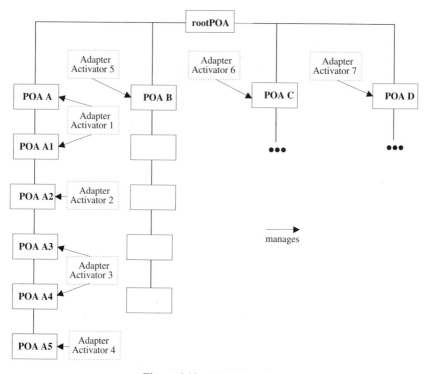

**Figure 4.12** POA hierarchy.

AdaptorActivator 1, POA A3 will be created by AdaptorActivator 2, POA A4 and A5 by AdaptorActivator 3. After the target POA is created, the request will be delivered to this POA.

When the value of the request processing policy is USE_ACTIVE_OBJECT_MAP_ONLY, the POA must also have its servant retention policy's value set to RETAIN. This combination tells the POA to perform a look-up of its Active Object Map using the target object's oid. If a matching entry is found, a reference to the servant can be acquired, and the request will be passed to it. The POA's map has to be populated by explicitly pre-activating objects that will be used. $POA :: activate\_object()$ can be used for that purpose if its id assigment policy value is SYSTEM_ID. If the value is USER_ID, $POA :: activate\_object\_with\_id()$ is used instead.

When the combination is RETAIN and USE_DEFAULT_SERVANT, the POA should perform a look-up of the Active Object Map when a request arrives. When no entry matches, the request will have to be passed to a default servant for its processing. If the POA has no default servant registered with it, an exception is produced. Like the previous combination, the Active Object Map needs to be populated with objects that will be used. There are two types of default servants: per-interface default servant and for-all default servant [77]. In the former, the default servant is typically used for a POA instance which manages objects of a given interface. All requests are processed by the default servant, which handles only those for objects of a given interface. The for-all default servant is capable of processing all requests regardless the interfaces the target objects have.

Any POA with NON_RETAIN does not have an Active Object Map and requires its request processing policy value to be either USER_DEFAULT_SERVANT or USE_SERVANT_MANAGER. If NON_RETAIN is combined with USE_DEFAULT_SERVANT, all requests will always be delivered to a default servant since no Active Object Map exists. As before, an exception will be produced if there is no default servant registered.

If the policy combination is NON_RETAIN and USE_SERVANT_MANAGER, the POA will rely on its registered servant manager to incarnate the requested object. A servant manager is a custom-made class written by programmers. Its incarnating operation is called by the POA to return an implementing servant of the wanted object. There are two kinds of servant managers available: servant activator and servant locator. A servant locator is used in this combination, with preinvoke as its incarnating operation. An Active Object Map does not exist and servant locator is always called for every incarnation.

If the combination is RETAIN and USE_SERVANT_MANAGER, the POA will first attempt to locate the appropriate entry in its active object map. If not found, the servant activator's incarnate operation will be called to incarnate the target object. After incarnation is completed, the POA will receive the servant from its servant activator and pass the request to this servant. A new entry for this servant will be added to the Active Object Map for its usage in the next invocations.

POA's object activations can happen in three ways: explicitly (by calling $POA$ :: $activate\_object()$) or $POA$ :: $activate\_object\_with\_id()$), on demand (using servant managers), or implicitly (by setting implicit activation policy's value to IMPLICIT). The first two have been explained previously. Implicit activation occurs when operations that logically require an oid to be assigned to an inactive object's servant are executed. Examples of these kinds of operations are: $POA$ :: $servant\_to\_reference()$ and $POA$ :: $servant\_to\_id()$. Intuitively, two values can be chosen for this policy: IMPLICIT_ACTIVATION and NO_IMPLICIT_ACTIVATION. The default value is NO_IMPLICIT_ACTIVATION. IMPLICIT_ACTIVATION also requires the POA to have SYSTEM_ID and RETAIN.

An object's deactivation occurs when the object is deactivated explicitly (by calling $POA$ :: $deactivate\_object()$); its POA is deactivated (by calling $POA$ $Manager$ :: $deactivate()$); its POA is destroyed (by calling $POA$ :: $destroy()$); or deactivated by ORB/POA. The last deactivation is triggered internally by ORB/POA and it is unstandardized. When the POA has no servant manager registered, the object will be deactivated immediately without any etherealization process. POA will search for this object's entry and remove it from the Active Object Map. Etherealization also does not happen when function POAManager::deactivate and $POA$ :: $destroy()$ are called, if their `etherealize_objects` parameter is set to false. Care should be taken when a POA Manager is set to the inactive state, just before its server's shutdown, as this would also deactivate its POAs's servant managers and stop etherealizations from happening.

Both persistent and transient objects are supported in a POA. A POA's definition of transient object has been revised in [78]. It states that a transient object is an object that cannot outlive the POA instance in which it was first created. Lifespan policy deals with this by providing two policy values: TRANSIENT and PERSISTENT. If no value is specified at POA creation, TRANSIENT will be used. A POA with policy values of PERSISTENT and UNIQUE_ID assigns oids which are unique across all instantiations of the same POA.

**Servant**   POA supports both explicit and implicit servant registrations. The operation $POA :: activate\_object()$ or $POA :: activate\_object\_with\_id()$ can be used an explicit registration. These operations will activate an object by using a specified servant and register a new entry with the Active Object Map. Objects are implicitly registered if the POA's servant retention and request processing policies have the value of RETAIN and USE_SERVANT_MANAGER. A new entry is inserted into the Active Object Map after the incarnation process finishes. If the servant retention policy is NON_RETAIN instead, implicit registrations can occur when the servant locator is implemented with a map similar to the POA's Active Object Map.

The names of base classes and the operation signatures of POA servants are specified. Also, inheritance and delegation based approaches are better described and the servant's methods and its inheritance hierarchy are more clearly defined. At the end, the code's portability is significantly improved.

Collocation in POA is not specified because of its implementation specific nature. Beside location transparency, there are several other important issues that must also be considered in collocation, with interceptor and multithreading being some that are relevant to database adaptors. Like BOA, levels of collocation supports vary from one CORBA implementation to another.

**Object Grouping**   An object group in POA consists of the objects that are managed by a POA instance. Their grouping is based on characteristics shared by its member objects. An object is a member of a group if it is managed by the group's POA. Note that since the structure of nested POAs is hierarchical, the overall structure of their object groupings is also hierarchical. However, because an object's management responsibility is determined during its creation, this grouping is static. Despite this limitation, the same operations can now be performed on all members of a group. For example, consider a servant manager being used for request processing. Its POA will use the same incarnate and etherealize the operation to apply the same algorithms to all its objects. Unfortunately, no strategy has been specified for object grouping activation and deactivation. Proprietary supports from ORB vendors, if any, are also limited. Programmers usually have to produce their own "home made" strategy to devise object group activation and deactivation.

**Request Redirection**   POA facilitates request redirection with its $ForwardRequest$ exception. This exception contains the reference to an object to which a request should be forwarded. Assuming a GIOP based protocol is used, this exception will be returned to the client in a reply message with LOCATION_FORWARD reply status. In the POA specification, for example, *Forward Request* can be raised during object incarnation by its servant manager's incarnate (for servant activator) or preinvoke (for servant locator) operation.

**Multithreading and Concurrency Control**  POA's thread allocation is controlled by its thread policy. The value SINGLE_THREAD_MODEL does not use any of the thread allocation policies mentioned earlier. Instead, all requests will be processed sequentially in a single thread. The ORB_CONTROL_MODEL value implies that ORB is responsible for the thread allocations. Although the POA has a thread policy in its specifications, there are still some details missing. First, no description is given on how exactly a POA with an ORB_CONTROL_MODEL policy value can allocate requests to threads. The ORB might use one of the thread allocation policies previously mentioned or it might still use a single threaded model. The critical section problem is left unsolved, while the specifications on multithreaded servants are not provided. A POA's code portability cannot be guaranteed for multithread server; future POA revisions on this topic are expected.

## 4.4  DATABASE ADAPTORS

This section discusses issues related to POA-based database adaptors, but we will not describe solutions for these issues. The aim of this section is to provide appropriate details about the integration of CORBA and database technologies. Some solutions are provided in [95], which is a POA-based database adaptor, and [87], which is BOA-based adaptor; however, these will be not discussed in this book. Nonetheless, these issues are valid regardless of the basis adaptor adopted. For database adaptors which are not based on BOA or POA, this section can be used as a reference. Issues which are specific to an adaptor will be explicitly noted.

Persistency of objects is critical for many applications, such as banking and telecommunication applications. A POA does not deal with such a persistency; however, it can provide a nice framework for extensions for building database adaptors. There is no CORBA standard regarding database adaptors; however, because we believe that persistency is a very important issue, we would like to explain how the basics of POA can be extended to deal with persistency. As the reader may notice, persistency can also be achieved by using the OMG's Persistent Service. We have not chosen to explain this service because we believe that persistency should be transparent to the users, and therefore it needs to be addressed by the ORB (through POA) without any use of the services.

This section explains issues pertinent to development of a database adaptor. It starts off with the concepts and design, and includes the issues of a reference model, the selection of a basis adaptor, and architectural considerations. We continue with a discussion of the deficiencies of the present object model, followed by issues of the persistent object's identity, state, lifecycle, reference and its servant lifecycle. This section ends with performance, scalability and portability issues.

***Concepts and Design***    Furnishing persistency to CORBA applications demands an integration with database systems. An integration approach must be devised for this purpose. First, a set of concepts is needed to construct the nature of the approach taken. These concepts are obtained from the approach's reference model. A reference model provides an overall view of the problems. It also provides knowledge of the approach's entities and their elements, thus enabling an understanding of things which are involved in the approach and to proceed with the conceptualization task. Once this is done, the rest of the issues should be resolved in line with those concepts.

At the start of the design process, developers have to consider whether or not to build the database adaptor on top of an existing conventional adaptor. If they decide to do so, two adaptors can be chosen from: BOA and POA. Each has its own strengths and weaknesses. Starting from BOA promotes reusability of an ubiquitous adaptor. However, its specification is problematic, not portable and will be phased out. Consequently, choosing BOA would commit a database adaptor to be a proprietary and short-term solution. POA, on the other hand, is not yet widely available in the current systems. Major CORBA vendors (e.g., IONA and Inprise) have not released their POA supported ORBs. Selecting a POA will advantageously position a database adaptor as a long term and portable solution. One could also avoid BOA and POA altogether and build a database adaptor from scratch. This gives maximum freedom in the development at the expense of portability and standard compliance. The last design issue is the database adaptor's architecture. For complex and sophisticated software like a database adaptor, having an architecture is compulsory. An architecture organizes the comprising elements of the software into a structural form. A good architecture provides clarity, extensibility, and maintainability to the software.

***Object Model***    The CORBA object model defines concepts related to the object semantics and implementation objects. It does not address persistency since this feature is optional to CORBA objects and outside of its scope. Thus, this object model was not designed to model persistent objects, and consequently its semantic concepts such as types, interfaces, operations and attributes do not have persistent counterparts. Due to their absence, persistency syntax and semantics are undeclarable in IDL. As the result, the following issues are unsolvable: (i) how and when a CORBA object can be determined as persistent, (ii) what indicates its persistency, (iii) how and when a servant can be denoted as being capable of implementing a persistent object, and (iv) how non-persistent objects are treated. The last issue is particularly important in cases where persistent objects refer to transient objects.

One may extend the CORBA model to take persistent properties into account by adding new object semantics. An example of this approach is found in Secant's Persistent Object Manager [84]. While this solution is sensible, the introduction of these persistent semantics creates new IDL syntax and semantics which are foreign to existing applications. Unless their IDLs and implementation are changed, interoperability will be compromised. This creates an unwanted dilemma: extending the current object model could jeopardize interoperability, but without the IDL syntax and semantics persistency is left unfacilitated. Even if this problem is resolved, developers still have to be careful not to pollute the IDL with syntax or semantics derived from the database schema. Such design is prone to changes that occur from the schema updates.

One important aspect when considering persistency in CORBA environments is transparent persistency. Transparent persistency is the property in which persistency details are hidden at two levels: object level and implementation level. At the object level, clients should not be aware of the persistency of the objects. This is because CORBA allows interface-related information to be disclosed to the clients, but not its implementation-related information. Thus, persistence which is an implementation issue [80], should also be excluded from the client's view. Transparent persistency at the implementation level dictates that persistency details should not be revealed to the servants. The new object model is obliged to accomplish persistency in accordance to this transparent persistency property.

*Object Identity*   The oid of a persistent object is used for several purposes, such as identification, storage and restoration of states, and processing requests. In the first usage, the oid needs to be in the form of an uninterpreted sequence of octets. It must have information on how to differentiate one object from others. In the next case, the oid must be in a form which is adherent to its database product and paradigm. It has to contain information for storing and restoring the right state. In the last case, the oid ought to be in an application-dependent form. The oid is expected to contain sufficient information to have requests to their objects processed by the right application service. In each of the above cases, its information should be unique. After these facts are analyzed, questions are raised on what sort of information, form and structure a persistent oid will actually have and how the above heterogeneities are accommodated. These issues are crucial since they affect how persistent objects are bound, identified, and manipulated.

A more complex issue is found in the oid generation process. A new persistent oid must correspond to a stored state and a set of services. This is not difficult for objects that represent new data and/or new service. However, it is more complicated when legacy databases and applications come into the equation. A database adaptor is obliged to resolve this issue appropriately.

oid uniqueness is also of concern because of the information it must contain. Each item of information might be used to uniquely identify the right object, state and service. However, its combined values might not be unique for an oid. Additionally, the database adaptor must now deal with the possibility of having multiple sources of the information. Each might have its own generation methods and issues.

*Object State*   Issues in this section stem from the lack of details concerning the persistent object's state and its determination process. Persistent state determination selects which part of an object's state will be made persistent. Its method of selection and timing are the particular concern. How a persistent object's state can be accessed, especially if access to its values is restricted, should also be considered. Manipulating databases of different products and paradigms, to store and restore the state, is also problematic. Each database requires a different way of loading and sav-

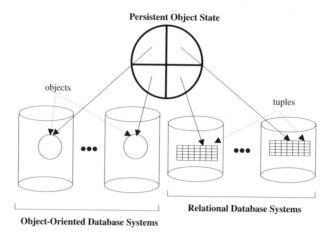

**Figure 4.13** Persistent object's state with multiple databases and paradigms.

ing the object's state. Most importantly, the database adaptor must know how to use RDBMS's tuple or ODBMS's object for storing and restoring the state. This is further complicated when there are multiple possible databases in which the state can be stored. It is the database adaptor's obligation to select which of the databases should keep the state. Locating the stored state is also harder, since the database adaptor must find which database that stores the state of a particular object.

Moreover, the adaptor must also determine which attributes of state should be stored. Whether or not it is capable of dealing with state fragmentation [83] is a matter of consideration. Objects which have their state fragmented and stored across multiple databases must be reconstructed before they can be accessed. This increases the difficulties in finding the right databases, storing and restoring objects, and manipulating their state.

***Object Lifecycle Events***   There are several issues which are common to object lifecycle events. Central to these is the issue of their integration with the storage steps of persistent objects. These steps are loading, inserting, querying, updating, and deleting the state of the objects. Exploitation of the basis adaptor, to manage a persistent object's lifecycle events, is significant in resolving the above issues. With respect to BOA, such integration must be accomplished in compliance with the CORBA standard. Last, but not least is the issue of the storage steps execution transparency of events. That is, how in programming terms can transparent persistency be imposed on the executions of these storage steps. There is a trade-off between the database information hiding and the performance which ought to be balanced to gain a suitable level of transparency and performance.

- *Event creation:* A persistent object comes into existence when its reference is created for the first time. During this process, the referenced object can either be activated at the same time (early binding) or later when the first request arrives (late binding) [34]. In both cases, the reference will be associated with the servant of the activated object. The selection of binding is important since it influences the length of time required to create a persistent object. Which binding(s) are available, how they are supported, and which one to choose are the points that need to be considered.

Besides this, one also has to realize that the creation of a persistent object is not always matched with a similar process being performed for the state and service. A database adaptor might have to act as a front end to the existing data and/or service. Therefore, the conventional meaning of "new object" needs to be redefined for persistent objects. Further, consider when new data does need to be inserted into the database. In this case, the timing of the insertion is the influencing factor to the server's response time. When this insertion is to be done is to be considered.

- *Event activation:* How persistent objects are activated is significant. As explained in the previous sections, BOA based objects suffer from lack of specification on this issue. Employing proprietary supports is usually the only way to fill this vacuum. It is highly desirable for BOA-based database adaptors to be able to navigate through this problem. In contrast, POA specifies several styles in activating its objects. Hence, the selection of the activation styles to be deployed and whether some/all of the styles can be used to activate persistent objects is to be considered.

- *Event querying:* Designing query facilities in a database adaptor requires a trade-off between performance and the hiding of database internal details. As database internals are better hidden, the performance degrades. A database adaptor should allow query facilities to be used without violating transparent persistency or causing its query performance to suffer. The location of query strings is equally important in relation to the previous issue. Query strings must exclusively exist in the database code fragments. What databases ( RDBMS/ODBMS/both), types of queries (pre- compiled/dynamic/both), and query manipulation language ( OQL/SQL/both) are supported influences the performance and applicability of the database adaptor. Furthermore, relevant standards should be followed while catering for proprietary extensions. How queries that return a collection of objects are handled needs to be considered as well.

- *Event update:* The first step in an update process is to determine the updatables. Pertinent to this step is the issue of granularity. A fine-grained granularity is selective and more efficient, whereas the coarser one is simpler but less efficient. This, along with the update timing of the stored data, are both the determining factors in an update's response time. Moreover, the cause of an update is significant in as much as it decides the controls over the update.

- *Event deactivation:* An active object will eventually be deactivated to reclaim the memory it occupies. Deactivations are governed by the memory management rules of its server. As mentioned earlier, neither BOA nor POA have these rules. One of the reasons is to avoid distributed memory management becoming part of the CORBA standard. This is due to its error prone and costly approaches. Thus, unless programmers provide their own object deactivation scheme, a server will crash because of memory exhaustion. The scheme devised might activate and deactivate objects several times, but it must observe the concepts of deactivation control, victim selection, deactivation safety and deactivation transparency.

Loosening the deactivation control amounts to less programming work since it lets the database adaptor take charge instead. However, it increases the reliance on the accuracy of its victim selection algorithm. The less accurate it is, the greater the chances of deactivating a still-in-use object. This is in conflict with the scheme's transparency and safety properties. A safe deactivation scheme guarantees the continuity and integrity of objects it deactivates, while a transparent deactivation scheme stops clients from being aware that such deactivation takes place. There are two kinds of deactivation safety: safety by state and safety by processing. A deallocation scheme is considered as safe by state if the state of objects it deactivates is preserved across their activations. Safety by processing protects a currently working object from errors and inconsistencies that might arise from their sudden deactivations. In particular, these properties must prevent cases where errors from the deactivations, which are triggered by clients/database adaptors, from being exposed and handled by the clients. This is because such actions increase the code complexity of the database adaptor's clients.

An object's deactivation process is always carried out in its lifecycle. This process is an ideal place to undertake any of the object's storage steps before it is finally deactivated. Deciding which storage step(s) should be included in an object deactivation is to be carefully contemplated.

- *Event deletion:* When a deletion occurs, it may or may not cause the deletion of its stored data and service as well. If the deletion triggers the removal of its data, the database will be located and the data will be removed. Crucial to the deletion's response time is the timing of the removal of stored data from the database. How a database adaptor determines when the deletion of data and/or service should take place and how the data can be removed needs to be answered.

**Object Reference**    A relationship between two objects is represented by an IOR. However, relationships in DBMS are represented differently. Relationships in RDBMS are symbolized by keys, while in ODBMS they are presented by database references. Such mismatches must be bridged before an IOR can be used to access its persistent object.

Generating IORs is the responsibility of an adaptor. This usually requires the information pertinent to the referenced object to be encapsulated inside the IOR. Furthermore, in order to preserve the relationships that a persistent object has, all the IOR's of the relationships must persist as well. Their referential integrity must be maintained so that they are still usable when they are restored. Referential integrity is conserved if references are not dangled, that is, pointing to a non-existent object. Also important is how to acquire references to remote CORBA objects when the references are not available locally. How oids can be made available during an IOR creation and how IORs of stored persistent objects are provided to the application are questions to be answered. How the mechanism providing IORs can fit into the application's code also needs to be considered. The above issues are to be solved in accordance with the IOR's transparent storability [87]. Transparent storability is a feature where converting an IOR to its usable form, that is, to string before it is stored or to a CORBA reference when it is retrieved, is not required. In other words, code that provides the actual application service are not aware that such IOR is actually stored in the database. How a database adaptor conserves this property is yet to be solved. In essence, IORs of persistent objects must be managed in such a way that they behave and perform similarly to a normal object.

***Servant Lifecycle Events*** Issues in the servant lifecycle events are focused on providing actual programming language logic to the objects. As CORBA has several programming language bindings, solving these issues clearly rests upon the programming language's capability. This section discusses all of these issues below; they are applicable regardless of what programming language is used.

- *Event instantiation:* Objects with multiple servant classes have problems with their servant instantiations. Having multiple choices of the servant class is relevant when an object is to provide the same service in different ways. The reasons might be because of better performance, support for previous service, and so on. However, each of these servants might be implemented in a different approach—POA/TIE/DSI. Parameters of their constructors could be distinct and require them to be passed with different values. Some of the constructors have no parameters at all (zero/null constructor), while others have multiple parameters. When dealing with the existing code, these servants may already have factories to carry out their instantiations. A database adaptor is compelled to cope with these variables before it is able to instantiate these servant classes. Although not crucial, adding and removing the selectable servants can cause minor irritations. Usually, the relevant code has to be manually changed and recompiled. A more convenient way of handling these tasks is needed to speed up the entire editing process.
- *Event incarnation:* A persistent object's incarnation restores the object's state from its database and prepares the object with the state as loaded. There are two choices in relation to the servant that is used to incarnate. The first option is to use an already instantiated servant, while the second option instantiates a new one. Choosing which option should be taken is the problem in incarnating. When the second option is chosen, the selection of an existing servant to use is another issue. A database adaptor might have to be careful not to cause a servant to over-incarnate. This is to avoid a servant being overloaded with the requests of its objects. It is especially true in cases where threads are used in the servant. Likewise, finding the database that stores the persistent object's state is hard

particularly when there are multiple databases at the back-end. Furthermore, a database adaptor must load the object's state, set it with this state, and finally activate the object.

Two kinds of initialization steps can be identified in an incarnation process: steps related to restoring the object's state and those pertinent to the business logic. The former is more likely to be similar for all applications than the latter. Therefore, the same set of code could be used to handle the former's steps. This raises the possibility of automating the task of restoring the object state for servants in all applications. If there are multiple servants to choose from, each of them might have unique initialization steps. The adaptor should be able to execute the right initialization steps for a particular servant. A mechanism to automate both steps is required, whilst allowing their customizations.

Incarnation is a potentially dangerous step for the concept of separation of concern. A naive programmer would write the incarnation code without separating code fragments related to the database from others. However, since they are very closely related, separating them is not an easy task. The design of a database adaptor should be aimed at simplifying this task.

- *Event etherealization:* Similar to incarnation, two kinds of steps can happen in an etherealization process; the object's storage and business logic processing steps. The etherealization's problems resemble those of the incarnation as well. It is compulsory for the database adaptor to be able to prepare the object before it is etherealized. This might involve one or several storage steps. The storage steps are similar from application to application, compared to the business related steps. Hence, automation is a possibility. The existence of multiple servants might also coincide with the presence of their dissimilar etherealization steps. The adaptor should select the right steps for an appropriate servant. The customization and the automation of both steps are to be facilitated in their mechanism. The issue of enforcing the separation of concern also needs to be tackled. Recall from the previous chapter that etherealization may or may not happen. This could cause problems to objects that rely on the etherealization to perform their storage step(s). The adaptor should be able to cope with this problem, while maintaining the state's consistency of those objects.

- *Event destruction:* A servant destruction in some BOA based products could be used to provoke its object deactivation. However, caution must be exercised when destroying a servant of the POA or other BOA-based products. An accidental destruction could cause the objects implemented by the servant to be forcefully unimplemented without their proper deactivations. The servant's destruction event is ready to be used for the execution of its object's storage step(s). The selection of what storage step(s) should be performed in the destructor requires some consideration.

### *Performance, Scalability and Code Portability*    Increasing scalability and the performance of a database adaptor is more likely to stretch CORBA standard to its limit. More improvement can only be gained from employing proprietary extensions. However, such use works against the portability of the server's code. Unless

standardized mechanisms are used, this problem remains as the stumbling block in realizing a scalable, performance minded and portable database adaptor. The issues below describe problems encountered when developing database adaptors with those goals. Some of the issues described below are not directly related to the database adaptor, but rather to the overall server. They are there because a database adaptor can play a pivotal and influential role in attaining those goals for the server.

Clients measure a server's performance according to its response time and availability. A response time is the time elapsed from the invocation of a remote object until its reply is received. Availability is the server's probability of failing or becoming unreachable [22]. Clearly, a low response time and higher availability are very desirable. Speeding up a server's response calls for the reduction of time consumed by all steps in an object invocation. These optimizable steps are illustrated in Figure 4.14. A server's availability is enhanced if the server failures can be minimized.

The first optimizable step is marshaling and unmarshaling steps on the client side. There are two factors that influence the time taken to complete those steps: message size and the IDL data types it contains. More data to be transferred means a larger message, which at the end prolongs the time taken [34]. Increasingly complex and structured data types also play an adverse role on the response time. The delivery rate/call latency is dependent on the ORB products used. The rate is usually uncontrollable except if modifications are made to the source code of the ORB product being used. Lowering the response time of a database adaptor is much harder than lowering it in a conventional adaptor counterpart. The processing time of a database adaptor is longer due to the database operations that have to be performed. For example, in an object activation, the database is accessed to load the object's state. For a remote method invocation, the database might be queried/updated. If an object's state is cached, the database operation will perform faster than its remote method invocation. Hence, there is a significant time difference existing between these two; as a result, access to fine-grained data via a remote method invocation would incur

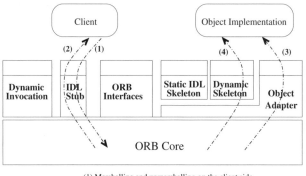

(1) Marshalling and unmarshalling on the client side
(2) Requests and replies delivery
(3) Object adapter processing
(4) Unmarshalling on the server side

**Figure 4.14**    Optimizable steps of the flow of a request and its reply.

unacceptable overhead [87, 99]. If data is uncached, database operations could slow down the entire invocation process. Instantiation of the classes involved (e.g., servant class) is also effectual, especially in interpreted programming languages like Java. A massive number of instantiations decreases the response time of a database adaptor. The last optimizable step is the processing time of an implementation object. A heavily loaded implementation object has a sluggish response time, which slows the server down. Thus, managing the request load of an implementation object is also essential. The number of requests and replies contributes to the overall server performance. A decline in their numbers automatically improves the server's response. This is because it eliminates the need to perform the steps for their requests and replies.

Availability of a server with a database adaptor should be resolved at two levels: server level and database level. Failures at the first level are classified as omission failure, response failure, and crash failure [22]. An omission failure is a failure in which a server fails to respond to a request. Response failure is divided into two classes: value failure and state transition failure. The former happens when the server returns a wrong value, while the latter has the wrong effect on resources (e.g., sets the wrong values to data items). Crash failure is repeated omission failure and includes all kinds of server crashes. At the database level, failures range from transaction failures to physical and catastrophic failures. At the first glance, there seems to be no connection between these failures and the database adaptor. However, due to its closeness to the implementation objects, it is logical for a database adaptor to at least accommodate any fault tolerance mechanisms that are being used by its server.

Scalability is the characteristic where the system and application software do not need to change when the scale of the system increases [22]. In servers with database adaptors, scalability concentrates on their capacity to bring about reasonable performance as the number of persistent objects, databases, and requests grows. Thus, some optimization techniques need to be devised to enable the database adaptor to cope with an increase of these variables.

In order to avoid a database adaptor becoming a proprietary solution, it should be built on existing standards. However, unstandardized parts of a database are the potential problems when moving to different environments (different DBMS and/or ORB products). These parts might come from the DBMS or CORBA side. In the DBMS, they can be found in queries, database-generated oids, and so on. From CORBA these parts can be found in optimization techniques such as threading.

## 4.5  SUMMARY

In this chapter we have presented one of the main components of the CORBA architecture, the object adaptor, and explained the importance of including such an adaptor within CORBA. We have also explained the main architectural differences between the BOA and POA adaptors. Based on technical issues related to object adaptors, we provided an analysis of both BOA and POA and showed their strengths and weaknesses. In the last section of this chapter we provided details of the issues that need to be taken into account in order to build database adaptors.

## 4.6 REVIEW QUESTIONS

- What is the advantage gained from placing an object adaptor between an ORB and implementations?
- What are the three steps in dispatching a request on the server side, assuming SSI is used?
- Compare the strengths and the weaknesses of using a default servant with those of using a servant manager.
- What is the difference between servant activator and servant locator?
- What is a persistent and a transient object?
- Why do vendors provide proprietary solutions (e.g., loader classes in IONA's Orbix) for loading inactive objects in BOA?
- What is the difference in the relationship between servant and object lifecycle in BOA, compared to that in POA?
- Which has a better support in multithreading: BOA or POA? Justify your answer. What is the problem with POA's multithreading support?
- Explain the concepts of incarnation and etherealization.
- Does the incarnation in an object activation corresponds to an etherealization in its object deactivation? Justify your answer.

## 4.7 EXERCISES

- What are the possible problems that could occur when a request bypasses interceptors which are used to provide security and access control.
- What is the consideration behind the use of USER_DEFAULT_SERVANT request processing policy?
- CORBA applications often need to store the states of their objects persistently in databases. The simplest approach would be to include in the servant classes of those objects all the necessary codes (SQL query strings, etc.) that access these databases, in order to manipulate (load, delete, edit, etc.) their object states. What is the main problem with this approach?
- What are the problems that occur if a database adapter is not built based on any of the CORBA adapters?

# CHAPTER 5

# CORBA Interoperability

CORBA specification provides a list of guidelines for implementing ORB products. The concrete realization of these guidelines is left to ORB vendors to fill. All CORBA compliant ORB products follow the same guidelines, but have different implementation details from each other. In the earlier versions of CORBA standard (CORBA 1), some aspects of the ORB such as low-level protocols used for inter-ORB communication were left unspecified. As a result, ORBs of different vendors were not always able to communicate with each other. OMG realized this problem and issued an RFP (Request For Proposal) asking vendors to submit proposals to standardize the inter-ORB communication. A specification called Universal Networked Object (UNO) was adopted and has been revised several times ever since. This specification introduces concepts such as domains, bridges, interoperability protocols, and Interoperable Object References (IOR).

This chapter describes the OMG's interoperability standard; the next section overviews the interoperability issues. Later sections provide details about domains (Section 5.2), bridges (Section 5.3), interoperability protocols (Section 5.4), and IOR (Section 5.5). The aim of this chapter is to provide additional technical details to the ones proposed in Chapters 2, 3, and 4. This chapter does not provide a complete cover of the topic related to the issue of CORBA interoperability. Points which are deemed to be important are discussed in more detail. For additional information, the reader may refer to the OMG's specification.

## 5.1 OVERALL PICTURE

Interoperability is the ability of a client of a given ORB to invoke an OMG IDL-defined operations on objects on other ORBs, where all these ORBs are independently developed. It is used when requests must travel from one ORB to another. Three factors motivate the introduction of the interoperability standard. The first factor is ORB implementation diversity, that is, differences in the way the ORB specification is implemented to address a variety of user needs. Application environments might be partitioned into different ORBs, based on the application requirements such as security. This creates ORB boundaries which divide the applications around the ORB being used. For example, one secure ORB might be used to mediate access to private objects, while another ORB is used to delegate requests to public objects.

Some objects are accessed over long distances, with global visibility, longer delays, less reliable communication, and must be active for a long period of time. Other objects are closer, are not accessed from elsewhere, provide higher quality service, and have shorter lifetime. As a result, their ORB varies in scope, distance, and lifetime. Interoperability is achieved with a combination of interoperability protocols, which govern rules and formats used to communicate; bridges, which translate requests from one domain to another; and IOR, which provides a standardized way to manipulate CORBA objects. Note that bridges are used only when requests must travel from one domain to another domain.

## 5.2  DOMAIN

A domain is a distinct scope, within which common characteristics are exhibited, common rules are observed, and over which a distribution transparency (e.g., location transparency) is preserved. It allows a system to be divided into a collection of components which have some common characteristics. They are related to each other by either containment (one domain inside another) or federations (two domains are joined in a manner agreed to and set up by their administrators). Each domain provides an abstraction and further distinction of the ORB's functionality scope. Its boundary is defined as the limit of the scope in which a particular characteristic is valid or meaningful. A characteristic is said to traverse a domain's boundary if it is translated to its equivalent in that domain. A domain can be modelled as an object and become a member of other domains. An object is said to be a member of a domain if it has the characteristic of the domain. An object can be a member of several domains, regardless their kinds, causing the domain member sets to overlap.

Domains are usually administrative or technological in nature. Administrative domains include naming domain, trust group, resource management domain, referencing domain (the scope of an object reference), network addressing domain (the scope of a network address), security domain (the extent of a particular security policy), transaction domain (the scope of a given transaction service), and other run-time characteristics of a system. Examples of technology domains are representation domain (the scope of a message transfer syntax and protocol), type domain (the scope of a particular type identifier), and other build time characteristics. Figure 5.1 illustrates an example of two CORBA objects sharing the same domains.

An ORB might have multiple domains within its functionality scope, such as different access domains, each having a different access control. The ORB itself can be a domain if ORB products used are from different vendors. A domain might span several ORBs, with each being a distinct scope and having its own characteristics, rules and transparency; for example, one access control domain for all objects handled by all ORBs. Most domains of an ORB usually have the same scope as their ORB's. Whenever two ORBs mediate a request from a client to a server, the request might not just move through these ORBs, but it might also cross to another domain boundary. This is because the client resides in a domain which is different from the server's domain. Thus, for the interoperability to succeed, the issues of do-

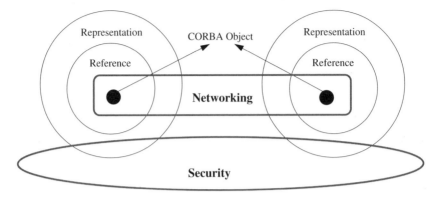

**Figure 5.1**   Two CORBA objects sharing same domains.

main boundary traversal must be resolved. For example, consider a request is being delivered from a client to a server via two identical ORBs which share one protocol. If the client resides in an access control domain different from the one of the server, the request's permission must be translated to its equivalent in the server's access control domain. Otherwise, the request would only be passed from the client's ORB to the server's ORB, without any transformation required.

## 5.3   BRIDGE

A bridge is conceptually a mapping mechanism which transforms requests expressed in terms of a domain's model to the one of destination model. It is used as an answer to the ORB and domain boundary traversal problems. Its role is to ensure that content and semantics are mapped from the form appropriate to one domain to that of another. The result is that users of any given ORB only see their appropriate content and semantics.

Figure 5.2 shows two techniques of bridging requests: *mediated bridging* and *immediate bridging*. The first one is a technique of bridging which transforms elements of interaction relevant to the domain from its internal form to an agreed common form at the boundary of each domain. The scope of agreement of a common form can range from a private agreement between two particular ORBs or domains to a universal standard. Multiple common forms might exist, with each optimized or oriented for a different purpose. Selecting which one should be used can be decided statically (administrative policy agreed between ORB vendors. or between system administrators), or dynamically (for each object or on each invocation). This bridging technique can be implemented as specifically compiled (similar to stubs), generic library code (like encryption codes), or intermediate bridges to the common form. The latter technique is a method of bridging that transforms elements of the interaction relevant, directly from the internal form of the source domain to the internal form of the target domain, at the boundary of each domain. This technique has the potential to be optimal since no mediation is required. However, this comes at the

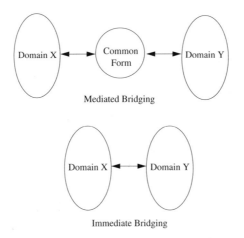

**Figure 5.2**   Mediated and immediate bridging techniques.

cost of the interoperability's flexibility and generality. Immediate bridging is usually applicable when the domain boundaries are purely administrative, that is, no technology changes. For example, when the domains are security domains handled by two similar ORBs, no common intermediate form is necessary.

Some applications require the traffic of requests which are being bridged to be constrained, controlled, and monitored based on certain policies. Such bridging is called policy-mediated bridging. An example of its application is found in domains which perform audits of their external access or provide domain-based access control, based on some security policies. Fully transparent bridging might be highly undesirable and resource management policies might even need to be applied for restricting some types of traffics during certain periods. Objects in certain domains of particular types might be made inaccessible to other domains. Traffics might have to be analyzed and some knowledge about them might be required in order to enforce particular security policies.

Bridges can be implemented as in-line and request level bridge, based on their bridging level, the level on which the bridging process occurs. An in-level bridge is a bridge which is implemented inside of the ORB, while a request level bridge is implemented by the application code outside the ORB instead. Request level bridges are further divided into two types: half and full bridge. A half bridge is a request level bridge that relies on another half bridge to connect to another ORB. It receives requests from clients in one ORB and transmits them in an agreed-upon format and agreed-upon protocol to another half bridge in another ORB. A full bridge is a request level bridge that spans two ORBs. It is used when the transformation is purely internal to one execution environment, using the shared programming environment's binary interface to CORBA and OMG-IDL defined data types. A full bridge appears to be another kind of in-line bridge from outside the execution environment. This is because the full bridge's environment is the only one that knows the techniques used to construct the bridge. However, full bridges more easily support portable policy mediation components, due to their use of only standard CORBA APIs.

Request level bridges could be implemented as interface-specific or generic bridges. The former support only predetermined IDL interfaces and aremdeveloped by using IDL-compiler generated stub and skeleton interfaces. The latter are capable of bridging requests for server objects with arbitrary IDL interfaces by manipulating interface repository, DII, and DSI. Programmers who wish to develop generic request level bridges should use several interfaces. The first one is DII which allows bridges to invoke objects whose interfaces are unknown when the bridges are developed or deployed. DSI enables bridges to handle invocations on proxies whose represented objects' interfaces are unresolved when the bridges are developed. Other important interfaces are interface repositories which are consulted when using DII and DSI and object adapters which are used to create proxies. The last interface is CORBA object references which supports operations that fully describe their interfaces and create tables mapping object references to their proxies and vice versa.

## 5.4   INTEROPERABILITY PROTOCOLS

In order to provide interoperability, several protocols have been specified by OMG, including GIOP, IIOP, and ESIOP. These protocols are used as the basic infrastructures for higher level interoperability services.

GIOP (General Inter-ORB Protocol) is an abstract protocol which provides a blueprint to implement a concrete interoperability protocol based on a transport protocol. GIOP is independent of any particular transport protocol. Its abstract nature means that this protocol cannot be used immediately for inter-ORB communications. Instead, it must be first mapped onto a specific transport layer. There are three versions of GIOP specification: GIOP 1.0, 1.1, and 1.2. The first revision of GIOP 1.0 adds support for message fragmentation for a more efficient marshaling. The next revision, GIOP 1.2, incorporates bidirectional communication for communication through a firewall, especially in cases where servers must also be clients. The explanation in this section is based on GIOP 1.2 specification and consists of the following elements: CDR, message format, and transport assumptions.

### Common Data Representation

CDR (Common Data Representation) is a transfer syntax for mapping OMG IDL into bi-canonical low-level representation for on-the-wire transfer between ORBs and Inter-ORB bridges. CDR has several important characteristics:

- *Supports both big-endian and little-endian byte orderings.* CDR-encoded data contains a flag which indicates the appropriate byte ordering. This allows big-endian and little-endian machines to send their data in their native format. Message originators determine which ordering should be used to send the data. The receivers are responsible to swap bytes that comprise the data. The byte swapping occurs whenever the ordering used by the receivers is different from the originators.

- *Aligns primitive types on natural boundaries.* CDR aligns primitive datatypes according to the number of bytes allocated to represent their values. For example, IDL's short is allocated two bytes to represent its value and aligned on a 2-byte boundary. This approach is less efficient in terms of bandwidth because of its use of bytes padding, a technique which is used to fill unused space of the bytes allocated to represent a datatype's value. Nevertheless, CDR is faster since a primitive value need not be reformatted based on the number of spaces actually used.
- *Lack of self-identification.* CDR-encoded data contains no information that can be used to describe its datatype(s). Both senders and receivers must agree on the datatype(s) of the data being sent; otherwise a misinterpretation could occur.
- *Supports complete IDL mapping.* CDR provides descriptions on how all IDL datatypes are represented. It supports primitive datatypes, constructed datatypes, pseudo-object datatypes, object references, and all user-defined datatypes.

IDL datatypes are encoded in one or multiple octets. An octet is a collection of eight bit values. For big-endian, the MSB (Most Significant Byte) starts at octet 0, while the opposite is true for little-endian. For example, big-endian and little-endian representation of increasing value one to eight is shown in Figure 5.3.

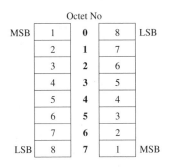

**Figure 5.3**  Big-endian and little-endian encoding layout.

The following is a description of CDR encoding rules for some of the commonly used IDL datatypes.

- *Primitive datatypes.* Figure 5.4 and interoperability-long illustrate the encoding layout of short and long datatypes.

**Figure 5.4**  Encoding layout of a short value.

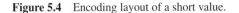

A short value occupies two octets, while a long value requires four octets. Both are aligned at their natural boundaries (Fig. 5.5).

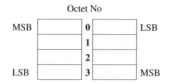

**Figure 5.5**  Encoding layout of a long value.

- *Constructed datatypes.* IDL struct is an example of constructed datatypes. Consider the following IDL declaration:

```
struct Address {
    string state;
    string street;
    string country;
};
```

Each string member is encoded with an unsigned long which indicates the string length in octets, including the terminating NULL, followed by the actual string value, also terminated by NULL. Figure 5.6 illustrates an example of a string value encoding for 'VIC' in big-endian:

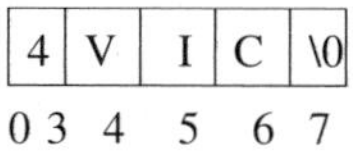

| 4 | V | I | C | \0 |
|---|---|---|---|---|

0 3  4   5   6  7

**Figure 5.6**  Encoding layout of a string.

An IDL struct itself is encoded as a sequence of structure members in order of their IDL declarations. Each member is encoded based on their datatype encoding rules. For example, Figure 5.7 depicts the big-endian encoding of a struct which contains 'VIC' in its state, 'Grattan' in its street, and 'Australia' in its country.

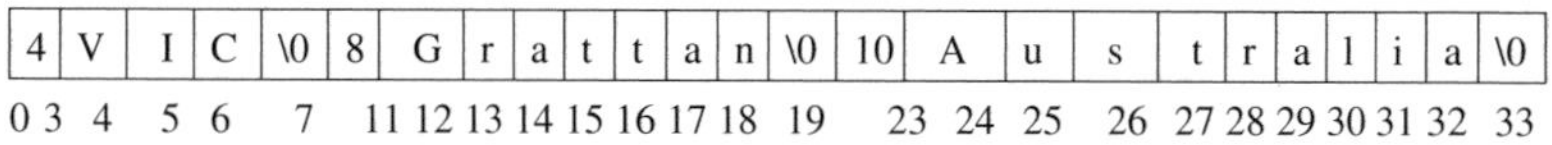

| 4 | V | I | C | \0 | 8 | G | r | a | t | t | a | n | \0 | 10 | A | u | s | t | r | a | l | i | a | \0 |
|---|---|---|---|----|---|---|---|---|---|---|---|---|----|----|---|---|---|---|---|---|---|---|---|----|

0 3 4  5 6    7    11 12 13 14 15 16 17 18  19    23 24 25  26 27 28 29 30 31 32  33

**Figure 5.7**  Encoding layout of a structure.

- *Named types.* Enumerated types are examples of named types. An enumerated type value is encoded as an unsigned long. For example, consider the following enumerated type:

```
enum ParamMode { IN, OUT, INOUT };
```

the encoding for OUT value is an unsigned long value which contains the ordering number of OUT, that is, two.

- *Template types.* sequence is an example of template types. Its encoding sequence starts with its length in unsigned long, followed by the sequence values. For example, consider the following declaration:

```
typedef sequence<short> shortSeq;
```

The big-endian encoding for a shortSeq whose members are initialized with values from one to five is illustrated in Figure 5.8.

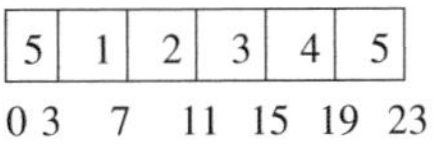

**Figure 5.8**    Encoding layout of a sequence.

## Message Formats

GIOP specification defines eight types of messages: *Request, Reply, CancelRequest, LocateRequest, LocateReply, CloseConnection, MessageError, Fragment.* The first four are administrative messages, while the latter are used in object invocations. Figure 5.9 illustrates the structure of a GIOP message.

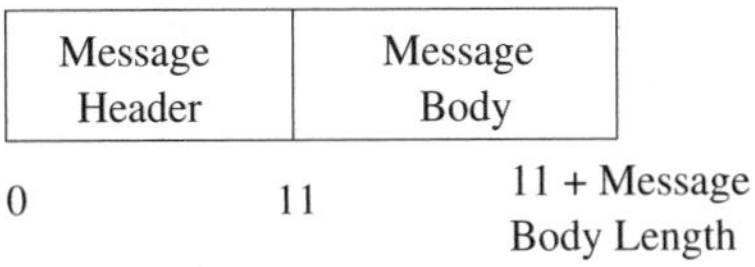

**Figure 5.9**    GIOP message structure.

A GIOP message starts with a message header followed by a message body. An IDL declaration for the message header is as follows:

```
module GIOP {
  struct Version {
  octet major;
  octet minor;
  };

  enum MsgType_1_1 { // Revised in GIOP version 1.1
     Request, Reply, CancelRequest, LocateRequest, LocateReply,
     CloseConnection, MessageError, Fragment
  };
```

```
struct MessageHeader_1_1 { //Revised in GIOP version 1.1
    char magic[4]; // Magic number
    Version GIOP_version;
    octet flags;
    octet message_type;
    unsigned long message_size;
};
    ...
};
```

The structure of a message header in big-endian ordering is depicted in Figure 5.10.

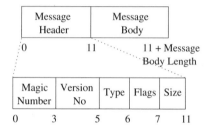

**Figure 5.10** Message header structure in big-endian.

A message header is the 12-bytes length part at the start of a GIOP message. The first 4 bytes of the header always contain the string 'GIOP'. The next byte is the major version number, while the latter one is the minor version number, and followed by one byte for flags. The least significant bit of the flag byte indicates the byte ordering used. If the rest of the message is encoded in big- endian, this bit has a value of 0. Otherwise, this bit will have a value of 1 for little-endian ordering. The second least significant bit indicates fragmentation. If this message is a complete message, or is the last message in a sequence of fragments, then the bit will have a value of 0. A message which is a fragment with more fragments to follow will have this bit set to 1. Byte 7 indicates the message type and is filled with the order number of $MsgType\_1\_1$, for example, 0 for Request message, 1 for Reply message, and so on. The last four bytes are 4-byte unsigned long, which indicates the size of the message body, minus the 12-byte message header, but including any alignment gaps. The GIOP message body is a variable length part of the message whose exact content is different from one message type to another. The rest of the GIOP discussion explains the message body's content for each message type.

**Request Message** Request message is sent by a client whenever it wishes to invoke an operation of an object. Figure 5.11 depicts the content structure of GIOP Request message.

As illustrated, the message body for a GIOP Request message consists of Request message header and Request message body. The IDL declaration for Request message header is provided below:

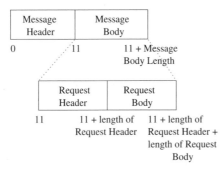

**Figure 5.11**   Content structure of request message.

```
module IOP {
  ...
  typedef unsigned long ServiceId;

  struct ServiceContext {
    ServiceId context_id;
    sequence<octet> context_data;
  };

  typedef sequence<ServiceContext> ServiceContextList; };

  module GIOP {
    ...
    struct RequestHeader_1_1 { // Revised in GIOP version 1.1
    IOP::ServiceContextList service_context; unsigned long request_id;
    boolean response_expected;
    octet reserved[3];
    sequence<octet> object_key;
    string operation;
    Principal requesting_principal;
  };
  ...
};
```

service_context is a sequence of ServiceContext used to transmit information specific to a certain context of a service transparently in each request. An example of its usage can be found in transaction and security service. request_id is used to associate a particular request with its particular reply. Clients could send multiple requests to servers and receive their replies in a random order. The use of request_id prevents a reply message from being misused to respond to a request. Clients are responsible for generating this value uniquely in the scope of a connection. response_expected is set to true if a reply is expected to be returned from the server as a response to the request message. Otherwise, the member should be set with the boolean value of false instead. reserved member is a three bytes sized member reserved for future use. object_key identifies the target server object where the request message must be delivered to. operation member encapsulates the name of the operation being invoked. For example, the operation name to retrieve the value of an attribute called serviceList is Reply message header *get_serviceList*(). The last member, *requesting_principal*(), indicates the identity of the sending client and is used to support *BOA* :: *get_principal*() operation. The Request's message body contains in and out parameters for the request. It could also be followed with Context if the declaration of the operation being invoked has a Context clause. Similar to IDL's struct, the parameters are encoded according to the orders in which they are declared. Each of these parameters is encoded by the rule specified by CDR for its datatype.

**Reply Message**    A server that receives a Request message whose request_ expected is set to true must respond by sending a Reply message. Figure 5.12 illustrates the content structure of a GIOP Reply message.

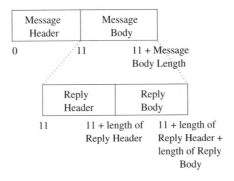

**Figure 5.12**    Content structure of reply message.

As shown, the message body of a Reply message consists of the Reply message header and Request message body. The IDL declaration for the message header is as follows:

```
module IOP {
  ...
  typedef unsigned long ServiceId;

  struct ServiceContext {
    ServiceId context_id;
    sequence<octet> context_data;
  };

  typedef sequence<ServiceContext> ServiceContextList; };

  module GIOP {
  ...
```

```
enum ReplyStatusType { NO_EXCEPTION, USER_EXCEPTION,
                       SYSTEM_EXCEPTION, LOCATION_FORWARD };

struct ReplyHeader {
  IOP::ServiceContextList service_context;
  unsigned long request_id;
  ReplyStatusType reply_status;
};
  ...
};
```

As in Request message, service_context is used to send information specific to a service context. request_id contains the request id obtained from the Request message header's request_id, thus associating the Request message with its Reply message. reply_status indicates the status of the operation invocation. If it contains NO_EXCEPTION, this means that the request has been processed successfully. The Reply message body will contain the return value and all out and inout parameters. Each of them is encoded according to its IDL declaration order and to the CDR rules defined for its datatype. Value USER_EXCEPTION indicates that a user exception has been raised. Reply message with this value will have its message body containing the repository id of the exception. SYSTEM_EXCEPTION indicates that the server or its ORB has raised a system exception. Its Reply message body contains the following structure:

```
struct SystemExceptionReplyBody {
   string exception_id;
   unsigned long minor_code_value;
   unsigned long completion_status;
};
```

exception_id is the exception's repository id. minor_code_value holds vendor-specific system exception minor codes. It is not used by standard system exceptions and has been deprecated by OMG. completion_status indicates where the error occurred. If its value is 1 this means the operation has been invoked successfully, but an error occurred during the return. Value of 0 indicates the exception is raised before the operation is successfully invoked. Lastly, value LOCATION_FORWARD indicates that the request cannot be processed by the server and should be forwarded to the another object instead. The reference to this object will be contained in the message body.

**CancelRequest Message**   This message tells the server not to send any reply after the request has been processed. However, this message does not cancel currently running request processing. The Reply message might still be sent and the client must be prepare to accept the message or any exception from the server. Figure 5.13 shows the content structure of GIOP CancelRequest message.

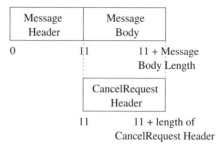

**Figure 5.13** Content structure of CancelRequest message.

A CancelRequest message contains only a message header with IDL declaration of:

```
struct CancelRequestHeader {
    unsigned long request_id;
};
```

request_id is the id of the request that needs to be cancelled.

**LocateRequest Message**   Clients use LocateRequest messages to determine the validity of an object or whether the server containing the object is capable of receiving requests or what address requests should be sent to. Figure 5.14 depicts the content structure of GIOP LocateRequest message.

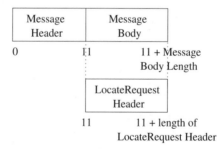

**Figure 5.14** Content structure of LocateRequest message.

As illustrated, LocateRequest contains only a message header of the following declaration:

```
struct LocateRequestHeader {
    unsigned long request_id;
    sequence<octet> object_key;
};
```

`request_id` of LocateRequest message associates the message with a LocateReply message in the manner similar with the association between Request and Reply messages. `object_key` identifies the object being located by the LocateRequest message.

**LocateReply Message**    The use of this message is to respond to a LocateRequest message. Figure 5.15 describes the content structure of GIOP LocateReply message pictorially.

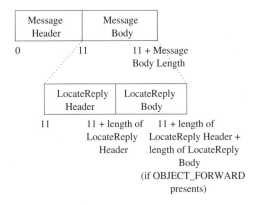

**Figure 5.15**    Content structure of LocateReply message.

The IDL declaration of LocateReply message header is given below:

```
enum LocateStatusType { UNKNOWN_OBJECT, OBJECT_HERE, OBJECT_FORWARD };
struct LocateReplyHeader {
   unsigned long request_id;
   LocateStatusType locate_status;
};
```

`request_id` is filled with a value obtained from LocateRequest's `request_id`, while `locate_status` holds the status of the attempt to locate the wanted object. It can contain three possible values. The first one is UNKNOWN_BJECT which indicates that the server does not know the desired object. The next possible value is OBJECT_HERE, with which the server can directly receive the requests for the wanted object. A LocateReply message with a `locate_status` value of UNKNOWN_OBJECT or OBJECT_HERE has no message body. If OBJECT_FORWARD is present, then the reference of the wanted object will be inserted into the LocateReply message body.

**CloseConnection Message**    A server uses this message to inform its clients that it is about to close the connection. A new connection must be established if clients want to communicate with the server again later. An example of its usage is found when a server is overloaded or about to reach its connection limit. Without this message, clients might confuse a normal connection closing with the abnormal ones, such as those that happen when a server crashes. This type of GIOP message contains no GIOP message body, only a GIOP message header. See Fig. 5.16.

**Figure 5.16**    Content structure of CloseConnection message.

***MessageError Message***    MessageError message is sent in response to messages which are not properly created: invalid version number, invalid message type, invalid magic value, etc. No GIOP Message body exists. See Fig. 5.17.

**Figure 5.17**    Content structure of MessageError message.

***Fragment Message***    A Request or Reply message that must be sent as fragment messages is broken into a normal message with its fragment bit set to 1 and a sequence of fragment messages. All of these fragment messages must also have their fragment bits set to 1, except for the last one. Figure 5.18 illustrates the content structure of a fragment-type message.

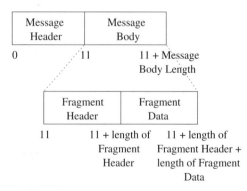

**Figure 5.18**    Content structure of Fragment message.

## Transport Assumptions

An interoperability protocol based on GIOP specification is implemented on top of a transport protocol. The following are assumptions regarding the behavior of this protocol:

- *Connection oriented.* Messages sent using connection-oriented transport proto-col require no embedded destination addresses. Instead, a connection handle is returned after the connection is established and used for message deliveries.

- *Reliable.* The transport protocol must guarantee that messages are delivered in the order in which they were sent, at most once, and their successful deliveries are acknowledged.

- *Viewable as a byte stream.* The transport protocol must not have message size limits, fragmentations, or alignments enforced.

- *Have reasonable orderly shutdown notification.* The transport protocol must be able to notify the other communication end about abnormal connection shut-down. This happens when clients or servers crash, network connectivity is lost, etc.

- *Have a TCP/IP mappable connection initiation model.* The transport proto-col's connection initiation model must be mappable to the TCP/IP's model. The model is described briefly next.

  Servers do not actively initiate connections, but listen or are prepared to receive requests for connections. A client that wishes to establish a connection must know the server address and send a connect request to it. The listening server might create a new connection or reject the request, for reasons such as insufficient resources. Either side is able to close the connection once it is established.

### 5.4.1   Internet Inter-ORB Protocol

IIOP (Internet Inter-ORB Protocol) is a concrete GIOP interoperability protocol based on TCP/IP. All CORBA compliant ORBs must support this protocol either as their native protocol or through half-bridges. IIOP is commonly used as the proto-col of choice in communicating with other ORBs. In order to map the abstract GIOP onto TCP/IP, OMG specifies how TCP/IP addresses information inside IOR. The in-formation allows clients to establish a connection to the server by manipulating the IOR before sending requests. The IDL declaration for this addressing information is shown below:

```
module IIOP {
  struct Version {
    octet major;
    octet minor;
  };

  struct ProfileBody_1_1 { // Revised in IIOP version 1.1
    Version iiop_version;
    string host;
    unsigned short port;
    sequence<octet> object_key;
```

```
    sequence<IOP::TaggedComponent> components;
  };
...
};
```

iiop_version indicates the IIOP version supported. host is the name of the host machine. The name can be specified as an Internet host name (e.g., www.hostname. com) or as an Internet IP address (e.g., 123.123.123.123). port member is used to specify the port number where the server listens for incoming requests. object_key is used to identify the object where requests should be sent to. components contains additional information which will be used by some newer CORBA features, such as wide character code sets. More details on this member are provided in the IOR section.

### 5.4.2   Environment Specific Inter-ORB Protocol

ESIOP (Environment Specific Inter-ORB Protocol) is a concrete GIOP protocol which is used to communicate in a particular environment. An ESIOP is optimized for a specific environment and may be chosen over TCP/IP. However, ESIOP is optional and could be proprietary. As a result, its availability is limited and at least one more protocol should be supported as the second choice. An example of ESIOP is DCE-CIOP (DCE-Common Inter-ORB Protocol) which makes use of a subset of DCE-RPC facilities and parts of GIOP specification.

***Message Transports***   DCE-RPC defines connection-oriented and connection-less protocols for establishing communication between a client and a server. It supports multiple underlying transport protocols and multiple outstanding requests to multiple CORBA objects over one single connection. Messages can also be fragmented, allowing ORBs to manage a buffer which contains a large amount of marshaled data. Interactions between ORBs are made in the form of remote procedure calls on one of two DCE-RPC interfaces: pipe-based or array-based interfaces. The first one has its messages transmitted as pipes of uninterpreted bytes. The use of this interface has the following characteristics: efficiently sends a large amount of data, buffering complete messages is not compulsory, marshaling and unmarshalling can be performed simultaneously with the message transmission, ORB controls message encoding and data marshaling, and DCE client and server stubs can be used to implement DCE-CIOP. This interface is optional since not all DCE-RPC implementations provide enough support for pipes. Messages of the second interface are transmitted as arrays of uninterpreted bytes. The interface is an alternative to the previous interface when the DCE-RPC implementations do not sufficiently support pipes. The existence of array-based interface support in all client and server ORBs is compulsory. Using this interface over the first one offers no advantage. However, the pipe-based interface is preferred over the array-based one since messages can be transmitted without precomputing their lengths. Both of these interfaces have invoke and locate operations. The former is used in operation invocations, while the latter finds server processes.

***Data Representation*** DCE-CIOP messages represent OMG IDL datatype values in CDR. Their message headers and bodies are delivered as OMG IDL data types values and also encoded in CDR. The messages are sent via DCE-RPC pipes or arrays. On the other hand, DCE-IDL defined operations use Network Data Representation (NDR) encoding. The way CDR represents OMG-IDL primitive datatypes is similar to how NDR represents DCE-IDL datatypes. In fact, there is almost a one-to-one equivalent of NDR's primitive types to those of CDR. For example, OMG IDL's short and long correspond to DCE-IDL's short and long. Some OMG IDL datatypes such as constructed types have no correspondent in the DCE IDL.

***Message Formats*** There are four types of DCE-CIOP messages that can be exchanged. The first one is Invoke Request which is used to send an invocation request. It contains information such as target object, target operation, the principal, the operation context, a service context, and in and inout parameter values. An Invoke Response message is sent as a response to an Invoke Request message. This message indicates the status of the invocation and returns a `ServiceContext`. If the invocation is successful, the return value, and out and inout are returned. If it fails, an exception is returned. If the object is at a different location, the object's binding information is returned instead. The next type of message is Locate Request which is used to send requests to locate server processes. It contains information which identifies the target object and the target operation. The last message type is Locate Response which is used to response to a Locate Request. It holds information that indicates whether the object's location is in the current server process, or elsewhere or even unknown. If the object is elsewhere, its RPC binding information will also be returned. Each of these message types have their message formats start with a field containing the byte ordering used in the CDR encoding of the rest of the message. The CDR byte order of a message must be the same with the NDR byte order used by DCE-RPC to transmit the message.

## 5.5 INTEROPERABLE OBJECT REFERENCE

An object is manipulated through its references. These references should contain potential information that is crucial to bridges in performing their job. The first information is whether or not object references are actually null, that is, do not point to any object. The object type—the interfaces that a referenced object implements—is the next information needed. A list of protocols that can be selected to communicate with the referenced object is also important. It facilitates the selection of a protocol which is optimized to communicate with the referenced object efficiently. Information about available ORB services is needed to reduce or eliminate negotiation overhead in selecting them. In order to provide the above information, OMG standardizes the structure of the object references as IOR. Its IDL declaration is shown below:

```
module IOP {
  typedef unsigned long ProfileId;
  const ProfileId TAG_INTERNET_IOP = 0;
  const ProfileId TAG_MULTIPLE_COMPONENTS = 1;

  struct TaggedProfile {
    ProfileId tag;
    sequence<octet> profile_data;
  };

  struct IOR {
    string type_id;
    sequence<TaggedProfile> profiles;
  };

  typedef unsigned long ComponentId;
  struct TaggedComponent {
    ComponentId tag;
    sequence<octet> component_data;
  };

  typedef sequence<TaggedComponent> MultipleComponentProfile;
};
```

As shown above, the IOR structure is declared as an IDL struct called IOR. Its type_id contains the most derived interface (i.e., the interface at the end of the referenced object's inheritance tree) of the referenced object. A null is represented as having an empty profile with its type_id holding a string which contains only a single terminating character. The latter can also be used to represent the org.omg.CORBA.Object interface. Profiles is a sequence of protocol specific tagged profiles; each supports at least one protocol. An IOR must have at least one profile which can be used to drive a complete invocation using any of the supported protocols. A bridge between two domains may need to know the detailed content of the profiles for those domains. Each tagged profile contains a tag encapsulated in its tag member. Vendors must reserve tag values from OMG before using them for proprietary protocols. If clients cannot interpret these proprietary tag values, their profiles will be ignored. Thus, the existence of proprietary protocol information will not jeopardize interoperability.

If the tag value is TAG_INTERNET_IOP, then its profile_data will have the IIOP::ProfileBody structure which was explained earlier in the IIOP section. If the tag contains a value of TAG_MULTIPLE_COMPONENTS, then profile_data will hold MultipleComponentProfile which in turn contains service-specific information. MultipleComponentProfile is a sequence of TaggedComponent structure, each having tag and component_data. Similar to values of tag in the TaggedProfile, vendors must also request OMG to allocate the tag values of the TaggedComponent's tag before using those values. component_data contains the actual information pertinent to a particular tag value. For example, if the tag value is TAG_ORB_TYPE, the component_data contains information to identify a particular ORB of a vendor. This tag enables the use of proprietary features and optimizations. Other tags are also specified for purposes like describing security mechanisms, codeset (for wide character supports), alternative IIOP address of the referenced object, and so on.

## 5.6 SUMMARY

In this chapter we described interoperability standardized mechanisms used to communicate with ORBs of different vendors. Bridges transform requests that cross their domains to the target domains' forms. Interoperability protocols facilitate communication between two ORBs on top of a particular transport protocol. Each of them is a GIOP mapping onto specific transport protocol. IIOP is a commonly used interoperability protocol which is based on TCP/IP. OMG also permits the use of the Environment Specific Interoperability Protocol (ESIOP) such as DCE-ESIOP. This type of protocol is optimized for a particular environment, making it an ideal choice for communication in that environment. IORs allow objects to be accessed without worrying about the underlying communication details. Information embedded in the IORs is relevant to one or multiple services and/or protocols. Proprietary features and optimizations can also be accomplished by manipulating the embedded information.

## 5.7 REVIEW QUESTIONS

- What is interoperability? Why is it so important? Explain the factors that motivate interoperability.
- What is a domain? Explain boundary traversing and different categories of domains. What is the use of domain in relation to the ORB's functionality scope?
- Why must the issue of domain boundary traversal be resolved for interoperability to succeed?
- What is a bridge? What is its role in interoperability? What are the techniques in bridging a request? What is policy-mediated bridging? Explain the different types of bridges?
- What is GIOP? What does its abstract nature mean? What are different types of GIOP messages?
- What must a person who wants to create a new interoperability protocol do in relation to GIOP?
- What is IIOP? How is an IOR used to identify a particular ORB product?
- What is ESIOP? Why is it usually chosen as a second choice protocol?
- How are multiple protocols supported in IOR?
- Explain how clients deal with tag values that they have no idea about.

## 5.8 EXERCISES

- After looking at the content of an IOR, one would realize that no information about the lifetime status (e.g., whether or not the object is still active, etc) of object referenced by this IOR is embedded inside the IOR. Why does OMG not include this information inside the IOR?

- When IIOP was not available, how could one make sure two CORBA applications would be able to communicate with each other?

# CHAPTER 6

# CORBA Caching

For many distributed data-intensive applications, the default remote invocation of CORBA objects by clients is not acceptable because of performance degradation. Caching enables clients to invoke operations locally on distributed objects instead of fetching them from remote servers. This chapter describes a design and implementation of a specific caching approach for CORBA-based systems using Orbix. The proposed caching solution is a generic one that can be implemented in any other ORB platform, such as OrbixWeb and Visibroker.

Caching has been extensively studied in several areas, such as databases, the World Wide Web, and conventional distributed systems. However there is a very little work done in the area of CORBA. This chapter proposes a summary of some of the techniques proposed in CORBA caching [104, 105][67], and later describes in detail a generic approach that deals with the issues of object eviction and object consistency. An FIFO-based removal algorithm is discussed, and this uses a double linked structure and hash table for eviction. A variation of optimistic two phase locking for consistency control is proposed. This protocol does not require a lock at the client side by using a per-process caching design. Based on experiments made, for a 1000 objects per-client invocation, when the number of clients increases to 20, no-caching approach will result in server saturation; when the number of clients equals 15, caching with half buffer will save up to 45% of access time and caching with full buffer will save up to 50% of access time.

Because caching is an implementation issue for CORBA systems, OMG has not provided any standard. Caching relates to the way proxies (e.g., client proxy and server proxy) and the ORB perform invocations.

## 6.1 OVERALL PICTURE

Chapters 2 and 3 provided details of the CORBA architecture as well as how to develop distributed applications. It was mentioned that CORBA has several advantages over existing communication protocols (e.g., RPC, socket), and in particular, with regard the issue of transparency, such as location transparency (i.e., clients do not worry where the objects are located, that is, the host and the address), operating system transparency (clients do not need to know the underlying operating systems on which the ORBs are installed), and programming language transparency (clients do not need to know the different languages used to implement the different servers). However the enforcement of these different types of transparency (by the ORB) causes performance problems, such as message overhead and frequent remote invocations. On the other hand, distributed applications, such as telecommunication and avionics control, require high bandwidth and low latency, high speed and portability [37]. For example, telecommunication systems require high speed as well to increase efficiency of work. Using existing ORBs for such applications may lead to poor performance due to excessive marshalling/demarshalling overhead, data coping, and high-level of function call overhead.

Whereas CORBA implementations can be optimized along the lines of efficient and data copying [36, 37], it is the default behavior of CORBA applications that causes significant latency. Network latency is often the significant component of application invocation latency. By default, a CORBA client application will perform a remote invocation for every request. For many distributed data-intensive applications, this is an unacceptable performance overhead. However, by caching remote objects, it is possible to reduce the number of network invocations during critical client processing. Inter-transaction caching allows clients to retain the contents of the cache across transaction boundaries. Inter-transaction caching requires a cache consistency protocol to ensure that a client's view of the data is globally consistent. Tradeoffs must be made during protocol selection to ensure that the cost of maintaining the cache does not eliminate the gain made by caching. Typically this is dependent upon the workload that the application is expecting.

When dealing with CORBA caching, one important aspect is the granularity aspect. Introducing caching is to allow CORBA objects to be used as fine grained application objects, rather than processing interface versions of internal objects (i.e., attributes). If CORBA objects are used only at process boundaries, then there is a need to write a mapping between the internal application and interface objects. This approach is error prone, complex, adds an extra layer of maintenance and is an additional performance overhead.

Very little work has been done with the caching approach in CORBA environments. The only work in the area we are aware of is the one proposed by Mowbray [67]. This approach includes an object caching technique that intercepts any remote invocations within the client if the object is locally available. Objects are migrated to clients via a distributed cache manager (with a single retrieve and single update operation). The cache manager is hard-coded for a specific set of related IDL interface types, which performs coarse-grained shipping using an IDL interface for a single retrieve operation and a single update operation. One major problem of this approach is that it is an "informal one." It does not present an implementation, testing or performance analysis of the approach. Also, this approach does not guarantee one copy serialization of objects updated, that is, consistency across different caches, which is not acceptable for most of the distributed applications.

The aim of this chapter is to propose a comprehensive view of the issues related to CORBA caching as well as a detailed caching technique that can contribute to improving the ORB performance. These issues involve object eviction and object consistency. Object eviction is considered when the client buffer is full (with cached objects); therefore, the decision to be taken is to decide which object to evict so the frequency of later remote of invocation is reduced. Object consistency is considered when "real" data is updated in the server. Therefore, the issue is to make sure that all clients have consistent copies of the data in the server, that is, the most up- to-date data. On one hand, by caching objects locally in the client workspace, good performance can be gained. On the other hand, caching has its own problems and limitations. Evicting a "wrong" object can have deep consequences on the performance of a system. Also, when dealing with applications where the frequency of updates is high, more messages are issued to make the copies of data consistent, and this has an impact on the overall performance.

This chapter describes an enhanced version of the existing removal algorithm (FIFO) using a specific data structure, a doubly linked queue structure with hash table. This chapter also describes a concurrency control algorithm without retaining or assigning locks for objects at the server side. Instead of locking operations in the client side, they are locked in the server side. The proposed algorithms were tested in Orbix [104, 105], as shown in the later sections, and there is substantial gain of performance improvement of client applications

The following section provides a technical summary of the existing approaches that deal with the issues of cache replacement and data consistency. Section 6.5 discusses a caching architecture as well as the different algorithms for cache replacement and data consistency in the context of CORBA environments. Section 6.7 provides details about the design of the proposed algorithms. Section 6.8 proposes a series of tests which demonstrate the performance improvement when caching is used in combination with CORBA applications.

## 6.2   CACHING ISSUES AND TECHNIQUES

In CORBA, all client invocations are routed by the ORB to specific implementations called servant classes. Based on the information contained within the object reference (or IOR), the local ORB will decide to invoke the operation either locally or remotely. Clients do not need to know about the location of the object, the programming language used to implement operations in the server, or the communication protocol to be used to communicate with a remote server. The ORB provides location and distribution transparency.

However, the demultiplexing strategies used by ORBs can impact their performance significantly. Conventional ORBs demultiplex client requests to the servant in several steps [36]: (1) the OS protocol stack demultiplexes the incoming client request multiple times through the data link, network and transport layers to the OS kernel and the ORB core; (2) the ORB core uses the addressing information in the client's object key to locate the appropriate adapter, servant and the skeleton of the target IDL operation; (3) the IDL skeleton locates the appropriate operation, demarshals the requests buffer into operation parameters and performs the operation up-call. Demultiplexing client request through all these layers is expensive. The major problem of this layered demultiplexing is that it induces bad performance as it increases the latency by increasing the number of times that an internal table must be searched. This can also lead to priority inversions.

In addition to the problem related to demultiplexing, ORB latency overhead stems from long chains of intra-ORB function calls, excessive presentation layer conversions and data copying, and non-optimized buffering algorithms used for network reads and writes. Scalability impediments are due to inefficient server demultiplexing techniques and the lack of integration with OS and network features. These inefficiencies prevent developers from using CORBA for life critical applications such as real time avionics, telecommunication call processing and medical imaging [37].

The degradation of ORB performance can also be due to unnecessary access to remote objects by applications. As mentioned in Section 6.1, caching these objects will remove the need for excessive access to a remote server and therefore improve the performance of remote execution of operations. Figure 6.1 shows two clients accessing data from the cache storage; as a result, the network congestion is reduced and the performance is increased. If the data is not cached, then the cache manager will request to retrieve the object from the server and cache it locally. One of the main tasks of the cache manager is to increase the probability of having objects in the cache when they are requested.

However, caching has its own problems. One of them is concerned with the selection of the object to be evicted when the buffer is full. The selection of a victim for eviction is quite complex because the use of a specific strategy may have a great impact on performance. Another problem is that the data in the server can be updated and therefore make the cached objects inconsistent. Local cached objects will need to be updated, and this may also affect the performance of ORB because of a large number of messages.

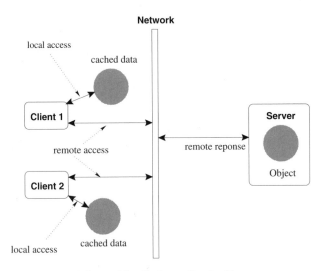

**Figure 6.1** Cache at client's side.

## 6.3   CACHE REPLACEMENT

When a cache buffer is full, some data must be evicted. Which data need to be evicted remains an issue for the developers. Here we discuss some of the main existing removal algorithms [113].

***Least Recently Used***   The LRU (Least Recently Used) algorithm is probably the most widely used cache replacement algorithm for handling objects. The least recently used objects will be removed as many as required to have a sufficient space for the newly accessed object. This may involve one or many replacements. Each time an object is accessed, the object is promoted to the head of most frequently used chain and some actions need to be taken to keep track of the accessed data item. Since a list with sorted order is used, the cost of keeping the object in order will degrade the performance.

- *Page cache design:* As shown in Figure 6.2, a page which is fetched from the server is put in the middle of the usage chain at page position $O$ (e.g., Page $O$). If a later transaction refers to the page $O$, then it is promoted to the top of the usage chain N. Whenever a new page enters the cache, the page at the bottom of the chain (e.g., Page $A$) is evicted. Clients always send whole pages to the server when committing a modified object [106].
- *Object cache design:* As shown in Figure 6.3, the page $W$ received from the server in response to a fetched request is placed in the middle of the usage chain which is the same as page cache design. However, when an object in a page (in the middle of Page $O$) is referred to, only that object is promoted to the top of the chain. When a new page enters the cache, some objects at the bottom of the chain are evicted. Clients send only the modified object to the server in a transaction commit message [106].

***SIZE Policy***   Objects are removed based on their size, with the largest object removed first. As for the LRU algorithm, some techniques are required to keep the data size in order. If two objects have equal size, which is generally rare, then the order

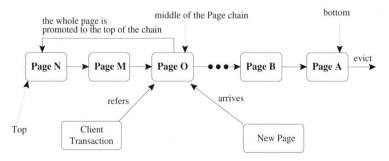

**Figure 6.2**   Page cache design.

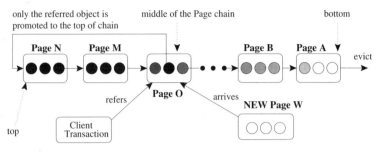

**Figure 6.3**   Object cache design.

of removal is based on their last access time [4]. One of the major limitations of this approach is to keep track of the object size as well as the access time.

***LRU-MIN***   This approach is a hybrid approach which combines LRU and the SIZE policy. The removal of larger sized objects is preferred, which reduces the number of objects replaced. If an incoming object (say S) is too big to fit in the cache, then an object of the same size or larger than S will be removed. If no objects can be found in the cache (with the same size or bigger), then objects are removed according to the LRU strategy: objects with size greater than S/2 are first chosen, then later objects with size greater than S/4, then objects of size at least S/8 will be deleted, and so on until sufficient free cache space is been created [4]. This algorithm requires an exhaustive search as well as the use of an efficient relocation algorithm in order to put together the smaller free spaces.

***LRU-THOLD***   This is a variant of the LRU algorithm. The LRU-THOLD algorithm avoids caching of large objects (or documents), which requires replacing a large number of existing smaller size objects. The difference with the LRU algorithm is that no objects larger than a threshold size can be cached [1].

***FIFO***   FIFO (First In, First Out) is the queue algorithm in which the first object in the queue is pruned off when the buffer is full. The new object is appended to the tail of a queue. If the object from the middle of the queue is addressed, then the cost of updating or removing the object will be expensive. Some appropriate mechanisms are required to efficiently remove objects from the middle of the queue.

***Object Live Time Algorithm***   An object live time is added to objects to indicate their life duration. When the live time expires, the object becomes stale. This algorithm is particularly for World Web Wide caching, in which the cached data has an expiration time. When the time expires, the browser will fetch a new copy of data from the Internet. Generally, it is not possible to associate a lifetime with an object copy when the object is written because the time of the next write to the object is not known [3]. Neither HTTP nor Gopher has any provision for a server notifying the cache when a page changes, so the cache object must be estimated a time period during which it believes the page will not change. In the context of CORBA, this algorithm is nearly useless, because the critical object in CORBA cannot be estimated by the program or the end user.

### 6.3.1  Caching Consistency Algorithms

As mentioned earlier, the data in a server can be updated, but this makes the cached objects inconsistent. Some techniques are used to control the cache consistency problem, such as locking of objects. Such techniques are particularly efficient when data is locked for short time. When the locks are used for long period, locking mechanisms become inappropriate. Instead, optimistic concurrency control based on forward and backward validation is used. Operations on objects are not transactions, that is, they require a very short time to be processed; therefore, locking is a better approach when dealing with CORBA cached objects. The focus in this section is on the recent locking approaches proposed in the literature.

***Callback Locking***   This algorithm first appeared in the Andrew file system to maintain the consistency of cached files [50]. Using this mechanism, a client must obtain a lock from the server before accessing a data page rather than at the commit time. The lock is retained even after a transaction is terminated. Therefore, there is no need for the client to contact the server to check object validity or to acquire a lock when a transaction accesses a cached object with the appropriate lock. When a transaction accesses a cached object without a retained lock (i.e., client's first request or cache object has been evicted from cache buffer) or with the wrong lock (the transaction wants to update an object that has only a read lock), it will need to obtain a proper lock from the server. The server broadcasts a message to all clients that have inappropriate locks associated with this object and requests them to release the locks. A client releases the lock requested by the server immediately if the object has not been accessed by the current transaction on the client. Otherwise, it waits until the current transaction terminates to release the lock. The server cannot grant the requested lock until all incompatible locks on the object are released [110].

***Server-based Two Phase Locking***   With this approach, the server's copy of each object (or page) is treated as the primary copy of that object. Client transactions must obtain the proper lock from the server before they are allowed to access a data item the same as the Callback Locking. But clients are not allowed to cache locks across transaction boundaries. A variant of this approach, called `Caching 2PL`, is proposed that allows data to be cached at clients across transaction boundaries. Consistency is maintained by using the "check-on-access" policy: when a transaction requests a read lock for a page that is cached at its client side, it sends the Log Sequence Number found on its copy of the page along with the lock request. The server responds to the lock request with the latest copy of the page along with the response, if it determines that the site's copy is no longer valid. In Caching 2PL, deadlock detection is performed exclusively at the server. Deadlocks are resolved by aborting the youngest transaction involved in the deadlock [17]. An algorithm similar to Caching 2PL is currently used in the EXODUS storage manager [16].

***Optimistic Two Phase Locking (No-Wait Lock)***    The O2PL schemes allow inter-transaction caching of data pages and an optimistic form of lock caching. They are based on a read-one, write-all concurrency control protocol for replicated data in distributed databases. The O2PL algorithms are optimistic in the sense that they defer the detection of conflicts among locks cached at multiple sites until transaction commit time. In these algorithms, each client has its own local lock manager from which the proper lock must be obtained locally before a transaction can access a data item at that client. This differs from Caching PL in that client assigns locks locally. Client updates are performed locally, but they are not permitted to migrate back to the server's buffer until the associated update transaction enters its commit phase. The client's read operation is executed locally as well, in case there is a cache miss(data not found in cache or data is invalid), the client requests the server to obtain the latest copy of the data. The server is responsible for keeping track of where pages are cached in the system. The client informs the server when it drops a page from its buffer pool by piggybacking that information on the next message that it sends to the server. Thus, the server's data is conservative.

When an updating transaction is ready to enter its commit phase, it sends a message to the server containing a copy of each page that has been updated. The server then acquires exclusive locks on these pages on behalf of the transaction. Once these locks have been acquired at the server, the server sends a message to each client that has cached copies of the updated pages. These remote clients obtain exclusive locks on their local copies of the updated pages on behalf of the committing transaction. Once all the required locks have been obtained, specific actions are taken. It can be invalidated by a message or updated with the latest data item [17].

- *Invalidation phase:* During this phase, a committing update transaction acquires update-copy locks on all copies of the updated pages. At the server, these locks enable the committing transaction to safely update data. On other clients, however, they enable it to safely invalidate cached copies of the page. Once all updated pages have been invalidated, these other clients send a prepared-to-commit message back to the server, release their update-copy locks, and then drop out of the commit protocol. The server can commit the update transaction when all sites containing cached copies of the updated data have responded. At that moment, only the server and the client that originated the update have copies of the updated data [17].
- *Propagation phase:* The propagation O2PL keeps all clients informed of any changes made to the data resident in their local caches. As in O2PL Invalidate, a committing update transaction acquires update-copy locks on all copies of pages to be updated. In this case, these locks are used to enable the committing transaction to safely update its data on every machine that holds a copy of the

updated data. Since updates must be installed on the server and all clients atomically, O2PL Propagation employs a two-phase commit protocol rather than the one-phase commit that suffices for O2PL Invalidate. Also, the prepare-to-commit messages that the server sends to clients in this case must include copies of the relevant updates. These updates are installed during the second phase of the commit protocol to avoid overwriting valid cached pages before the outcome of the update transaction is certain [17].

### 6.3.2  Other Issues

In addition to the above two issues, there are other aspects that need to be taken into account when designing a caching approach. These aspects involve, for example, cache storage, cache organization and invalid access prevention.

- *Cache storage:* In some network file systems, such as Andrew [50], clients' file caches are kept on their local disks. In the Sprite network file system, file data is cached in the main memory for the following reasons: i) the main memory caches permit workstations to be diskless, which makes them cheaper and quieter; ii) data can be accessed more quickly from a cache in main memory than a cache on disk; iii) physical memories on client workstations are now large enough to provide high hit ratios. As memories get larger, main memory caches will grow to achieve even higher hit ratios; iv) the server caches will be in main memory regardless of where client caches are located. Memory-based caching can also have three levels: local client memory, remote client memory, and server memory. The first two levels require a remote access operation to fetch the cache data; thus it is not recommended.
- *Cache organization:* In the ScaFDOCS system [56], two schemes for client caching are mentioned: per-node caching and per-process caching. The former allows clients in the same node to share the cache data, whereas the latter enables clients to have their own caching manager.
- *Invalid access prevention:* When a cached data becomes stale, some action needs to be taken either to leave the stale data unchanged until the next event or to remove the stale data from the cache. Franklin et al. [32] described two schemes: avoidance and detection. The *avoidance-based scheme* ensures that all cache data is valid, while the detection scheme allows stale data to remain in client caches and ensures that transactions are allowed to commit only when they do not access such cache data. *Detection base schemes* are lazy; they require that the transaction check the validity of cache data. Stale data is kept in the cache for some period. If the next transaction refers to the stale data, then it is updated without re-assigning the space for it. In case of a full cache buffer, if the stale data is in the head of the queue, then it is removed. While the avoidance based scheme is positive, it guarantees that all the invalid data will be removed immediately so that it will not have a chance to access invalid data.

## 6.4 THE CACHING APPROACH

As described in Sections 6.3 and 6.3.1, there are four main types of removal algorithms: LRU, Size, FIFO and object live time algorithm. LRU-Min and LRU-THOLD are variants of LRU. Since the LRU algorithm will have one or many replacements, the cost will be higher. For the Size algorithm, in case of objects having the same size, this approach is not realistic because objects with the same size have equal priorities and therefore not useful to be used in CORBA environments. The FIFO algorithm has a limitation when dealing with the update of objects in the middle of chain. The algorithm which uses object live time is hard to estimate because the time for the next update action on the object is unknown. However, an appropriate extension of the FIFO approach to better deal with object updates can be beneficial for CORBA caching. This chapter will show how to extend the FIFO approach to include an appropriate data structure (e.g., double linked list) to improve some of its limitations.

Table 6.1 summarizes the characteristics of the different locking consistency protocols. This table shows that Caching 2PL always accesses the remote server. Frequent remote access will degrade the performance of the whole system. The Callback Locking retains the lock even after a transaction terminates, which will induce poor performance unnecessarily. The Optimistic 2PL can be considered as the most appropriate consistency algorithm for CORBA environments. It has a callback feature and it does not retain a lock. Assigning locks in the client side, as is done by the Optimistic 2PL, will have the same drawbacks as the Callback Locking. Therefore the implementation of a lock manager at the client side is impractical. A design of an algorithm based on the optimistic 2PL with some enhanced features, such as the use of per-process design (i.e., each client has its own cache manager), is one of the most appropriate solutions for CORBA environments.

Regarding the issue of cache storage, we use the client memory as a cache storage. Figure 6.4, which shows some experiments performed in [104, 105], found that the cost of access time can be reduced by caching using memory. With data size equal to 10000 bytes, remote access time requires 6.91872 milliseconds, while caching using memory only needs 0.9421923 milliseconds. By using memory caching, 86.3% of the access time is saved. The concurrency control and replacement algorithms are

**TABLE 6.1   Summary of Different Lock Mechanisms**

| Algorithms | retain lock | client assign lock | callback action | event trigger remote access |
|---|---|---|---|---|
| CallBack | YES | NO | YES | Cache Miss Wrong lock |
| Caching 2PL | NO | NO | NO | Always |
| Optimistic 2PL | NO | YES | YES | Cache Miss Commit time |

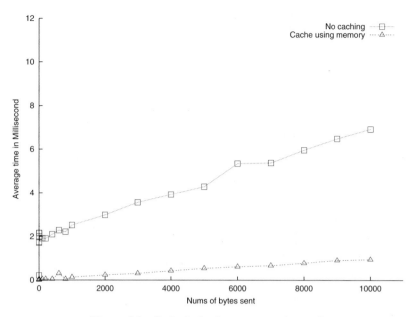

**Figure 6.4**   Cache design in memory and no cache.

not of concern at this stage. How the performance can be increased using the above algorithms is discussed in a later section.

One of the advantages of a per-node caching scheme is that object faulting and consistency-related actions only need to be done for a single copy at a node. However, when multiple clients access the cache data, some lock mechanisms are required in the client side to protect the shared data. To simplify the lock control at client side, the per-process scheme is selected for the approach described in the remaining sections of this chapter. For invalid access prevention design, removing stale objects may make room in the buffer, but the cost of reallocating space for the same object when it is accessed next time will be expensive. However, detection-based algorithms can be improved by using a callback strategy. Then the stale data will not be accessed. So we implement the detection-based scheme using a server callback strategy. When the data is stale, the client knows there is no need to access that data.

## 6.5   ARCHITECTURE

This section describes an architecture and a model for CORBA caching. We present the main components in this caching architecture and later show how they communicate with each other. The cache architecture has the following components: cache manager, evictor, server manager, monitor and lock manager. As shown in Figure 6.5, this architecture is based on a single server and multiple clients. Each client has its

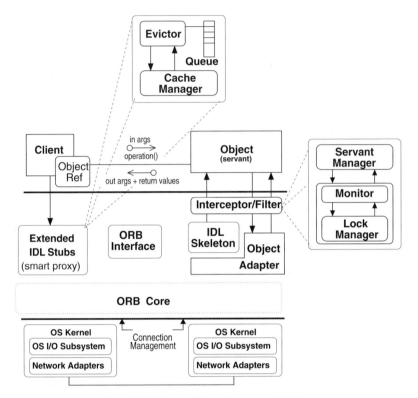

**Figure 6.5** The caching reference architecture.

own evictor and cache manager. The cache organization design is based on a per-process approach.

- The cache manager is responsible for deciding whether the client should perform local access or remote access. When a client makes a read request, the cache manager will contact the evictor first. If the data is found and it is valid, the cache manger will then return the data to the client. All write requests are passed through to the server.
- The evictor is responsible for cache replacement. When the cache buffer is full, some cache data items need to be evicted. At the beginning, the evictor is empty. When a client first performs a read operation, it fetches data from the server side and an evictor is created. In the next read operation, the client will contact the cache manager. It is the task of the cache manager to contact the evictor first; if data is not found or is invalid, it will then contact the server for the data and put the latest data into the evictor.
- The server manager is responsible for coordinating the server resource and callback operation. When the client contacts the server for the first time, a cache manager is constructed on the client side. The server manager is informed that

a cache manager is created at the same time. If one client makes a write request, the server manager will notify all the clients that the data is updated, and invalidate the data.

- The role of the monitor is to manage consistency of the cached objects. It is an independent process which monitors the operations accessing the server and includes an enhanced optimistic lock algorithm.
- The lock manager will lock the operation before accessing the server site's data. The operation will be unlocked once it is finished. The design of the lock manager is illustrated later in the next section.

Figure 6.6 shows the interaction between each component of the caching architecture. The client first makes a read request. The request is handled by the caching manager. The caching manager contacts the evictor, and because the evictor is empty at the beginning of the process, the caching manager decides to contact the server for an object copy. The monitor intercepts a client request and tells the lock manager to assign a lock for the operation. The lock manager first checks the operation and assigns the proper lock. Then the operation is passed to the server. The server processes the request. The monitor notices that the server finishes a processing operation; then it commands the lock manager to unlock the operation. The lock manager again checks the operation, and frees the lock associated with the operation. The object returned by the server is sent to the caching manager. The caching manager then creates an entry in the evictor and returns the copy to the client. If the client makes a read request again, the request is passed to the caching manager. After contacting the evictor, the caching manager knows the object is in the evictor and it is valid; it then

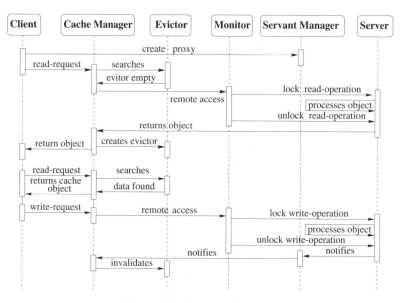

**Figure 6.6**   Sequence diagram.

fetches the object from the evictor. The object is then sent to the client. The client decides to make a write request this time. The caching manager makes a remote access request to the server. The monitor again intercepts the request and informs the lock manager. The lock manager assigns the proper lock and the request is processed in the server. The monitor notices the operation is done by the server; then it asks the lock manager to unlock the operation. The information of the updated object is passed to the server manager. The server manager broadcasts an invalidate message to all the caching managers. The caching manager in each client invalidates the object in the evictor. After the object is updated in the evictor, the client may continue to make more requests.

## 6.6 CACHING MODEL

This section discusses the details of the CORBA caching approach proposed in [104, 105]. A generic algorithm, which deals with various caching issues (cache management, eviction, callback strategy, filtering and locking algorithms) is described.

### Cache Management

The cache manager manipulates the client resources such as cache object and communicates with the evictor and the server objects. The algorithm below describes the main operations of the cache manager.

```
---- Cache Management -------------------
check whether there is an invalidate operation and process if yes
if read operation
  if Evictor not empty
      Hash_search() the key
      if key found and the object is valid
         fetch the object and promote the object to the tail of chain
      end if
  else
      make remote call to server
      get the object
      if evictor is empty
         create evictor
      else
         hash search the object key
         if object key is found and is valid
            validate the object with latest value
         else
            hash insert the new object into evictor
         end if
      end if
  end if
end if
```

```
else
    remote access to server
    get the object
    invalidate object in evictor
end if
```

## Eviction

The evictor uses a double-linked list with an FIFO based algorithm. When an object is dropped from the evictor, the client will not inform the server. If the next operation of the client requires an object which is not available in the evictor, the client will contact the server for the import of the object. The FIFO chain in the evictor is a double linked list. A hash table is constructed to find the object quickly. The hash function is based on a string search with some improved features. One of these features is to convert the string value into integer and perform $hash(n)$ searches to find the correct slot of the object. At the same time, the object key is retained as string format. If the object location is empty, it returns an empty location. In the case of conflicts, a linear search will be performed on the object.

```
----  hash algorithm ------------------
if evictor is empty
     return not found
else if object is in the top of queue
     return the object found
else if object is the latest accessed object
      return the object found
else if object is at the tail of queue
     return the object found
else
     perform hash(n) to find the object
     if object is found
        return the object
     else
        perform a linear search to find the object
     end if
end if
```

The object we are looking for in the evictor may be in the middle of the queue. In this case, the hash function is called to search the key. If the key is found, the object link with the previous object and with the next object in the queue will be removed. Also, the object found is then promoted to the tail of queue. Whenever a new object arrives, and if the cache buffer is full, the first object in the queue will be removed, otherwise the new object is appended to the end of the queue. When a server wants to invalidate an object in the evictor and the object is not found, the evictor will simply ignore the server notice. If the object is found in the evictor, it will be invalidated. Further operations can be taken either by keeping the object in the cache or removing it immediately. The removal algorithm for eviction is given below.

```
---- removal algorithm ------------------
if object is in the evictor
    promote the object to the tail of queue
else if evictor is full
    evict the first object in queue
else
    perform hash function to find the proper location for the object
    put object into the hash_table and append the object to the tail
      of queue
end if
```

## Callback Strategy

The server manager is responsible for manipulating server resources and callback strategies. The server will notify all other clients when the object is updated at the server side by using the invalidation protocol. The invalidation message size is far smaller than the update size. In the update protocol, the latest copy of the object is sent to all the clients when this object is updated. Using the invalidating protocol reduces the network congestion, since the clients do not need to check the validity of each object with the server.

```
---- Callback algorithm ------------------
If client proxy creates
    store the proxy information into database
end if
monitor process
If there is an request coming from client
    lock manager check the operation and assign lock
    server process the request
    lock manager unlock the operation
    if write operation
        call back all the clients
    end if
end if
```

## Filtering and Locking

The lock manager is a part of the monitor. It assigns locks to operations when they access the server data. It also unlocks operations once they have finished processing with the data. Because operations process the data quickly, at least quicker than transactions, there is no need to retain the lock on the cache data. This proposed algorithm is a combination of Caching 2PL and O2PL, where each client does not have its own local lock manager. The lock manager is located on the server side. In a read operation, when the client accesses the local cache data, no lock is required. If the cache data is not found in the cache buffer or the cache data is invalid, then the client needs to make a remote access call to the server. The lock manager, which is implemented in the server, assigns a Log Sequence Number according to the operation.

The lock manager will need to know what data is operated on in each operation. In a write operation, the client always makes a remote call to the server to update the data on the server side (the primary data copy). This is done in such a way that the server does not need to wait for all the other clients which are holding the data to reply or send ready-to-commit request to it. This approach differs from O2PL in that the client updates are not performed locally, which will save numerous messages being exchanged between clients and server to confirm the lock. The server is responsible for keeping track of the object's location in the system. Clients don not inform the server when they drop an object from their buffer pool. Once an operation refers to an object and the object is not found at cache buffer, it will contact the server immediately for a copy.

## 6.7  DESIGN

This section describes an Orbix implementation of the proposed caching approach, a workload generator, testing and results.

### Interface and UML design

The implementation of the caching approach will be illustrated by a simple example, a distributed banking application. The IDL interface for this application is given below. We consider a scenario when a banker interface creates Account objects and the register interface is used to tell the server that a client proxy is created, and regAccount interface will notify the client when an update happens.

```
struct Statement{
    string holder;
    string address;
    float balance;
    long hosts[4000];
    long num;
};
typedef sequence<Statement> seqStatement;
interface account {
    readonly attribute float balance;
    void setStatement(in any s, in long num);
    void getStatement(out any s, in long num);
    void makeLodgement (in float f);
    void makeWithdrawal (in float f);
};
interface bank {
    account newAccount (in string name) raises (reject);
    void deleteAccount (in account a);
};
```

```
interface cacheCallback {
  oneway void invalidate (in string key);
};
interface registerProxy {
  oneway void signOn (in cacheCallback proxy);
  oneway void signOff (in cacheCallback proxy);
};
interface regAccount : registerProxy, account {
};
```

## Caching Manager

The caching manager illustrated in Figure 6.7 is located at the bottom of the UML diagram. It inherits almost all the classes and is generated by the Orbix standard proxy factory class (AccountProxyFactoryClass). A single instance of the proxy factoryclass needs to be created if a user-defined proxy (caching manager) is constructed. Orbix will communicate with the factory whenever it needs to create a proxy of an interface in three ways: (i) when a reference to an object of that interface (e.g., Account) is passed back as out or inout parameter or a return type, or when a reference to a remote object enters an address space via an in parameter; (ii) when the :: _bind() function is called; and (iii) when the function $CORBA$ :: $Orbix.string\_to\_object()$ is called for that interface. The following is the implementation of caching manager class;

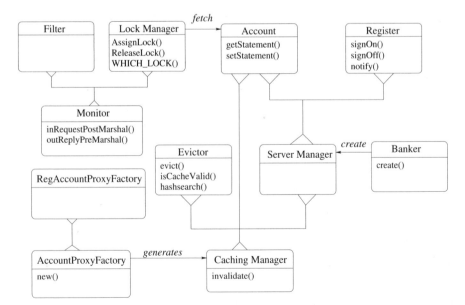

**Figure 6.7**   UML class diagram.

```
//  Code fragment of AccountProxy (Caching Manager) class

import org.omg.CORBA.Any;
import org.omg.CORBA.SystemException;

public class AccountProxy extends _AccountProxyImplBase {
   _tie_cacheCallback m_self;

   // notify the server manager that a client proxy is constructed
   m_self = new _tie_cacheCallback(this);
   signOn(m_self);

   void getStatement(Any s, int num) throws SystemException {

      char[] key;
      Times  T;

      checkPending();
      key = new char[11];
      assignKey(num,key,'s');
      if(!isEmpty()){
         int pos= -1;

         if(hash_search(key,pos)) {
            if(isCacheValid()) {
               cacheHit++;
               s = get_cache();
               updateCacheTimeStamp(T.set_timestamp());
               return;
            }
         }
      }

      try { // data not in cache
         cacheMiss++;
         getStatement(s,num);
         updateEvitorManger(T.set_timestamp(), s, key);
      }
   }
}
```

## Monitor and Lock Manager

A filter is used to intercept processes. With the filter, a programmer can specify
additional code to be executed before or after the execution of an operation. Orbix's
filters do not comply with the standard OMG's specifications. There are two types of
filters: per-process filters and per-object filters. A *per-process filter* allows control of
all applications and attributes calls leaving or entering a client's or server's address

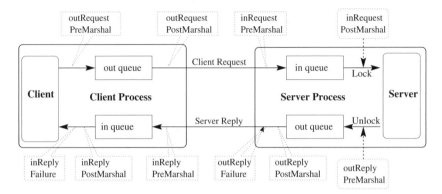

**Figure 6.8** Orbix's filter diagram.

space, while the *per-object filter* only concerns individual objects. A per-process filter is used to implement the monitor. The Orbix's filter is illustrated in Figure 6.8.

The Filter class has ten methods to monitor the transaction and reception of an operation. The operations *out Request PreMarshal()*, *out Request Post Marshal()*, *inReply PostMarshal()* and *inReply PreMarshal()* are in the client's address space. The *out Request PreMarshal()* operations are used before the operation's parameters have been added to the request queue. *out Request Post Marshal()* is used after the operation's parameters have been added to the request queue. *inRequest PreMarshal()*, *inRequest Post Marshal()*, *out Reply PreMarshal()* and *out Reply PostMarshal()* are in the server's address space. *inRequest pre Marshal()* is used before the operation has been sent to the target object and before the operation's parameters have been removed from the request queue. *inRequest PostMarshal()* is used before the operation sent to the target and after the operation's parameter has been removed from in-queue. The *out Reply PreMarshal()* is used before the return value has been added to the out queue. *out Reply Post Marshal()* is used after the return value and out parameter have been added to the out-queue. The other two methods, *out Reply Failure()* and *inReply Failure()*, are used when there is a failure during the process.

The *inRequest PostMarshal()* and *out Reply PreMarshal()* are used for locking and unlocking operations. We have implemented them by inheriting the super class Filter and rewriting the *inRequest PostMarshal()* and *out Reply Pre Marshal()* methods so that they will perform appropriate functions.

```
// Code Fragment of Lockmanager

public class Mutex_t {
  // This class implements C++-alike mutex_t
}
```

```
public class LockManager {

    protected Mutex_t Sharedata[1000];
    protected int    counter; // total numbers of lock assigned
    protected int    index;   // current lock number

    public void AssignLock(int n)  {...};
    public void ReleaseLock(int n) {...};
    public int  WHICH_LOCK(const char * func) {...};
}
}
```

The lock manager is using the Solaris mutex to protect share data. The maximum share lock limit is 1000 different objects in the lock manager. The method WHICH_LOCK is used to assign lock number to different function call.

## Evictor

The evictor is composed of object, hash table and an FIFO queue. Only pure object design is illustrated here; details about the page design are not considered. The object in CORBA environments is designed by using the struct type which is mapped to the C++ struct. Figure 6.9 shows the object structure. The data member inside struct is an object identity key, object state which shows an object's current status whether it is valid or not, object value, object access time, link pointer to the previous object and link pointer to the next object. The double links inside the object are used for quickly removing the object from the link. Each object is considered as a CORBA::Any type, because objects with different types cannot be linked together. CORBA provides a generic type ANY which suits this purpose.

Figure 6.10 shows how the evictor is implemented. When a client refers to an object with key S6, a hash function is performed. If the data with key S6 is found, the object can be promoted to the top  of the FIFO chain immediately. In this case,

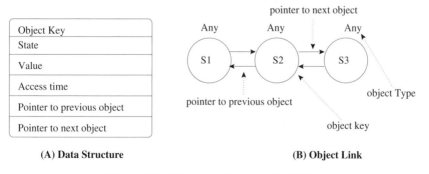

| (A) Data Structure | (B) Object Link |

**Figure 6.9**   Object structure and object link.

**Hash table**

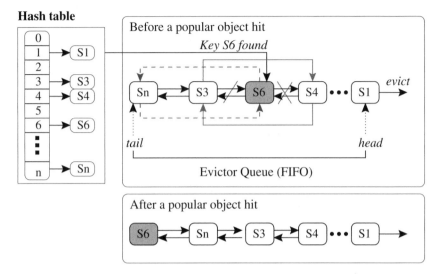

**Figure 6.10** Evictor pattern.

the previous link(S3) and forward link(S4) are destroyed. A new link with the and the data S6 is constructed in the tail of the queue.

```
// Code fragment of Evictor class
public class Evictor {
   protected class LINK {...}
   protected LINK first_;   // the head of queue
   protected LINK last_;    // the tail of queue
   protected LINK current_; // last accessed object in queue

   public int  isCacheValid() {...} // check whether the cache is valid
   public int  hash_search(const char * key,
                           int * pos ) {...} // search object key in queue
   public void createFIFO() {...} // create queue
   public LINK evict( ) {...} // evict object from evictor queue
   public void updateEvitorManger() {...} // update the information
                                          // of evictor
}
```

## Server Manager

The server manager class inherits from the register class which allows the server manager to callback the clients. The callback happens only if one of the clients performs a write operation. Only the write operation is shown below:

```
// Code fragment of Server Manager class
import org.omg.CORBA.Any;
```

```
void setStatement(const Any s, int num) {
   String key = new String();
   acc.setStatement(s,num,pe);
   assignKey(num,key,'s');
   notify(key); // broadcast the invalidate message to client
                // based on the object key
}
```

## 6.8  TESTING

This section shows the different tests made on the proposed CORBA caching approach.

### Workload Generation

There are different workloads, such us the one using databases, the World Wide Web, and distributed file systems. Although it is hard to generate a perfect workload, the designed workload is based on the initial purpose-evaluation of the distributed application. Thus, distributed file systems workload is suitable for this purpose. The distributed file system workload (Princeton workload) [15] is selected for the evaluation of banking system with a few modifications. The workload is described by the following parameters: number of object invocations per client, inter-access times, object creation rate, temporal locality, access type and transfer data size.

- *The number of object invocations per client:* In Princeton trace, the number of object invocations per client is 50000 objects which will take up 16 hours. Due to the resource limitation in the used OS system, a 1000 objects invocation per-client is used.
- *The inter-access times:* Within some period, a request of the client will be made. The inter-access time in Princeton workload is one second. Since 1 second is too long for all of the testing, we take 0.1 second in the workload.
- *Object creation rate:* Every time a request is generated, the request can be on the same existing object or a new object. The object creation rate decides how many new objects should be created. In [3], it suggests 0.5% for an object creation rate. This is found to be insufficient for evaluating the system. Matt [15] suggests 4.16% for a file creation rate. An object creation rate of 5% is chosen.
- *Temporal locality:* The temporal locality suggests which object needs to be accessed in the previous generated object. However, the previous accessed time used in [3] is too long. Based on the number of selected objects, we recalculate the figure as shown in Table 6.2.
- *Access type:* The access type determines the read and write operations of the object. The read-write rate of 4:1 in [3] is selected for the workload generation.
- *Data transfer size:* We use the average data size of 16 KB in the Toronto study [35].

**TABLE 6.2 Temporal Locality**

| Percentage | 1000 objects Chosen object accessed in the last $n$ seconds |
|---|---|
| 46.4% | 3 |
| 53.4% | 6 |

The inter-access rate decides the timestamp of an operation generated by the event. Once the event is generated, the object creation rate is used to determine whether a new object should be created or just access an existing object. In the case of accessing an existing object, the access type is generated by the access type rate read-write 4:1. The temporal locality is applied after the object is determined to be object accessing rather than object creating. The first object is created without determining its creation rate.

## Testing and Result

The tests presented here are those proposed in [104, 105]. Before the test experiment is set up, a buffer size test is performed. When the buffer size increases, the cache miss rate decreases. A full buffer size is defined to be a point when the miss rate ceases to decrease when the buffer size is increased. Figure 6.11 shows the full buffer

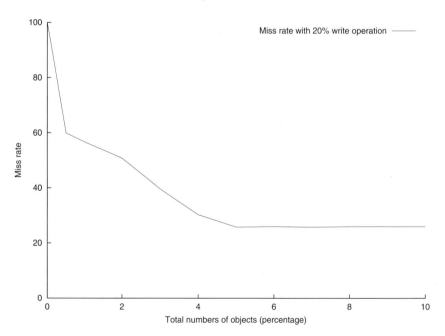

**Figure 6.11** Miss rate decreases with the increase of buffer size.

size for 1000 objects is 60 objects. Half of that size is selected, which has around 30 objects as the buffer size. The experiments are conducted on Solaris 2.6 operating system. The available memory in the server side is 250 MB. Each client has 30 objects and 60 objects buffer size separately. The maximum number of clients is 20. Current network bandwidth is 10 MB.

As shown in Figure 6.12, the performance of the caching approach is obviously better than that of the no-caching approach for 1000 objects with average data size equal to 16 KB. Caching with half buffer size can save up to 45.5% of the access time, while caching using full buffer size can save up to 50% of the access time. A full buffer size caching only shows slightly better performance than it yields in the half buffer size caching. This because when eviction takes place, the hash table is very efficient. Both the half buffer caching and full buffer caching outperform the no-caching. From Figure 6.12, we found that when the number of clients increases to 20, the no-caching approach causes exhaustive invocations on the server side and the server becomes saturated. Then memory used in the server reaches the current limit 250 MB, and the server crashes. On the other hand, the caching will not reach the current memory limit in the same situation. This is because many read requests are handled on the client side. This proves the previous opinion that caching reduces network congestion.

For the problem of a server crashing in the no-caching approach, this can be caused by the lack of memory. More tests were conducted in [104, 105] to measure the performance when numbers of object invocation per-client increased or decreased. A 500 objects invocation per-client and 1500 objects invocation per-client

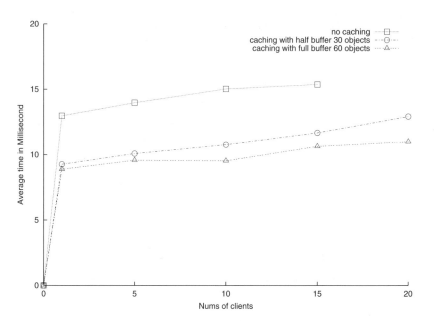

**Figure 6.12**  Client invocation of 1000 objects.

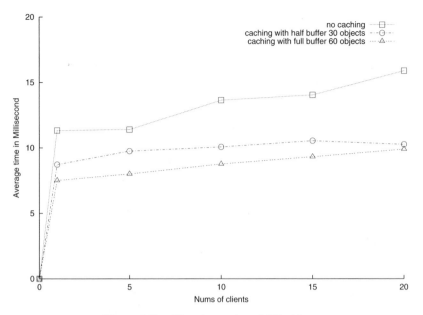

**Figure 6.13**    Client invocation of 500 objects.

are performed in the experiment. A new temporal locality for each 500 objects and 1500 objects is recalculated separately. The full buffer size and half buffer size the same as in the previous figure, which is 60 objects and 30 objects separately. From the Figures 6.13 and 6.14, the caching approach was found to outperform the no-caching approach. This is because many client requests are performed locally if the object is cached on the client side. Only when the object is not found on client side or the object is invalidated, Will the client perform a remote request. This is contrasted with the no-caching approach as it causes more network congestion when the number of objects is increased. For 1500 objects invocation per-client, the no-caching crashes the server when the number of clients equals 5. By monitoring the process, we realized that it reached the current memory limit, whereas the caching approach is consistent.

The experiment shows that full buffer caching is always better than half buffer caching. This is because full buffer caching has less eviction or no eviction. The probability that the object can be fetched in the full buffer size caching side is higher than that of half buffer size caching. This is because full buffer size caching has more available space for objects.

The result is affected by the workload as well, since the 500 objects invocation per-client has fewer objects created, in which operation on the same object is higher than 1000 objects and 1500 objects. In the implementation of the evictor, if the object is referred to frequently, then the object can be fetched quickly since it is always at the tail of the queue. No further operation is needed, also since 30 and 60 objects

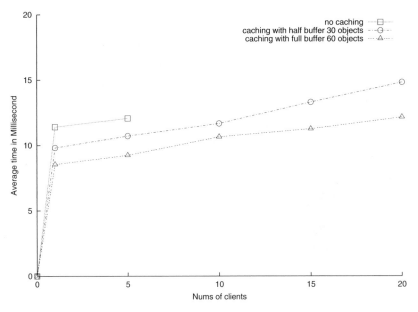

**Figure 6.14** Client invocation of 1500 objects.

in the 500 objects invocation per-client have more space. As a result, the 500 object invocation has less access time than that of the 1000 objects and 1500 objects.

## 6.9 SUMMARY

This chapter reviews some of the existing techniques used in The caching approach. An appropriate eviction algorithm for CORBA caching is described, and this is based on an extension of the FIFO algorithm to include a double-linked list and hash table. In this extended algorithm, if an object is referred in the middle of the queue, the object can be removed quickly from the queue. Consistency algorithms based on locking mechanism were analyzed and a variation algorithm of the Optimistic 2PL is described. In this algorithm, clients are not required to get a lock or retain a lock, while at the same time it remains consistent by using a per-process design. An interceptor is introduced to the lock mechanism, so that locking can be application independent. This goal is achieved by implementing a monitor process which intercepts all the requests from the clients, and locks the operation based on the data attribute on which it operates.

To test the performance, existing workloads were carefully studied and a distributed workload based on a distributed file system was described. To work efficiently, a workload generator is implemented. The generator iterates on each client side to generate a different workload set. The performance shown in the experiments indicates that caching is feasible. With increasing numbers of clients, the performance is significantly increased. Full buffer caching is slightly better than half buffer caching. This shows that the eviction algorithm is efficient. At the same time, both the full buffer caching and half buffer caching approaches outperform the no-caching approach. Performance is significantly increased in the caching design.

## 6.10  REVIEW QUESTIONS

- Explain what usually causes poor performance in CORBA applications.
- Explain two important issues in caching.
- Explain briefly the problem(s) that occur in each existing cache replacement algorithm which have been discussed in this chapter.
- When should lockings not be used to maintain cache consistency? Justify your answer.
- What are three other issues that must be taken into account when designing a caching approach?
- Compare the characteristics of callback locking, server-based two phased locking, and optimistic two phase locking.
- What is the advantage and the problem of a per-node caching scheme?
- What is the responsibility of each component of the caching architecture explained in this chapter?
- What happens if an evictor does not exist in the caching architecture?
- How can the Callback strategy used in this caching approach reduce network congestion?

## 6.11  EXERCISES

- Discuss briefly how the eviction of "wrong" objects can have deep consequences on the performance of a system. (Hint: relate this to the I/O cost involved when accessing database entries.)
- How could one make the proposed caching approach be more portable to other CORBA compliant ORB products?

# PART III

# CORBA SERVICES

# CHAPTER 7

# Naming Service

This chapter provides details of the CORBA Naming Service, with examples given to show how this service is used in distributed object environments. Section 7.1 provides the basic background about the naming service and describes some well-known case studies (e.g., DNS and X.500). Details about the OMG Naming Service, including a detailed description of the operations for name resolution, name binding/unbinding and creation/deletion of context, are given in Section 7.2.

## 7.1 BACKGROUND

A naming service is a generic directory service that provides similar functionalities as the White Pages, such as finding an address of a person when his/her name is known. Given a name of an object, the naming service is responsible for returning the reference to that object. Names for objects are very useful because they can be used to externally identify objects and therefore make it easy for the user to remember and find them. This becomes very important when distributed environments become more and more open with a very large number of inter-connected systems.

Names require management. They can be treated uniformly, each within its own name space, and require the following management and administrative functions:

- *Name space structuring*: The structure of a name space must be defined as a design decision, and this reflects the naming policy adopted.
- *Name allocation*: At some level or in some context, a name should be unique; for example, an IP address must be unique in a network. Name management includes the activity of administering and allocating the unique part of a name to a particular entity. The name space may be partitioned so that names can be independently allocated by multiple management agents without conflicts.
- *Name registration*: This is a function of directory service management which includes the activity of making persistent the information which permits mappings between names and entities. An example is a name to address mapping. This is critical information, so it must be complete, accurate and readily available.

A naming service enables attributes such as addresses of resources or objects to be obtained when given their names. It manages the naming space using specific operations. In this section we give an overview of the naming service in distributed systems and we later present two case studies, DNS (Domain Name Service) and X.500 Directory Service.

### 7.1.1 Naming

Names, in a system, are generally used to enable users to locate and communicate with the entities on which they operate. Names may refer to a variety of resources such as computers, services, ports and individual objects. Names are known by the users, and the naming service provides a mapping of these names to the (system) identifiers of the corresponding resources. System identifiers provide efficient access to appropriate resources, and more importantly they are fixed-length bit strings.

Names cover three different concepts: symbolic names, unique identifiers, and addresses. The former are ordinary names through which users identify the entities on which they wish to perform their operations. A symbolic name could indicate location information (e.g., $laser\_printer@Computer\_Room$) or may be location independent (e.g., Amazigh Tari 1999). Unique identifiers are those used by systems to refer to persistent entities. They provide immutable identifiers, which are efficient for system use. Addresses enable a support system to locate the physical location of an entity.

Figure 7.1 illustrates an example where names are used to locate objects in a distributed system, such as files. The file identifier, which in this case contains the port identifier and the identifier of the file within the server, is resolved. Several mappings are performed to access the file: mapping its textual file onto a resource identifier, mapping this to a port identifier and service-specific identifier, and mapping the port identifier to a network address, and the service-specific identifier on the resource in the appropriate server.

The association between a name and an object is called *binding*. A naming service is responsible for managing a database binding between a set of textual (i.e.,

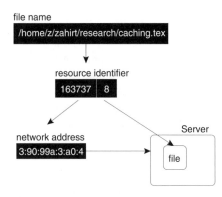

**Figure 7.1**   Names used to locate resources.

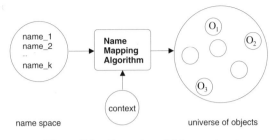

**Figure 7.2**   General model for naming.

human-readable) names and attributes of objects. This service provides the operation *resolve()* that looks up attributes in the database for a given name. Other operations are also supported by the naming service: for example, creating new bindings with new names, deleting bindings and listing names. For large scale applications, the database bindings are distributed in several sites and also replicated to improve the availability of the service.

When names are used, the naming service needs to associate names with particular objects. In any particular naming system, names are chosen from a name space, which is comprised of an alphabet of symbols together with syntax rules that specify which names are acceptable in this name space. As shown in Figure 7.2, a name mapping algorithm associates some (not necessarily all) names of the name space to some (again, not necessarily all) values in a universe of values. A value may be an object, or it may be another name from either the original name space or from a different name space.

Performing the name mapping algorithm to determine a value that is associated with a name is, as mentioned earlier, known as resolving the name. This is generally controlled by an additional parameter, known as a context. For a given naming system, there can be many different contexts, and a single name of the name space may map to different values when different contexts are used. For example, in ordinary discourse when I refer to "you," "here," or "Mary" the meaning of those names depends on the context in which I utter them. The most common implementation of a context is a table of particular name to value (object) mappings, which are known as bindings, since they have been fixed in advance of lookup. One thus describes a name as being bound to a value in a particular context. For example, a telephone book is a context that binds personal names to telephone numbers. A name that is not bound in a context is said to be free in that context. There are usually several contexts, so the interpreter must specify which one to use.

Conceptually, there are three operations associated with a naming system:

- *Resolve (name, context)*: When an interpreter encounters a name of an object, it identifies an appropriate context. It resolves the name in that context, and it substitutes the corresponding value for the name as it continues interpretation.
- *Bind (name, value, context)*: This operation proposes a new binding; the status result reports whether or not the proposal is acceptable to the naming system.

- *Unbind (name, value, context)*: This operation removes an existing binding, again with a status reporting of success or failure.

Different naming systems have different rules about uniqueness of name to value mappings. Some naming systems have a rule that a name must map to exactly one value in a given context, while in other naming systems one name may map to several values, or one value may have several names, even in the same context. The name mapping algorithm plus a single context does not necessarily map all names of the name space to values; therefore, a possible outcome of performing the name mapping algorithm can be a not found result. In some systems, a possible outcome can be a list of values. In practice, there are three commonly used name mapping algorithms: *simple table lookup*, *path name resolution*, and *search*.

### 7.1.1.1  Simple Table Lookup.
When the implementation of a context is a table of {name, value} pairs, the name mapping algorithm becomes a simple lookup of the name in that table (with an appropriate access method, such as an index or hash-table, when the table is too large). Binding a name to a value consists of simply adding that {name, value} pair to the table. When a naming system uses table lookup contexts, it is immediately apparent how different contexts may contain different bindings for the same name.

Several real world examples are based on the table lookup, such as:

- The registers of a processor are named with numbers. The value is the register itself and the mapping from name to value is accomplished by wiring. This name does not identify the contents of the register, although those contents may also have a name in a program that uses the register. Thus in the sentence "The value of X is currently in register two," "two" names a physical register, and "X" names its contents.

- Storage cells (individual memory locations) in a virtual memory are similarly named with numbers known as addresses. The algorithm for mapping generally involves lookups in page tables, which provide bindings from blocks of addresses (pages) to blocks of contiguous storage cells. When multiple virtual memories are used to enforce modularity, each virtual memory is a distinct context; a given address usually refers to a different storage cell in each virtual memory. Storage cells can also be shared among virtual memories, in which case the same storage cell may have the same (or different) addresses in different virtual memories, depending on the bindings in the page tables.

- The file system of a personal computer involves names and contexts at several levels: disk sectors, file storage regions, files, and directories are all named objects. Directories are examples of table lookup contexts. A particular file name may appear in several different directories, bound to either the same or different files.

- Ports of a data communication system such as the Internet are usually named with two distinct naming systems. The first one, used inside the network, involves a name space consisting of numbers in a fixed length field, and maps to physical entrance and exit points of the network. A second naming system, used by clients of the network, maps a more human-friendly name space of character strings to port names of the first name space.

***7.1.1.2 Path Names.*** A path name is the second most commonly encountered in naming algorithms. A path name is a name that explicitly includes a reference to the context in which it should be resolved. A path name involves some syntax that separates its components. Some examples of path names are:

```
zahirt.cs.rmit.edu.au
/home/z/zahirt/corba
Chapter 4, section 3, first paragraph
First paragraph of Section 3 of Chapter 4
```

The two last examples suggest that different naming systems place the component names in opposite orders, and indeed the first three examples also demonstrate both orders. The order of the components comes into play in the interpretation of the path name, which is most easily explained recursively: all but the least significant component of a path name is an explicit context intended to be used to resolve that least significant component.

Path names are usually used to identify objects that are organized in a hierarchical structure. Contexts are treated as objects, and any context may contain a name to object binding for any other object, whether a context or not. The name interpreter identifies one context to use as the root, and it then resolves all absolute path names by following a path from the root to the first named context in the path name, then the next, etc., until it reaches the object that was named by the original path name. It similarly can resolve relative path names by referencing to a variable containing the absolute path name of the current context.

***7.1.1.3 Search.*** Simple table lookups and recursive path name resolution may be the two most common forms of name resolution, but there are many situations which involve more elaborate schemes with multiple table lookups: search. Search is typically involved, for example, when a compiler creates a binary program that imports a named interface from a library of subroutines and functions. A search is also often involved when the user of a desktop computer types a command that refers to a program and some data object, or double clicks on an icon.

Still search is a widely used mechanism. In addition to being used by the loader to locate programs in libraries, search is used by user interfaces to locate commands whose name is typed by the user, by compilers to locate interfaces, and by documentation systems to locate documents. Additionally in a programming language with nested environments, a variable that is free in the current context gets bound by a search of hierarchically containing contexts.

## 7.1.2 Case Studies

So far we have seen some implementations of the basic functions of a naming service in several environments. This section provides a description of two case studies, namely DNS and X.500, which may help the reader to understand the implementation issues of the naming service within the context of distributed systems.

### 7.1.2.1 Domain Name System (DNS).   DNS provides naming of computers and services in the Internet. DNS is a very general name management and name resolution system that hierarchically distributes the management of names to different naming authorities, and it also hierarchically distributes the job of resolution of names to different name servers. Its design allows it to respond rapidly to requests for name resolution, to scale up to very large numbers of stored records and very large numbers of requests. It is a quite robust, in the sense that it provides continued, accurate responses in the face of many kinds of network and server failures. The basic interface to DNS is quite simple, that is, value = dns_resolve (domain_name), which is a little different from the standard resolve interface. There is no context argument because there is only one, global, context for resolving all Internet domain names, and it is wired into *dns_resolve()*. The primary use for DNS is to associate human-friendly character string names, called *domain names*, with machine-oriented binary network attachment point identifiers: in other words, IP addresses. The term domain is used in a very general way in DNS: it is simply a set of one or more names that have the same hierarchical ancestor. This means that naming regions are domains, but it also means that the personal computer is a domain with just one member.

In the usual DNS implementation, binding is not accomplished by invoking *bind()* and *unbind()* (to delete the binding) operations as in the general naming model, but rather by using a text editor or database generator to create and manage tables of bindings. These tables are then loaded into DNS resolvers by some behind-the-scenes method as often as their managers deem necessary. One consequence of this design is that changes to DNS bindings do not often occur within seconds of the time you request them; they typically take hours, instead. Domain names are path names, with components separated by periods (called *dots*, particularly when domain names are read aloud) and with the least significant component coming first. A typical domain name is goanna.cs.rmit.edu.au.

The name resolution operation of DNS is conceptually simple, but it has several elaborations that enhance its performance, scalability, and robustness. For example, when presented with a domain name, *dns_resolve()* sends that domain name to a root name server, whose network attachment point it somehow knows. The root name server extracts the most significant component of the domain name (in the example, au) and looks up just that component in its tables. The binding that it finds there is to the network attachment point of another name server that handles all names that end in au. The root responds by sending back a message saying "the name server for the au domain is at network attachment point Z."

This sequence repeats for each component of the original path name, until *dns_resolve()* finally reaches the name server for cs.rmit.edu.au. That name server has a record for the network attachment point of goanna.cs.rmit.edu.au, so it sends back a message saying "goanna.cs.rmit.edu.au is at network attachment points." *dns_resolve()* returns this result to its caller, which can go on to initiate some network protocol with that network node. The server that holds a name record for a domain name is known as the naming authority for that domain name. In this example, the name server `cs.rmit.edu.au` is the naming authority for the `goanna.cs.rmit.edu.au` domain, as well as all other domain names that end with `cs.r.mit.edu`. Note that this definition of naming authority means that the naming authority for the name of a name server is different from the naming authority for the names managed by that server. Thus the root name server is the naming authority for the domain name `au`, while the `au` name server is the naming authority for all domain names that end in `au`.

### 7.1.2.2  *X.500 Directory Service.*

X.500 is a directory service which is defined by CCITT and ISO standards organizations to be used by individuals and organizations to make available a wide range information about themselves and the resources they wish to offer for use in the network. X.500 is specified as an Application Level Service in the Open Systems Interconnection (OSI) set of standards.

The X.500 directory is organized under a common "root" directory in a tree hierarchy (called *Directory Information Tree*, i.e., DIT) of: country, organization, organizational unit, and person. An entry at each of these levels must have certain attributes; some can have optional ones established locally. Each organization can implement a directory in its own way as long as it adheres to the basic schema or plan. Each local directory is called a *Directory System Agent* (DSA) and can represent one organization or a group of organizations. The DSAs are interconnected from the Directory Information Tree (DIT). The user interface program for access to one or more DSAs is a Directory User Agent (DUA). DUAs include who is, finger, and programs that offer a graphical user interface. X.500 is implemented as part of the DCE in its Global Directory Service (GDS).

X.500 directory model is a distributed collection of independent systems which cooperate to provide a logical data base of information to provide a global directory service. Directory information about a particular organization is maintained locally in a Directory System Agent (DSA). This information is structured within specified standards. Adherence to these standards makes the distributed model possible. It is possible for one organization to keep information about other organizations, and it is possible for an organization to operate independently from the global model as a stand alone system. DSAs that operate within the global model have the ability to exchange information with other DSAs by means of the X.500 protocol. Each DSA provides information for the global directory. Directories are able to locate, in the hierarchical structure discussed above, which DSA holds a certain portion of the directory. Each directory manages information through a defined set of attributes and in a structure defined as the *Directory Information Base* (DIB). A DSA is accessed by means of a DUA which interacts with the directory by communicating with one or more DSAs as necessary to respond to a specific query. DUAs can be an IP protocol such as whois or finger, or a more sophisticated application which may provide a graphical user interface access to the DSA. Access to a DSA can be accomplished by an individual or automated by a computer application.

In addition to the directory model, the X.500 standard defines the information model used in the directory service. All information in the directory is stored in "entries," each of which belong to at least one "object class." The object classes to which an entry belongs defines the attributes associated with that particular entry. Some attributes are mandatory white others are optional. System administrators may define their own attributes and register these with the regulating authorities, which will in turn make these attributes available on a large scale. Every entry has a *Relative Distinguished Name* (RDN), which uniquely identifies the entry. An RDN is made up of the DIT information and the actual entry. The directory operates under a set of rules know as the directory schema. This defines correct utilization of attributes, and ensures an element of sameness throughout the global Directory Service.

An example of an entry under "RMIT University" will have the following structure under X.500:

@c = AUS @o = RMIT University @ou = Staff @cn = Zahir Tari

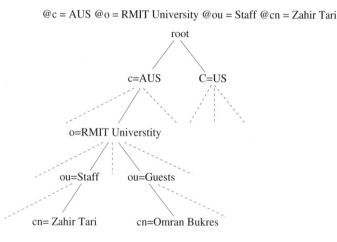

## 7.2 FUNCTIONS

This section provides some insight into the OMG Naming Service [72]. As with other naming services, this service allows one or more logical names to be associated with an object reference. A server that holds an object reference can register it with the naming service. The name can subsequently be used by clients of that server to find the object. Client applications can use the naming service to obtain the first object reference by using the logical name assigned to that object.

The OMG Naming Service is designed around a syntax-independent, in-memory hierarchical name structure that can be used with any of the established naming conventions, such as in Unix syntax (where names are organized in a hierarchy, separated with slashes, and they can be almost any length), DOS syntax (where names are separated by backslashes and with a length of "8 dot 3" characters), and X.500 syntax (where names are separated by commas and space between names is allowed). The OMG Naming Service provides a multilevel name structure, and the clients are responsible for inserting the name separators (e.g., slashes, backslashes) before displaying the compound name.

As for other naming systems, the association of names to objects defines *name bindings* and these are persistent within *naming contexts*. In the previous section, we saw the different ways these bindings are made persistent (e.g., tables), but this issue is an implementation one; therefore, there is no reference to it in the OMG specification document for the naming service [72]. Names are unique within each naming context; however, different names can be bound to an object in the same or different contexts at the same time. There are no absolute names. A name binding is always defined relative to a naming context. To resolve a name is to determine the object associated with the name in a given context. To bind a name is to create a name binding in a given context.

Because a context is like any other object, it can also be bound to a name in a naming context. Binding contexts form the structure of a graph called the *naming graph* which is a directed graph with nodes and labelled edges where the nodes are contexts. A naming graph allows more complex names to reference an object. Given a context in a naming graph, a sequence of names can reference an object. This sequence of names, called a *compound name*, defines a path in the naming graph to navigate the resolution process. Figure 7.3 shows an example of a naming graph, where the directed edges are object references. The nodes of the graph are like the type of the edges, where solid nodes represent application objects and others are

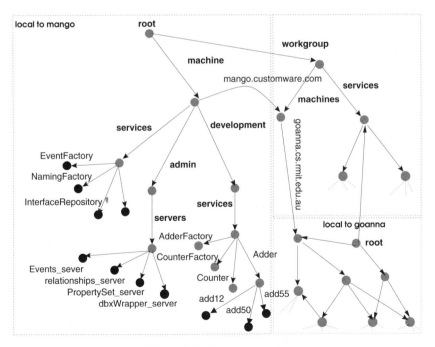

**Figure 7.3**   A naming graph.

contexts. Depending on the systems used, the graph can be a hierarchy as in Unix or DOS, or just an ordinary graph with cycles. As illustrated in this example, there are several root naming contexts, one local to mango server and the other one for goanna server, which is a general rule for naming graphs. As we will see in a later section, there is a specific operation of the ORB idl interface that returns the root of the naming graph for a given ORB daemon running a specific server.

Also, in the proposed example of Figure 7.3, even though the graph seems like it is built as one unique graph, it is actually a union of a set of naming sub-graphs (more precisely, a federation of naming graphs): one sub-graph is located in goanna, the other ones in mango, etc. These sub-graphs can be located in different machines, local or remote, supporting different conventions, such as DOS or Unix conventions. Clients can transparently access to objects in these different sub-graphs using the API of the naming service, which will be covered later.

Let us start now by introducing more details about the OMG IDL of the naming service. Many of the operations defined in a naming context take names as parameters. Names have a structure and they are ordered sequences of components. A name with a single component is called a *simple* name; a name with multiple components is called a *compound name*. Each component except the last is used to name a context; the last component denotes the bound object. The notation

```
name =  [component_1 , component_2 , ..., component_k]
name[0]    = component_1
name[2]    = component_2
...
name[k-1] = component_k
```

indicates the sequences of components. A name component consists of two attributes: the identifier attribute and the kind attribute. As shown below for the IDL for a compound name, both the identifier attribute and the kind attribute are represented as IDL strings. The kind attribute adds descriptive power to names in a syntax-independent way [72]. The values of this attribute can be c_source, object_code, executable, pdf, or anything that can give additional information about the objects users are looking for. This allows applications that use syntactic naming conventions to identify related objects. For instance, Unix environments use suffixes such as .c (for c_source) and .o (for object_code). Applications (such as the C compiler) depend on these syntactic conventions to make name transformations, for example, to transform a C file adder.c into adder.o. Obviously, the OMG naming system does not interpret, assign, or manage the values of the kind attributes. Only the specific application may make policies about the use and management of these values.

Referring to the example of Figure 7.3, a name can have the following form:

```
name =  [component_1 , component_2 , component_3, component_4]
name[0].id = ''machine''
name[1].id = ''development''
```

```
name[2].id = ''services''
name[3].id = ''Adder''
```

The example refers to the naming context which is the sub-context of the context that has a name "services." In the general case, the OMG idl for name is as following:

```
typedef string Istring;
struct NameComponent {
   Istring id;
   Istring kind;
};

typdef sequence <NameComponent> Name;
```

The lack of name syntax is especially important when considering internationalization issues. Software that does not depend on the syntactic conventions for names does not have to be changed when it is localized for a natural language that has different syntactic conventions,unlike software that does depend on the syntactic conventions which must be changed to adopt to new conventions. To avoid issues of differing name syntax, the naming service always deals with names in their structural form, that is, there are no canonical syntaxes or distinguished meta characters. It is assumed that various programs and system services will map names from the representation into the structural form in a manner that is convenient to them.

OMG Naming Service provides several operations for navigating and updating the naming graphs: binding objects, name resolution, unbinding, naming contexts, deleting contexts, and listing a naming context. To simplify the description of these operations, we will first provide below the IDL of the CORBA Naming Service, without the details of the exceptions, for example. Later we will go through the different operations of the IDL and illustrate their use on the example of Figure 7.3.

```
interface  NamingContext {
   ...
   void bind(in Name n, in Object obj) raises(...);
   void bind_context(in Name n, in NamingContext nc) raises(...);
   void rebind(in Name n, in Object obj) raises(...);
   void resolve(in Name n) raises(...);
   void unbind(in Name n) raises(...);
   void list(in unsigned long how_many,
             out BindingList bl,
             out BindingIterator bi) raises(...);
   NamingContext new_context() raises(...);
   NamingContext bind_new_context(in Name n) raises(..);
   void destroy() raises (...);
};
```

### 7.2.1 Name Resolution

Before any operation is performed on a naming context, say services of the naming graph of Figure 7.3, the reference to this context object needs to be found. Because of the structure of the naming graph, the references of all context objects along the path that joins the root of the naming graph and the context in which the operations need to be applied (i.e., services) are to be retrieved (i.e., resolved). In general cases, if $r_1 \longrightarrow r_2 \longrightarrow \cdots \longrightarrow r_p$ is a directed path of the naming graph, where $r_1$ is the root context and $r_p$ is the name of context in which we are looking for the reference, then all the references of the contexts $r_i, 2 \leq i \leq p - 1$, need to be found. By using the operation

```
Object resolve (in Name n)
    raises (NotFound, CannotProceed, InvalidName);
```

on a given context object of the directed path, say the context object with the name $r_j$ ($2 \leq j \leq p - 2$), will return the reference to the context object with the name $r_{j+1}$. For instance, if the reference of the context machine is o-machine, then the reference o-services to the context services can be found as follows:

```
CORBA::Object obj3;
CosName::NamingContext o-services;
CosName::Name name;    // initialisation of the name
name.length(1);
name[0].id = CORBA::string_dup(''services'');
obj3 = o-machine->resolve(name);

// we assume that all checkings are done before down-casting
o-services = CosName::NamingContext::_narrow(obj3);
```

To obtain a reference to the root context of a naming graph, this needs to be done by using a specific operation of the ORB idl, that is, *resolve_initial_references()* operation, as follows:

```
CORBA::ORB orb = CORBA::ORB_init(argc, argv);
CORBA::Object obj1;
CosName::NamingContext o-initial;
obj1 = orb->resolve_initial_references(''NamingService'');
o-initial = CosName::NamingContext::_narrow(obj1);
```

To obtain the reference to the context "machine," the operation *resolve()* needs to be applied on the object o-initial with the name of the context as a parameter.

```
CORBA::Object obj2;
CosName::NamingContext o-initial // one obtained above;
CosName::Name name;    // initialisation of the name
name.length(1);
```

```
name[0].id = CORBA::string_dup(''machine'');
obj2 = o-machine->resolve(name);

// we assume that all checkings are done before down-casting
o-machine =  CosName::NamingContext::_narrow(obj2);
```

As the reader may see, the operation *resolve*() was applied twice: one time on the object reference o-initial to obtain the reference to the to the naming context machine; and the other time on the object reference o-machine to obtain the reference to the naming context services. This process can be simplified by directly applying the operation *resolve*() on the object o-initial with the appropriate name (as a path machine $\longrightarrow$ services).

```
CosName::Name name;
name.length(2);
name[0].id = CORBA::string_dup(''machine'');
name[1].id = CORBA::string_dup(''services'');
obj2 = o-initial->resolve(name);
o-services =  CosName::NamingContext::_narrow(obj2);
```

As for the general case illustrated at the beginning of this section, where $r_1 \longrightarrow r_2 \longrightarrow \cdots \longrightarrow r_p$ is a directed path of the naming graph, where $r_1$ is the root context and $r_p$ is the name of context in which we are looking for the reference, then it will be enough to create a CORBA name with a length $p - 1$, as the following example illustrates:

```
CosName::Name name;
name.length(p-1);;
name[0].id = CORBA::string_dup(''r2'');
name[1].id = CORBA::string_dup(''r3'');
...
name[p-1].id = CORBA::string_dup(''rp'');
... // apply resolve as in previous examples
```

### 7.2.2  Binding and Unbinding Names

The *bind*() operation assigns a name to an object in a given naming context. This object can be a context object or an application object. Naming contexts that are bound using bind do not participate in name resolution when compound names are passed to be resolved. The syntax of this operation is as follows:

```
void bind(in Name n, in Object obj)
   raises(NotFound, CannotProceed, InvalidName, AlreadyBound);
```

As for the *resolve*() operation, the operation *bind*() can be used several times within a directed graph to assign a name to an object within a specific context. Alternatively, the operation can be applied only once with a specific value for the name to represent the complete path. In the example below, we will be using the operation only once to bind a given name add-71 to an object (say new-obj, which can be of any type) within the naming context Adder.

```
CORBA::Object new-obj = ... // it can be of any type
CosName::Name name;
name.length[4];
name[0].id = CORBA::string_dup(''machine'');
name[1].id = CORBA::string_dup(''development'');
name[2].id = CORBA::string_dup(''services'');
name[3].id = CORBA::string_dup(''Adder'');
o-initial->bind(''add-71'', new-obj);
```

The operation *rebind*() is used to force the creation of a new binding whether or not that biding is already in use. This is a safer call than the *bind*() operation, which fails (with an exception AlreadyBound (when the binding already exists). In the case of the *rebind*() operation, if the binding with a specified name already exists, it is simply dropped. This operation is generally useful when the user wants to ensure that a binding is created whether or not the binding already exists.

The operation *unbind*() removes a binding within a naming context. This means that the object still exists; however, it cannot be found within the context in which the operation *unbind*() is used. Obviously, this object can be found from any other context if bindings have been created (probably with different names). The following example reverse the above procedure and unbinds the name "add-71" from the context Adder.

```
CosName::Name name;
name.length[4];
name[0].id = CORBA::string_dup(''machine'');
name[1].id = CORBA::string_dup(''development'');
name[2].id = CORBA::string_dup(''services'');
name[3].id = CORBA::string_dup(''Adder'');
o-initial->unbind(''add-71'');
```

If the operation *unbind*() is applied on a context, such as Adder, than all the content of this context can no longer be found unless that context is accessible from other contexts. To unbind the context Adder, the procedure is similar to the previous example.

```
CosName::Name name;
name.length[3];
name[0].id = CORBA::string_dup(''machine'');
name[1].id = CORBA::string_dup(''development'');
name[2].id = CORBA::string_dup(''services'');
o-initial->unbind(''Adder'');
```

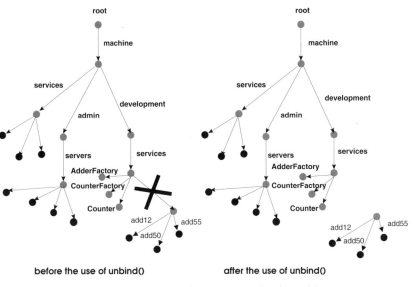

**Figure 7.4**   Deleting of the binding related to Adder.

A naming graph is similar to the one proposed in Figure 7.4. All of the information related to the disconnected graph containing the objects add12 and add50 is no longer accessible from any other naming context. In most situations, this result with dangling context sub-graphs is not appropriate because the information related to these graphs is lost. Therefore, it is generally useful to check whether there is another binding from a context before deleting a binding.

### 7.2.3   Creating and Deleting Naming Contexts

The OMG Naming Service supports two operations to create new contexts: *new_context*() and *bind_new_context*(). The former returns a naming context implemented by the same naming server as the context on which the operation was invoked. The new context is not bound to any name. The latter operation creates a new context and binds it to the name supplied as an argument. The newly created context is implemented by the same naming server as the context in which it was bound (i.e., the naming server that implements the context denoted by the name argument excluding the last component).

Let us assume that we want to create a sub-context within the context Adder with a name SpecialAdder. As mentioned earlier, this can be done in two ways using the two different operations. If the operation *new_context*() is used, then we will proceed as follows:

```
CosNaming::Name name;
name.length[4];
name[0].id = CORBA::string_dup(''machine'');
```

```
name[1].id = CORBA::string_dup(''development'');
name[2].id = CORBA::string_dup(''services'');
name[3].id = CORBA::string_dup(''Adder'');

// we first get the context Adder
CosNaming::NamingContext ContAdder;
CORBA::Obj obj4;
obj4 = o-initial->resolve(name);
ContAdder = CosNaming::NamingContext::_narrow(obj4);

// create a context
CosNaming::NamingContext newCont;
NewCont = ContAdder->new_context();

// assign a name
CosNaming::Name newName;
newName.length[1];
newName[0].id = CORBA::string_dup(''SpecialAdder'');
ContAdder->bind_context(newName,NewCont);
```

This creation of the new context and later the assignment of a name to it can be done in one step by using only one operation, that is, *bind_new_context*():

```
CosNaming::NamingContext newCont;
CosNaming::Name name;
name.length[5];
name[0].id = CORBA::string_dup(''machine'');
name[1].id = CORBA::string_dup(''development'');
name[2].id = CORBA::string_dup(''services'');
name[3].id = CORBA::string_dup(''Adder'');
name[4].id = CORBA::string_dup(''SpecialAdder'');
newCont = o-original->bind_new_context(name);
```

The removal of a context is done by using the operation *unbind*(), as illustrated in the previous section. As mentioned, if the binding is deleted, it will be difficult to retrieve the content of the context unless there are references to it from other contexts.

As mentioned earlier, the *unbind*() operation deletes only the binding, and is shown in Figure 7.4. The information related to the disconnected sub-graph will be in the server, unless this sub-graph can be accessed from another context or the same context with a different name. To correctly destroy a context, that is, both delete the context as well as remove the bindings, another operation needs to be used. This operation is the *destroy*() operation. When this is used on the context Adder of Figure 7.1, *destroy*() will produce a structure of the naming graph as depicted in Figure 7.5. Obviously, the remaining applications objects are no longer accessible, given there are no bindings from another context.

Figures 7.5 and 7.6 show a general example of a naming graph and illustrates the differences between the operations *unbind*() and *destroy*() on a given naming con-

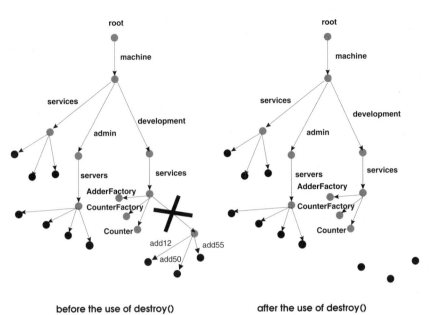

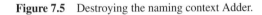

**before the use of destroy()**          **after the use of destroy()**

**Figure 7.5**  Destroying the naming context Adder.

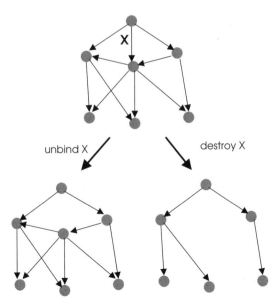

**Figure 7.6**  *unbind*() and *destroy*() operations.

text. As mentioned earlier, these operations need to be used carefully to avoid having objects that cannot be accessed anymore. Obviously, the OMG Naming Service does not guarantee this type of safety. It is the responsibility of the users to make sure that their objects, whether they are context or application objects, are accessible.

### 7.2.4   Listing the Context of a Naming Context

The *list*() operation allows a client to iterate through a set of bindings in a naming context. It returns at most the requested number of bindings in a list of type BindingList. If the naming context contains additional bindings, the operation returns an iterator (of type BindingIterator) with the additional bindings. If the naming context does not contain additional bindings, the binding iterator is a null object reference. The IDL is given below:

```
enum BindingType {object, ncontext};
struct Binding {
    Name binding_name;
    BindingType binding_type;
};

typedef sequence <Binding> BindingList;
void list (in unsigned long how_many,
    out BindingList bl, out BindingIterator bi);
;
```

### 7.3   SUMMARY

In this chapter we provided a detailed description of the OMG Naming Service, and gave an example of how to use such a service with OrbixWeb. We first showed the real importance of the use of names within distributed systems, and in particular, we showed how existing systems implement such functions of naming services (e.g., resolve function). To provide a better understanding of the different structures of a naming service, we explained the architecture and operations of two well-known systems, namely, the DNS (Distributed Naming Service) used in the Internet, and X.500 Directory Service which is widely adopted by the industrial community.

The different functions of the OMG Naming Service were described and appropriate examples were shown. These functions covered binding and unbinding of names, creation and deletion of naming contexts, and finally the function that lists the content of the a naming context. Exercises are given at the end of this chapter to help readers practicing with the OMG Naming Service. We suggest that the reader have a look at the OMG specification in case additional information is needed (e.g., the complete description of the IDL).

## 7.4   REVIEW QUESTIONS

- What are the management functions required by names?
- What is binding? What is the relationship between the binding and a naming service? What are the three conceptual operations provided by a naming service?
- Explain the three mainly used name mapping algorithms and illustrate their differences.
- Explain the difference between the CORBA Naming Service and existing distributed naming services in relation to its name space structuring.
- Explain the similarities between the CORBA Naming Service and existing distributed naming services.
- What is the advantage of having a lack of name syntax in the CORBA Naming Service?
- Explain the difference between a simple name and a compound name.
- Describe the following operations of the CORBA Naming service: $bind()$, $rebind()$, $resolve()$, and $bind\_new\_context()$.
- Explain the name resolution process in DNS.
- Explain how the X.500 Directory Service is organized.

## 7.5   EXERCISES

- Provide a code fragment that does the following: get the initial reference to the naming service, bind an object named boundObject in the context of $r_1 \longrightarrow r_2 \longrightarrow r_3$, and unbind this object.
- Provide a code fragment that does the following: get the initial reference to the naming service, get the context $r_2$ from the previous question, create a new context called $r_{3new}$, and delete $r_3$ context.
- Explain some cases where multiple names are bound to a single object.
- Explain how different types of entries in an X.500 Directory Service name hierarchy can be translated to that of OMG Naming Service.

■■■■■■■ **CHAPTER 8**

# Trading Object Service

In Chapter 7 we saw how objects can be found by using the CORBA Naming Service when their names are known. One problem that may arise is that the users do not have details about the names that are associated with different objects, but they have details about their (external) properties, such as the cost of printing a file. To enable the creation of objects in such a way, another service is defined, called the trading service, that is responsible for locating objects when the values of their properties are known.

This chapter explains the details of the CORBA Trading Object Service (TOS). Before introducing the different elements of the TOS, we will show an example of how a TOS is used. The JTrader, which is a CORBA-compliant syntax will be used to illustrate the use of different trader operations, such as registering and importing a service type. Section 8.3 provides details about the elements of the CORBA TOS, and Section 8.4 explains the trading policies, such as scoping policies, associated with CORBA traders. Because query routing is very important when dealing with large-scale distributed applications, in Section 8.5 we explain the underlying model of the OMG query propagation mechanism and later show how this mechanism can be extended to deal with dynamic information related to service offers. Finally, in Section 8.6, we provide a short description of some existing CORBA TOS implementations.

## 8.1 OVERALL PICTURE

### 8.1.1 Basic Concepts

The general function of a trading service is to provide facilities for service providers to advertise services and for clients to search and locate services available in a distributed system dynamically. An object that provides trading services in a distributed system is called a trader. A *trader* can be seen as the third-party object which analogously provides a "Yellow Page" type of service. It enables a match-making facility for service providers and service users. Service users look for a service based on its type or characteristics instead of its name. Just like a Yellow Page which acts as an index system to provide information according to general categories, a trader provides a classification scheme for distributed objects, and more importantly, it enables runtime advertising and retrieval of services under proper trading contexts.

**Figure 8.1**   A network of traders.

A simple picture of the interaction between traders, clients and servers is depicted in Figure 8.1. Services provided by service providers can be advertised, that is exported, to a trader. The information advertised by the service providers is known as *service offers*. They describe a service using a set of *service properties*, such as name, value and mode triples. The object placing the advertisement is called the *exporter*. Exporting a service is therefore performed by an assertion made by the server and will consist of the following details: (i) the service identifier, (ii) the methods of the objects of the corresponding server (service types), (iii) the service properties (attribute types/values), (iv) the location of the service. (In some sophisticated architectures, the location of the service is maintained by a *Locator*, which is an important component of a Trader architecture).

Opposite of the service offer, a service request is issued by clients, called *importers*, in order to find service offer(s) which satisfy its required matching constraints. The service request is made with following details: (i) service type (e.g., the kind of service the client wants), (ii) service properties (expressed by the matching constraints), and optionally (iii) searching and scoping policies (e.g., the preference criteria or the extent of the search).

Both the service offer and the service request operations are mediated by traders. In the case of a service offer, the trader needs to acquire sufficient details about the offer in order to store the service in the type repository (usually defined as a database). The amount of details required by the trader is necessary both for the trader to know (i) how to store the service offer during the registration, and later, (ii) how to accommodate the search of the service offers from the repository according to the service request. Because the same service type can be available in different traders, traders will need to route the service requests to other traders by following the forward links of the trading graph. The *routing graph* is a subgraph of the trading graph which involves only those traders that have received the service request, as shown in Figure 8.2. When the original constraints of the service request are satisfied, the traders of the routing graph return the result by following the path of links to the routing in the opposite direction until reaching the original trader (which have started the invocation of the service request). As we will see in later sections, specific

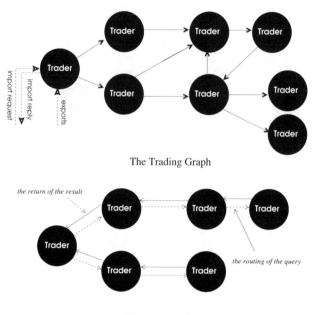

The Trading Graph

The Routing Graph

**Figure 8.2**  Trader query routing.

policies are described in the OMG document [73] on the links between the traders (e.g., hopcount) to allow the routing of trader queries along specific paths of a trading graph. When the object references are returned, the importer can interact with the service providers.

A simple example illustrating the use of traders is the printing example. In such a case, the exporter can be a printer that exports its printing service with a set of service properties suitable for the printing service, such as cost, speed and quality. Examples of service offer properties are the service offer's expiration time and owner. The importer can be a user who wishes to print a report with a lower cost and within a certain time. If the cardinality constraint, that is the number of printers specified by the user to satisfy the original constraints, are not yet satisfied, then the local trader will route the query to the remaining traders using specific information regarding within the links of the trading graph. Using this graph, traders share information about service offers amongst each other, and they can act recursively as clients to each other.

Although the described view of service trading seems to be simple, there are several approaches when dealing, for example, with the returned service offers and persistency. Most of the traders, such ODP-based traders [86][63], return all of the service matchings found in the type repository. A few approaches, such as [109], re-turn a single (best) selection. The return of a single (best) selection saves the client from having to browse through a long list of retrieved results. However, when the (best) selection cannot be found, it is sometimes suitable to return a group of service offers, which together can meet the service request. It is generally up to the client to decide within its service import policy on the number of service offers it wants for every service request.

In most of the existing trader architectures [49, 69], service offers are registered within a trader and are often stored in a database (as the type repository). This way of dealing with persistency of service offers may cause the trader to become a service bottleneck instead of being a service mediator. Other approaches, such as in [109], keep the service references of those objects within the traders (in a file). Client requests are to be done by the trader in consultation with all the service offers through their interfaces. In other words, the trader decentralizes its exclusive right on its type repository and lets the service matching be done by a bidding process between the service offers and trader itself, whichever service provides the best matching will be selected. This approach has the advantage that the burden of service mediation is being decomposed and distributed to the service offers themselves, but the potential disadvantage is that, if a trader has many registered service offers, inter-communication costs can be prohibitively expensive due to the negotiation and deliberation process needed for choosing a final bid by the trader.

### 8.1.2 OMG vs. ODP

The history of traders can be traced back to October 1994 when the International Standard Organization (ISO), in conjunction with the International Electrotechnical Commission (IEC), released a working document on traders [59]. In March 1996, ISO and IEC issued another draft on the ODP trading function. Three months later, OMG also released its trading service specification [73], which is largely based on the ODP TFS [7]. Some of the ODP trading specifications were not appropriate to use in the context of CORBA, and therefore needed to be changed. Some of the problems were related to the fact that the ODP trading specifications do not allow for the re-use of services, such as the query service, except in a hidden implementation-dependent manner. Also, the operations provided many parameters that are irrelevant within a CORBA environment.

***The OMG View***   The OMG view of the trading service is to "facilitate the offering and discovery of instances of services of particular types." [73] OMG considers a trading service as a service object in itself. It is invoked to allow its clients to discover services that become available. It uses the key operations of "export" and "import" on a trader of services. OMG's specification document on the object trading service states two main considerations about the trader's functionalities: (i) a trader "facilitates the offering and the discovery of instances of services of particular types"; (ii) a trader "enables export and import, facilitates the discovery of, and late binding to services." The first point implies that the trader has knowledge of the service (or object) life-cycle. It must be ready to accept frequent exports and de-registrations in order to keep up to date. An environment in which a trader is to work has the potential to be dynamic. Under such conditions, behavior within the environment should not be predicted as services may come and go very frequently and unexpectedly. The second point suggests that there is a large degree of automation in the activities of importing and invoking service offers. The service offers are rigidly type-matched with precise behavior descriptions. If this were not the case, then there could be problems due to invoking an unwanted service. In general, programs are written and used in the precise knowledge of the expected behavior.

***The ANSA View*** "The activity of choosing services, such that they match some service requirement. The choice is based on the comparison of the specification of a service required (provided by a prospective consumer) and the service specifications supplied by service providers or their agents."[24] This is the same as the OMG view. However, there are a number of key differences in trader operation which are a consequence of the differences in the ODP and CORBA paradigms. An interesting difference is that the OMG computational model requires that a reserved function name be made available as part of the ORB bootstrap. This allows all users of the ORB to access the name without having to look it up via the naming service. The calls are direct to the trader through one of a series of interfaces that give a specialized interface according to the desired function. Alternatively, a client of an ANSA trader makes the calls directly to a trader context and from there, all operations are carried out. The client can navigate to different contexts and search for the appropriate service. This has the disadvantage that all user operations, from client to administrator, use the same interface. Therefore, the operations that each type of user needs are not shielded from those who do not need them. This is what OMG tackles by providing more than one interface to the same trader. The other implication from the ANSA document in this regard is that when services are exported, they are stored in the specified context. This shifts the responsibility of clustering to the client, which is undesirable for a user-friendly, useful trader.

## 8.2 AN ILLUSTRATIVE EXAMPLE WITH JTRADER

This section shows the use of the OMG Object Trading Service. We first give a brief discussion of the way CORBA functions, and later describe the process of advertising a service with a trader and sending a query to a trader to find services. The example uses stock trading as the service offer and an investor as the user of the service. The programs are written in Java using JTrader version 0.2 and ORBacus ORB version 2.0.4.

### 8.2.1 Definition of a Service Offer

The service that we wish to export to a trader is a StockBroker service. The IDL specification below shows the service type model of the stock trading service we want to export. Note that this is only a description of the service that we want to export.

```
service StockBroker
{
 interface Broker;
 mandatory readonly property string firm_name;
 mandatory readonly property float minimum_charges;
 mandatory property float commission_rate;
};
```

The StockBroker service is provided by a Broker object. It is comprised of three properties, the firm name, the minimum amount of commission charged and commission rate. A service provider has to provide values for all three properties as they are defined as "mandatory" properties. The firm name and minimum commission rate cannot be changed after the service is advertised. The property mode of "commission_rate" is not defined as "readonly" because we will use the commission rate to demonstrate the use of dynamic properties. The interface below defines the behavior of a Broker who sells shares to the public with a commission.

```
interface Broker
{
   readonly attribute string firm_name;
   readonly attribute float minimum_charges;
   readonly attribute float commission_rate;
   boolean buy_share(in string share_code,
     in unsigned long amount) raises(StockNotFound);
}
```

The services provided can be a function of an object, a product from a factory or a professional service from a firm. It is not necessary to have the same object for the service that we are going to offer. For example, we can offer a service of type Share that has properties to define its share price, lowest share price, highest share price and par value. This service type can return the same Broker object so that users can use the *buy_share*() function to buy the share in mind. The interface is compiled by using the IDL compiler which generates three types of files: "holder" type, stub files, and object or server implementation skeleton files. Orbix's Java IDL compiler generates seven Java source files from the Broker interface: _BrokerRef.java, Broker.java, _BrokerHolder.java, _BrokerOperations.java, _boaimpl_Broker.java, _tie_Broker.java, _dispatcher_Broker.java. Each of these files contains a type in the form of an Java interface or a Java class. Table 8.1 gives a brief description of the roles of each file.

When ORBacus Java IDL compiler jidl is used, five Java source files are generated from the same IDL interface: Broker.java, BrokerHolder.java, _BrokerImpl Base.java, BrokerHelper.java and StubForBroker.java. The purpose of Broker file is similar to the _BrokerRef file generated by OrbixWeb IDL compiler. StubForBroker implements the operations defined in the interface Broker. Both the OrbixWeb Java IDL compiler and ORBacus Java IDL compiler generate a holder class for the interface. The _BrokerImplBase class defines operations that must be implemented by a class in the server.

**TABLE 8.1  OrbixWeb IDL Compiler Generated Files Description**

| | |
|---|---|
| _BrokerRef | A Java interface; the methods of this interface defines the Java client view of the IDL interface. |
| Broker | A Java class which implements the methods defined in interface _BrokerRef. This class provides functionality which allows client method invocations to be forwarded to a server. The primary role of this Java class is to transparently forward client invocations on Broker operations to the appropriate Hello implementation object. |
| _BrokerHolder | A Java class which defines a Holder type for the class Hello. This is required for passing Broker objects as **inout** or **out** parameters to and from IDL operations. |
| _BrokerOperations | A Java interface which maps the attributes and operations of the IDL definition to Java methods. These methods must be implemented by a class in the server. |
| _boaimpl_Broker | An abstract Java class which allows server-side developers to implement the Broker interface using one of two techniques available in OrbixWeb; this technique is called the BOAImpl approach to interface implementation. |
| _tie_Broker | A Java class which allows server-side developers to implement the Broker interface using one of two techniques available in OrbixWeb; this technique is called the TIE approach to interface implementation in OrbixWeb. |
| _dispatcher_Broker | A Java class used internally by OrbixWeb to dispatch incoming server requests to implementation objects. Application developers do not require an understanding of this class. |

In the rest of this section, we will be using the ORBacus jidl compiler. We will build the BrokerImpl class to implement all of the operations defined in the _BrokerImplbase class.

### 8.2.2  Service Export

A server application is needed to service client requests. The server application has to obtain an ORB pseudo-object reference. This serves two purposes.

First, it initializes itself into the ORB environment to serve clients. Second, the ORB pseudo-object reference is needed for use in future ORB operations. Applications can be initialized in one or more ORBs. When an ORB initialization is complete, its pseudo reference is returned and can be used to obtain other references for that ORB. Applications call the init operation to obtain an ORB pseudo reference.

```
ORB orb = ORB.init(args, new Properties());
BOA boa = orb.BOA_init(args, new Properties());
```

Through the ORB we can obtain an object reference to a trader. This can be done in three ways. If the trader is registered as an initial service of the orb, we can use the ORB's *resolve_initial_references*() method to resolve the TradingService initial reference. The second method is to get a reference of the trader through the CORBA Naming Service. The third way is by obtaining the trader object reference from persistent storage. In this example, we obtain a stringified trader reference from a file. The basic procedure to obtain a trader object reference is shown in the code below.

```
// obtain a trader object reference
org.omg.CORBA.Object obj = <...>;
org.omg.CosTrading.Lookup trader =
  org.omg.CosTrading.LookupHelper.narrow(obj);

org.omg.CosTrading.Register register = trader.register_if();
```

We want an instance of the Register interface to advertise a service with a trader. The primary object associated with a trading service is an instance of the Lookup interface. Therefore, an object of the the Lookup interface will need to be found. Then an object of the Register interface through the Lookup object will be retrieved. The TOS specification specifies a TraderComponents interface from which all the five trading object interfaces inherit. This interface contains five readonly attributes, namely *lookup_if*, *register_if*, *link_if*, *proxy_if* and *admin_if*, which represents the five components of a trader. Section 8.3 will provide more details about these components. The IDL compiler generates functions that return the value of these five attributes. A trader implementation does not have to implement all of the five interfaces. A *nil* object reference is returned to the client if the trader does not support a request interface. We can obtain a register object by invoking the function *register_if*() of the Lookup object.

```
org.omg.CosTrading.Register register = trader.register_if();
```

The service offer can now be prepared to be exported to the trader. First, it is important to make sure that the trader knows about the service type to be exported. To do so, a message *describe_type* will be sent to the *Service Type Repository* (STR) of the trader to check whether a service type exists in the database. If the service type is not in the STR, the system will throw an exception. We obtain an object reference to the STR in the same way that we obtain the register object reference. Each of the implementations of the five trader interfaces have the function *type_repos*() which returns an object reference to a STR.

```
// find the reference to STR
org.omg.CORBA.Object obj = trader.type_repos();
ServiceTypeRepository repository =
 ServiceTypeRepositoryHelper.narrow(obj);
```

The registration of a new service within STR can be done as following:

```
// assuming there is no super type for this service
String superTypes[] = new String[0];

// define the properties of the services type
PropStruct properties[] = new PropStruct[3];

properties[0] = new PropStruct();
properties[0].name = "firm_name";
properties[0].value_type = orb.create_string_tc(0);
properties[0].mode = PropertyMode.PROP_MANDATORY_READONLY;

properties[1] = new PropStruct();
properties[1].name = "minimum_charges";
properties[1].value_type =
 orb.get_primitive_tc(org.omg.CORBA.TCKind.tk_float);
properties[1].mode = PropertyMode.PROP_MANDATORY;

properties[2] = new PropStruct();
properties[2].name = "commission_rate";
properties[2].value_type =
 orb.get_primitive_tc(org.omg.CORBA.TCKind.tk_float);
properties[2].mode = PropertyMode.PROP_NORMAL;

repository.add_type(typeName, BrokerHelper.id(),
 properties, superTypes);
```

The above procedure ensures that the service type that we want to advertise exists in the STR. If we advertise a service type which does not exist, we will get an UnknownServiceType exception from the trader. *BrokerHelper.id*() returns the specific identification number for the Broker interface to be associated with the service type. As we mentioned before, a service can have super types from which it inherits. If a query for a service does not require an exact type match, the trader will consider the subtypes of the request type when searching for matches. In this example, we assume that StockBroker does not have any super types. As such, we create an empty super type list to pass to the STR.

A query to a trader returns a list of object references that can provide the service a user is looking for. We thus need to have the object reference ready when we advertise the service. We create an instance of BrokerImpl instead of Broker because the latter is just an interface which cannot be instantiated.

```
BrokerImpl aBroker = new BrokerImpl();
```

The code below shows the procedure involved in preparing a service to be advertised with the trader.

```
// prepare the broker properties to register
org.omg.CosTrading.Property [] properties =
  new org.omg.CosTrading.Property[3];
properties[0] = new org.omg.CosTrading.Property();
properties[0].name = "firm_name";
properties[0].value = orb.create_any();
properties[0].value.insert_string(aBroker.firm_name());

properties[1] = new org.omg.CosTrading.Property();
properties[1].name = "minimum_charges";
properties[1].value = orb.create_any();
properties[1].value.insert_float(aBroker.minimum_charges());
```

The procedure involved in advertising a service that has a dynamic property is different from a usual service advertisement. The job of providing a value for the dynamic property *commission_rate* is delegated to an object which implements the IDL interface CosTradingDynamic::DynamicPropEval. In our case, a RateEval object is used to provide the value for this property. The DynamicPropEval interface provides *evalDP()* function which is invoked by the trader when it examines a service that contains dynamic properties. The role of this function is to return a dynamic property value for the trader to examine. The implementation of this function is dependent on the service provider. It can obtain a value from the database or derive the value from a mathematical calculation. In our example, the constructor of the RateEval provides a commission rate for this property when it is created and the function *evalDP()* returns the value to the trader when the service is being examined. The implementation of this function is shown in the program below.

```
public org.omg.CORBA.Any evalDP(String name,
      org.omg.CORBA.TypeCode returned_type,
      org.omg.CORBA.Any extra_info)
        throws org.omg.CosTradingDynamic.DPEvalFailure
{
  org.omg.CORBA.Any commissionRate = null;
  if( !name.equals("commission_rate"))
    throw new org.omg.CosTradingDynamic.DPEvalFailure(name,
    returned_type, extra_info);

  commissionRate = orb.create_any();
  commissionRate.insert_float(rate);
```

```
    return commissionRate;
}
```

To prepare a dynamic property, a DynamicProp structure must be created as the value of the *commission_rate*. This structure contains the object reference of a RateEval object, a CORBA TypeCode indicating the type returned for this property. and a CORBA Any containing information needed by the RateEval object.

```
// create dynamic property.
// RateEval object will provide the actual value
properties[2] = new org.omg.CosTrading.Property();
properties[2].name = "commission_rate";
properties[2].value = orb.create_any();
org.omg.CosTradingDynamic.DynamicProp dyProp =
 new org.omg.CosTradingDynamic.DynamicProp();
dyProp.eval_if = new RateEval(orb,aBroker.commission_rate());

dyProp.returned_type =
 orb.get_primitive_tc(org.omg.CORBA.TCKind.tk_float);
dyProp.extra_info = orb.create_any();
DynamicPropHelper.insert(properties[2].value, dyProp);
```

As mentioned before, we need to specify a service type name under which we want the service advertisings to fall. We advertise three Broker objects under three different service type names to demonstrate the service type matching problem in traders. The names chosen are StockBroker, ShareBroker, and ShareTrader. As we will see from the query result later, the trader will only return a service that has an exact type match.

After we have prepared all the necessary components, we can use the Register object that we obtained through the Lookup object to advertise or export the service with the trader. The export function returns an identification number for the offer if the export process is successful.

```
String id = register.export(aBroker, typeName, properties);
```

### 8.2.3 Service Import

The steps involved in importing a service from a trader are straightforward. All CORBA-compliant traders must support the Lookup interface. We concentrate on the query operation of the Lookup interface in this section. This operation requires nine parameters which are of types ServiceTypeName, Constraint, Preference, PolicySeq, SpecifiedProps, unsigned long, OfferSeq, OfferIterator, and PolicyNameSeq, respectively. We will explain each of these parameters in later sections.

ServiceTypeName is a string that specifies the type of service the user is looking for. In this example, the investor is looking for a service of type ShareBroker.

```
// service type
String type = "ShareBroker";
```

Constraints specify the group of advertised services that a user is interested in. These constraints are expressed in the form of a string. In this example, the investor is only interested in share brokers who charge a commission of less than twenty percent.

```
constraint = new String("commission_rate < 0.2");
```

A Preference parameter states the order in which a user prefers to have the matched services returned, this is, to ensure that the returned services are those of greatest interest to the user.

```
// set preference.
// Options available are first, random,
// max (expression), min (expression), and with (expression)
String preference = "first";
```

The PoliciesSeq parameter allows the importer to specify how the search should be performed as opposed to what sort of services should be found in the course of the search.

```
// set the policies. Only a few policies are provided here
org.omg.CosTrading.Policy policies[] =
 new org.omg.CosTrading.Policy[9];

// set exact_type_match policy
anyType = orb.create_any();
anyType.insert_boolean(false);
policies[0] =
 new org.omg.CosTrading.Policy("exact_type_match", anyType);
 ...
```

The SpecifiedProps parameter defines the set of properties describing offers that are to be returned with the object reference. There are three possibilities: the importer wants one of the properties, all of the properties, or some of the properties.

```
// properties that the trading services should
// return with each matched offer, which is all at here.
org.omg.CosTrading.LookupPackage.SpecifiedProps desiredProps =
 new org.omg.CosTrading.LookupPackage.SpecifiedProps();

desiredProps.all_dummy((short)0);
```

The returned offers can be returned in one of two ways or a combination of both:

- The parameter of type OfferSeqHolder holds a list of offers and the OfferIt-eratorHolder parameter is a reference to an interface at which offers can be obtained.

- A "how_many" parameter of unsigned long type states how many offers are to be returned via the OfferSeqHolder variable. Any remaining offers are available via the iterator interface. If the "how_many" exceeds the number of offers to be returned, then the OfferIteratorHolder variable will have a value of nil.

If any cardinalities or other limits were applied by one or more traders in responding to a particular query, then the parameter of type PolicyNameSeqHolder will contain the names of the policies which limited the query.

```
// set up variables to hold the search result
org.omg.CosTrading.OfferSeqHolder offers =
 new org.omg.CosTrading.OfferSeqHolder();
org.omg.CosTrading.OfferIteratorHolder iterator =
 new org.omg.CosTrading.OfferIteratorHolder();
org.omg.CosTrading.PolicyNameSeqHolder limits =
 new org.omg.CosTrading.PolicyNameSeqHolder();
```

We can invoke the query operation after we have prepared all the required parameters.

```
// perform the query
trader.query(type, constraint, preference,
 policies, desiredProps, 20, offers, iterator, limits);
```

The code below tests whether a query returns any result.

```
// no match result
 if (offers.value.length == 0 && iterator.value == null)
 {
 System.out.println("No offer found");
 System.exit(0);
 }
```

The trader returns one offer of type "ShareBroker" although there are three service offers in the trader that match the request. This is because the other two objects are advertised under different service type names. Although they have the same interface and behavior, the trader does not consider them to be compatible service types.

### 8.2.4 Result Manipulation

The trader returns a list of object references that have satisfied the specific requirement. This is where the limitations of CORBA greatly reduce the usefulness of TOS. Users generally have two ways of using an object reference returned from a query. The client can either invoke an operation on the object by calling stub routines that are specific to the object or by constructing a request dynamically through the CORBA Dynamic Invocation Interface (DII). The ORB then locates the appropriate implementation code, transmits the parameters and transfers control to the implementation object through an IDL skeleton or a dynamic skeleton. In performing the request, the object implementation may obtain some services from the ORB through the object adapter. The control and output values are returned to the client when the request is complete.

Dynamically typed programming languages, like Smalltalk, do not need to know the returned object type to make an invocation on it. However, static type binding programming languages, like C++ and Java, do need to know the object type to invoke an operation on the object. A client can use a Helper class to narrow the object reference to its type and invoke the operation statically if the object type and the function name and parameters are known to the user. This method is very practical because it is difficult for a user to know the return service type in advance. In this way, the user can send a request to the Naming Service to look for an object that matches the specified type. The following code shows the use of static operation invocation.

```
Broker broker = BrokerHelper.narrow(offers[i].reference);
```

To perform a dynamic invocation on an object, we need to get an object of type Request from the object. CORBA Object classes define the function _request() to return a Request object. This function takes in a parameter which is the name of the function that we want to invoke. We can see the problem with DII in this case. The DII allows the invocation of operations on an object without knowledge of its type. However, it does require the client to know the exact syntax of the operation name. In our example, we have to make the assumption that all the compatible service types have the operation buy_share(). This assumption cannot stand except when there is a standard defined for the service type naming and object interfaces associated with the service type.

```
org.omg.CORBA.Request request =
offers[i].reference._request("buy_share");
```

We need to put values into the request object. First we have to obtain an empty NVList object which holds the parameters to the operation request. NVList contains a list of NamedValue elements. A NamedValue contains a name and a value, where the value is of type Any and is used in the DII to describe the arguments to a request. We can get a reference to the NVList in the request object by invoking the arguments function on the request object.

```
// create a NVList object which will contain the
// parameter to the operation request
org.omg.CORBA.NVList list = request.arguments;
```

The NVList provides functions to prepare parameters for the invocation. We would like to buy 100 BHP shares from a stock broker in this example. The function *buy_share*() takes in a share code and the amount to buy as its parameters. We will use *add_value*() function to insert these two parameters into the named value list.

```
// assume we want to buy 100 BHP shares
org.omg.CORBA.Any valueA = orb.create_any();
valueA.insert_string("BHP");
list.add_value("share_code", valueA,
 org.omg.CORBA.ARG_IN.value);
org.omg.CORBA.Any valueB = orb.create_any();
 valueB.insert_long(100);
list.add_value("amount", valueB,
 org.omg.CORBA.ARG_IN.value);
```

We can invoke the request on the object once the parameters have been inserted into the Request object.

```
try { request.invoke(); } catch(Exception e) {}
```

## 8.3  ARCHITECTURE

After introducing some concepts related to the CORBA Trading Object Service and showing an example on how to use it, in this section, we will provide details of all the components of a CORBA Trader.

Figure 8.3 shows the different components that take part in the OMG Trading Service: *Lookup*, *Registry*, *Admin*, *Link*, and *Proxy* interfaces that are intended to provide specific trading tasks. An interface is graphically represented with a rectangle and includes a name, a list of attributes, and a list of operations. A trader does not need to provide all of these interfaces to be inter-operable with other traders. If a trader is intended to provide only a query service, a trader with Lookup alone will be sufficient to achieve the requirements. Traders that provide only the Lookup interface are called query traders. Those traders that provide Lookup and Registry interfaces are called simple traders. A stand-alone trader provides only the interfaces Lookup, Registry, and Admin. Those traders that provide Lookup, Registry, Admin, and proxy are called proxy traders, and full-service traders are those that implement all the interfaces of a trader.

To configure a trader's functionality in order to obtain a specific type of trader, the interface TraderComponents is provided and contains five readonly attributes. A trader's functionality can be configured by composing the defined interfaces in one of several prescribed combinations.

```
interface TraderComponents {
  readonly attribute Lookup lookup_if;
  readonly attribute Register register_if;
```

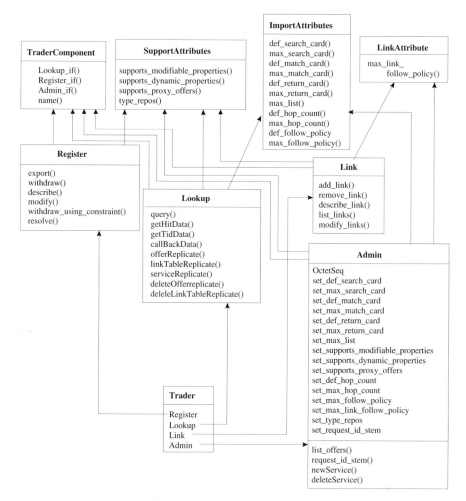

**Figure 8.3** Class diagram of trader.

```
    readonly attribute Link link_if;
    readonly attribute Proxy proxy_if;
    readonly attribute Admin admin_if;
};
```

The composition is not modelled through inheritance, but rather by multiple interfaces to an object. Given one of these interfaces, a way of finding the other associated interfaces is needed. To facilitate this, each trader functional interface is derived from the TraderComponents interface. The five read-only attributes provide a way to get a specific object reference. The implementation of the operation *_get_ < interface > _if* () must return a null object reference if the trading service in question does not support that particular interface.

In addition to the ability of a trader to select specific functionalities to support, a trader may also choose not to support modifiable properties, dynamic properties, and/or proxy offers. The functionality supported by a trader implementation can be determined by querying the readonly attributes in the interface SupportAttributes, which has the following IDL:

```
interface SupportAttributes {
    readonly attribute boolean supports_modifiable_properties;
    readonly attribute boolean supports_dynamic_properties;
    readonly attribute boolean supports_proxy_offers;
    readonly attribute TypeRepository type_repos;
};
```

where:

- *supports_modifiable_properties* informs whether the trader supports properties that can be modified or not. If this attribute is set to true, the service provider can modify properties relating to their service registered in the trader. If this attribute is set to false, the trader will not let the service provider modify the properties of the services that have been registered.

- *supports_dynamic_properties* informs whether the trader supports properties to be declared dynamic or not. If set to true/false, the trader will not hold the data relating to the dynamic properties, rather the service provider will hold the information. The trader will dynamically query the service provider each time the trader wants to know the property value.

- *supports_proxy_offers* informs whether the trader supports proxy offers to be registered or not. If this attribute is set to FALSE, then the trader will not let proxy offers be registered.

- *type_repos informs* whether the trader supports an interface repository or not. If the trader supports the type repository, the type_repos attribute is set to hold a reference to interface repository. This type repository is used by the trader implementation to enquire on the interface repository. If the trader does not support type repository, this attribute is set to hold null.

Each trader can be configured with default and maximum values of certain cardinality and link follow constraints that apply to queries. The values for these constraints can be obtained by querying the attributes in the interface ImportAttributes which holds the traders query policies. These policies can be altered by the administrator. If there are missing policies, the trader takes the default policy value. When the user policy exceeds the maximum policy value, the trader silently sets the policy value to the maximum allowable policy value. Every time a query is made to the trader, the trader checks both the trader policies and the query policies to respond accordingly.

```
interface ImportAttributes {
  readonly attribute unsigned long def_search_card;
  readonly attribute unsigned long max_search_card;
  readonly attribute unsigned long def_match_card;
  readonly attribute unsigned long max_match_card;
  readonly attribute unsigned long def_return_card;
  readonly attribute unsigned long max_return_card;
  readonly attribute unsigned long max_list;
  readonly attribute unsigned long def_hop_count;
  readonly attribute unsigned long max_hop_count;
  readonly attribute FollowOption def_follow_policy;
  readonly attribute FollowOption max_follow_policy;
};
```

When a trader creates a new link or modifies an existing link the *max_link_ follow_policy* attribute will determine the most permissive behavior that the link will be allowed. The value for this constraint on link creation and modification can be obtained from the following interface LinkAttributes. Whenever a query is made, the trader checks if the query "link follow" policy exceeds its maximum link follow policy. If it does, the trader silently sets its value to maximum link follow policy value.

```
interface LinkAttributes {
  readonly attribute FollowOption max_link_follow_policy;
};
```

### 8.3.1   Trader Components

This section provides more details regarding the different modules supported by a trader. Figure 8.4 summarizes the list of these modules.

**Figure 8.4**   OMG trader modules.

***Lookup Module*** Being one of the main components of a trader, the function *query*() (see IDL of Lookup) searches the trader's local database and remote trader's databases for the relevant service which satisfies the given constraints. This query takes in the service type, constraints, preference, policy sequence, specified properties, and number of services. It then returns the sequence of offers, offer iterator, and limits applied. For example, if a client wishes to buy a sports shoe, in particular from the Adidas company, and he/she wishes to know if there are any stores in Melbourne, Australia, which can offer him the best value for the money, say, offering at least a discount of 10%, the client will issue the following query to the trader:

```
location = Melbourne,
service type = shoe-shop,
brand = Adidas,
and discount >= 10
in decreasing order of discount.
```

The trader will check its local database for any matching offers and then query remote traders in the network depending on the local traders policies and the query policies. The local trader gathers all the results from the remote traders and displays them to the user in the format preferred. The client can then choose a shop and make the purchase.

The OMG IDL of the interface Lookup is:

```
interface Lookup: TraderComponents,SupportAttributes,ImportAttributes{
  typedef Istring Preference;
  enum  HowManyProps {none, some, all };
  union SpecifiedProps switch (HowManyProps) {
   case some: PropertyNameSeq prop_names;
  };

 void query (in ServiceTypeName type, in Constraint constr,
      in Preference pref, in PolicySeq policies,
      in SpecifiedProps desired_props,
      in unsigned long how_many, out OfferSeq offers,
      out OfferIterator offer_itr,
      out PolicyNameSeq limits_applied);
```

The service type, declared as in `ServiceTypeName type`, is the name of the service the client is looking for. For instance, a client may be looking for book shops or restaurants. Constraints, declared as in `Constraint constr`, are the properties which the service has to satisfy before the trader returns the service to the client. These constraints give the desirable properties of the services which the trader has to take into consideration before returning to the client. Preference, declared as in `Preference pref`, gives the order in which to return services. For example, the client is looking for inexpensive hotels. When they give the preference as 'min price', the trader displays all the hotels that satisfy their requirements in increasing order of price. If "pref" does not obey the syntax rules for a legal preference expression, then an IllegalPreference exception is raised.

Policy sequence, defined as in `PolicySeq policies`, is a set of instructions to the trader to follow specific policies while looking for the services. These are explicit instructions to the trader. If any of the policies are not mentioned, the trader takes the default values of the local trader. Specified properties, declared as in `SpecifiedProps` *desired_props*, represent those properties of the service which the trader has to display to the client so as to let client make decisions on which service to select. Number of services, specified by the clause in unsigned long how_many, advises the trader to look for the maximum of the requested number of offers. All those services that satisfy the client's requirements will be returned through a sequence of offers, declared in out `OfferSeq offers`. The trader also returns the iterator *offer_itr* to let the client iterate through the returned offers. The argument limits_applied gives the client the names of all policies which limit the query.

Search policies for a trader can be specified by using the provided structure `LookupPolicies`, which is defined as follows:

```
struct LookupPolicies {
    unsigned long search_card;
    unsigned long match_card;
    unsigned long return_card;
    boolean use_modifiable_properties;
    boolean use_dynamic_properties;
    boolean use_proxy_offers;
    TraderName starting_trader;
    FollowOption link_follow_rule;
    unsigned long hop_count; boolean exact_type_match;
};
```

- The *search_card policy* indicates to the trader the maximum number of offers it should consider when looking for type conformance and constraint expression matches. The lesser of this value and the trader's max_search_card attribute is used by the trader. If this policy is not specified, then the value of the trader's def_search_card attribute is used.

- The *match_card policy* indicates to the trader the maximum number of matching offers to which the preference specification should be applied. The lesser of this value and the trader's max_match_card attribute is used by the trader. If this policy is not specified, then the value of the trader's def_match_card attribute is used.

- The *return_card policy* indicates to the trader the maximum number of matching offers to return as a result of this query. The lesser of this value and the trader's max_return_card attribute is used by the trader. If this policy is not specified, then the value of the trader's def_return_card attribute is used.

- The *use_modifiable_properties policy* indicates whether the trader should consider offers which have modifiable properties when constructing the set of offers to which type conformance and constraint processing should be applied. If the value of this policy is TRUE, then such offers will be included; if FALSE, they will not. If this policy is not specified, such offers will be included.

- The *use_dynamic_properties policy* indicates whether the trader should consider offers which have dynamic properties when constructing the set of offers to which type conformance and constraint processing should be applied. If the value of this policy is TRUE, then such offers will be included; if FALSE, they will not. If this policy is not specified, such offers will be included.

- The *use_proxy_offers policy* indicates whether the trader should consider proxy offers when constructing the set of offers to which type conformance and constraint processing should be applied. If the value of this policy is TRUE, then such offers will be included; if FALSE, they will not. If this policy is not specified, such offers will be included.

- The *starting_trader policy* facilitates the distribution of the trading service itself. It allows an importer to scope a search by choosing to explicitly navigate the links of the trading graph. If the policy is used in a query invocation it is recommended that it be the first policy-value pair; this facilitates an optimal forwarding of the query operation. A "policies" parameter need not include a value for the starting_trade policy. Where this policy is present, the first name component is compared against the name held in each link. If no match is found, the InvalidPolicyValue exception is raised. Otherwise, the trader invokes *query()* on the Lookup interface held by the named link, but passing the starting_trader policy with the first component removed.

- The *link_follow_rule policy* indicates how the client wishes links to be followed in the resolution of its query. Section 8.5.1 discusses this aspect in detail.

- The *hop_count policy* indicates to the trader the maximum number of hops across federation links that should be tolerated in the resolution of this query. The parameter at the current trader is determined by taking the minimum of the trader's max_hop_count attribute and the importer's hop_count policy, if provided, or the trader's def_hop_count attribute if it is not. If the resulting value is zero, then no federated queries are permitted. If it is greater than zero, then it must be decremented before passing on to a federated trader.

- The *exact_type_match policy* indicates to the trader whether the importer's service type must exactly match an offer's service type; if not (and by default), then any offer of a type conformant to the importer's service type is considered.

**Registry Module**   This interface is used by exporters who wish to export or advertise about their services or withdraw their advertised services. A service can be registered or withdrawn through this module. The registry module provides six functionalities: export, withdraw, describe, modify, withdraw (using constraint), and resolve.

A trader will need to keep persistent in its local database certain information, including the references of the different offers and their corresponding properties. A null value for a particular property will mean that that this particular property is not defined. All mandatory property columns are defined as "NOTNULL" which makes it mandatory to insert a value.

The IDL definition of the Register interface is defined below. In the following discussion, we will provide details of the different functions of such an interface.

```
typedef string OfferId;
typedef sequence<OfferId> OfferIdSeq;

interface Register: TraderComponents,SupportAttributes {
  struct OfferInfo {
  Object reference;
  ServiceTypeName type;
  PropertySeq properties;
  };

  OfferId export(in Object reference,
          in ServiceTypeName type, in PropertySeq properties)
  void withdraw(in OfferId id)
  OfferInfo describe(in OfferId id)
  void modify(in OfferId id,
        in PropertyNameSeq del_list,
        in PropertySeq modify_list)
  void withdraw_using_constraint (in ServiceTypeName type,
        in Constraint constr)
  Register resolve(in TraderName name)
}
```

The export function is used to register a service. The exporter has to supply the service reference, its service type and properties of the service. These properties are used for matching the constraints of the clients. All the services registered in the trader have a unique Id. The export function assigns this Id to the service every time a new service registers itself with the trader.

Service providers wishing to advertise their services invoke the export operation passing the service reference, the service type and the property sequence. The trader stores this information in its local database and returns a unique number relative to this trader of type OfferId. Export will perform the following checks [73]:

- The reference parameter carries information that enables a client to interact with a remote server. If the trader wishes to consider a certain type of reference as unacceptable, it may return an InvalidObjectRef exception.
- The type parameter identifies the service type, which contains the interface type of reference. If the string representation does not obey the rules for the identifiers, then an IllegalServiceType exception is raised.

- If the type is syntactically correct, but a trader is unable to unambiguously determine that it is of recognized type, then an UnknownServiceType exception is raised.

- If the trader can determine that the interface type of the reference parameter is not the subtype of the interface type specified in type, then an InterfaceTypeMismatch exception is raised.

- The properties parameter contains a sequence of name value pairs that describe this offer. If any of the property names defined in the property name sequence do not obey the syntax for the PropertyNames, then an IllegalPropertyName exception is raised.

- If the type of the property value is not the same as the declared type, then a PropertyTypeMismatch exception is raised.

- If an attempt is made to assign a dynamic property value to a read-only property, a ReadonlyDynamicProperty exception is raised.

- If the properties parameter omits any property declared in the service type which is mandatory, then a MissingMandatoryProperty exception is raised.

- If two or more properties with the same property name are included in the properties parameter, then a DuplicatePropertyName exception is raised.

When dealing with the implementation of the export function, after performing the above checks, this function will get a new transaction number for the transaction to store in its database. It then invokes the function $newOffer()$ (on the database). This function will store the reference and properties; it will then generate an Id that will be unique to the trader. The id is returned to the exporter which could be used as an identity for the offer. The interaction diagram of the export function is shown in Figure 8.5.

The describe function takes the unique Id of the service and returns the description of the service. This function is invoked by a service provider or the administrator who wishes to know details of an offer denoted by a particular offerId. This function returns an OfferInfo structure. This structure holds the object reference, its service type and the properties related to a particular offerId, which was registered by the exporter. This function takes offerId, which is originally returned by the export function, as an argument to avoid a call to this function by malicious clients. Figure 8.5 shows the different steps of the function describe():

- If the string representation of the offer id does not obey the rules of the offer identifiers, an IllegalOfferId exception is raised.

- If the offer id is legal, but the trader cannot find the offer within the database, an UnknownOfferId exception is raised.

After performing the above checks, this function invokes the function $getOffer()$ on the database, which returns an offer. An Offer is a structure with an object reference and a list of properties. After getting the service type for offerId by invoking

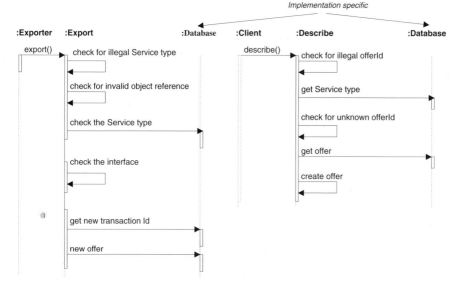

**Figure 8.5**   Export and describe functions.

$getServiceType()$ on the database, this function creates an OfferInfo structure and returns it to the caller.

The remaining functions of the Register interfaces are the withdraw (with or without constraints) and modify functions. The former is used to deregister the service. The service which wants to deregister itself has to pass its unique Id to this function. This function takes the offerId and checks for the matching offers in the database. If a match exists, the trader removes the entry of the offer, otherwise it throws an appropriate exception. This function takes offerId, which was originally returned by export function to avoid a call to this function by malicious client,s as its argument. Figure 8.6 shows the different steps of such a function.

The administrator of the trader may no longer be interested in all of the services which satisfy a particular constraint. The administrator will invoke the function $withdraw\_using\_constraint()$ constraint on a particular service type. A trader checks through its database to see if there are any services of the particular service type matching the constraint. If so, it removes all of the entries relating to that particular service, otherwise it throws an appropriate exception.

The modify function is used to modify the properties of the service. It is quite reasonable that the services may have some extra properties or may delete some properties in the course of time. This modify function reflects these changes in the trader database.

A client may want to refer to the trader that is known by a name rather than by object reference. The operation resolve is used to resolve a context relative name for another trader. When the trader cannot resolve the name, it throws an appropriate exception. When there is a match, it returns a reference to the Register interface.

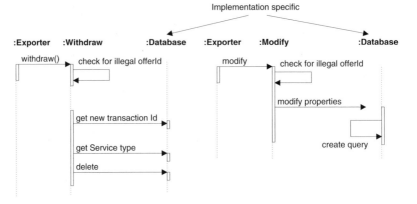

**Figure 8.6** Withdraw and modify functions.

The function resolve takes in a sequence of name components and returns a reference to Registry. This function performs the following checks:

- If the contents of the parameter cannot yield legal syntax for the first component, then the IllegalTraderName exception is raised.
- If no match is found for the linkName, or the trader does not support links, UnknownTraderName is raised
- If the Register interface is not null, then the trader binds to the Register interface and invokes resolve, but passes the TraderName list with the first component removed. If it is null, then a RegisterNotSupported exception is raised.

When the trader matches the first name component and there are no names left over, a reference to the register interface is returned. Intermediate traders return this register interface to the client in a recursive manner.

***Admin Module*** Federated traders are autonomous, meaning each trader administers itself and is not influenced by external traders. The administrative module has various parameters that define the policies of the trader. These parameters can be modified to reflect the changes in the trader's policy. Apart from these policy parameters, the administrator supports two functions: the list offers and the list proxies.

```
interface Admin: TraderComponents,SupportAttributes,
        ImportAttributes,LinkAttributes {
  typedef sequence<octet> OctetSeq;
  readonly attribute OctetSeq request_id_stem;
  unsigned long set_def_search_card (in unsigned long value);
  unsigned long set_max_search_card (in unsigned long value);
  unsigned long set_def_match_card (in unsigned long value);
  unsigned long set_max_match_card (in unsigned long value);
  unsigned long set_def_return_card (in unsigned long value);
```

```
unsigned long set_max_return_card (in unsigned long value);
unsigned long set_max_list (in unsigned long value);
boolean set_supports_modifiable_properties (in boolean value);
boolean set_supports_dynamic_properties (in boolean value);
boolean set_supports_proxy_offers (in boolean value);
unsigned long set_def_hop_count (in unsigned long value);
unsigned long set_max_hop_count (in unsigned long value);
FollowOption set_max_follow_policy (in FollowOption policy);
FollowOption set_def_follow_policy (in FollowOption policy);
FollowOption set_max_link_follow_policy (in FollowOption policy);
TypeRepository set_type_repos (in TypeRepository repository);
OctetSeq set_request_id_stem (in OctetSeq stem);
void list_offers (in unsigned long how_many,
     out OfferIdSeq ids, out OfferIdIterator id_itr)
void list_proxies (in unsigned long how_many,
     out OfferIdSeq ids, out OfferIdIterator id_itr)
}
```

The list offers Id's of services registered in the local database. This function takes in the number as its parameter and returns a sequence of Id's and an iterator to it so that Admin can iterate on the returned Id's. The list proxies return the set of Id's of proxy offers registered in the trader.

***Link Module***    This module provides a means to interact with the remote traders in the federation. It provides four functions: add link, remove link, describe link and modify link.

```
interface Link:TraderComponents,SupportAttributes,LinkAttributes {
   struct LinkInfo {
     Lookup target;
    Register target_reg;
     FollowOption def_pass_on_follow_rule;
     FollowOption limiting_follow_rule;
   };

   void add_link(in LinkName name, in Lookup target,
        in FollowOption def_pass_on_follow_rule,
        in FollowOption limiting_follow_rule );
   void remove_link(in LinkName name);
   LinkInfo describe_link(in LinkName name);
   LinkNameSeq list_links ();
   void modify_link(in LinkName name,
        in FollowOption def_pass_on_follow_rule,
        in FollowOption limiting_follow_rule );
}
```

The add link function creates a new link between the local trader and a remote trader. A trader is connected to a number of federated traders through the links. Every time a new trader is known to the local trader, a link is created between the local trader and the known trader. Every link has an associated name which will be in the context of the trader, and has policies that describe the link. These link policies can be modified by the modify link function. A description of a link can be obtained by invoking the describe link function. Remove link removes the link associated between the local trader and remote trader.

- The function *add_link*() is used to dynamically add a new link, which takes in linkname, target reference, def_pass_on_follow_rule, and limiting_follow_rule. Each trader is independent in assigning names to the link. A linkname will be unique in the context of trader. Each link has to follow rules, which have to be obeyed by the trader while querying the remote trader. The def_pass_on_follow_ rule parameter specifies the default link behavior for the link if no link behavior is specified on an importer's query request. If the def_pass_on_follow_rule exceeds limiting_follow_rule, then a DefaultFollowTooPermissive exception is thrown. The parameter limiting_follow_rule specifies the most permissive link follow behavior that the link is willing to tolerate. A limitingfollowTooPermissive exception is raised if this parameter exceeds the trader's attribute of max_link_follow_policy at the time of the links creation.

- This function removes all knowledge of the target trader. The target trader can no longer be used to resolve, forward, or propagate any trading operations from this trader. This function takes in the link name as a parameter and returns void. The exception IllegalLinkName is raised if the link name is not valid. The UnknownLinkName exception is raised if the named link is not in the trader.

- The function *describe_link*() returns information about the link held in the trader. It takes in the link name and returns LinkInfo. LinkInfo is a structure comprised of Lookup interface, Register interface, default_follow_behavior and limiting_follow_behavior of the link. Link name identifies the link whose description is required. An IlegalLinkName exception is raised for an invalid link name.

- The function *list_links*() returns a list of the names of all trading links within the trader.

- Finally, the function *modify_link*() can be used to change the existing link following behaviors of an identified link. The name and the Lookup reference cannot be changed. It takes in def_pass_on_follow_rule, limiting_follow_rule and returns void. The parameter def_pass_on_follow_rule specifies the new default link behavior for this link. If the def_pass_on_follow_rule exceeds the limiting_follow_rule, then a DefaultFollowTooPermissive exception is raised. limiting_follow_rule parameter specifies the new limit for the follow behavior of this link. The LimitingFollowTooPermissive exception is raised if the value exceeds the current max_link_follow_policy of the trader.

**Proxy Module** Proxy services are like normal services that have a service type and properties, but do not have a direct object reference. An object reference is obtained by querying the lookup of the proxy offer. This module has three main functions: export proxy, withdraw proxy and describe proxy.

```
interface Proxy:TraderComponents,SupportAttributes {
  typedef Istring ConstraintRecipe;
  struct ProxyInfo {
   ServiceTypeName type;
   Lookup target;
   PropertySeq properties;
   boolean if_match_all;
   ConstraintRecipe recipe;
   PolicySeq policies_to_pass_on;
  };

  OfferId export_proxy(in Lookup target, in ServiceTypeName type,
    in PropertySeq properties, in boolean if_match_all,
    in ConstraintRecipe recipe, in PolicySeq policies_to_pass_on)

  void withdraw_proxy(in OfferId id)
  ProxyInfo describe_proxy(in OfferId id)
}
```

Like normal service offers, proxy offers have a service type "type" and named property values "properties." However, a proxy offer does not include an object reference at which the offered service is provided. Instead, this object reference is obtained when it is needed for a query operation; it is obtained by invoking another query operation upon the "target" Lookup interface held in the proxy offer. The "recipe" parameter tells the trader how to construct the constraint expression for the secondary query operation to "target." This permits the secondary constraint expression to be made up of literals, values of properties of the proxy offer, and the primary constraint expression.

If a query operation matches the proxy offer (using the normal service type Matching, property matching and preference algorithms), this primary query operation invokes a secondary query operation on the Lookup interface nominated in the proxy offer. Although the proxy offer nominates a Lookup interface, this interface is only required to conform syntactically to the Lookup interface; it need not conform to the Lookup interface behavior specified above.

## 8.3.2 Service Type Repository

The service type is a very important element of trading services in distributed systems. A trader compares the service request type with service offer types to find matches for a request. An importer has to specify a service type when requesting a service. Similarly, an exporter also needs to supply a service type when advertising a service offer with a trader. When a trader is designed, problems in uniquely identifying and comparing service types have to be solved.

A (trading) service has a type, called service type, which is a sort of meta-information about the service. It's comprised of an interface type that defines the computational signature of the service interface, and zero or more named property types: <service_type_name, service_interface, set_of_properties>. Properties of a type describe the characteristics of the type and the rules that govern its usage. A property has a name, a type, and a property mode. A property mode can be normal, read only, mandatory, or mandatory read only. Exporters do not need to provide a value for a normal property when advertising a service. However, the exporters must provide a value for a mandatory property. If a service type contains a read only property, the value of the property cannot be changed later. A mandatory read only property has the strongest specification. The exporter must provide a value for the property and the value cannot be changed subsequently.

The value of a property in a service offer might change frequently. It is too troublesome and inconvenient for an exporter to withdraw and re-register a service offer every time the value of a property in the offer changes. The share price is an example of these frequently changing properties. Instead of supplying a static value for this property, exporters can give instructions to traders to find out the value dynamically.

The TOS supports dynamic properties where the value of a property is not held within a trader. Instead, the property contains a reference to an object implementing an OMG trader DynamicPropEval interface. The DynamicPropEval interface only supports one operation, the evalDP operation which is responsible for returning a value for the property. This function needs to know the name, the returned type and any extra information about the dynamic property. When the value of the property is required, the trader invokes the evalDP operation on the object reference. Depending on the server object implementation, it might look up the value in a database or compute the value on the fly.

There is no restriction on the type of a dynamic property. However, a trader must support the dynamic property functionality for an exporter to be able to advertise a service offer with dynamic properties. A client can make a query to a trader with the function *support_dynamic_properties*() to find out whether the trader supports dynamic properties. As dynamic properties involve an extra step and introduce overhead in obtaining the value for a property, the importer can specify whether a trader should consider offers with dynamic properties when searching for matched services. As mentioned earlier, the value of a read-only property cannot be changed after it has been initialized. Therefore, a service type cannot have any dynamic read only attributes.

Similar to inheritance in object-oriented programming, service types can be related in a hierarchy that reflects type inheritance. This hierarchy can be used to decide whether a service type can be substituted by another service type. The TOS specification [73] lists the rules for service *type conformance* as follows: given two service types X and Y, X is said to be a subtype of Y if and only if:

- The interface type associated with X is either the same as, or derived from, the interface type associated with Y.
- All the properties defined in Y are also defined in X.

- For all properties defined in both X and Y, the mode of the property in X must be the same as, or stronger than, the mode of property in Y.

- All properties defined in X that are also defined in Y shall have the same property value type in X as their corresponding definitions had in Y.

Information about service types is stored in a Service Type Repository (STR). The type repository supports the storage, retrieval and management of type descriptions. In most of the implementations, a database system is used as an STR, which needs to take into account non-functional aspects, such as performance and scalability, using appropriate techniques of indexing [31], clustering [23], and query routing [103] to produce better performance and scalability for critical distributed applications.

Users must provide the full details of a service type to register it within the STR, such as the type name, an interface associated with the type, a list of type properties and super types for each of the service types. The IDL structure of the STR system is as follows:

```
module CosTradingRepos {
  interface ServiceTypeRepository {
  // local types
  typedef sequence<CosTrading::ServiceTypeName> ServiceTypeNameSeq;
  enum PropertyMode {PROP_NORMAL, PROP_READONLY,
          PROP_MANDATORY, PROP_MANDATORY_READONLY };
  struct PropStruct {
    CosTrading::PropertyName name;
    CORBA::TypeCode value_type;
    PropertyMode mode;
  };
  typedef sequence<PropStruct> PropStructSeq;
  typedef CosTrading::Istring Identifier;

  // IR::Identifier
  struct IncarnationNumber {
   unsigned long high;
   unsigned long low;
  };

  struct TypeStruct {
   Identifier if_name;
   PropStructSeq props;
   ServiceTypeNameSeq super_types;
   boolean masked;
   IncarnationNumber incarnation;
  };
  enum ListOption {all,since};
  union SpecifiedServiceTypes switch(ListOption) {
    case since IncarnationNumber incarnation; };
```

```
// attributes
readonly attribute IncarnationNumber incarnation;

// operation signatures
IncarnationNumber add_type(in CosTrading::ServiceTypeName name,
   in Identifier if_name, in PropStructSeq props,
   in ServiceTypeNameSeq super_types )

void remove_type(in CosTrading::ServiceTypeName name)
ServiceTypeNameSeq list_types(in SpecifiedServiceTypes which_types);
TypeStruct describe_type(in CosTrading::ServiceTypeName name)
TypeStruct fully_describe_type(in CosTrading::ServiceTypeName name)
void mask_type(in CosTrading::ServiceTypeName name)
void unmask_type(in CosTrading::ServiceTypeName name)
```

The operation *add_type()* enables the creation of new service types in the service type repository. The caller supplies the "name" for the new type, the identifier for the interface associated with instances of this service type, the property definitions for this service type, and the service type names of the immediate super-types to this service type. The operation *mask_type()* permits the deprecation of a particular type (i.e., after being masked, exporters will no longer be able to advertise offers of that particular type). The type continues to exist in the service repository due to other service types being derived from it.

### 8.3.3 Dynamic Property Evaluation

The part of the IDL which specifies the use of dynamic properties is the following:

```
module CosTradingDynamic {
  interface DynamicPropEval {
    any evalDP(in CosTrading::PropertyName name,
         in TypeCode returned_type, in any extra_info);

  struct DynamicProp {
    DynamicPropEval eval_if;
    CORBA::TypeCode returned_type;
    any extra_info;
  };
};
```

The DynamicPropEval interface allows dynamic property values in a service offer held by the trader. When exporting a service offer (or proxy offer), the property with the dynamic value has an "any" value which contains a DynamicProp structure rather than the normal property value. A trader which supports dynamic properties accepts this DynamicProp value as containing the information which enables a correctly typed property value to be obtained during the evaluation of a query.

The export (or export_proxy) operation raises the PropertyTypeMismatch if the returned_type is not appropriate for the property name as defined by the service type. Readonly properties may not have dynamic values. The export and modify operations on the Register interface and the export_proxy operation on the Proxy interface raise the ReadonlyDynamicProperty exception if dynamic values are assigned to readonly properties. When a query requires a dynamic property value, the evalDP operation is invoked on the eval_if interface in the DynamicProp structure. The property name parameter is the name of the property whose value is being obtained. The returned_type and extra_info parameters are copied from the DynamicProp structure. The evalDP operation returns an any value which should contain a value for that property. The value should be of a type indicated by returned_type.

If the trader does not support dynamic properties (indicated by the trader attribute supports_dynamic_properties), the export and export_proxy operations should not be parameterized by dynamic properties. The behavior of such traders in such circumstances is not specified by this standard.

## 8.4  CONSTRAINTS, POLICIES, AND PREFERENCES

### Policies

The interaction between traders, exporters and importers is affected by trading behaviors of the trading objects. Both TOS and ODP TF use the concept of policy to provide a framework for describing the behavior of a trader. Policies are rules that affect trader behavior at run time. A policy has a name and a value assigned to that policy. For example, a hop_count policy, of an unsigned long type, specifies how many times a query can propagate to other traders. OMG's Trading Service defines policies for traders and importers, but not for exporters.

### Importer Policies

An importer sends its policies as a query operation's parameter to a trader. Table 8.2 describes eight importer policies that a trader must support. In this section we have a particular interest in the exact_type_match policy as the trader will consider the subtype of the request type as a match when the importer does not require an exact type match.

### Scoping Policies

A trader's policies are stored in the attributes of the trader. Trader policies are specified initially when the trader is created, and can be modified or interrogated later by the user. A trader specifies its default policies to be used when an importer does not specify any policies in its service request. A trader also has maximum policies to place limitations on what the trader will do. Table 8.3 lists out the traders' default and maximum policies.

**TABLE 8.2  Importer Policies**

| Policies | Description |
|---|---|
| **search_card** | the maximum amount of service offers to be searched for a particular request. |
| **match_card** | the upper bound of matched offers to be ordered by a trader. |
| **return_card** | the number of matched offers to be returned to a user. |
| **link_follow** | the link follow behaviour for a trader. The value of this policy can either be: always follow links, follows the links when there is no matched service found in the local trader, or do not follow any links. |
| **starting_trader** | the user specifies a trader to process its request by providing a reference of the trader. The trader who receives the request has the obligation to forward the request to the specified trader even though the user has specified a policy to search offers in local trader only. |
| **request_id** | an identifier for a query operation. |
| **exact_type_match** | specifies whether an importer is looking for an exact type match of the request service type. |
| **hop_count** | specifies how many times a request can be propagated to other traders. |

A link specifies a limiting follow rule limiting_follow_rule to limit the chaining behavior when a link is created. The limiting follow rule indicates whether a forwarded request should be propagated further by the target trader. The value of the limiting rule could be: always propagated further(always), propagated further if there is no matched service in the target trader(if_no_local), or do not propagated the request to other traders(local_only). The always option has the highest value followed by the

**TABLE 8.3  Trader's Default and Maximum Policies**

| Default Policies | Maximum Policies |
|---|---|
| def_hop_count | max_hop_count |
| def_follow_policy | max_link_follow_policy |
| def_match_card | max_match_card |
| def_search_card | max_search_card |
| def_return_card | max_return_card |

**TABLE 8.4  Preferences**

| Preference | Description |
| --- | --- |
| `max <expression>` | The expression can refer to properties of the offer. The matched offers are returned in a descending order. |
| `min <expression>` | The expression can refer to properties of the offer. The matched offers are returned in an ascending order. |
| `with <expression>` | The expression is a boolean expression. It can refer to properties of the offer. The matched offers that have a true value precede those that have a FALSE value. |
| `random` | The order of returned matched offers is in random. |
| `first` | The matched offers are returned in the order as they are discovered. |

if_no_local and local_only. The max_link_follow_policy is used to specify an upper limit on the value of a link's limiting follow rule at the time of creation or modification of a link. If the maximum link follow policy has a value of local_only, then a propagated request to a trader would not be forwarded further even though the link has an always follow policy.

There are general rules regarding the use of importer and trader policies. If an importer does not specify a policy for a service request, the trader uses its default policy. In the case of an importer policy exceeding the limitation (maximum) policy specified by the trader, the trader's limiting policy overrides the importer policy.

## Preferences

Preferences are used to determine the order in which matched services return to user. Table 8.4 lists the five possible ways a user can order the matched services.

## Constraints

Importers use a service type name and constraints to specify the service offers in which they have an interest. The constraints are specified in a constraint language. OMG has specified a Constraint Language to be used in its trading service, but proprietary query languages can also be accommodated. The name of a proprietary query language has to be placed between two angle brackets($<<>>$) at the start of the constraint expression. The trader evaluates each service offer against the constraint. An offer is considered a match only if the constraint expression evaluates to a TRUE value.

Standard constraint language has constructs including comparative functions, substring matching, set membership, and mathematical and logical operators. The constraint expression can refer to properties of a service offer and thus enable importers to find a potential service offer on the basis of its properties. However, constraint expressions are operated only on properties of the standard data types like boolean, short, unsigned short, long, unsigned long, float, double, char, string and sequences of these data types. This does not mean that a service offer cannot contain complex property types, but complex types cannot be referred to in a constraint expression. For example, a query looking for service offers that have a cost of less than 50 will look like "cost < 50".

## 8.5  QUERY PROPAGATION

In this section we discuss the basic OMG's TOS query routing and show a possible extension to deal with important issues, such as scalability.

### 8.5.1  CORBA Query Routing

The trader linkage allows arbitrary directed graphs of traders to be produced, which may introduce two types of problems [73]: (i) a single trader can be visited more than once during a search due to it appearing on more than one path (i.e., distinct set of connected edges) leading from a trader; and (ii) cycles can occur. Figure 8.7 shows an example of a trading graph with has a cycle which may lead to repeated querying of the same trader, and therefore result in an infinite loop: A $\longrightarrow$ B $\longrightarrow$ C $\longrightarrow$ A. When an importer queries the trader A, A passes the same query to B, and in turn, B passes the query to C, and C passes the query to A. This process may be repeated indefinitely, which leads to an infinite loop unless there is a means to detect and avoid it.

To ensure that a search does not enter into an infinite loop, a hop_count is used to limit the depth of links used to propagate a search. The hop_count is decremented by one before propagating a query to other traders. The search propagation terminates at

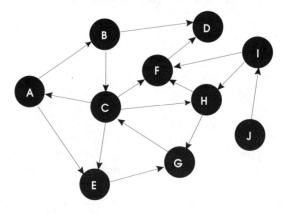

**Figure 8.7**    A trading graph with cycles.

the trader when the hop_count reaches zero. To avoid the unproductive revisiting of a particular trader while performing a query, a RequestId can be generated by a source trader for each query operation that it initiates for propagation to a target trader. The trader attribute of request_id_stem is used to form RequestId.

```
typedef sequence<octet> OctetSeq;
attribute OctetSeq request_id_stem;
```

A trader remembers the RequestId of all recent interworking query operations that it has been asked to perform. When an interworking query operation is received, the trader checks this history and only processes the query if it is the operation's first appearance. In order for this to work, the administrator for a set of federated traders must have initialized the respective request_id_stems to non-overlapping values. The RequestId is passed in an importer's policy parameter on the query operation to the target trader. If the target trader does not support the use of the RequestId policy, the target trader need not process the RequestId, but must pass the RequestId on to the next linked trader if the search propagates further.

To propagate a query request in a trading graph, each source trader acts as a client to the Lookup interface of the target trader and passes its client's query operation to its target trader. The following example illustrates the modification of hop_count parameter as a query request passes through a set of linked traders in the trading graph of Figure 8.8. We assume that the link follow policies in the traders will result in always_follow behavior.

- A query request is invoked at the trading interface of T1 with an importer's hop count policy expressed as hop_count = 4. The trader scoping policy for T1 includes max_hop_count = 5. The resultant hop_count applied for the search, after the arbitration action that combines the trader policy and the importer policy, is hop_count = 4.

- We assume that no match is found in T1 and the resulting follow policy is always, that is, T1 is to pass the request to T3. A modified importer hop_count policy of hop_count = 3 is used. The local trader scoping policy for T3 includes max_hop_count = 1 and the generation of T3_Request_id to avoid repeat or cyclic searches of the same traders. The resultant scoping policy applied for the search at T3 is hop_count = 1 and the T3_Request_id is stored.

- Assuming that no match is found in T3 and the resulting follow policy is always, the modified scoping parameter for the query request at T4 is: hop_count = 0 and request_id = T3_Request_id.4. Assuming that no match is found in T4, even though the max_hop_count = 4 for T4, the search is not propagated further. An unsuccessful search result will be passed back to T3, to T1, and finally to the user at T1. Of course, if a query request is completed successfully at any of the traders on the linked search path, then the list of matched service offers will be returned to the original user. Whether the query request is propagated through the remaining trading.

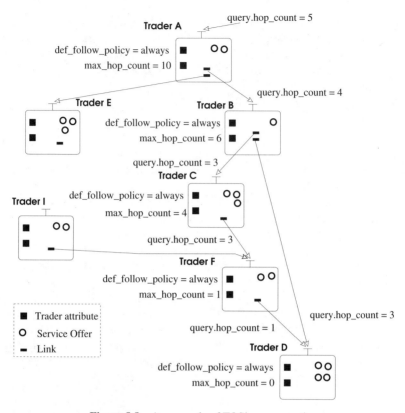

**Figure 8.8**    An example of TOS's query routing.

## 8.5.2   Semantic-based Query Routing

One of the main characteristics of the information maintained by traders is that they keep changing in the course of time. The stock market is a good example where the price of shares keeps changing and new shares are continually introduced to the market. Making use of static information about a particular trader, as is the case in the current specification of the CORBA trader, does not lead to effective query routing. The information recorded in the attributes of traders (e.g., max_hop_count) and queries (e.g., hop_count) is static by nature and therefore does not change to reflect the new information added to the STRs (e.g., new shares, update of share price) of traders. In this way, an identical query will always be propagated in the same way, which makes the Lookup operation useless because it does not return updated information, which may be available in other traders that have not been visited.

To address such a problem, the approach proposed in [103] suggests making use of dynamic information about the traders, where each trader keeps information locally relating to the services remote traders can offer. Each trader holds two types of information: (i) a *linkTable* table which holds references to all traders that the local trader has links to, and (ii) a *callback* table that holds references to all traders which are linked to this local trader. When a trader adds a new link, it creates a new table in its local database, which holds all service types and hit factor information of the linked trader. At the same time, the linked trader also stores the address of the trader that has a link to it. Whenever new data is added to the database, for example, a new offer is registered or exported, all the traders can pass queries to the trader to update themselves to reflect this change. This can be achieved by getting all the trader references from the callback table, and calling an appropriate function for all of references to reflect the change. In turn, other traders that have links to it will be notified. This process maintains up to date information about the linked traders at the local level. When a trader is queried, it gets references of all traders that have the potential to return offers from locally stored information. A trader will first query the trader that has the highest hit factor for a particular service type, and then the trader that has the second highest hit factor, and so on. This delays or avoids querying traders that have the least chance of returning the particular service type offers.

Routing algorithms are used to decide the target traders for the query, based on the hit factor [103]. The calculation of a hit factor is based on the number of offers and their relative distance from the trader. When a trader claims that it can address $N$ number of offers, it means that this trader can give access to $N$ number of offers both locally and remotely via this trader. It is not sufficient to decide the target trader based on the number of offers it can give access to. For example, suppose there are two traders A and B. A has 500 offers of a particular service type and can address 100 offers of the same type remotely from a trader 1 hop away. B has 5 offers locally and can address 1000 offers remotely from a trader 100 hops away. It is advisable for the local trader to pass a query to A rather than B, even though B can address 1005 offers, as A would take less time to query. The hitfactor is calculated by the following formula:

$$\text{HF} = \text{HF} + (\text{no\_of\_offers} \times e^{-\lambda \times n}),$$

where $\lambda$ is the arbitrary factor which determines the nature of the curve, and $n$ is the number of hops away. When new offers are added to a trader, HF for that particular service in a local trader increments by no\_of\_offers, since for a local trader, $n = 0$. So, the factor no\_of\_offers $\times e^{-\lambda \times n} = $ no\_of\_offers $\times 1$. For a remote trader, HF for that particular service is added to by a factor of no\_of\_offers $\times e^{-\lambda \times n}$, where $n \geq 1$.

Let us consider the example of Figure 8.7. Assume that we have 100 exporters exporting 100 services of type $x$ to trader D. At the first stage, traders B and F receive this update information and increment their corresponding service hitfactor by $100 \times e^{-\lambda}$. Suppose, we take the factor $\lambda = 1$, then the value becomes $100 \times e^{-1} = 36.78794$. Hence, traders B and F increment their hit factor of type $x$ by 36.78794 in the appropriate tables. Trader B in turn, sends this information to A and trader F sends it to C and H. Traders A, C and H are two hops away from trader D. Thus, their corresponding hitfactors are incremented by $100 \times e^{-1 \times 2} = 13.53352$. This process continues until there are no other traders to pass on this update, or the trader decides not to propagate this update any further. If we look closely at the graph, trader A receives the update message from B and updates itself by incrementing HF by 13.53352. But trader C again informs trader A in the next stage and asks for an increment of HF by $100 \times e^{-1 \times 3} = 4.978706$. Hence, two updates have taken place for the same transaction. This leads to inconsistent HF tables, which is not acceptable. To avoid this, a *transactionId* which is unique in a trader federation is used.

When an STR gets updated due to the addition or deletion of services, all other traders which hold information relating to this trader have to update themselves to reflect the change in the repository. The trader broadcasts this information to the federated traders, which update themselves recursively. Due to the presence of cycles, a trader may undergo an update twice as demonstrated above. To overcome this problem, each trader, before broadcasting, generates a unique transactionId to represent this change. When this update message is passed on to the remote traders in the federation, traders who have already processed the update message will have stored this transactionId. When the remote trader is asked to process an update, it first compares the update transactionId with the ones that have been stored in its repository (i.e., those which have already been processed or seen). If there is a match, the trader just ignores it, otherwise it makes the change. When the remote trader processes the update, it stores the transactionId in its database to avoid future inconsistencies.

## 8.6 TOS IMPLEMENTATIONS

There are several implementations of the CORBA Trading Object Service [7, 112, 9]. [7] built a trader on top of the CORBA Naming Service. Traders were implemented by using the X.500 protocol as a database to store and search for information about service offers [112]. [9] added a service locator which incorporated DCE cell and X.500 functionality for the retrieval of resource access information given the resource name.

A number of trader prototypes have been implemented for the DCE platform by [68] [8]. DCE functions already available are unsatisfactory and lack important mechanisms, such as type management, to support service management and mediation in open distributed environments.

Although the TOS specification was not released until mid 1996, a few CORBA-compliant traders have been implemented by various commercial vendors, including IONA (for OrbixTrader), DSTC (for Object Trader), Nortel (for RCP-ORB), Suite Software (for SuiteValet), ICL (for DAIS), and Mark Spruiell (for JTrader). Several prototypes were developed by academic institutions, including TAO Trader (Washington University), and DOK Trader (RMIT University).

### 8.6.1 JTrader

JTrader creates a service type list that it will consider when matching service offers. It checks whether the importer looks for an exact type match. If it does, then the initial request service type is the only service type in the search type list. If an exact type match is not specified, it will find all the compatible service types and add them to the search type list. JTrader defines compatible service types as the initial request service type and all of its subtypes. It does so by examining the super types of all the service types in the service type repository. If the service type being examined is a subtype of the initial request type, it is added to the search type list.

The trader then goes through each element in the search type list. It finds all of the service offers that match the service type and puts them into a potential service offer list. The trader goes through the search type list again to search for proxy offers that match the request service and adds the returned service offers to the potential list. The trader takes the search_card value into consideration while searching for matched services. The search_card defines the amount of service offers a trader should search in order to find matching services. After it gets all of the potential offers, the trader matches the offers with the constraint and puts the results into a matched service list. It checks with the match_card value to make sure that it does not match more offers than the match_card specified. The items in this list are put in the returned lists in the user's preferred order.

JTrader is not fully compliant with the OMG trader in the sense that it does not check for the starting_trader policy value. If the importer provides a value for this policy, the trader is obligated to forward the request to the target trader. The argument for not implementing this policy is that JTrader does not support the Link interface which provides functions for a trader to interact with other traders in a trader federation. However, the OMG trader lists the starting_trader as one of the "standard" scoping policies and a trader does not need to support the Link interface to forward a request to the target trader. The target trader object reference is provided as a policy value and the trader does not need to know about the target trader. One of the reasons for having a trader forward a query to a second trader is because the importer does not have the right to access the target trader but the initial trader does. The importer can ask the initial trader to make a query on the target trader in order to gain access to services available in the target trader.

### 8.6.2 TAO Trader

The TAO Trader first checks whether the query has specified a starting_trader policy. It forwards the query to the target trader if a trader reference is provided. Because the TAO Trader also supports the Link interface, it checks whether a federated query is returned to it. The TAO Trader's matching process is different from JTrader. It finds all the offers that match the request service type and then iterates through the offers to match them with the constraints of the query. If the offer matches the constraint, it is added to the matched offers list in the order preferred by the importer. The search_card and match_card values are evaluated during the matching process.

The trader proceeds to search for compatible service types if the importer does not specify an exact type match. The efficiency of the trader can be improved if the trader checks whether it has reached the search_card and match_card limits before it retrieves all of the subtypes and checks for matched services. Subtype searching is more efficient in the TOA Trader due to the use of an incarnation number. The service type repository generates an incarnation number for every new service type. It is impossible to have a subtype that has a larger incarnation number than its super type since the incarnation number is generated in ascending order. In this case, the trader only checks for service types that have a larger incarnation number than the request type.

Unlike the JTrader's implementation, the TAO Trader performs a search for offers of a type once it discovers it is a subtype of the request service type. The result is added to the matched list in the user preferred order and the trader checks the next service type until it reaches the search_card or match_card limits, or it has examined all of the service types in the repository. The matched offers are then returned to the user in the specified format.

### 8.6.3  DOK Trader

The DOK-Trader [23, 103] implements all of the CORBA TOS's interface, with a special emphasis on performance and scalability. Two main issues were addressed: clustering and routing. The routing approach [103] was partially described in Section 8.5.2. Here we summarizse the clustering approach for service offers [23] within a trader's STRs.

The clustering of service offers is performed within a hierarchy of contexts by specialization of property sets. It provides a meaningful clustering scheme, centered on semantics, rather than schematics. The basis of the scheme is to cluster services on their properties, which give service offers their semantics. Service offers which have similar properties, irrespective of service type, are related by being clustered into one or more contexts. Each context has associated to it a set of properties. Each member of a context is said to share the set of properties of that context.

The two offers share one or more properties, then they can be viewed in a similar context. This is the reasoning behind the notion of context, and is the basis of the clustering technique. Each context has a set of (i.e., zero or more) offer property objects bound to them. A context contains a cluster which holds service offers pertaining to the context. The following rule is the basis of the clustering technique: all the offer objects bound to a context must contain a property set which is equal to, or a super-set of, the property set that the context holds. Contexts are related in a hierarchical manner, called a *specialization graph*. The term specialization is used because the more properties that are bound to a context, the more specialized, or detailed are the offers that are members of it. Figure 8.9 shows an example context structure. For the purpose of simplicity, property object references are denoted as: $p_1$, $p_2$, and so forth.

The clustering algorithm attempts to make service offers members of the most specialized contexts possible. The algorithm works by pushing the offer down the levels of the graph until it cannot be pushed any further (i.e., the offer cannot become a member of any sub-contexts). Offers only exist in the lowest, most specialized, context possible.

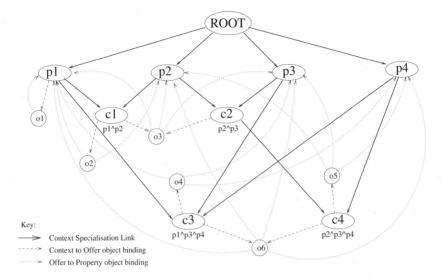

**Figure 8.9**    An example context.

*Clustering.*    When a new offer is bound to a cluster, it triggers a procedure that checks all of the offers for property commonalities, apart from the properties of its context. If a number of those offers have some properties in common, other than the properties of that context, then a specialized context can be created for those common offers. This new context becomes a specialization of the context that was checked. This type of specialization is controlled by the specialization threshold. Specializations are created when the number of services in common within a cluster exceeds this value. The specialization threshold value needs to be adjusted in order to optimize performance. If set too high, it will result in large clusters. If set too low, it will result in a large specialization graph. Ultimately, it has be tuned to the specific needs of the trader.

*Specialization graph re-structuring.*    When a new context is created, it must be linked in to the existing graph in a way that allows it to be accessed through any of its properties. To elaborate, a cluster inherits its super-context's properties plus has its own additional properties. The new context can be accessed via the link to the context that created it, and also needs to be linked to the properties it does not inherit. During re-structuring, the graph must be searched in order to find the appropriate context(s) to link to. This can be done as cheaply as finding a context to add a service offer to. There are some special cases where a new context needs to be linked between two pre-existing contexts (i.e., it becomes a specialization of one context and a generalization of another). Fig. 8.10 shows an example of graph restructuring. It also shows that there is a link that becomes redundant and is destroyed.

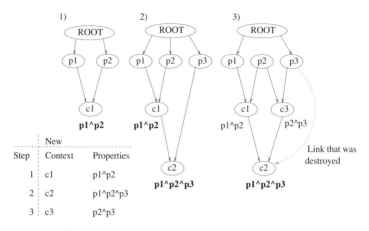

**Figure 8.10**    Restructuring a specialization graph.


## 8.7  SUMMARY

A Naming Service provides appropriate functions for locating objects within distributed environments. This is done by using (useful) names that are known by the users. The functions of such a service are important; however, they are not sufficient because users may not know or may not remember all of the names of objects, especially in large scale distributed applications. She/he may only know certain attributes (or properties) of such objects. Using the functions of a Trading Service, users can find such objects based on the values of certain properties attached to these objects. Such values are not stored by objects within servers. They are like meta-data that characterize the internal structure and data of objects. The values of properties are managed by the type repository of the Trading Service.

The Trading Service does not replace the Naming Service. These services have complementary roles within distributed environments, and in particular, within CORBA environments. Depending on what functionalities the users are looking for, these two services can be used either separately or in combination.

In this chapter, we started with a description of the role of the Trading Service in distributed systems. We then explained the differences between the ODP and OMG views with regard to the trading architecture and functions. To better understand some of the basic ideas of the OMG Trading Service, we preferred to give first an example with a specific Trading Service (JTrader) and later go into details in the description of the different components of the OMG Trader. JTrader was one of the first CORBA-compliant Trading Services, and several extensions were proposed later on to deal with specific issues of service trading, such as performance and semantic issues of offers.

Details of the OMG Trading Service were provided, including (i) the architecture and (ii) the constraints and policies, and (ii) the query propagation. We showed how a CORBA trader statically routes queries to its neighbors by using information they have (e.g., max_hop_count), as well as the information related to queries (e.g., query hop_count). We explained how such a routing mechanism has a few limitations when dealing with dynamic environments. We then proposed an extension of the OMG routing approach to deal with the dynamic information contained within traders of trading graphs.

In the last section of this chapter three different implementations of the OMG Trading Service were described: JTrader, TAO's trader and DOK-Trader. All of these traders are CORBA compliant in the sense that they support the OMG specification. However, they differ in their implementation of such specification. The first trader supports the basic functions of the OMG service, the second provides an extension of the service to deal with QoS features (such as realtime), and the last trader deals with performance and scalability issues of the OMG Trading Service.

## 8.8 REVIEW QUESTIONS

- What is the general function of a trading service? Why must the trader have sufficient details of an offer in order to store the service in the type repository?
- What does the term exporting in a trading service mean? What are the assertions made by the server when exporting a service?
- What does the term importing in a trading service mean? What are the details made along with a service request when importing a service?
- Explain the trader approaches in relation to the returned service offers and persistency.
- Why are some ODP trading specifications inappropriate to use in the context of CORBA? What are the two main considerations about the OMG trader's functionalities? What do they imply? Explain the key differences in the trader operations of ODP and OMG Trading Service.
- What are the five interfaces specified in the TOS specification? What does each of them do?
- Explain briefly about "importer policies" in OMG Trader Service.
- Explain briefly about "scoping policies" in OMG Trader Service.
- Must all of five interfaces specified in the OMG Trading Service be implemented by a trader implementation? Justify your answer. *Hint*: Relate the justification with the different combinations of interfaces which are implemented by traders.
- Briefly explain Service Type Repository including the operations in its interface.

## 8.9 EXERCISES

- Provide the IDL service specification and the code fragment for exporting a Bank object to a service called BankingService. The object has the following

IDL interface:

```
interface Bank {
    readonly attribute string name;
    readonly attribute float interest;
    attribute float    monthly_charge;
};
```

The Bank interface is implemented by BankImpl class with all of its attributes are being mandatory. Its interest attribute is a dynamic property whose value is provided by the function evaluator of a class called interestEvaluator. Assume no Bank object has ever been exported before and no super type exists in the BankService. *Hint*: The code fragments in this chapter should provide sufficient detail for this task.

- Provide a code fragment to import all the Bank objects with the following conditions: their interest attributes must be greater than 0.1, preference must be first, exact_type_match must be set to FALSE, and only ten offers should be returned. The code fragment must also check if there is at least one offer returned, otherwise it should display a message and exit. Hint: the code fragments in this chapter should provide sufficient detail for this task.

- Describe briefly how trading service can be applied to the area of e-commerce.

# CHAPTER 9

# Event Service

This chapter provides an insight into the CORBA Event Service, including a description of its components, a way of implementing them for an object request broker, and finally the list of problems which can be encountered in the design of such a service. This chapter may help readers not only understand the details of the CORBA event channel, but also grasp the technical issues related to the implementation of the event channel in the context of object-request brokers.

This chapter describes the core CORBA specifications of the event channel and presents a high level view of its basic architecture along with the many benefits of CORBA. The CORBA Event Service is discussed in Section 9.1. Section 9.2 reviews some of the existing approaches based on the Push and Pull models. Section 9.3 provides details of the architecture of the CORBA event channel, and Sections 9.4 and 9.5 go in depth in the discussion about the untyped and respectively typed event channels. Section 9.6 provides an analysis of the existing CORBA Event Service. Section 9.7 finally discusses some of the required extensions needed by the CORBA Event Service to deal with different QoS issues.

## 9.1  OVERALL PICTURE

An event service allows components to dynamically register or unregister their interest in specific events. The service defines a well known object called an *event channel* that collects and distributes events among components that know nothing about each other. Subscribers connected to the event channel receive the events asynchronously. The uses of the event service are many and any communication between objects that fits into the Publish/Subscribe pattern can make use of the event service. In this model of distribution, inserting the event channel as a third party between the client and server provides a high degree of decoupling.

In an event service, there are both suppliers and consumers of information. The event channel does the actual de-coupling between suppliers and consumers. It consumes events from the suppliers and supplies events to the consumers. The mode of communication can be one to one, one to many or many to many. The important aspect is that all events received from suppliers are broadcast to all consumers for specific event channels, called untyped channels. For the typed event channels, the principle is the same but only relevant to the suppliers and consumers that are interested in a particular IDL interface. Furthermore, multiple event channels are supported working independently of each other. An event is defined as any piece of data that has been generated as a result of some activity.

The OMG event channel communication is based on the Publish/Subscribe paradigm and may be achieved by using any of the following three communication technologies [101]: *unicasting*, *broadcasting*, and *multicasting*. Unicasting is a point-to-point method, which is a communication that links two processes. An example of a unicast protocol is the TCP/IP stack. Broadcasting is a method of communication that allows one process to send messages to all other processes on the network. Multicasting allows one process to selectively send a message to be delivered to a select group of processes that form the active group. CORBA shields the programmer from interfacing with these lower level facilities by higher level protocols such as IIOP.

There are several examples relating to the practical use of an event service. Some of these examples are from the aviation industry (e.g., Boeing [13]) and digital libraries. In the context of the aviation industry, an avionic generally has a logical and a physical device. Certain groups of devices are distributable, others are not. Some are active, some are passive. The software is run by events generated by the various controllers and components. The avionics infrastructure can benefit from the use of CORBA, and in particular, of the Event Service. Event-based execution is the way control flow happens. The idea is to keep the event control and dependency knowledge within each of the components. The Event Service allows for the easy definition and addition of pluggable entities. This helps in reducing the number of entities and their inter-dependencies.

In the context of digital libraries [30], suppliers are the providers of documents. Hence the different kinds of electronic documents correspond to the more general term object in the model. Providers are typically scientific publishers. A scientist usually follows the publications in a few journals and conference proceedings, those that fit into his/her research area. He/she scans the table of contents of the new issue, reads a few abstracts and carefully studies one or two of them. This is exactly where an alerting service becomes useful and more and more publishers are offering such a service.

Yet another pattern of accessing scientific literature involves browsing in the local library, where, for example, some journal that is not read regularly is quickly scanned for papers of interest, with perhaps one read carefully. However, browsing in the vast number of electronic documents spread over thousands of servers is completely unreasonable. A profile is a filter predicate. In the context of digital libraries, this is a retrieval query executed periodically without explicit intervention by the user. Only the results are presented. Of course, a single user may define more than one profile. The event service decouples this process and allows several servers to communicate asynchronously with the clients via their profiles. The suppliers may push or pull their objects.

In several business activities which often evolve unpredictably and asynchronously, a model of a tightly coupled client and its server communication is not inadequate. The CORBA Event Service offers the ability to de-couple the clients and servers and provides an event-driven, connectionless communication. The event service roughly aims at transferring data between objects. An application can then send events to the event service and not worry about the recipients that would be interested in receiving the message. The event channel manages the registration of receivers and the delivery of the event to applications that are interested in receiving the event.

## Push and Pull Models

There are suppliers of information and consumers of information. The heart of OMG's Event Service is the event channel. Alone, the event channel is the consumer to the suppliers, and the supplier to the consumers. The event channel accepts connections from one or many suppliers, and one or many consumers. The key is that any event received from one of the suppliers is transmitted to every consumer. Furthermore, multiple event channels are supported working independently of each other. An event is defined as any piece of data that has been generated as a result of some activity. The event channel allows users to connect one or several suppliers with one or several consumers. Using the event channel means that we get a symmetric relationship between suppliers and consumers: It is possible, for example, to let the producer use the push model and the consumer use the Pull model on the same event channel.

The CORBA Event Service supports two models of operation—a Push model and a Pull model, which are described in detail in Section 9.2. Both models govern how suppliers communicate with an event channel, and how an event channel communicates with consumers. In a push model, a push supplier sends an event to the event channel by using a CORBA push operation. This is unsolicited, event-driven processing to the event channel. However, the event channel also supports a Pull model, acting as a client to the suppliers, polling the suppliers for information. Such pulling can be based on time intervals. On the consumer side, both Push and Pull models are supported by the specification.

The data communication itself is done through normal method calls, and there is a choice whether the producer initiates the transfer (the push model) or the consumer (the Pull model). Mainly intended for sending messages that announce events, this service is done either via generic push/pull method calls that can take the Any data type, or via the typed event channel on specific IDL interfaces.

## Untyped and Typed Channels

There are two models in the CORBA Event Service specification, the untyped and typed channels. These models will be detailed in Sections 9.4 and 9.5. In the untyped event channel, event data is delivered via the IDL Any type. Events are passed to all connected consumers. In the typed event channel, the callers can use an application-specific IDL interface for supplying and consuming events. This allows applications to overcome the limitation of sending untyped data over the event channel, thereby minimizing type errors. The supplier and consumer must have prior knowledge of the nature of the interface. The use of objects has become an accepted basis for distributed programming. Strongly typed interfaces enhance ease of programming, correctness, reusability and portability.

The untyped and typed event channels support the following delivery models: (i) the canonical Push model (where the supplier pushes events to the channel, which in turn pushes the events to the consumers), (ii) the canonical Pull model (where the event channel pulls the events from the supplier and in turn the consumers pull the events from the event channel), (iii) the hybrid Push/Pull model (where suppliers push events to the event channel but consumers pull events from the event channel), and (iv) the hybrid Pull/Push model (where the event channel pulls events from the suppliers but the event channel pushes the events to the consumers).

While there are several implementations of the CORBA Event Service (see Section 9.6), they all differ from the standard by providing a specialization for a particular requirement. There are some that provide real time performance, while others use multicast protocols for message delivery. The common thread is that they all deviate and extend the standard with proprietary enhancements. Also, there are no reference implementations of the typed event service.

This chapter goes beyond a description of the OMG specifications of the CORBA event channel. We propose a full description of the different aspects of the event channel and ideas about how such a channel can be implemented in existing CORBA platforms. A list of problems that a designer of a CORBA event channel may face when implementing such a system is discussed. For example, in the untyped channel, Orbix handles the type Any, when used as a parameter or as a return value from an operation, in a very peculiar manner. Parameters of type Any are marshalled and un-marshalled by the ORB's object adaptor. This creates a problem for the event channel because the marshalling/unmarshalling code (for the object type contained within the type Any) in the skeleton and/or stub, has to be statically linked into the event channel. This defeats the purpose of de-coupling the suppliers from the consumers. Also, the implementation of the type Any is ORB dependent. This hampers the interoperablity of omniORB2 and Orbix, a problem which can be overcome once Orbix implements the new OMG type *DynAny*; omniORB2 already does. For the typed event channel the CORBA-compliant operation $CORBA :: ORB :: create\_operation\_list()$ is not supported by several systems (e.g., Orbix2.3MT), and this operation is critical to the typed event channel as it allows for dynamically determining the operation parameter modes and types. It is therefore useful for marshalling and unmarshalling of the incoming and outgoing requests.

## 9.2   PUSH AND PULL MODELS

This section looks at the Publish/Subscribe paradigm and existing work along with implementations of event communication based on this paradigm. Also, we briefly look at some of the uses of the Publish/Subscribe model in order to get a better understanding of the practical importance and requirements of the event channel real environments.

Distributed control in a network using computers has, in the past, employed polling by using fetch-execute feedback cycles:

```
while (true) do begin
  probe the environment;
  call event procedure;
end
```

Event-based programming, on the other hand, offers the benefit of notification instead of busy-probing. The program tells the environment to inform it when something happens, and when that something happens it reacts accordingly. A program can set up multiple event handlers to deal with different things happening independently. These event handlers can operate in different threads concurrently, which leads to a natural concurrent design. Also, the program does not waste cpu-cycles by busy-probing; therefore, the program itself is free to do other useful things. Event-based programming provides a simple model for component interaction that is useful for distributed control problems such as resource reservation and allocation.

The following are some of the aspects of the event-based model. (i) Events are represented as a hierarchy of classes. (ii) Event delivery uses the Publish/Subscribe paradigm, with the potential of using adapters as proxies. Publishers announce events, and Subscribers receive event notification. (iii) Event listeners register with one or more Publishers or proxies to receive events from them. (iv) Event publishers each maintain a list of subscribers. Events are sent to subscribers by calling an individual method on each subscriber. (v) Event proxies can behave as event Publishers or as event Subscribers as needed. They can even subscribe to other proxies and so on.

*Event proxies* are often employed as intermediary event subscribers that can reside between the actual event publishers and the event subscribers that actually want to act on the events generated. Proxies themselves can be chained compositionally, with the ability to set up customizable event-triggering networks. As proxies, adapters can be delegated one or more useful applications such as: (i) provide filtering events; (ii) provide aggregation of events, like a mailing list digest facility; (iii) provide the ability to forward and/or translate events; (iv) provide a persistence store and archive events; (v) provide security features such as maintaining access control to one or more subscribers; (vi) demultiplex multiple event sources to a single listener; (ix) offer default behavior for event listener methods; and (x) provide ordering capabilities, such as total ordering or causal ordering.

There have been efforts by other agencies and companies to standardize the Publish/Subscribe services, and some of the more important and successful efforts are outlined below. The Java Multicast Object Bus (iBus) is a middleware product from Softwired Inc[1]. It is a Java-based middleware product allowing Java applications and

---

[1] http://www.softwired.ch/

components to exchange arbitrary kinds of events or objects. The iBus is a piece of software that embodies the idea of a ubiquitous information medium using a channel abstraction similar to radio transmission. Applications tune into channels to send or receive data in near real time. The Generic Multicast Service (GTS) is useful for reliable group communication; it also offers a reliable order-preserving multicast. An event service based on GTS can harness the group communication and order preserving facilities of GTS. There is also an event service specification proposed for the Distributed Computing Environment (DCE) by the OpenGroup[2].

## iBus—The Java Multicast Object Bus

iBus[3] is pure Java; object bus middleware for the instant delivery of event objects via reliable IP multicast and TCP. iBus provides a Publication/Subscribe API and can be extended with new quality-of-service features. iBus provides the following communication features: multicast, point-to-point, non-blocking, blocking, request-reply and as well as coordination features such as failure-detection, tracking subscription/unsubscription and fault-tolerance.

Spontaneous networking is supported allowing applications to be written in a location independent way. iBus applications can be relocated from one machine to another without affecting their peer applications. The iBus architecture has no single point of failure, and there are no daemon applications that need to be present. iBus provides a quality of service framework in which applications only pay for services they need: programmers can request qualities of service such as reliable multicast, reliable point-to-point communication, channel membership notifications, message compression, and encrypted communication. The iBus protocol composition framework allows programmers to extend iBus with as yet unsupported communication protocols and qualities of service.

The QoS features such as reliable multicast, unreliable multicast, and encryption are implemented as Java classes. A quality of service is expressed as a list of protocol objects. The core of the iBus is a channel; the main job of the channel is to administer the producer and consumer objects. Like the CORBA Event Service channel, events pushed on to the channel are received by all connected consumers. An iBus is described by a URL. The URL encodes everything that is relevant to a channel, such as the communication protocol to be used, the QoS, the network address and a topic string describing the events on the channel. The protocol and QoS objects are linked as depicted in Figure 9.1. By specifying several channels and each demanding a different quality of service, suppliers and consumers may use multiple qualities of service simultaneously.

## 9.2.1  DCE Event Management Service (XEMS) [81]

The XEMS Preliminary Specification defines a common event model, together with a binding to DCE RPC, and a proposed binding to CORBA IDL. Their intention is

---

[2]http://www.opengroup.org/
[3]http://www.softwired.ch/

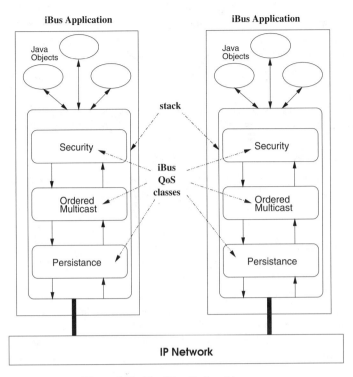

**Figure 9.1**    The iBus QoS architecture.

to make the XEMS compatible with the CORBA notification service. A preliminary
look at the XEMS gives the impression that it is very similar to the CORBA Event
Service; this is true only at a very superficial level. The XEMS differs widely from
the CORBA Event Service, and mainly the DCE XEMS has a good elaboration for
filtering and persistence in the specification and mandates policies by specifying
them in the event services manager. The characteristics of DCE XEMS are:

- XEMS involves two or more channels, centralizing the functionality associated
  with reliable delivery.
- XEMS includes filtering mechanisms. The interface to suppliers ensures that
  only suppliers that are authorized to insert events are allowed. On the side of
  the client the filters are based on event type and and the criteria for receiving an
  event. Clients can only receive events for which they are authorized.
- XEMS provides persistence, so that events that are not delivered to consumers
  are stored in an events repository. A consumer may act as a proxy for a centralized logging facility.

- Filters are akin to the select statement in SQL and ODMG queries. An event will be passed to the consumers only if it passes all the criteria specified in the filter that were registered by the client.
- The consumer/supplier registry also maintains state information about active consumers and suppliers.
- Consumers may disconnect without losing events as events will still be collected for the consumers and passed on when the consumer reconnects at a later time.
- The schema repository contains information for typed events.
- The event services manager is responsible for managing the activities of the event service.

## 9.3   ARCHITECTURE

This section is specifically dedicated to the CORBA Event Service. It provides a high-level description of this service.

The CORBA event channel plays the role of a mediator between the suppliers and consumers. There are two roles defined for objects in the event service: objects that produce data are suppliers and objects that process the event data are consumers. Standard CORBA requests are used to communicate data between the suppliers and consumers. There are two orthogonal approaches to initiating event communication between the suppliers and consumers. They are the Push model and the Pull model as depicted in Figure 9.2. The Push model allows a supplier of events to initiate the transfer of event data; the Pull model allows the consumer of events to request the event data from the supplier.

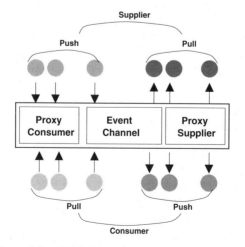

**Figure 9.2**   CORBA event service: A high-level view.

The communication of events can be either generic by means of the *push* or *pull* operations or it can be typed via operations defined in OMG IDL. The event data to be passed can be defined in any manner desired and is passed by means of parameters. The event channel allows for multiple suppliers to communicate with multiple consumers asynchronously. The channel is both a consumer and supplier of events. It manages the object references to supplier and consumers, and it also acts as a proxy consumer to the real suppliers and as a proxy supplier to the real consumers. For more advanced architectures, channels can serve also serve as a replicator, broadcaster and multicaster that forward events from one or more suppliers to one or more consumers. However, any event channel must be capable of supporting all four models and their combinations, of event receiving and dispatching.

There are four types of event communication models: the *push model* (which involves the interfaces PushConsumer and PushSupplier), the *pull model* (which supports the interfaces PullConsumer and PullSupplier), the *hybrid push/pull model* and the *hybrid pull/push model*. The event channel object is responsible for managing the communication of events from the suppliers to the consumers; it does this through proxies. All four event models follow the same connection and disconnection protocols. The IDL of the basic event channel interface is provided below.

```
module CosEventComm {
  exception Disconnected { };
  interface PushConsumer {
    void push (in any data) raises(Disconnected);
    void disconnect_push_consumer();
  };
  interface PushSupplier {
    void disconnect_push_supplier();
  };
  interface PullSupplier {
    any pull() raises(Disconnected);
    any try_pull (out boolean has_event) raises(Disconnected);
    void disconnect_pull_supplier();
  };
  interface PullConsumer {
    void disconnect_pull_consumer();
  };
};
```

## Canonical Push Model

In this model, the suppliers push events to the event channel proxy push-consumers. The event channel proxy push-suppliers, in turn, push the events to the connected consumers via the *push*() operation (see Figure 9.3).

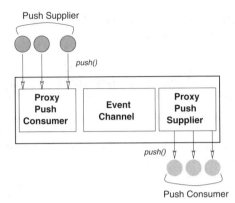

**Figure 9.3** The canonical push model.

### 9.3.1 Canonical Pull Model

In this model, the event channel proxy pull-consumers, pull events from the connected pull-suppliers. The proxy pull-suppliers, in turn, let the connected pull-consumers, pull events via the *pull*() and *try_pull*() methods (see Figure 9.4).

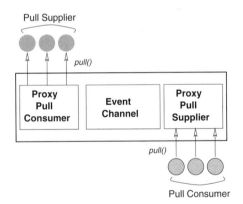

**Figure 9.4** The canonical pull model.

### Hybrid Push/Pull Model

In the Hybrid Push/Pull Model, the connected suppliers push events on to the proxy push-consumers in the event channel object. The proxy pull-supplier objects, in turn, let the connected pull-consumers, pull events via the *pull*() and *try_pull*() methods (see Figure 9.5).

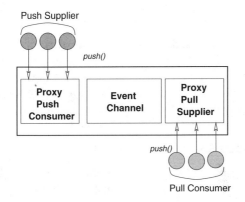

**Figure 9.5**    The hybrid push/pull model.

## Hybrid Pull/Push Model

In the Hybrid Pull/Push Model, the event channel proxy pull-consumers pull events from the connected pull-suppliers. The event channel proxy push suppliers, in turn, push the events to the connected consumers via the *push*() method (see Figure 9.6).

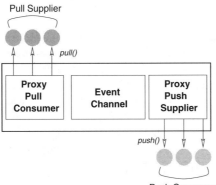

**Figure 9.6**    The hybrid pull/push model.

## 9.4 UNTYPED EVENT CHANNEL

### 9.4.1 Design Aspects

The core of the event channel for both the typed and untyped event channel follow the same connection, administration and disconnection procedure. The IDL syntax for the untyped event channel is listed In this section, and we will explain the purpose of the various interfaces and the related issues.

## Channel Creation

The event service specification does not mandate a policy for the event channel creation, nor does it explicitly advocate a supplier or consumer connection policy to an instance of the event channel. Suppliers and consumers are free to connect to any event channel once they have an object reference to an event channel object. The creation of objects within the event channel is based on the factory pattern [44].

## Channel Administration

There is a single instance of each of the consumer and supplier administration objects. As show in the IDL of the Event Channel, the administration interface within the channel is used to get the object references to the proxy supplier and consumer objects which will receive and dispatch events. The event service specification does not specify an explicit interface for the creation of channels but does provide for an operation $CosEventChannelAdmin :: EventChannel :: destroy()$ to terminate a channel.

```
interface EventChannel {
   ConsumerAdmin for_consumers();
   SupplierAdmin for_suppliers();
   void destroy();
};
```

There are two types of administration interfaces, one for supplier administration and another for consumer administration. The administration objects perform two major functions: first the actual creation and deletion of the proxy objects, and second, assisting in the management of the events. For the consumer proxies, the supplier administration object provides a backward reference to the central event channel event queue on to which the proxy consumers push the arriving events. In the case of the supplier proxies, the event channel object pulls an event from its central event queue. Then it requests the consumer administration object to broadcast it to the individual proxy supplier queues.

```
interface ConsumerAdmin {
   ProxyPushSupplier obtain_push_supplier();
   ProxyPullSupplier obtain_pull_supplier();
};
interface SupplierAdmin {
   ProxyPushConsumer obtain_push_consumer();
   ProxyPullConsumer obtain_pull_consumer();
};
interface ProxyPushConsumer: CosEventComm::PushConsumer {
   void connect_push_supplier(
         in CosEventComm::PushSupplier push_supplier)
      raises(AlreadyConnected);
};
```

```
interface ProxyPullSupplier: CosEventComm::PullSupplier {
  void connect_pull_consumer(
        in CosEventComm::PullConsumer pull_consumer)
     raises(AlreadyConnected);
};
interface ProxyPullConsumer: CosEventComm::PullConsumer {
  void connect_pull_supplier(
        in CosEventComm::PullSupplier pull_supplier)
     raises(AlreadyConnected, TypeError);
}
interface ProxyPushSupplier: CosEventComm::PushSupplier {
  void connect_push_consumer(
        in CosEventComm::PushConsumer push_consumer)
     raises(AlreadyConnected, TypeError);
};
```

Below is a description of the methods present in the individual administration object interfaces.

- *Supplier Administration.* All supplier administration within the channel is done via the CosEventChannelAdmin::SupplierAdmin interface. Suppliers can obtain the proxy consumer object references via this interface. The push-suppliers will obtain the reference from *CosEventChannelAdmin* :: *SupplierAdmin* :: *obtain_push_consumer*() and the pull-suppliers will obtain the reference from the *CosEventChannelAdmin* :: *SupplierAdmin* :: *obtain_pull_consumer*().

- *Consumer Administration.* All consumer administration within the channel is done via the CosEventChannelAdmin::ConsumerAdmin interface. Consumers can obtain the proxy supplier object references via this interface. The push-suppliers will obtain the reference from *CosEventChannelAdmin* :: *ConsumerAdmin* :: *obtain_push_supplier*() and the push-consumers will obtain the reference from the *CosEventChannelAdmin* :: *ConsumerAdmin* :: *obtain_pull_supplier*().

### Connection of Suppliers and Consumers

In order to connect to the proxy objects the suppliers and consumers, both call the relevant connect operation on the proxy interface that was obtained from the administration object. For example, the PushSupplier object connects to the ProxyPushConsumer object via the *connect_push_supplier*() operation, passing a reference to itself. The PullConsumer object connects to the ProxyPullSuplier object via the *connect_pull_consumer*() operation. If the proxy objects already have suppliers and consumers connected they raise the AlreadyConnected exception. Even though the proxy objects are created by the administration objects, the proxies are activated only after the suppliers and consumers perform a connect operation. If a PushSupplier calls the ProxyPushConsumer push operation without connecting first, the ProxyPushConsumer throws a Disconnected exception. The situation is similar for the ProxyPullSupplier object *pull*() and *try_pull*() operations.

## Disconnection of Suppliers and Consumers

Here again the event service specification is vague on the specifics and there is no mandatory policy. The suppliers and consumers are free to disconnect at any time. The channel object may also disconnect any of the suppliers or consumers arbitrarily. The policy followed in this design is to let the suppliers and consumers decide when to disconnect. The event channel object will not initiate a disconnect, except when it is itself explicitly destroyed.

### 9.4.2   Implementation Aspects

A multi-threaded model will be useful for the implementation of the event channel because it makes for better throughput, but on the down side it does lead to more programming complexity. In order to coordinate the various activities of a concurrent design, the use of different control and locking mechanisms, such as mutexes and semaphores, can be useful. The management of connected suppliers and consumers, the storage and dispatching of events all require different appropriate data structures which are discussed below. As new events arrive and are dispatched, the event management issues that can be raised are:

- *Thread Model.* Since multiple suppliers and consumers may connect to an event channel object, each supply or consume events asynchronously. A multi-threaded model can be chosen for the event channel. The thread model for the untyped event channel is the thread per object model which is the active object pattern [61].

  For every supplier and consumer that connects a separate thread is started to service the connection. The event channel object itself runs in a separate thread. This thread is responsible for broadcasting the events to the connected consumers. The memory management of the events is handled by a separate thread. This thread is associated with the ConsumerAdmin object. It monitors the events that are broadcast and deletes the associated data structures and objects, once they have been successfully broadcast to all connected consumers. From the implementation point of view, the thread per object model in Orbix can be implemented by inheriting from the CORBA::ThreadFilter class [5]. This derived class sits between the incoming requests before they are unmarshalled and dispatched to the target object on the server.

- *Dead Lock Prevention.* There are several situations where a deadlock can occur because of the multithreaded design of the event channel: for instance, if an incoming request comes in from a supplier/consumer to disconnect, while the channel is "blocked" on the request portion (push/pull) of an invocation from the same supplier/consumer. The causes of potential deadlocks can be when a consumer/supplier is added/ deleted, an event is added/broadcast, or during garbage collection of events. (i) When suppliers and consumers are added to the SupplierAdmin object or the ConsumerAdmin object, access to the data structures, needs to be synchronized and regulated via semaphores and mutexes. (ii) For the addition/broadcast of events, as events arrive from the suppliers, the addition to the central event queue, has to be synchronized via semaphores as there may be a conflict, since the queue data structure holding the events is monitored and accessed by different threads. These threads are the supplier objects thread, channel event broadcast thread and the garbage-collection thread. (iii) For the garbage collection of event objects, there is a garbage collection thread associated with every channel object. All events are monitored by the garbage-collection thread, and when their reference count reaches zero, the objects are disposed of and the associated memory freed.

- *Data Structures.* All the events can be stored in FIFO queue data structures, and the connected suppliers and consumers are stored in an Array type of data structures. There will be no ordering of events within the event channel except FIFO; Therefore, a queue can be suitable data structure for storing and retrieving events. The Standard Template Library (STL) [97] can be used for the common data structure representations such as hash_map, queue and lists.

- *Memory Management.* When an event arrives from a supplier, only a single instance of the event object is maintained; a reference is passed from the supplier to the central event channel object. The central event channel object broadcasts the event. During the broadcasting operation the event channel object increments the reference count of the event, for every connected consumer. It then puts the event on the garbage-collection queue and the proxy supplier event queue. The proxy suppliers all have their own independent event queues. These queues are maintained by the proxy supplier object. Every time an event is successfully passed to a consumer, the proxy supplier object reduces the reference count of the event and removes it from its event queue. The garbage-collection thread monitors the garbage-collection queue at fixed time intervals. Those events that have a reference count of zero are deleted and the resources reclaimed.

## Supplier Interface

Supplier objects that connect to the event channel are managed by the SupplierAdmin object. The proxy consumer objects add the events received from the supplier objects, to the global event queue, that is, maintained in the EventChannel object. The global event queue is managed by the EvenChannel object and is a blocking queue data structure. If there are no consumers attached or the number of events in the queue crosses a hard-coded threshold value, then adding events to the queue will block the caller.

The supplier admin object also keeps track of the number of suppliers connected, as shown in Figure 9.7. The proxy consumer objects are created by SupplierAd-

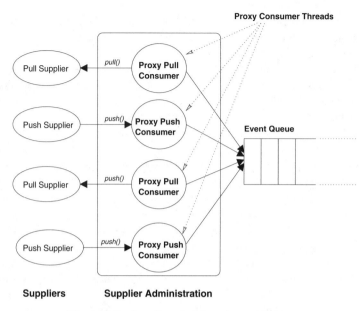

**Figure 9.7** Supplier administration architecture.

min when the suppliers request connection via the *obtain_push_supplier*() and *obtain_pull_supplier*() operations. The proxy consumer object is added to the collection. At the time of disconnection the supplier object informs the consumer object by calling the *disconnect_push_consumer*() and the *disconnect_pull_consumer*(), respectively. The consumer objects call the *remove*() operation in the SupplierAdmin object to inform it about the disconnection request. The supplier admin object then removes the disconnected supplier from its collection. The addition and removal of suppliers is coordinated by using semaphores and mutexes.

- *Pull Supplier Interface.* The Pull Supplier interface requires that the Pull Supplier first obtain the SupplierAdmin reference from the event channel object and then obtain a reference to the ProxyPullConsumer object. The Pull Supplier has to then connect to the ProxyPullConsumer object by passing its reference to the ProxyPullConsumer, so that it can then start to pull events from the Pull Supplier. The events pulled from the Pull Supplier are put on the central event queue, maintained by the event channel object, Figure 9.8.

- *Push Supplier Interface.* The Push Supplier interface requires that the Push Supplier first obtain the SupplierAdmin reference from the event channel object and then obtain a reference to the ProxyPushConsumer object. The Push Supplier has to then connect to the ProxyPushConsumer object by passing its reference to the ProxyPushConsumer. After the connection, the Push Supplier object can start pushing events to the ProxyPushConsumer object. The events received by

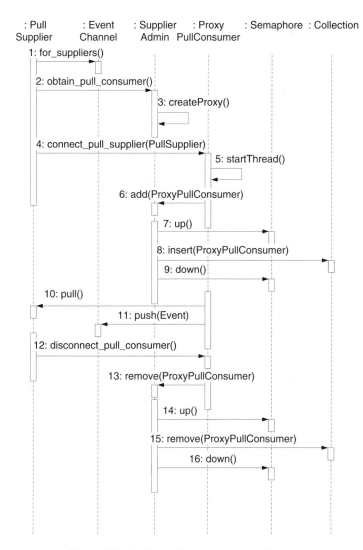

**Figure 9.8** Pull supplier message trace diagram.

the ProxyPushConsumer object are passed on to the central event queue maintained by the event channel object, Figure 9.9.

## Consumer Interface

The consumer objects that connect to the event channel are managed by the ConsumerAdmin object. The event channel object broadcasts the events received from the suppliers, to the ProxyConsumer objects, that are registered with the Con-

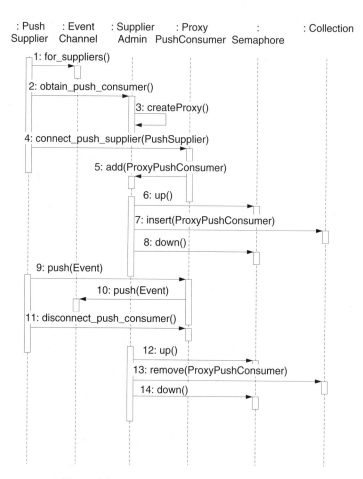

**Figure 9.9**  Push supplier message trace diagram.

sumerChannelAdmin object. The event queues in the proxy supplier objects are non-blocking. Therefore, any event received from the suppliers is guaranteed to be broadcast to the proxy supplier objects. After an event has been successfully passed to the consumer, the proxy supplier object reduces the reference count associated with the event. Broadcast events are not disposed of by the proxy suppliers but are managed by a garbage-collection thread.

As shown in Figure 9.10, the ConsumerAdmin object also keeps track of the number of consumers connected. The proxy supplier objects are created by the ConsumerAdmin object when the consumers request connection via the *obtain_push_consumer*() and *obtain_pull_consumer*() operations. The proxy supplier object is added to the collection. At the time of disconnection the consumer objects inform the supplier objects by calling the *disconnect_push_supplier*() and the *disconnect_pull_supplier*(), respectively. The supplier objects call the *remove*() operation in the ConsumerAdmin object to inform it about the disconnection request.

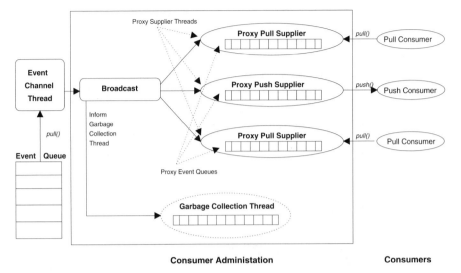

**Figure 9.10**    Consumer administration architecture.

The supplier admin object then removes the disconnected consumer from its collection. The addition and removal of consumers is coordinated by using semaphores and mutexes.

The proxy supplier objects can be in three states, DISCONNECTED, DISCONNECTING or CONNECTED. If the proxy supplier is in the state CONNECTED then a request to connect will throw an AleadyConnected exception.

- *Pull Consumer Interface.* The pull consumer interface requires that the pull consumer first obtain the ConsumerAdmin reference from the event channel object and then obtain a reference to the ProxyPullSupplier object. The pull consumer has to then connect to the ProxyPullSupplier object by passing its reference to the ProxyPullSupplier. After the connection the pull consumer object can start receiving events from the ProxyPullSupplier object. If there are no events pending in the ProxyPullSupplier queue, then the pull operation will block until an event is available, Figure 9.11.

  During the pulling of events from the proxy supplier the proxy pull supplier can be in any of the two states: WAITINGFOREVENT or EVENTREADY. It is necessary to keep track of these states in case a multithreaded pull consumer initiates a disconnect from the proxy pull supplier while another thread is blocked trying to pull events. In this situation the proxy pull supplier disconnect operation first informs the *pull*() operation of the disconnection request, by changing the state to DISCONNECTING. After the *pull*() operation aborts the request, it enters into the DISCONNECTED state.

- *Push Consumer Interface.* The push consumer interface requires that the push consumer first obtain the ConsumerAdmin reference from the event channel object and then obtain a reference to the ProxyPushSupplier object. The push con-

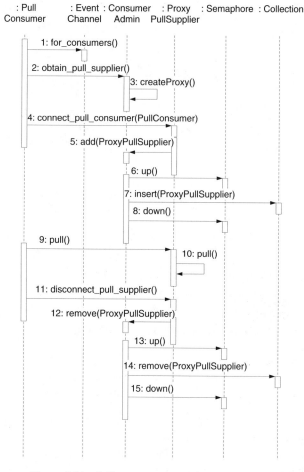

**Figure 9.11** Pull consumer message trace diagram.

sumer has to then connect to the ProxyPushSupplier object by passing its reference to the ProxyPushSupplier. After the connection, the push consumer object
can start receiving events from the ProxyPushSupplier object, Figure 9.12.

## Event Manager

The event channel object is responsible for queueing all incoming events and then
broadcasting them to the connected consumers via the proxy suppliers (see Figure 9.13). The event channel object upon creation starts a separate thread to handle
the broadcasting of events. Flow control is implemented using mutexes; the broadcast thread blocks waiting for consumers to connect. The event queue also has a

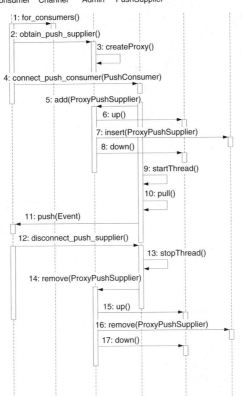

**Figure 9.12**    Push consumer message trace diagram.

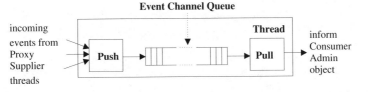

**Figure 9.13**    Event queue architecture.

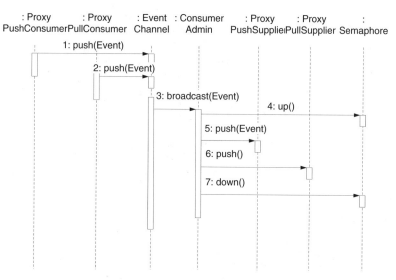

**Figure 9.14** Event manager message trace diagram.

configurable threshold value, specifying the number of events it will accept, before it will block suppliers that attempt to push incoming events (see Figure 9.14).

## 9.5 TYPED EVENT CHANNEL

### 9.5.1 Design Aspects

The creation of a typed channel is the same as an untyped channel. The administration issues are also the same. The communication of events does not use the type Any but is through IDL interfaces. This allows the applications to pass data that can be defined in the IDL interfaces, thus overcoming the shortcomings of using type Any to pass events. In order to facilitate the communication using the IDL interfaces the following interfaces are introduced in the OMG specification, Typed EventChannel,TypedConsumerAdmin, TypedSupplierAdmin, TypedPushConsumer, TypedPullSupplier, TypedProxyPushConsumer and TypedProxyPullSupplier. The IDL interfaces, for the Type event service are listed below.

```
module CosTypedEventComm {
  interface TypedPushConsumer : CosEventComm::PushConsumer {
    Object get_typed_consumer();
  };

  interface TypedPullSupplier : CosEventComm::PullSupplier {
    Object get_typed_supplier();
  };
```

```
};

module CosTypedEventChannelAdmin {
  exception InterfaceNotSupported { };
  exception NoSuchImplementation { };
  typedef string Key;
interface TypedProxyPushConsumer :
  CosEventChannelAdmin::ProxyPushConsumer,
  CosTypedEventComm::TypedPushConsumer { };
interface TypedProxyPullSupplier :
  CosEventChannelAdmin::ProxyPullSupplier,
  CosTypedEventComm::TypedPullSupplier { };
interface TypedSupplierAdmin : CosEventChannelAdmin::SupplierAdmin {
  TypedProxyPushConsumer obtain_typed_push_consumer(in
      Key supported_interface) raises(InterfaceNotSupported);
  CosEventChannelAdmin::ProxyPullConsumer
      obtain_typed_pull_consumer(in Key uses_interface)
        raises(NoSuchImplementation);
};
interface TypedConsumerAdmin: CosEventChannelAdmin::ConsumerAdmin {
  TypedProxyPullSupplier obtain_typed_pull_supplier(in
      Key supported_interface) raises(InterfaceNotSupported);
  CosEventChannelAdmin::ProxyPushSupplier
      obtain_typed_push_supplier(in Key uses_interface)
      raises(NoSuchImplementation);
 };
interface TypedEventChannel {
  TypedConsumerAdmin for_consumers();
  TypedSupplierAdmin for_suppliers();
  void destroy();
};
interface TypedFactory {
    TypedEventChannel create();
};
};
```

The benefit of using IDL interfaces is that it allows applications to decide on the data that is to be passed on each event. One of the obvious benefits is that it makes for better static type checking. The IDL interfaces are identified by a Key; this is a parameter of type string which uniquely identifies a particular IDL interface. The IDL interfaces are persistent within the Interface Repository. The Typed-SupplierAdmin and TypedConsumerAdmin objects obtain the IDL description from the Interface Repository server. This interface description is used to create a DSI (Dynamic Skeleton Interface) object in the case of the TypedProxyPullSupplier and TypedProxyPushConsumer. For the TypedProxyPushSupplier and the TypedProxy-PullConsumer a DII (Dynamic Invocation Interface) request is made by the created objects, Figure 9.15.

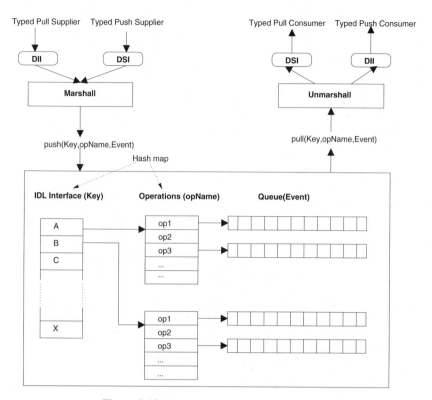

**Figure 9.15**   Typed event channel architecture.

The flow control issues are the same as for the untyped event channel. The difference is in the event management. Unlike the untyped channel the typed channel can accept events on multiple operations, for the same interface simultaneously. The same conditions apply for the broadcasting of events. The design therefore requires separate event queues for each operation defined in the IDL interface, for both the proxy consumers and proxy suppliers. All incoming events are marshalled into a generic data structure along with the type information that will be required for unmarshalling. This marshalled event is then pushed onto the central typed event channel interface operation queue. Like the untyped event channel the typed channel also uses the same technique to broadcast the events to the TypeProxySuppliers. The TypeProxySuppliers unmarshal the events before dispatching the events to the typed consumers. In order to maintain separate queues for the operations, the key that represents the IDL interface is used as the key for the hash table.

There are some important differences in the Typed Push and Typed Pull Models. The Pull model of communication is a little more complex than the Push model. This is because the server object from which the events have to be pulled must automatically modify the IDL interface and provide operations to pull events. The two operations are $pull\_op()$, which blocks if there are no events pending and $try\_op()$, which checks if there is an event pending and if not returns false, else true along with the pending event. For example if there is an Interface **I** then the new interface will be pull <I>.

```
Interface I {
  oneway op(in Object a);
};
```

is transformed to pull <I>:

```
Interface pull<I> {
  pull_op(out Object a);
  boolean try_op(out Object a);
};
```

There are also restrictions on the operation parameter passing modes. All operations must be one way; they need not be declared as such but should follow the semantics of one way operations. The parameter passing modes for the pull and try operations have to be the *out* mode only.

In the rest of this section, we will re-explain some the important steps of the DSI and DII, which were already covered at the beginning of this book. The DII and DSI mechanisms are important for implementing the typed event channel.

***DSI—Dynamic Skeleton Interface.***    Since the event channel cannot know in advance what interface the suppliers and consumers want to use for communication, the server objects to facilitate communication have to rely on the DSI mechanism rather than the normal static skeleton interface. All such dynamically created objects have to inherit from the CORBA::DynamicImplementation class and override its single method *invoke*(). The newly created object then has to be registered with the BOA or POA. In order to pass a reference to the object that is created dynamically, an IOR (Interoperatable Object Reference) is created which has the following format:

host:serverName:marker:IR_host:IR_server:interfaceMarker

where *serverName* is the server host name; *marker* the unique object marker within the type; *IR_host* is the IFR server host name; *IR_server* is the name of the IFR server ie. IFR; and *interfaceMarker* is the name of the IDL interface or Key.

***DII—Dynamic Invocation Interface.***    For TypedProxyPullSupplier and the TypedProxyPushConsumer objects that have to invoke operations on remote objects, the invocations requests have to be constructed dynamically from the IDL interface. The sequence of steps is: (i) Request object is constructed; (ii) the Request object is populated with the object reference, the name of the operation/attribute, and the parameters to the operation; and (iii) the request is invoked.

### 9.5.2 Implementation Aspects

The core design of the untyped and typed event channels is the same. The differences are noted below:

- *Thread Model.* The thread model is Thread per object [93]. A new thread is created for each instance of the proxy objects in the typed event channel.
- *Marshalling and Unmarshalling.* As the events are received on the different IDL interfaces registered with the typed event channel, the typed proxy consumers marshal the event parameters into a generic data structure along with the type information of the parameters for unmarshalling. The typed proxy suppliers unmarshal the events before dispatching to the connected consumers.
- *Data Structures.* The typed event channel can receive events for all the operations that may be present in the IDL interface. Therefore, separate queues have to be maintained for these separate operations. This necessitates the augmentation of the simple queue (FIFO) that is used in the untyped event channel. The typed event channel uses two hash map data structures to maintain the different queues. The first hash table maps to another hash table that is keyed on the operation names present in that particular IDL interface. Each value of the hash table points to the queue (FIFO) for that operation. So in order to push or pull events to and from the central queue, two parameters are required: first, the IDL interface Key and second, the operation name.

### Typed Supplier Interface

The typed Supplier objects that connect to the event channel are managed by the TypedSupplierAdmin interface. The typed proxy consumer objects add the events received from the typed supplier objects to the global typed event queue that is maintained in the EventChannel object. The incoming events are identified by the key and the operation name. Since the typed channel interfaces inherit from the untyped event channel Interfaces, the protocols for connection and disconnection are similar. For obtaining the object references two new interfaces and methods are introduced. The TypedPushConsumer interface has one method—get_typed_consumer(), which returns the reference to the DSI object.

- *Typed Pull Supplier Interface.* The typed pull supplier first obtains the proxy pull consumer object from the SupplierAdmin interface. The typed pull supplier passes the key as the parameter to identify the IDL interface it will support, after informing the event channel of the IDL interface the supplier will support. The supplier then connects to the proxy pull consumer by passing its object reference in a connect function call. The typed proxy consumer object first looks up the interface in the IFR, and upon a successful reference passes the key to the event channel for the purpose of storing events for the interface identified by the Key. The proxy consumer then starts a thread that makes DII calls on the Interface identified by the Key; after retrieving the events it marshals the events

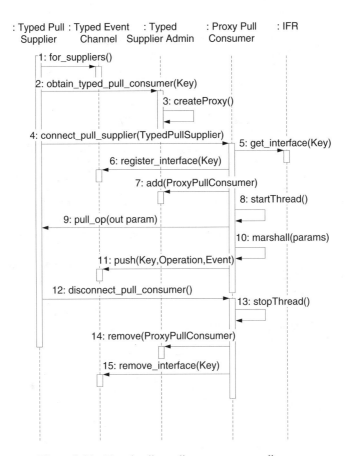

**Figure 9.16**    Typed pull supplier message trace diagram.

and pushes them onto the event queue that is maintained by the EventChannel object, Figure 9.16.

- *Typed Push Supplier Interface.* The typed push supplier first obtains the typed proxy push-consumer object from the the SupplierAdmin interface. The typed push supplier passes the key as the parameter to identify the IDL interface it will be pushing events on to. The supplier then obtains an object reference to the object that will accept events on the Interface identified by Key. The typed proxy push-consumer looks up the IDL interface in the IFR, then it creates a DSI object for the Interface, registers the key with the event channel and returns the newly created dynamic object reference that will accept a push request from the push-supplier. When it receives events from the push supplier the proxy push-consumer marshals the events and pushes them on to the event queue that is maintained by the event channel object, Figure 9.17.

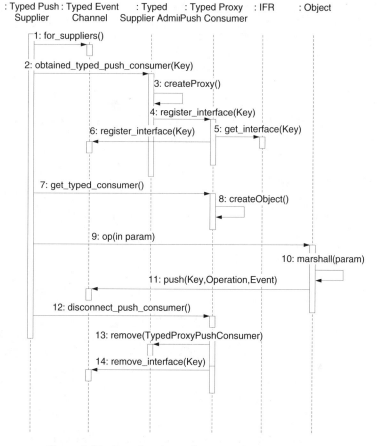

**Figure 9.17** Typed push supplier message trace diagram.

## Typed Consumer Interface

The typed supplier objects that connect to the event channel are managed by the TypedSupplierAdmin object. The typed proxy consumer objects add the events received from the typed supplier objects to the global typed event queue that is maintained in the EventChannel object. The incoming events are identified by the key and the operation name. Since the typed channel interfaces inherit from the untyped event channel Interfaces, the protocols for connection and disconnection are similar. For obtaining the object references, two new interfaces and methods are introduced. The TypedPullSupplier interface has one method—Object get_typed_supplier(), which returns the reference to the DSI object.

- *Typed Pull Consumer Interface.* The typed pull consumer first obtains the typed proxy pull-supplier object reference from the ConsumerAdmin interface. The typed pull consumer passes the key as the parameter to identify the IDL interface from where it will be pulling events. The consumer then obtains an object reference to the object that will supply events on the Interface identified by Key. The typed proxy pull-supplier looks up the IDL interface in the IFR, then it creates a DSI object for the Interface, registers the key with the event channel and returns the newly created dynamic object reference that will supply pull requests from the pull consumer. When a request for an event arrives the DSI server retrieves an event from its local event queue, unmarshals the event, converts all parameters to OUT parameters and returns the events to the pull consumer, Figure 9.18.

- *Typed Push Consumer Interface.* The typed push supplier first obtains the proxy push-supplier object reference from the ConsumerAdmin interface. The typed push consumer passes the key as the parameter to identify the IDL interface it will support, after informing the event channel of the IDL interface the consumer will support. The consumer then connects to the proxy push-supplier by passing its object reference in a connect function call. The typed proxy supplier object first looks up the interface in the IFR, and upon a successful reference

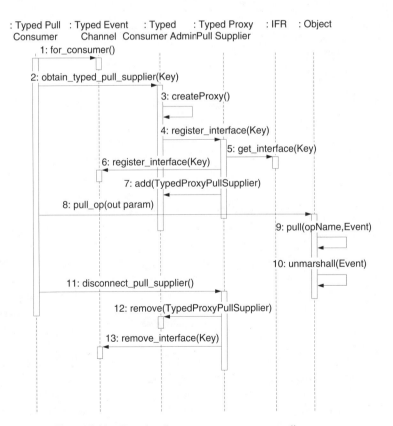

**Figure 9.18** Typed pull consumer message trace diagram.

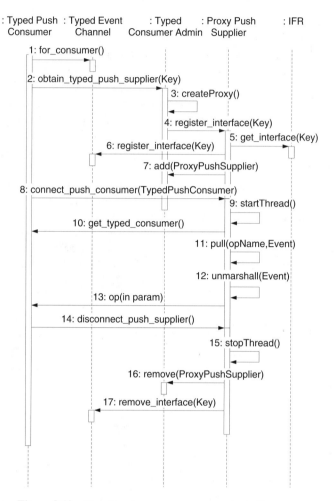

**Figure 9.19**  Typed push consumer message trace diagram.

passes the key to the event channel for the purpose of retrieving events for the Interface identified by the key. The proxy supplier then starts a thread that makes DII calls on the Interface identified by the key, and after retrieving the events from its local queue, it unmarshals the events and pushes them on to the typed push consumer. All the parameters are converted to IN parameters, Figure 9.19.

***Typed Event Manager.***   The typed event channel object is responsible for queueing all incoming events and then broadcasting them to the connected consumers via the DSI and DII Suppliers. The event channel object upon creation starts a separate thread to handle the broadcasting of events. Flow control is implemented by using

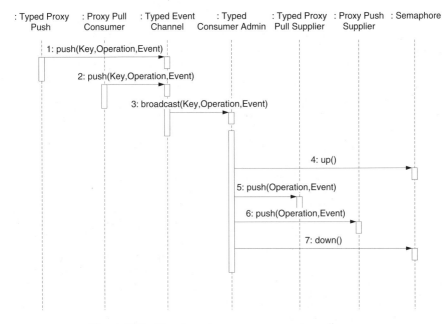

**Figure 9.20**    Typed event manager message trace diagram.

mutexes; the broadcast thread blocks waiting for consumers to connect. The event queues have a configurable threshold value, specifying the number of events they will accept before they will block suppliers that attempt to push incoming events on to the individual operation queues. For the typed event channel there is more than one queue for queueing the events. In fact, for every interface there is a hash_map that takes a string key as a parameter and this maps to another hash_map. The second hash_map is the hash table for the operations specified in the interface. For every operation the hash_map maps to a queue of events for that particular operation. Therefore, to access any event requires two indirect operations. The first mapping is based on the interface key and the second on the operation, as in Figure 9.20.

## 9.6  CORBA EVENT SERVICE IMPLEMENTATIONS

This section provides a description of some of the implementations of the CORBA Event Service within the following distributed object systems: OrbixTalk, TAO's event service, Electra, and CyberBus.

### 9.6.1  OrbixTalk

Iona's OrbixTalk implementation is similar in some respects to the event service specification. However, instead of using point-to-point communication, it uses IP Multicast, which is much more efficient and scalable. Using OrbixTalk, the world of applications is divided into talkers (publishers) and listeners (subscribers). OrbixTalk allows shared information to be organized into a hierarchical structure of topics, each of which is identified by an OrbixTalk topic name. In this way, an application can determine which information it is interested in and inform OrbixTalk by using the topic name. The application employs negative acknowledgments to make sure that a request is delivered to every object that has subscribed to it. However, it does not provide totally ordered multicast, not does it provide virtual synchrony. Also, requests can get lost under high load situations or when a receiver detects that it has missed a message after the sender has discarded that message from its internal message queue.

Talkers generate messages and listeners receive them. Consequently, any particular stream of messages is unidirectional, from one or more talkers to one or more listeners. If a listener wishes to, in some sense, "reply" to an message which it has received, it must either use a normal ORB invocation back to the talker, or establish a second stream of messages in the opposite direction to the first. Thus, a single message stream can simultaneously have more than one talker and more than one listener. In general, M talkers can issue messages via the same message stream to N listeners, without any of the talkers and listeners having explicit knowledge of each other. One of the advantages of this is that new talkers and listeners can be added easily. The talker does not have to maintain a list of listeners.

To understand the roles of talker and listener in terms of the client-server model, note that talkers generate messages, and listeners receive and act on these messages. Therefore, a talker is a client while a listener is a server. OrbixTalk architecture includes three parts, an OrbixTalk talker, an OrbixTalk listener and a Directory Enquiries Server. Briefly, a talker application wishes to talk on a topic. The OrbixTalk network first checks to see if the topic name has been translated to a Multicast address. If not, a request is sent to the Directory Enquiries Server requesting the IP Address for the topic name. The Directory Enquiries Server looks up the name and returns the IP Address of the IP Multicast group if it has it or allocates a new one if it does not. The talk message is then multicast to the group.

A listener application calls the OrbixTalk network to listen, passing it a topic name. Again, the OrbixTalk network performs the topic name translation as above. Messages arriving on this topic are passed to listeners listening on that topic.

### 9.6.2 TAOs Event Service

TAO's Event Service [91] is an attempt to augment the CORBA Event Service specification with some additional features, such as real-time event dispatching and scheduling, periodic event processing, and efficient event filtering and correlation mechanisms. It is part of the TAO system, which is a real-time ORB end system that provides end-to-end quality of service guarantees to applications by vertically integrating CORBA middleware with OS I/O subsystems, communication protocols, and network Interfaces [92].

The event service runs on real-time OS platforms (e.g, $V \times Works$ and Solaris 2.$\times$) that provide real-time scheduling guarantees to application threads. The TAO event channel is a specialized extension to the standard for a very specific application domain, such as avionics, telecommunications, process control, and distributed interactive simulation. Applications in these domains have very strict real-time requirements, which are implemented in the TAO ORB, and the event channel extensions make use of these real-time facilities.

- *Guarantees for real-time event dispatching and scheduling.* TAO extends the CORBA Event Service interfaces by allowing consumers and suppliers to specify their execution requirements and characteristics. These parameters are used by the channel's dispatching mechanism to integrate with the system-wide real-time scheduling policy to determine event dispatch ordering and preemption strategies.
- *Specification for centralized event filtering and correlation.* TAO's Event Service provides filtering and correlation mechanisms that allow consumers to specify logical OR and AND event dependencies. When those dependencies are met, the event service dispatches all events that satisfy the consumers' dependencies.
- *Support for periodic processing.* TAO's Event Service allows consumers to specify event dependency timeouts. It uses these timeout requests to propagate temporal events in coordination with system scheduling policies.

The priority-based event dispatching and preemption is done by the dispatching module. Below we list some of its important components and functions.

- *Run-time Scheduler.* The Dispatching Module collaborates with the Run-time Scheduler to determine priority values of the event/consumer tuples. Given an event and the target consumer, the Run-time Scheduler determines the priority at which the event should be dispatched to the consumer.
- *Priority Queues.* The Dispatching module maintains a priority queue of events for each preemption priority used by the Run-time Scheduler. When an event/consumer tuple arrives, it is inserted into the queue corresponding to the preemption priority.
- *Dispatcher.* The dispatcher is responsible for removing the event/consumer tuples from the priority queues and forwarding the events to consumers by calling their push operation. The positioning of the events in the priority queue is determined by the Run-time scheduler by assigning different priorities to the event/consumer tuples.

### 9.6.3 Electra

Electra [64] is a CORBA v2.0 ORB supporting the implementation of reliable distributed applications. Electra objects can be replicated to achieve fault tolerance. Electra permits combining equally-typed object implementations running on different machines to an object group. A CORBA object reference can be bound to an object group and requests will be transmitted by a reliable multicast. Object groups can be used for active replication, efficient data distribution from one sender to many receivers, object migration, and for more. The replication degree of an Electra object can be increased dynamically at run time, while clients are firing operations that update the internal state of the objects. Objects that join a replication group automatically obtain a copy of the current internal state of the group members. Electra runs on communication subsystems like Horus, Ensemble, and ISIS. All of the ORB and RPC code is based on a generic virtual machine that abstracts the functionality provided by systems like Horus and ISIS, for example, communication endpoints, process groups, message passing, threads, and semaphores. To map the operations of the Virtual Machine onto the underlying communication subsystem, a specific Adaptor Object is implemented. This is called the Adaptor Model. Presently, there is an Adaptor Object for Horus and one for ISIS. To port Electra to another subsystem, an Adaptor Object is written and plugged into the architecture. None of the code residing above of the adaptor needs to be modified for that.

### 9.6.4 CyberBus

Cyberbus is an event management software that allows objects to interact By using the Publish/Subscribe paradigm. Supplier objects push events on the bus; consumer objects subscribe for events they are interested in. A CyberBus object can be both a producer and consumer at the same time. A consumer can also request an event directly from a producer by using a pull request. The producers use a subject to label events and encapsulate the event object into a posting data structure. The events are then multicast by the Cyberbus. The CyberBus is not based on the CORBA event service model but does try to solve the same problem. It offers reliable, asynchronous communication, failure detection and fault tolerance.

CyberBus makes use of the CORBA Any data type and CORBA sequences to package data for transmission over the bus. Downcall methods are invoked by the implementor of a CyberObject. Up-call methods, on the other hand, are invoked only by CyberBus to deliver postings or to inform a CyberObject of the failure of another CyberObject. Programmers are discouraged from invoking up-calls directly. The CyberBus subject is a simple *char*∗ and is represented as follows: /usr/joe/group/whiteboard. CyberBus allows a CyberObect to subscribe to many subjects and also allows for the use of wildcards in subjects. Event data needs to be encapsulated into a posting data structure before it can be shipped over the CyberBus. A posting consists of the subject it is addressed to and a list of name value pairs:

```
struct nameValueElem {
  CORBA::String_var name; // name of value (optional)
  CORBA::Any value;       // application specific data
};
```

```
struct posting {
    CORBA::String_var subject; // subject associated with the posting
    namedValueElemSeq data; // a CORBA sequence of nameValueElems
};
```

CyberBus guarantees that every operational object that has subscribed for that subject will receive a copy of the posting (reliable multicast). In the case of pulling events from producers, CyberBus provides a pull mechanism. The consumer calls the operation *CyberBus* :: *pull*() with a parameter that is the subject that it is interested in; this operation behaves like a blocking multicast RPC.

CyberBus also supports the concept of groups. It is accomplished by assigning a single name to a set of CyberObjects. CyberBus delivers special upcalls to the members of a CyberGroup when an object joins or leaves a group. The members of a CyberGroup cooperate tightly to achieve a common goal such as active replication, primary/backup, load sharing or mutually exclusive access to a an external resource. CyberBus supports state transfer between the members of a CyberGroup. CyberObjects join a group by calling the *plug*() operation. When programming CyberBus applications one can ensure that each CyberObject sees postings, failure notifications and subscribe/unsubscribe notifications in exactly the same order. They share a consistent view on failures and on CyberGroup membership.

### 9.6.5   Orbix+ISIS

IONA has provided a facility for integrating group communication and "Virtual Synchrony" into their ORB Orbix by incorporating the ISIS toolkit. ISIS is a distributed group communication toolkit that implements the Virtual Synchrony model. This was originally proposed by Birman in [12]. Virtual Synchrony guarantees that the behavior of a distributed application is predictable regardless of partial failures, asynchronous messaging and objects that join and leave the system dynamically. The core of the model is a failure suspector service and a group abstraction.

Orbix+ISIS (O+I) offers a CORBA-compliant distribution model for actively replicated process groups. Applications can be developed by using the traditional Iona Orbix C++ bindings, and then converted to being Orbix+ISIS servers. O+I has group membership services, including heartbeat detection, join and exclusion primitives. It supports total message ordering [58], as well as less stringent (but more efficient) causal ordering, leaving the choice up to the developer. It supports a general cooperative group computing paradigm, and while it is primarily intended for high availability, it can be used by any applications that need a totally ordered ("Virtually synchronous") computing model. Being network-based, it has no proprietary hardware dependencies. It is supported on multiple common platforms (HPUX, Solaris, IBM AIX, Windows NT), and groups can be composed of server processes running on heterogeneous combinations of these platforms. ISIS groups can be distributed over Wide Area Networks, allowing for geographic diversity.

In addition to its standard active replication model, Orbix+ISIS also supports a Coordinator/Cohort model. While this model can still fully mask failures from clients as in the active replica model, it does so in a "lazy" replication style, which can be considerably more efficient, depending upon the size of state to be transferred relative to the cost of computing that state from the client inputs. Coordinator/Cohort can also be a useful load balancing tool, since a group can nominate different members to be coordinators for different client operations simultaneously.

Orbix+ISIS integrates the two separate products in two ways. First, it replaces the TCP/IP layer in Orbix with the ISIS reliable transport software. The result is new options availability and reliability options for developers. ISIS is a message-oriented middleware with high-availability features. ISIS manages the states of objects in different locations on a network. ISIS can guarantee that the same message delivered to two (or more) objects running in different locations will produce the same result. This capability can be used to support a fault-tolerant configuration for a set of objects - two identical sets of objects executing in parallel, with one set taking over if the other fails. In addition, ISIS is useful in recovering from failures. In case of an outage, the ISIS software transfers the current state to replicas and resynchronizes the system-wide state. Lastly, the ISIS system can make an ORB itself (as opposed to applications that use an ORB) fault-tolerant. Iona and ISIS have designed a set of templates, an IDL code generator, and programming conventions to make Orbix+ISIS transparent to C++ developers. The only change for developers will be the addition of "call backs" to their application code. Call backs are required to support interaction via the ORB.

Finally, Orbix+ISIS has an event stream model which decouples the client and server in an interaction and funnels their operations through an event queue. This queue can optionally store messages persistently and is itself implemented as an actively replicated ISIS group. This yields a CORBA- based Publish/Subscribe mechanism, with fully ordered, guaranteed message delivery to intended recipients, whether they are executing at the time of transmission or not. Object perISIStance is achieved by using database specific adapters. The Orbix adapter approach is explained below.

The Orbix approach to providing persistence is by using object adapters. An object database adapter provides a tight integration between the ORB and persistent object implementations. An object adapter mediates between the ORB, the generated skeletons and the object implementation. With the assistance of skeletons (or of the DSI), it adapts the object implementation interface to the ORB-private interface. Orbix Adapters are implemented by using the Orbix filter hooks. Orbix references are used to load objects from a persistent store when necessary. The objects are registered in their constructor, and the transactions are also managed by the database adapter.

## 9.7  DISCUSSION ON QOS ISSUES

One of the important issues in event service is the QoS requirement. At the current stage of the OMG specification, a few aspects need to be addressed:

- *Persistence*. The OMG standard does not mandate that event channels provide persistence. In the event of a server shutdown due to a problem, the event channel may lose events. For the untyped channel which uses the type Any for communicating events there is an added problem of incompatibilities between the implementation between different ORB's. This problem should be solved when the type DynAny is widely available.
- *Filtering*. The standard OMG Event Service does not specify any filtering capabilities. This means that all events are passed to all connected consumers. In the current situation, filtering has to be implemented on the side of the consumers.
- *Increased End System Utilization*. Since the event filtering is performed on the side of the client the network utilization increases. This could be avoided by proving a filtering mechanism in the event channel interface.

There are no QoS Service guarantees in the specification. This makes it very difficult to anticipate all the possible application requirements and therefore implement a general solution which would be universally applicable. Different applications have different QoS requirements, e.g, in aviation controllers the real time requirements are very stringent; in stock market applications ordering of events is very important. In general, an event channel should provide persistence, so that events that are not passed to consumers should be stored for future delivery.

To extend the CORBA Event Service to work on a domain specific application, the following QoS features can be added.

- *Scalability*. In order to make the event channel scalable one technique would be to use multicasting or group communication. This can be done, for example, by using the ISIS toolkit with additional interfaces to the design for interfacing to the low level facilities of the toolkit. Orbix+ISIS features are transparent to the client program; fault-tolerant object group behavior does not require changes to the client code. A server implementation class gains fault-tolerant object group behavior by inheriting from a base class [60]. Orbix+ISIS provides base classes for two types of object groups, active replication and event stream.
- *Persistence*. The events that need to be stored in persistence storage. This can be either using a database adaptor, similar to the one described in Section 4.4 of Chapter 4, that is, by extending the Portable Object Adaptor to manage persistency of objects within a database system [95]. Another alternative is to use the CORBA Persistency Service.
- *Ordering of Events*. Currently, the ordering of events is first- come first-serve at the event channel. The originating time is not taken into consideration. In order to provide total or causal ordering [58], a different queueing mechanism will have to replace the simple queue that stores the events on the event channel. Guaranteeing "stronger" QoS levels like total-order is expensive with respect to message latency. The latencies on total-ordered messages can be very high [11]. The interface between the suppliers and the event channel would also require modification to accommodate these changes.

- *Garbage Collection.* This is an issue that affects the ORB's in general. GIOP has no concept of sessions and does not permit servers to distinguish between orderly and disorderly client shutdown. As an example if a client (supplier or consumer) crashes or loses connectivity before it gets a chance to initiate a disconnect, the server objects do not have a means to detect this. The objects on the server then tend to hang around forever. If too many such objects accumulate, this tends to have a negative impact upon the performance of the server.

- *Filtering of Events.* This issue has been addressed in the CORBA Notification Service and the same mechanism could be used to provide event filtering in the event service.

- *Realtime Event Channel.* For realtime requirements it is better to use a realtime ORB that provide realtime guarantees to clients and servers. So the typed channel should be ported to existing realtime ORB's such as TAO and Electra. There are already untyped event channels for these to realtime ORB's

## 9.8  SUMMARY

For many complex distributed applications, one-to-one communication is just not acceptable. De-coupling those who provide events (suppliers) and those who consume events (consumers) is just appropriate. Suppliers do not need to know the consumers of their events. They just need to have a "letter box" where they can put their events (letters or messages) and later consumers can pick them up when they are ready. These consumers may be also informed about the events (letters or messages) which concern them. The CORBA Event Service provides such "letter box" style functionalities and it enables many-to-many communication.

In this chapter we discussed the advantages of of the OMG Event Service. Before proposing details about such service, we described some of the Publish/Subscribe mechanisms. The untyped and typed event channels were detailed and examples were given. To complement the description of the OMG specification of such a service, we provided details about how such a service can be implemented as well the problems that can be encountered during the implementation (not use!) of the service. At the end of the chapter, a few implementations of the OMG Event Service were described, such as OrbixTalk, TAO's realtime event channel, Electra, CyberBus, and Orbix+ISIS.

## 9.9  REVIEW QUESTIONS

- Briefly explain the event channel. *Hint*: Relate the event channel with subscribers, publish/subscribe pattern, and decoupling.
- What is an event? Briefly explain the decoupling provided by an event channel. Briefly explain the different kinds of event channels.
- Explain the three communication technologies that use the OMG event channel.

- Explain briefly how the push and pull models work.
- What is the difference between typed and untyped event channels in terms of interfaces used to access events? Briefly explain delivery models that can be used by these event channels.
- What are the problem with the current implementations of CORBA event service? What is an event proxy? What kinds of applications adapters can be delegated with as proxies?
- Explain the implementation aspects of untyped event channels.
- Explain the implementation issues of typed event channels.
- Explain the QoS aspects that must be addressed at the current stage of the OMG specification.
- Explain the QoS features that can be added in order to extend the CORBA Event Service to work on a domain specific application.

## 9.10  EXERCISES

- Discuss the abilities that the Push and Pull models give to consumers. Provide an example for the ability each model gives.
- Discuss QoS issues of OMG event service specification when it is used to implement an event service in stock trading applications

# CHAPTER 10

# Object Transaction Service

This chapter describes the main elements of the CORBA Object Transaction Service (OTS), including the OTS architecture and its different components. At the end of the chapter, an example of a CORBA OTS is given, followed by a comparison with the Microsoft transaction server.

## 10.1 OVERVIEW

The concept of transactions is an important programming paradigm for simplifying the construction of reliable and available applications, especially those that require concurrent access to shared data. The concept was first used to protect data in a centralized database, but it has recently been extended to the broader concept of distributed computation. Transactions guarantee that the data will be consistent at the end of its execution, regardless of whether the transaction may have been executed concurrently with others (commits) and failures may have occurred during its execution (aborts).

OTS is a service under OMA that provides operations to control the scope and duration of a transaction. It allows multiple objects, potentially residing at different resource managers, to participate in a global atomic transaction and allows objects to associate their internal state changes with the transaction. OTS coordinates the completion of a distributed transaction by implementing presumed abort two phase commit (2PC) protocol across heterogeneous, autonomous, and distributed objects based systems [75]. OTS is the object-oriented counterpart of the procedural transaction processing (TP) monitors in distributed environments. TP monitors provide transaction management (ACID properties and resource management, database connection management, load sharing between software servers, etc.) in procedural environments, whereas OTS only provides the transaction management function through its object interfaces. The design of OTS is based on the X/Open reference model, except that the procedural XA [107] and TX [108] interfaces have been replaced with a set of CORBA interfaces defined in the CORBA Interface Definition Language (IDL). All inter-component communication is mandated to be via CORBA method calls on instances of these IDLs.

Transaction capabilities play a key role in several applications that require reliable processing. The OTS defines IDL interfaces that let multiple distributed objects on multiple platforms participate in atomic transactions. In this way, by using the OTS, ORBs can provide a seamless environment for running mission-critical components. The OTS allows applications already making use of a distributed object-oriented CORBA environment to make use of transactional behavior, thus increasing reliability and robustness. It also allows applications which must rely on transactional capabilities to be embedded in an ORB-based environment.

## 10.2 BASICS OF TRANSACTIONS

This section introduces the basic concepts related to transaction-based systems and describes in more details the different transactional models, including flat and nested models, and finally introduces the consistency protocols for these models. Transactions will be described in a format similar to the one used in the following example:

```
begin_transaction T:              begin_transaction INCREASE_BAL88
    op-1();                           :x = read(balance);
    op-2();                           :y = read(salary);
    ...                               write(balance, :y + :x);
    ...                               write(salary, :y + 100);
    ...
    ...                               :x = read(age);
    op-K()                            write(age, :x+1);
end_transaction T                 end_transaction INCREASE_BAL88
```

**Figure 10.1**  Structure and example of transactions.

where $op-1(), \ldots, op-K()$ are $read()$ and $write()$ operations and $:x$ and $:y$ are variables.

### 10.2.1 Concepts

The concept of transactions has been widely supported by a variety of existing systems, including data-oriented systems, such as databases, and process-oriented systems such as distributed systems. This concept has the same purpose in all these systems and is meant to "group" a set of operations, mainly read and write operations, into one logical execution unit called a *transaction*. However, as we will describe in later sections, operations within a transaction can also be regrouped to form sub-transactions (or child-transaction) of the original transaction (or parent-transaction). These types of transactions are called *nested transactions* as opposed to the conventional transactions called *flat transactions*.

Whether a transaction is a flat transaction or a nested transaction, the basic requirement is to enforce ACID properties [10, 43], which are *Atomicity, Consistency, Isolation*, and *Durability*. Atomicity property is the property that says all operations performed as part of a transaction are considered to be one atomic action—they are either all performed or none of them are. When a transaction commits, all the effects of the operations are completed and cannot be interrupted or undone. In the example of Figure 10.1, the operations within the transaction INCREASE_BAL88 have to be all or none applied, that is, update the current balance with the salary amount and later update the salary with 100, or none of them will be applied. When the transaction commits, all the updates are made persistent. When a transaction aborts (or is rolled back), all the operations are undone, and the state will match the state that existed and was relevant before any of these operations were performed.

Consistency refers to the property that transactions must guarantee that the data are transformed from one consistent state to another. Consistency of a state is defined by a set of constraints and variants which must be satisfied. The property of consistency enables an application that is implemented correctly to perform a set of operations guaranteed to create a new state satisfying these constraints. The isolation property of transactions is used in situations where multiple processing entities reference and change the same underlying resources and data. An executing transaction cannot reveal its results to other concurrent transactions before its commits. Ensuring isolation by not permitting incomplete results to be seen by other transactions solves the lost update problem. The following example illustrates this lost update problem for the two transactions *zahir_trans* and *jim_trans*:

```
balance = 200$
salary  = 1000$
begin_transaction zahir_trans
:x = read(balance);            200$
                        begin_transaction jim_trans
                          :z = read(balance);          200$
                          write(balance, :z+100);      300$
  write(balance, :x + 10)   210$
  end_transaction zahir_trans
                          x: = read(balance);
                        end_transaction jim_trans
```

Because *jim_trans* was able to see the balance and changed it after *zahir_trans* had read the balance, the transaction *zahir_trans* has lost the update that was performed by the other transaction, that is, it should have a balance of 240$ instead of 210$. One could say that a solution is to abort the transaction *zahir_trans* in order to retrieve a consistent state. If that is done, this will require that the transaction *jim_trans* to be aborted as well as those that have used the data since this transaction. This is known as cascading aborts. If a transaction permits others to see its incomplete results before committing and then decides to abort, any transaction that has read its incomplete values will have to abort as well.

When looking at *jim_trans* transaction, it is apparent that it was allowed to read an inconsistent value of balance. This occurred because it read the value in the time between *zahir_trans* reading and writing a new value—this is called an *inconsistent retrieval*.

To avoid the problem of lost updates and inconsistent retrieval, the system needs to enforce what is called *serializability* of the transactions. Two transactions are serializable if the interleaving of the operations of the transactions produces an effect as if the transactions had been performed one at a time. For example, the operations *zahir_trans* and *jim_trans* are not serializable because they cannot be interleaved. If interleaving is attempted, there will be a lost update and an inconsistent retrieval. In these situations, where there are conflicts between the transactions, one of the transactions needs to be aborted.

In general, given a set of transactions, say $T_1, \ldots, T_n$, these transactions are said to be serializable if the interleaving of their operations produces a serial order $T_{i_1}, \ldots, T_{i_n}$, where $i$ is a permutation on $\{1, \ldots, n\}$. In this case, the operations of $T_{i_1}$ will be performed first, then those of $T_{i_2}$, and so on until the transactions are completed.

The last property is the durability property which guarantees that the result of a transaction that commits is durable (persistent) and will never be lost (except in the case of catastrophes, such as destruction of the disk and all its backups). Durability is usually implemented by using a persistent storage mechanism, but the definition of transactional durability does not specify how this is done or place limitations on what implementation is used; it only specifies that the result set of a completed transaction must be durable.

These ACID properties apply to any transactional-based model, whether it is a flat transactional model or a nested transactional model. In a flat transactional model, transactions are only defined in terms of basic read and write operations. The transactions shown in Figure 10.1 are examples of flat transactions. Nested transactions relate to those that are defined in terms of other transactions, called *sub-transactions*. For example, the transaction INCREASE_BAL88 can be rewritten to contains two subtransactions, one that reads the balance and salary and updates them, and the other subtransaction that reads and updates the age. Because the operations of these subtransactions are not dealing with the same data items, they can be split and executed in parallel. Now the initial transaction of Figure 10.1 can be expressed in a nested transaction as in Figure 10.2 model.

In general, a nested transaction can be defined as a directed graph where nodes are subtransactions and a directed edge is defined between a parent transaction and

```
begin_transaction T:                begin_transaction INCREASE_BAL88
   begin_transaction T_1               begin_transaction UPD_SALARY
      op-1();                             :x = read(balance);
      op-2();                             :y = read(salary);
   end_transaction T_1                    write(balance, :y + :x);
   ...                                     write(salary, :y + 100);
   begin_transaction T_K               end_transaction UPD_SALARY
      op_k();                          begin_transaction INCREASE_AGE
      op_k+1();                           :x = read(age);
      ...                                 write(age, :x+1);
      op_n();                          end_transaction INCREASE_AGE
   end_transaction T_K              end_transaction INCREASE_BAL88
```

**Figure 10.2**  Structure and example of a nested transaction.

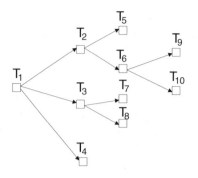

**Figure 10.3**    Nested transactions.

its sub-transaction. Figure 10.3 shows the general structure of a nested transaction $T_1$ which has three sub-transactions, $T_2$, $T_3$ and $T_4$. In turn, $T_2$ and $T_3$ has sub-transactions $T_5$, $T_6$ and $T_7$, $T_8$, respectively. Finally, $T_6$ has two sub-transactions, $T_9$ and $T_{10}$.

One obvious advantage of the nested transactional model is that it enables the systems to process sub-parts of a nested transaction in parallel and therefore increase the performance of the systems supporting such a model. Also, because sub-transactions belonging to different sub-graphs of a nested transaction can commit or abort without affecting the results of each other. In this way, the nested transaction $T_1$ can commit even if one of its sub-transactions, say $T_3$ is aborted. This offers more flexibility in managing complex applications without affecting their performance, such as rolling back unnecessary transactions because some of their sub-operations have not been committed. More details about the commit protocol in nested transaction are given in Section 10.2.3.

## 10.2.2 Concurrency Control Protocols

To allow atomicity and isolation, transactions must be scheduled so that all of their offset on shared data is serially equivalent. There are several concurrency control mechanisms which enable serializability of transactions. Here we will show two of these mechanisms, the pessimistic concurrency control and the optimistic concurrency control.

### 10.2.2.1 *Pessimistic Concurrency Control.* This concurrency control mechanism is used in several systems, including existing database systems. The idea is that before any transaction performs an operation on a data item, it must acquire a lock, which can be either an exclusive lock (in case of a write operation) or a shared lock (in case of a read operation). Locks that have been acquired by a transaction are released only by the transaction commits. The locking mechanism is generally implemented by using a lock manager which is responsible for the management of locks.

When a data item is locked by a given transaction, any other transaction that needs to access or update this item must wait until the lock is released. This creates a (waiting) dependency relationship between transactions, called the *Waiting Directed Graph* (WDG), where the nodes are transactions. In this case, a directed edge from a transaction $T_i$ to a transaction $T_j$ means that $T_i$ is waiting to acquire a lock on the data item that was locked by $T_j$. When a WDG does not have a directed cycle, the transactions are serializable. Otherwise, they are said to not be serializable, and therefore there exists a deadlock. One solution to solving the deadlock situation is to abort one of the transactions involved in the cycle. Since there may be several transactions, in some systems, priorities are assigned to transactions and the transaction with the lowest priority is aborted.

### 10.2.2.2 *Optimistic Concurrency Control.*

Locking data items generally restricts the accessibility of the data items, thereby reducing concurrent access to shared data items. This is generally not acceptable for several types of applications because it reduces their performance since transactions need to wait until locks are released by earlier transactions.

To avoid waiting for locks, a solution is to leave transactions performing operations on copies of the data items. Each transaction has two timestamps, one for the starting of the transaction (read phase) and the other for when the transactions ask to commit (validation phase). When a transaction has a "green" light to commit, it enters its last stage in which all the operations made on the copy of the data item are made persistent (write stage).

During the read phase, the operations of a transaction are performed on a copy of the data item. When the transaction wants to commit, the transaction manager checks whether this transaction has any conflict with other transactions and whether or not they have been committed. Here we describe two protocols to validate transactions in the context of the optimistic concurrency control: backward validation and forward validation.

- *Backward Validation.* In the context of this protocol, the operations a transaction that have asked to commit are checked with the operations of earlier transactions. Conflicts occur when the transaction has read a data item that has been updated by earlier transactions.

  Let us consider the example of Figure 10.4 which illustrates the different phases of the transaction $T_9$. When $T_9$ enters the validation phase, conflicts can only occur with the transactions $T_3$ and $T_5$. $T_{20}$ and $T_{10}$ have no conflicts with $T_9$ because they were committed before $T_9$ started its read phase. Therefore, $T_9$ reads data items after the two transactions committed. Regarding $T_1$, since this transaction has not yet committed, there will be no checking to perform. However, when this transaction enters its validation phase, it has to check if there is a conflict with the transaction $T_9$, if it has been allowed to commit.

  When the set of transactions that may enter in conflict with $T_9$ has been identified, it is called the *candidate conflict set* and is denoted as $CCS_{T_9}$; the second step is to check whether or not this transaction has read a data item that

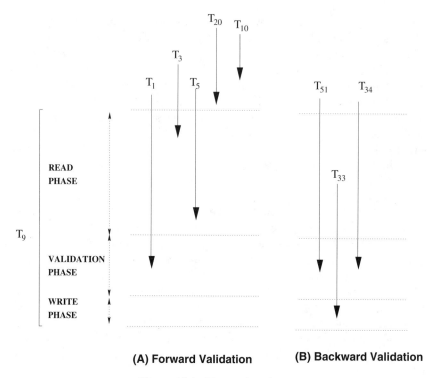

**(A) Forward Validation**        **(B) Backward Validation**

**Figure 10.4**    Transaction phases.

has been updated by the $CCS_{T_9}$'s transactions. In fact, if a $CCS_{T_9}$'s transaction has updated the data item before $T_9$ has performed the read, then this transaction does not have any conflict with $T_9$. The only ones that are in conflict with $T_9$ are those of $CCS_{T_9}$ which have updated data items after $T_9$ performed the read operation. We denote this subset of transaction as $CCS_{<T_9, backward>}$.

In general, given a transaction $T_i$, this transaction can start the write phase if and only if $CCS_{<T_i, backward>}$ is empty. If not, this will mean that this transaction will need to be aborted and started again.

- *Forward Validation.* In the context of this protocol, the transaction to be validated is checked with those transactions that are currently active, that is, those that have not yet committed when the transaction entered the validation stage. Conflicts may arise when the transaction has updated a data item that has been read by active transactions.

  Referring again to Figure 10.4, to validate the transaction $T_9$, the conflicts that need to be checked are with the following set $CCS_{<T_9, backward>} = \{T_{51}, T_{33}, T_{34}\}$, that is, the set of transactions that have not yet committed when $T_9$ started the validation stage. If one of the transactions of this conflict set has read a data item that has been updated by $T_9$, then either this transaction or $T_9$ needs to be aborted [46].

### 10.2.3 Commit Protocols

A commit protocol is used to synchronize updates on data items (that can be located in different servers) so that they either all fail or all succeed. This is done by centralizing the decision to commit but by giving each participant the right of veto. For flat or nested transactions there are several commit protocols, and here our focus will be on the two phase commit (2PC) and three phase commit (3PC).

#### *10.2.3.1 2PC Protocol for Flat Transactions.* This protocol is designed so the servers that contain the data items can commit or abort a transaction. Because of the atomicity property, if a part of a transaction is aborted by a given server, then the whole transaction must be aborted. To make sure that a transaction can be committed, one of the servers (called *coordinator*) will be responsible for checking with the other servers to determine if the transaction can commit. This is done in two phases, the CanCommit phase and the DoCommit phase. In the first phase, as shown in Figure 10.5, the coordinator sends a request to all the servers that are executing operations of the transaction. These servers are called *workers*, and they will work together with the coordinator to come up with a consistent final decision about the transaction.

When the workers receive the message CanCommit, they will send a reply as to whether they can or cannot commit the operations of the transactions. The coordinator analyzes the replies and decides to continue committing the transaction or to abort it. If one of the replies is negative, that is, one of the operations of the transaction cannot be committed, then the coordinator aborts the transaction. If all the votes are positive the commit protocol enters its second phase, the DoCommit phase, where

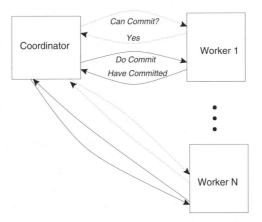

**Figure 10.5**    2PC protocol.

the coordinator asks each worker to commit the operations of the transaction. Every worker will act accordingly and apply the operations and inform the coordinator when all the operations are applied.

### 10.2.3.2 2PC for Nested Transactions.

The commit protocol for nested transactions is a little complex because when a subtraction wishes to commit, and since it does not necessarily have information about other sub-transactions, then it will commit even though one of it parents has aborted. In general, the top-level transaction can commit only if all of its provisionally committed child transactions can commit.

When a nested transaction wishes to commit (i.e., provisionally commit), it should report its status (as well as its descendants) to its direct parent. This process repeats until the top-level transaction receives all the information about all its sub-transactions. Let us consider the example of Figure 10.3 with additional information on the status of the sub-transactions, as shown in Figure 10.6. In this example, because $T_6$ has aborted, $T_9$ and $T_{10}$ should be aborted. But because these two transactions are not aware of the status of $T_6$ and $T_2$, they will try to commit even though their ancestors have aborted.

To avoid such a problem, each transaction will keep track of the provisionally committed sub-transactions as well as those that are aborted. This information is then passed to the parent transaction, which will in turn send information to its parents, etc. Table 10.1 shows the flow of information from one sub-transaction to its parent for the example shown in Figure 10.6.

During the 2PC protocol, the coordinator (the server that has initiated the top level transaction) sends a CanCommit? request to each of the workers and supplies the abort list. As mentioned earlier, based on the information in this list, each worker will

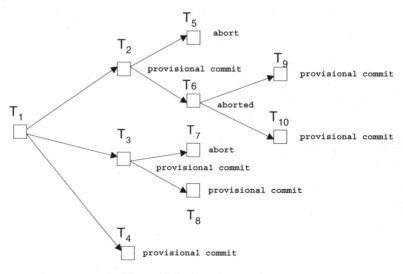

**Figure 10.6**   Nested transactions.

**TABLE 10.1**

| Transaction | Childs | Provisional Commit List | Abort List |
|---|---|---|---|
| $T_9$ | | $T_9$ | |
| $T_{10}$ | | $T_{10}$ | |
| $T_5$ | | | $T_5$ |
| $T_6$ | $T_9$ , $T_{10}$ | $T_9$, $T_{10}$ | $T_6$ |
| $T_7$ | | | $T_7$ |
| $T_8$ | | $T_8$ | |
| $T_2$ | $T_5$, $T_6$ | $T_2$ | $T_6$, $T_5$ |
| $T_3$ | $T_7$, $T_8$ | $T_3$, $T_8$ | $T_7$ |
| $T_4$ | | $T_4$ | |
| $T_1$ | $T_2$, $T_3$, $T_4$ | $T_2$, $T_3$, $T_4$ | |

decide whether to commit or abort by checking the status of the parent transactions. When a worker receives a CanCommit? message, it first checks the aborted list. If there is no aborted parent transaction in the list, then the worker sends a Yes vote to the coordinator. If there is, an abort votes in the list, then the transaction aborts. In the second phase of the 2PC, the coordinator collects the votes and sends a DoCommit request for those that have voted Yes. The coordinators must then commit those transactions.

The 2PC protocol for nested transactions allows a top level transaction to commit even though some of the sub-transactions have aborted. In the example of Figure 10.3, if the sub-transactions $T_2$, $T_3$, $T_8$ and $T_4$ can commit, then the top level transaction will commit.

### 10.2.3.3 Three Phase Comitt Protocol (3PC).

The main objective of the 2PC protocol is to make sure that a consensus is found regarding the commitment of a transaction among the different servers. This (consensus) provides a good basis for the consistency of data; however, it can induce a delay that is mainly related to the failure of the coordinator or one of the workers. Referring to Figure 10.5, if a worker has failed after a coordinator has voted, then this worker will be waiting until the coordinator restarts. The same problem occurs when a worker fails, then the coordinator will have to wait until the worker restarts.

To avoid such a delay, 2PC has been extended to include an additional phase, called the *PreCommit phase*, and the new protocol is called *3PC protocol*. The first phase of this protocol is similar to the 2PC. In the second phase, the coordinator collects the votes and makes a decision. If one of the workers votes No, then it sends an abort to all the workers. If the vote is Yes, then it sends a PreCommit request to all the workers to check whether or not the workers (who have voted yes) are still able to commit. Workers that have voted Yes will wait for the PreCommit or Abort request. For a given timeout, if the request is not received, the worker will assume that the coordinator has failed and either aborts the transaction or contacts the coordinator.

When a worker receives the PreCommit request, it votes a second time and sends the reply to the coordinator. The coordinator will collect the vote and decide to commit or abort the transaction. When it decides to commit, then it sends a DoCommit to all the workers, and they will carry out this commit.

## 10.3 OTS CONCEPTS

OTS service supports the concept of a transaction in the context of CORBA environments. It defines interfaces that allow multiple distributed objects to cooperate to provide atomicity. These interfaces enable the objects to either commit all changes together or to rollback all changes together, even in the presence of failures. It provides transaction synchronization across the elements of a distributed client/server application. The transaction service places no constraints on the number of objects involved. The transaction service does not require that all requests be performed within the scope of a transaction. OTS provides operations (i) to control the scope and duration of a transaction; (ii) to allow multiple objects to be involved in a single, atomic transaction; (iii) to allow objects to associate changes in their internal state with a transaction; and (iv) to coordinate the completion of transactions. OTS [75] provides the following features:

- Support for multiple transaction models, such as flat and nested transactions.
- Support for transactions that span heterogeneous object request brokers. Objects on these brokers can participate in a single transaction, and in addition, a single broker can support multiple transaction services.
- Support of existing IDL interfaces. A single interface supports both transactional and non-transactional implementations. To make an object transactional, it needs to use an ordinary interface that inherits from an abstract OTS class. This approach avoids an explosion of IDL variants that differ only in their transaction characteristics.
- Support of both implicit (system-managed) propagation and explicit (application-managed) propagation. With implicit propagation, transactional behavior is not specified in the operation's signature. With explicit propagation, applications define their own mechanisms for sharing a common transaction.
- Support for TP Monitors. A TP Monitor provides both efficient scheduling and the sharing of resources by a large number of users. It must be possible to implement OTS in a TP monitor environment.

### 10.3.1 Interface Hierarchy

Figure 10.7 shows the OMG's schematic view of a distributed transaction processing model. The model's principal concept is that a client may perform CORBA transactions on various types of servers by using invocations. The service usually establishes a so-called transaction context for this, which is unique to the client's session. The

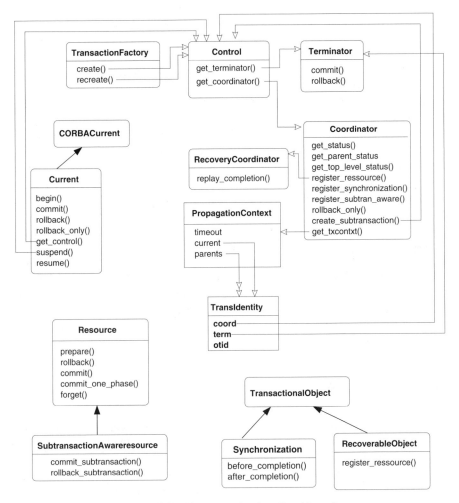

**Figure 10.7**   The transaction interface hierarchy.

transaction context is a way for the transaction service to monitor the vital signs of the transaction as it occurs.

The Current interface defines operations that allow a client of the OTS to explicitly manage the association between threads and transactions. It is provided to begin, commit, rollback, or obtain status monitoring information on transactions. It supports the notion of multiple client threads of operation occurring per transaction, which leads to the support of nested sub-transactions within a transaction via the use of these threads. The TransactionFactory interface enables the transaction originator to begin a transaction. This interface defines two operations, create and recreate, which create a new representation of a top-level transaction. The two operations actually return a Control object. The Control interface allows a program to explicitly manage or propagate a transaction context. It defines two operations, namely *get_terminator*() and *get_coordinator*(). The first operation returns a Terminator object which supports operations to end the transaction. The second operation returns a Coordinator object, which supports operations needed by resources to participate in the transaction. The Terminator interface supports operations to either commit or roll back a transaction. Typically, these operations are used by the transaction originator. The Coordinator interface provides mechanisms to coordinate the actions of the different participants involved in ongoing transactional operations. Examples of this are *create_subtransaction*() to setup new sub-transactions nested under the current parent transaction, or the registering of an external resource, using *register_resource* or *register_subtransaction_aware*(). The RecoveryCoordinator interface can be used by recoverable objects to coordinate recovery of the OTS-based system in the event of failure. It provides a *replay_completion*() operation that returns the current status of a transaction, whether or not it has committed successfully, rolled back, or is in some intermediate state, contingent upon other sub-transactions. The Resource interface defines the operations invoked by the Transaction Service during the 2PC. The Subtransaction Aware Resource interface is used with the nested transaction model. Its purpose is usually to help register a specialized callback resource object that will notify some recoverable object if a specified subtransaction completes successfully. Finally, the Transactional Object interface is used by an object to indicate that it is transactional. It is a marker interface and has no operations.

## 10.3.2   Context Propagation

A transactional originator has a choice to either use the indirect context management (and therefore implicit transaction propagation) or the direct context management (and therefore explicit transaction propagation). In the example below, *txn_crt* is an object supporting the Current interface. The client uses the *begin*() operation to start the transaction which becomes implicitly associated with the originator's thread control. The program later uses the operation *commit*() to end the transaction.

```
// Indirect & Implicit Propagation
...
txn_crt.begin();
...
Account->makeDeposit(10.00);
...
txn_crt.commit(false);
...
```

In the direct or explicit model, as shown in the example below, the transaction originator uses direct context management and explicit transaction propagation. The client uses an object from the interface TransactionFactory (see Figure 10.7) to create a new transaction and uses the returned Control object to retrieve the Terminator and Coordinator objects. As shown in the interface of Control objects, these objects do not directly support management of transactions. Instead, they support operations that return the Terminator and Coordinator objects. The former is used to commit or rollback a transaction. The latter is used to enable transactional objects to participate in the transaction. The two objects can be propagated independently, and therefore allow finer granularity control over propagation.

```
// Direct & Explicit Propagation
...
CosTransactions::TransactionFactory fac;
CosTransactions::Control ctr;
CosTransactions::Terminator trt;
CosTransactions::Coordinator crd;

// probably using _bind() to find the factory
fac = ...
ctr = fac->create(0);
trt = ctr->get_terminator();
```

Later on the client issues requests, some of which involve transactional objects (those that have their IDL interface inherit from `CosTransactions::Transactional Object`). The propagation of the context should be explicit, meaning the object ctr should be passed as an explicit parameter of the request:

```
...
// my_object is a transactional object
my_object->operation(arguments,  ctr);
...
trt->commit(false);
```

The client can use the object reference trt to commit the transaction. Basically a client can invoke any operation on any object during a transaction, but the object must be either transactional or recoverable for that operation to display transaction semantics.

### 10.3.3  Transactional Objects

A transactional client is a program that invokes operations of many transactional objects in a single transaction. Transactional objects are those objects whose behavior is affected by being invoked within the scope of a transaction. For instance, given a transaction $T_1$ which updates the balance of a customer, the corresponding object Account will be a transactional object. All of the transactional objects related to $T_1$ will define the context of the transaction. Those objects that are not affected by $T_1$ are called nontransactional objects. The difference between the transactional objects and those that are not is that changes on the former objects can survive any failure.

The example below shows two types of interfaces. The SpecialAccount interface is an object that inherits from TransactionalObject interface, and the context of the transaction is implicitly associated with the object's thread. The *makeDeposit()* operation performs some transactional requests on recoverable objects. The object acc is an example of a recoverable object.

```
// IDL
interface SpecialAccount : CosTransactions::TransactionalObject {
    ...
    void makeDeposit(in float amount);
    ...
}

interface OrdinaryAccount {
    ...
    void makeDeposit(in float amount);
}

// server side
void SpecialAccount_i::makeDeposit(CORBA::Float amount) {
{
    // find the appropriate account
    acc = ...
    balance = acc->get_balance();
    balance += amount;
    acc->set_balance(amount);
}

// end of a transactional operation
```

The operation to begin a transaction is executed by a pseudo-object located in the ORB. It sets up a transaction context, which the ORB automatically inserts as a parameter of each to every operation in the scope of the transaction until the transactional client invokes the corresponding end transaction operation. This is termed implicit transaction propagation. Transactional (and recoverable) objects look for the transaction context to determine whether a request is a part of a transaction. There is also a CORBA mode that supports explicit passing of the transaction context. This allows the originating transactional client, or any other object that receives the context from that objects, to extend the bounds of the transaction explicitly.

### 10.3.4    Recoverable Objects

Recoverable objects have persistent data that is managed as part of the transaction. Recoverable objects are transactional objects whose data is affected by committing or rolling back the transaction. A recoverable object owns the data and places it in a persistent storage and implements a failure-recovery mechanism. If a failure occurs during the transaction, during the restart procedure, the transactional object reads its saved data from the persistent storage, discovers that a transaction is in process, and participates in a commit/rollback protocol with the Transaction service.

A recoverable object registers a resource object with the transaction service to associate the changes made to its data with the transaction. The transaction service drives the 2PC protocol by issuing requests to the registered resources.

The client may call on transactional and recoverable servers during the course of a transaction. The recoverable server implements an object with a recoverable state that is invoked within the scope of the transaction, either directly by the transaction originator or indirectly through one or more transactional objects. Transactional objects, contained within transactional servers, refer to persistent data that may be modified in the course of the transaction. In addition a client can perform invocations on non-transactional objects, but these typically will not survive a failure and cannot be reversed if a rollback operation results. The behavior of objects within transactional servers may be affected by a transaction but is not recoverable in nature. Transactional servers do not participate in the completion operation (e.g., commit) of a transaction, but are capable of forcing the transaction to roll back.

Let us consider the following example to illustrate the concept of recoverable objects.

```
interface RecovrableAccount : CosTransactions::TransactionalObject,
        CosTransactions::Resource {
    ...
    void makeDeposit (in float amount);
    ...
}
```

Upon entering, the context of the transaction is implicitly associated with the object's thread. The pseudo-object Current is used to retrieve the Coordinator object associated with the transaction. As shown below, before registering the Resource, the object uses *has_transaction* and *is_same_transaction* operations on the coordinator crd to check whether it has already been registered for the same transaction. Here the object (i.e., this) is itself a Resource object and therefore the object recv (as RecoveryCoordinator) will be returned when calling $crd - register\_resource(this)$. As shown in Figure 10.7, rollback operation of recv can be invoked to re-establish the previous state of an object of RecoverableAccount.

```
void RecoverableAccount_i::makeDeposit(CORBA::Float amount)
{
    CosTransactions::Current cur;
    CosTransactions::Control ctr;
    CosTransactions::Coordinator crd;
    CosTransactions::RecoveryCoordinator recv;

    cur = new CosTransactions::Current();
    ctr = cur.get_control();
    crd = ctr->get_coordinator();
    // register the current object
    recv = crd->register_resource(this);
```

```
    ...
    // perform the usual operation
    balance = balance + 10;
    ...

    // end of the transaction operation
}
```

### 10.3.5 Transactional and Recoverable Servers

Figure 10.8 summarizes the whole architecture: when a transactional client begins a transaction, a transaction context is created when the transaction is started and transmitted to transactional and recoverable objects with each transactional request. Transactional objects propagate the transaction but are not involved in transaction completion. They may force rollback of the transaction. The Recoverable objects register Resource objects for the transaction completion. They may force rollback of the transaction. Finally, the Resource objects participate in the transaction completion (e.g., 2PC).

The OMG defines ten key interfaces inside the CosTransactions module. As shown in the previous section, these interfaces play a major role in managing the life-cycle of any and all CORBA transactions from beginning to end. Figure 10.9 shows the components of the OMG's OTS and how they work together to execute a transaction. A transaction client makes a request of the OTS to define the boundaries or a series of operations that constitute a transaction. It then invokes transaction operations (b) on transactional objects. During the transaction, requests can also be made (c) on recoverable objects.

Transactional objects can be used to implement two types of application servers, transactional and recoverable. A transactional server is a collection of one or more

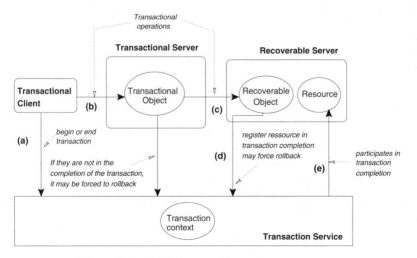

**Figure 10.8** CORBA transaction service components.

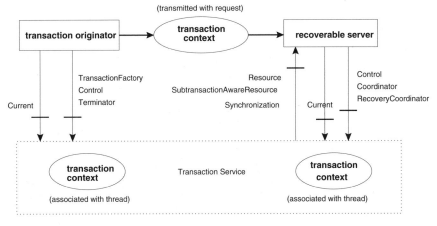

**Figure 10.9**   Major interfaces of the transaction service.

objects whose behavior can affect a transaction, but which has no recoverable state of its own. It implements recoverable changes using other recoverable objects. It does not participate in any way with the commit protocol of a transaction, but it may force the transaction to rollback in case of problems (e.g., stopping the server). A recoverable server is a collection of objects, in which at least one of them is a recoverable object. As shown in the previous section, a recoverable object participates in the protocols by registering one or more Resource objects (d) with the Transaction Service. The Resource implements the appropriate commit protocol (e.g. 1PC, 2PC).

## 10.4   TRANSACTION SCENARIO

Here we will show a typical transaction scenario, and the different phases are illustrated Figure 10.10.

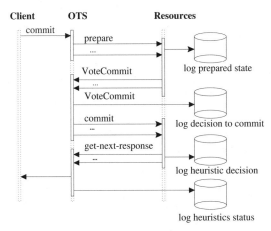

**Figure 10.10**   A typical transaction scenario.

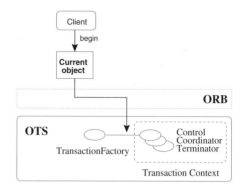

**Figure 10.11**   Phase 1.

*Phase 1.* As shown in Figure 10.11, the transaction originator starts the transaction by using the Current pseudo-object. The Transaction Service creates objects that represent the transaction (Control, Coordinator, Terminator) and are used to form the Transaction Context. The transaction context becomes implicitly associated with the client's thread.

*Phase 2.* The transaction originator issues requests to transactional objects (see Figure 10.12). The transaction context that is associated with the client's thread is propagated with the request and associated with the thread in which the method of the target object will be executing. Using the Current pseudo-object, the transactional object can inquire about the visiting transaction and in particular use this information to implement isolation of transactions.

*Phase 3.* Some transactional objects are also recoverable objects whose persistent data will be affected by the outcome of the transaction. A recoverable object uses the Current pseudo-object to retrieve the Coordinator of the transaction. As shown

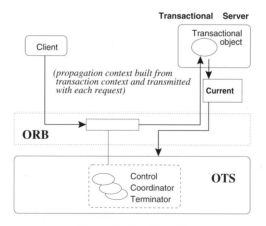

**Figure 10.12**   Phase 2.

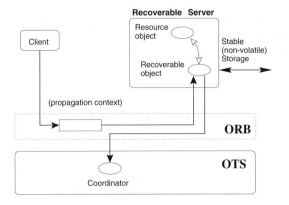

**Figure 10.13**   Phase 3.

in Figure 10.13, it registers a Resource object to notify its participation in the transaction.

*Phase 4.* When all the operations performed in the transaction have been completed, the transaction originator uses the Current pseudo-object to request the commitment of the transaction. As shown in Figure 10.14, the Transaction Service commits the transaction using the 2PC wherein requests are sent to the registered Resource object. In the first phase of the 2PC, prepare requests are sent to all registered Resource objects. Each Resource object returns a vote result to the Transaction Service which takes the decision either to commit or to roll back the transaction depending on the result of the votes. In the second phase of the 2PC,

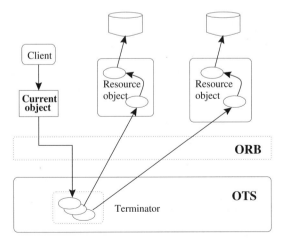

**Figure 10.14**   Phase 4.

commit requests are sent to all registered Resource objects that returned a vote to commit (presume here that the decision has been taken by the transaction service to commit the transaction).

## 10.5   OTS IMPLEMENTATIONS

This section describes two implementations of object-based transaction systems, one is CORBA compliant and the other one is not. The CORBA compliant is from Iona and it relates to the Orbix transaction monitor. The non-CORBA compliant is the Microsoft Transaction Service (MTS).

### 10.5.1   Iona Transaction Service

OrbixOTS was developed in collaboration with the Transarc Corporation to bring the powerful computing concept of transaction processing to distributed objects. As shown in Figure 10.15, OrbixOTS has a modular architecture that includes such services as distributed transactions and a Resource Manager that uses the XA protocol to integrate applications with databases or queueing systems. All interprocess communication takes place using Orbix. The architecture includes the OMG's Object Concurrency Control Service (OCCS), and services for logging and failure recovery.

The transaction manager is implemented as a link in library; hence transactional applications have an instance of the transaction manager that cooperates to implement distributed transactions. The transaction manager is linked-in (and there is no dedicated "transaction server") and there is no central point of failure. Application or resource failures during the two-phase commit protocol will block the committing transaction but will not stop new transactions from executing. The transaction manager is a full implementation of the CORBA's OTS interface, with additional advanced features such as nested transactions and clients and servers may be multithreaded.

OrbixOTS also provides a resource manager to support the X/Open XA interface. Many products support the XA interface including Oracle, Sybase, and Informix relational databases, as well as IBM's MQ Series queueing system. The OCCS is an advanced locking service that fully supports nested transactions and works in cooperation with the transaction manager. The OCCS implementation component is

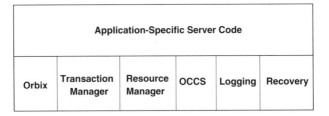

**Figure 10.15**   OrbixOTS server components.

linked into the application that is acquiring the locks. Hence, the OCCS is not a true distributed locking service, but since the interfaces are defined by using CORBA IDL, servers can be developed that export the OCCS interface to provide a server that effectively implements a distributed locking service.

Logging provides a durable record of the progress of transactions so that OrbixOTS servers can recover from failure. OrbixOTS permits both ordinary files and raw devices to be used for transaction logs. A transaction log may be expanded at runtime and it may be mirrored for redundancy. Also, an OrbixOTS server can provide a logging service to other recoverable servers.

The transaction log is used during recovery after a crash to restore the state of transactions which were in progress at the time of the crash.

An example of how the OrbixOTS is involved in coordinating a distributed transaction is given below. A hypothetical situation where two applications, each with their own database, are distributed by using Orbix. Applications could either be two separate software products or different parts of the same one, in different processes or machines. In this example, the scenario will have two applications A and B, where the application A wants to update its database and invoke an application B, which in turn will cause an update of B's database. OrbixOTS mediates between the applications, ensuring that the database updates are performed automatically.

- Application A begins a transaction by making a call on OrbixOTS (Figure 10.16). Application A is now in the context of a created transaction. Application A then registers with the OTS that it has a database that may be updated in the context of the transaction. This registration may be done automatically by the OTS.
- Application A proceeds to update its database, but does not commit this update, as the OrbixOTS is responsible for performing this step.
- Application A next invokes application B over Orbix, by making a call on a transactional object. This carries with it knowledge of the transaction that A has begun. B is said to join the global transaction.

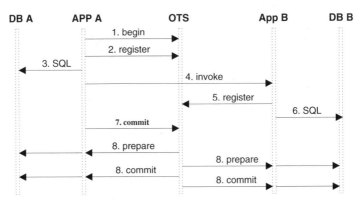

**Figure 10.16**  Interaction diagram.

- On receipt of the invocation, application B registers with the OrbixOTS that it has a resource that will need to be called back on transaction completion. As for application A, this registration step may be done manually or automatically.

- Application B now updates its database, and again defers the commit to the OrbixOTS. Control returns back to application A.

- Application A now requests completion of the transaction by invoking the commit operation on the OTS.

- The OrbixOTS now commits the transaction to both resources, using a two phase commit protocol.

Figure 10.16 shows the interaction diagram which summarizes the steps detailed above. Components of the systems are represented by vertical lines; horizontal lines represent calls from one component to another.

### 10.5.2  Microsoft Transaction Service

Microsoft Transaction Server (MTS) combines the services of a TP monitor with the philosophy of component software. MTS provides a server-centered environment for developing and deploying three-tiered applications based on Microsoft's Component Object Model (COM) technologies. It provides a container for in-process COM server components.

MTS is a container for server components. The services MTS provides are deferred activation, a sharable object context, and support for transactions. MTS allows the transaction requirements of each component it manages to be set administratively. This feature allows components to be written separately and then grouped as needed to form a single transaction. The work required to carry out a transaction, such as two-phase commit, is actually performed by a separate service, the Distributed Transaction Coordinator (DTC).

A traditional transactional application tells a transaction server that it should begin a transaction, makes changes, then tells the transaction server to commit or abort. But this traditional approach cannot be applied when the transactions are being performed by components. Since the primary goal of component-based development is to allow building applications from independently created parts, if each component is always used alone, the traditional transactional structure can be applied. But when multiple components are combined into a single transaction, each component cannot contain its own Begin Transaction request.

MTS can disallow a component to determine when a transaction begins. Instead, each component can be administratively configured to require a transaction. When a client creates a transaction-required component, MTS automatically starts a transaction. If that component then commits or aborts the transaction, MTS carries out the component's request. If the component creates another component, and the new component also requires a transaction, MTS can automatically include the changes made by the new component in the transaction. When the second component commits or aborts its work, MTS takes note but does not end the transaction, not until the parent component commits or aborts does MTS end the transaction. This approach allows the same component binary to be used in its own transaction or combined with others into a single transaction.

MTS supports automatic transactions, allowing clients to remain unaware of when transactions start and end. MTS also supports the approach in which the client indicates when a transaction begins and ends in traditional client/server transaction systems. MTS also accomplishes automatic and transparent transaction support using a context object. If a transaction needs to span the functions of two different objects, then MTS simply uses the same context object to coordinate the activities of both objects. This process allows the transaction semantics to be separated from the application code.

MTS transaction management logic is not necessarily defined within the application logic. The transaction semantics are defined declaratively when the components are assembled into an application package. An MTS application package is actually a group of related ActiveX components. In order to create an application package, the relationships between the individual components must be configured by using a tool called the MTS Explorer. The MTS Explorer generates the package and installs the runtime control information into the MTS catalogue As each component is configured, it is assigned a transaction attribute, which can take one of four values: Required, Supported, Not Supported, Requires New.

When a client application requests the creation of a new component, MTS determines the transaction status of the caller and the transaction requirements of the new component. If the caller wishes to propagate an existing transaction, then it creates the new component. By being created within the context object, the new component inherits the context object and the associated transaction.

Once the transaction context is established, the component carries out its function, based on requests from its client. When its work is completed, the component must tell the MTS executive that its task is complete. The component must determine whether to commit the transaction or abort the transaction, and then make the appropriate call to MTS to signal that its work is finished. To close the transaction, the component calls a method in the IObjectContext interface of its context object. If the transaction is ready to be committed, the component calls IObjectContext::SetComplete. If something has gone wrong and the transaction must be rolled back, the component calls IObjectContext::SetAbort.

If a component is part of a group of components, all collectively participate in a single transaction. In this case, each component will call SetComplete when its work is done, but MTS will not begin the commit process until all components within the transaction have called SetComplete. A component can be used in various ways, letting an application architect reuse the application code without rewriting the transaction control logic. This is because a component can either live within its own transaction or be part of a larger group of components, all of which belong to a single transaction.

Two phase commit for MTS applications is handled by DTC, which plays the role of transaction coordinator. DTC runs as a separate service on the same machine as MTS. When a client calls SetComplete, MTS delegates this request to the DTC. It is the DTC that actually carries out the work required to accomplish commitment and the two-phase commit process.

## 10.6   SUMMARY

The CORBA OTS offers robustness and reliability for critical applications. It provides typical TP monitors (such as TUXEDOS) for distributed object applications. CORBA OTS supports different models, including flat and nested transactional models. It also provides flexibility to customize the functionalities of the service for specific requirements.

This chapter explained in detail the CORBA OTS. We first provided some background on transactions, in particular a description of the transactional models (flat and nested), concurrency control protocols (pessimistic and optimistic), and commit protocols (2PC and 3PC). Later we described the different elements of the OTS architecture, including transactional and recoverable objects. We showed how these elements can be used according to two different modes of context propagation, implicit and explicit. Two major OTS systems were described at the end of this chapter: one is a CORBA compliant (i.e., Iona's OTS) and is widely used within industrial organizations; the other one is the Microsoft Transaction Service. Even though this is not a CORBA compliant, it shares many common aspects with the OMG's OTS.

## 10.7   REVIEW QUESTIONS

- What protocol uses OTS to coordinate the completion of a distributed transaction? Briefly explain the definition, different types, and properties of a transaction.
- Explain the lost update and inconsistent retrieval problems.
- Briefly explain the two concurrency control protocols discussed in this chapter. What is the assumption each of them makes?
- Explain how 2PC protocol for flat transactions, 2PC for nested transactions, and 3PC work.
- What is the reason behind the inclusion of an extra phase (i.e., PreCommit phase) in the 3PC?
- What are the features the OTS provide?
- What are the functions of the following OTS interfaces: Current, TransactionFactory, Control, Terminator, Coordinator, RecoveryCoordinator, Resource, SubtransactionAwareResource, and TransactionalObject?
- Compare indirect context management and implicit transaction propagation with direct context management and explicit transaction propagation in terms coding (i.e., IDL interfaces and their operations).

- Briefly explain transactional, non-transactional, and recoverable objects. How is a client invocation on non-transactional objects handled when a failure occurs?
- Give an example for each CORBA-OTS and non-CORBA OTS implementation. Explain a typical transaction scenario of OTS.

## 10.8  EXERCISES

- Compare the benefits and the drawbacks of using explicit and implicit context propagation in terms of their coding in a program.
- In OMG Transaction Service, is a transactional object also a recoverable object? Justify your answer.

# CHAPTER 11

# Object Query Service

The CORBA Object Query Service (OQS) allows declarative access to heterogeneous database systems, including relational databases, such as Oracle and Sybase, as well as object-oriented databases (ObjectStore and $O_2$). Users can invoke queries on collections of objects and the Query Service will return collections of objects that satisfy the given predicate. In this chapter we will not only describe the OQS, but also some of the main query processing techniques used in distributed databases. We believe that these techniques can be used to fully implement OQS.

There are, however, a few differences between query processing in distributed databases and CORBA environments. The major difference relates to the semantic meaning of "data sources." In distributed databases, data sources are generally stored as "tuples" of relations which are fragmented horizontally, vertically, or both at different sites. There is a centralized system that manages the distribution of data sources, and most of the processing, including query processing, is performed by central modules. CORBA has a different approach when dealing with data sources or processes. First, no distinction is made regarding the nature of the distributed objects; they can store data, perform operations, or both. Second, each server is autonomous and can support different language bindings (e.g., C++, Java) as well as different underlying systems (relational database system, file system, object-oriented database). Therefore, query processing techniques of distributed database systems need to be updated to deal with the specific requirements of CORBA environments.

This chapter does not propose solutions for query processing in CORBA environments, because they have yet to be developed. Instead we summarize the main ideas used in query execution and optimization in distributed database systems [83], and we show how these ideas can be used in the context of CORBA environments. This chapter also describes the architecture of the CORBA Object Query Service.

## 11.1 OVERALL PICTURE

For CORBA environments, dealing with database aspects is a very important issue because several organizations need to deal with persistent data sources as well as the facilities (e.g., query and transaction facilities) to manipulate these data sources. CORBA, with the object request broker, can provide communication across different database systems and therefore enable organizations to cross boundaries.

To deal with the management of data, or heterogeneous data sources, several issues must be addressed. The first one relates to the design of appropriate database wrappers which will provide a standard interface for different clients. These adaptors will be responsible for understanding local database systems and must be able to serve as a gateway between object request brokers and databases. Other issues relate to the design of database facilities to be used by CORBA clients to access and manipulate persistent data. OMG proposed a standard for such database facilities, including the query service, the transaction service and the concurrency control service. This chapter deals with the query service. Details about the different components related to this service can be found in the following chapters: database adaptor (Chapter 4), and transaction service (Chapter 10). In [95], the author proposed a POA-based adaptor with appropriate solutions for object activation/de-activation, pre-fetching and caching.

To integrate CORBA and database environments, issues such as optimization of the network access and the reliable access to a large number of data need to be considered. A simple two-tier architecture cannot adequately support these needs. A solution is three-tier client/server architecture with an explicit middle layer of software mediating between modern client workstations and exiting database systems. The client handles the presentation and local processing. The database system manages storage and retrieval of the respective data. The middle layer functions as an object application server that enables client applications to store and retrieve the data from a data server. The ORB will handle heterogeneity at the platform level, and in doing this it provides location and implementation transparency. It provides an infrastructure to integrate application components into a distributed system. The Object Query Service will provide the facilities to overcome the difficulty of accessing the database system with a better solution.

The integration of CORBA and database technologies enables clients to access CORBA objects that are stored in the persistent storage. Some of the advantages are:

- CORBA improves the ease of working across many boundaries: some database systems do not support a wide range of operating systems. The choice available may be only for that particular database server machine.

- Some database systems do not support multiple languages: If they do, then they do not allow interoperability between them. In object-oriented database systems, objects accessed by the client must be loaded in the client address space or client's machine. In CORBA, the client requests are processed on the remote object, and the result is returned back.

- In relational database management systems, clients make a query call to the database, thus exposing the relational schema to the clients; whereas in CORBA, objects export an interface defined in IDL to their clients. This allows ease of exporting an IDL interface rather than export the SQL interface. Moreover, the choice of the database management system is not revealed to the clients, an important issue when the systems and the clients are being written by different companies.

To deal with the management of data sources, OMG defined database-like services, such as query, transaction, concurrency control and persistency services. The Object Query Service enables clients to find objects whose attributes meet the search criteria that the client specified in the query. This service allows objects to be accessed from anywhere in a network without concern for the type of database that is being used, the operating system it is running on, or the programming language it is written in. In this way the user of CORBA can gain the advantage of implementing the system in a mix of technologies that use multiple machines and databases. OQS provides clients facilities to query data from heterogeneous storage systems (different types of database management systems) like ORACLE (relational database), ObjectStore (object oriented database) or a non-DBMSs (e.g., file systems, WWW servers).

Figure 11.1 shows how the OQS can be used in distributed environments. The first step consists of taking the database schema and wrapping it in an IDL. Wrapping means to develop an IDL specification that maps the database tables into IDL interfaces, with the respective DBMS type. Wrapping also means that appropriate adaptors must be used in the server side to deal with several issues, such as the communication between the ORBs and the databases. These technical issues are explained in Section 4.4 of Chapter 4. Global queries are expressed in a standard query language (such as ODMG's OQL) and then passed as strings to OQS. The syntax analyzer checks for the correctness of the received query. To facilitate the transformation of the global queries, and therefore optimize them, these queries are then transformed into algebraic expressions (called *execution plans*). An execution plan is typically a tree where the nodes are algebraic operations and the edges are links

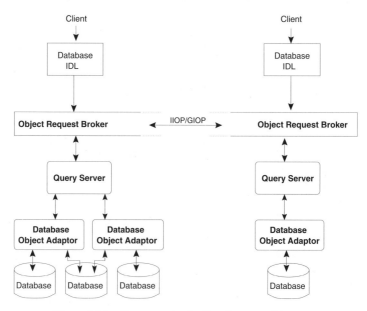

**Figure 11.1**   Query service in client/server architecture.

between the execution of the algebraic operations. The query optimizer, which is a part of the OQS, will then find the "best" global execution plan (GEP) which can be decomposed into a set of local execution plans (LEP). An LEP is an execution plan in which the data sources needed for the evaluation come from a single database server. Every query may have an infinite number of possible GEPs which are obtained by all possible re-arrangements of an original GEP. A variety of heuristic or cost-based optimization strategies within constraints imposed by the algebraic operators are then applied to reduce the number of GEPs to the most desirable ones. A "best" GEP is then selected and each LEP of the GEP is forwarded to the object adaptors which will translate them into specific (query) language to the relevant database servers on the network. When a database server receives a query, it executes it and then returns the result to the database adaptor. The adaptor then translates it into a standard format, and the result is further processed by the appropriate components of the query server (e.g., query evaluator).

From the specification point of view, OQS supports: (i) Basic operations on collections of objects, namely *selection, insertion, updating,* and *deletion.* These operations are part of the CosQueryCollection interface. (ii) Different types of objects, locally or remotely stored. They may be transient or persistent. (iii) Use of objects with arbitrary attributes and operations. (iv) Allowing the scope of the objects accessible in and via the collections that are the immediate operands of the query operations. (v) Querying and/or returning complex data structures. (vi) Operations on user-defined collections of objects. (vii) Operations on other kinds of collections and sets. (iix) The use of attributes, inheritance, and procedurally specified operations in the querying predicate and in the computation of results. (ix) The use of available interfaces defined by OMG-adopted specifications. (x) The use of relationships for navigation, including testing for the existence of a relationship between objects. (xi) An extensible framework for dealing with object queries. (xii) Independence of specific syntax and semantics of the query language used.

## 11.2 BACKGROUND ON QUERY PROCESSING

Important work has been done by the database community in designing efficient query services for distributed database systems, and in particular, the design and implementation of distributed query managers that are able to generate efficient query execution plans to coordinate the execution of the generated plans. This section overviews such work and describes concepts related to execution strategies and join operators.

### 11.2.1 Overview

The efficiency of a query manager basically depends on the integration between query execution module components (query scanner, query parser, query transformer, query functions and operators, query optimizer, query decomposer and query evaluator). This integration is performed through an interface between a declarative query language (e.g., predicate calculus) and a host programming language that is used to develop the required execution module components. The levels of integration are mainly categorized as loosely or tightly coupled approaches. In a loosely coupled approach, a query execution engine is introduced to take strings containing queries as their arguments. The execution engine parses and semantically evaluates a given query at run time. This approach also allows queries to be optimized at runtime.

A query manager has two main components: a query optimization engine and a query execution engine. A client query is first analyzed (by a parser) and then mapped (by a translator) into a sequence of algebraic operations to be implemented by the query execution engine. Algebraic operations involve operations such join, project, and select. A *query optimization engine* (or query optimizer) is a special planner module that employs different techniques (plan representation, search including directed search and pruning, dynamic programming, and branch-and-bound algorithms) to enhance the performance of the query processing by minimizing several variables, such as the response time, cpu, I/O, network time and effort (i.e., time and effort can differ due to parallelism), memory costs (e.g., maximum allocation or as time-space product), and a total resource usage. A *query execution engine* is used to define the space of possible plans that can be chosen by the query optimizer. Since query execution plans (QEP) are algebraic expressions, they can be represented as trees [40]. As shown in Figure 11.2, there are several tree shapes that QEPs can take, including left deep, bushy, and right deep. The QEPs can be divided into groups according to which shape of the query inputs (operands) it can evaluate. For example, when a user query is submitted, the query execution engine (using parser) generates a possible un-optimized query plan (i.e., tree structure). The query optimizer then maps or expands the initial query expression into a possible optimized query execution plan that operates directly on the stored database objects. The mapping or expanding process can be very complex and might require substantial search and cost estimation effort. This process may be iterated repeatedly until

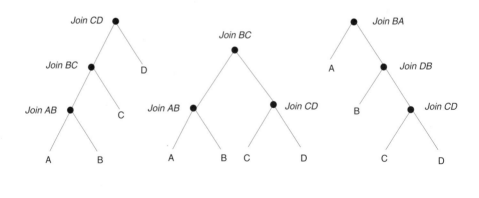

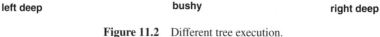

**Figure 11.2** Different tree execution.

a most optimized stage is reached. By using a simple tree traversal algorithm, the QEP is translated into a representation ready for execution by the database's query execution engine. The result of this translation can be (i) a compiled code, (ii) a semi-compiled or interpreted language, or (iii) semi-compiled or interpreted data structure.

A query can be a read-only query or update query. Both types of queries may include a search predicate to determine the database objects to be modified. Therefore query optimization and execution techniques will be applied to search and extract information from the database without changing the database. Queries can be implemented by using either interactive queries or embedded queries. Embedded queries are usually optimized when the program is compiled and used to avoid the optimization overhead when the program run. This type of optimization strategy is called *static optimization*. The static strategy concept is applied in different projects such as EXODUS [41] and later refined by using a dynamic optimization strategy [42, 66]. As indicated in the system R, there must be dynamic optimization mechanisms for storing the optimized plans and invalidating the stored plans when they become infeasible (i.e., index dropped from database). The invalidating and storing of a current valid plan is known as a cut point. The cut point between compile-time and run-time used in dynamic optimization techniques may be placed at any other point in the sequence of query processing steps.

A query can be nested or un-nested. Nested queries pose a few problems during the optimization stage because their processing requires special techniques to deal with (i) optimization rules and heuristics such as flattening, (ii) selectivity and cost estimation, and (iii) algorithms and their parallelization. Processing these types of queries requires more enhanced developing efforts, and includes: (i) the system architectures for complex query plans and parallel execution, (ii) the selection and aggregation algorithms, (iii) the relationship of sorting and hashing as it pertains to database query processing, (iii) special operations and other auxiliary techniques such as compression. As the purpose of query processing algorithms is to perform some kind of matching between database items (i.e., tuples, objects, attributes, etc), there is a need for concepts that can be implemented to perform operations (binary and unary operations) and sorting and hashing structures. These concepts affect many aspects of query processing from indexing and clustering over aggregation and join algorithms for centralized, distributed and federated database systems operations.

## 11.2.2 Execution Strategies

In a distributed database system, data is stored across several sites and the distribution is transparent for the user. The database system is responsible for the management of the data distribution. Relations can be stored across several sites and their access can incur message-passing costs. There are generally two techniques for storing relations and the third one can be a hybrid. In a horizontal fragmentation, each fragment consists of a subset of rows of the original relation and the union of the horizontal fragments must be equal to the original relation. In vertical fragmentation, each fragment consists of a subset of columns of the original relation and the collection of vertical fragments should be a lossless-join decomposition. In general, a relation can be fragmented, and each resulting fragment can be further fragmented.

The processing of queries in distributed databases has several more factors to be considered than in centralized databases. One of the crucial factors is the cost of transferring data over the network. Data includes intermediate files that are transferred to other sites for further processing, as well as the final result files that may have to be transferred to the site where the query result is needed. Although these costs may not be very high if the sites are connected via a high-performance local area network, they become quite significant in other types of networks. Therefore, query optimization algorithms for distributed databases have been focusing on reducing the amount of data transfer as an optimization criterion in choosing a distributed query execution strategy.

To estimate the cost of an evaluation strategy, in addition to counting the number of page I/Os, the cost model needs to take into account the cost of shipping the result tuples to the site where the query is posed from the site where the result is assembled.

Let us consider the following two relations which describe a department and its staff members. Every department has an id (deptid), a name (d_name) and an address (address). For every staff of a department, the department id, the staff id (staffid), its name (s_name) and its title (title) are recorded.

```
Department(deptid, d_name, address)
Staff(deptid, staffid, s_name, title)
```

Now we wish to query these relations and select all the names of the staff of the department of Computer Science. The expression of this query in relational calculus using SQL syntax is:

```
Select  s_name
From    Department D, Staff S
Where   D.deptid = S.deptid
and     D.d_name = ''Computer Science''
```

As shown below, two algebraic expressions can be derived from the query above, where $\sigma$, operators, respectively. These expressions are semantically equivalent (produce the same result), but they do not have the same performance (the time cost of evaluating the query). The semantic equivalence of algebraic expressions can be obtained by a series of transformations on the algebraic operators, such as the permutation of the operators $\sigma$ and $\bowtie$. The cost of evaluating the expression (2) below is cheaper than the option (1) because the join in the second option will be done on a reduced size of the relation Department (i.e., only computer science department will be used). In the first option, all the tuples of the relation will be considered and therefore this will increase the cost of the join.

**TABLE 11.1    Horizontal Fragmentation**

| Site | Relation |
|------|----------|
| $S_1$ | $\text{Department}_1 = \sigma_{deptid \leq 100}$ (Department) |
| $S_2$ | $\text{Department}_2 = \sigma_{deptid > 100}$ (Department) |
| $S_3$ | $\text{Staff}_1 = \sigma_{deptid \leq 50}$ (Staff) |
| $S_4$ | $\text{Staff}_2 = \sigma_{deptid > 50}$ (Staff) |

$$\prod_{s\_name} (\sigma_{d\_name=\text{``Computer Science''}} (\text{Department} \bowtie_{deptid} \text{Staff})) \quad (11.1)$$

$$\prod_{s\_name} (\sigma_{d\_name=\text{``Computer Science''}} (\text{Department}) \bowtie_{deptid} \text{Staff}) \quad (11.2)$$

Now if we are dealing with distributed data, the relations Department and Staff can be fragmented horizontally, vertically or both. Let us assume there are four sites where these relations are stored and horizontally fragmented. Table 11.1 describes the way the relations Department and Staff are horizontally fragmented. The site $S_1$, for example, contains only those tuples of the relation Department that have an id lesser than 100. Those with greater id are stored in the site $S_2$.

We assume that the result is expected at $S_5$. There are several equivalent distributed execution strategies for the above query. To make the idea simple to understand, we illustrate three strategies, as shown in Figures 11.3, 11.4, and 11.5. Strategy

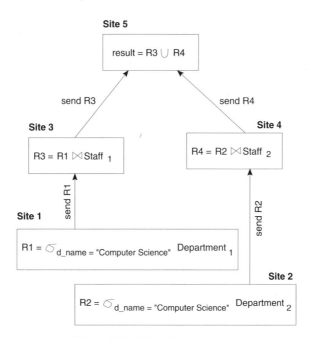

**Figure 11.3**    Execution strategy A.

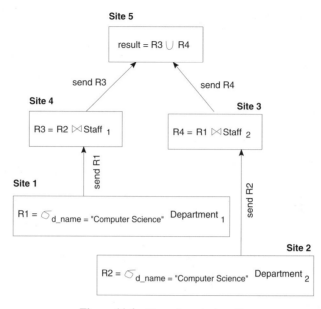

**Figure 11.4**   Execution strategy B.

A basically computes the selection of all Computer Science department at $S_1$ and $S_2$, respectively, within the relations $R_1$ and $R_2$. The sites 1 and 2 send the produced relations to $S_3$ and $S_4$, which in their turn will compute the join with their respective fragments of the relation Staff (i.e., $Staff_1$ and $Staff_2$). Finally, sites 3 and 4 will send $S_5$ the produced relations $R_3$ and $R_4$, which later joins them to generate the final result.

Strategy B illustrated in Figure 11.4 is similar to strategy A, except that site 1 will communicate the result to site 4 instead. In the same way, site 2 will transfer the partial result to $S_3$.

Another strategy is to send all the fragments of the relations to $S_5$ which will re-create all the complete relations (by union of the fragments) and later make an ap-

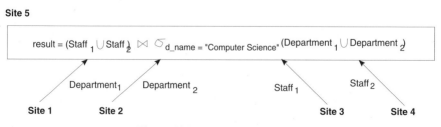

**Figure 11.5**   Execution strategy C.

propriate join between the relation Staff and Department. This strategy can be much more expensive in terms of total cost[1] than Strategies A and B. In strategy A, for example, only a reduced number of data will be transferred between sites (bottom to up of Figure 11.3) because all the selections and join (with smaller relations) are done earlier, and $S_5$ will then be working with a smaller data compared to $S_5$ of Strategy C. Without specific details, it is difficult to differentiate between the strategies A and B. However, if sites 1 and 3 are closer to each other (and similarly for sites 2 and 4), the strategy 11.3 will be better because it reduces the transfer cost.

To perform any choice between strategies, the query optimizer needs to access statistics on the database. These typically bear on fragments and include fragment cardinality and size as well as the number of distinct values of each attribute [83]. To minimize the probability of error, more detailed statistics such as histograms of attribute values are sometimes used at the expense of higher management cost.

### 11.2.3  Query Architecture

Figure 11.6 depicts the different steps of a typical query processing system.

- During the *query decomposition step*, the user query will go through different steps to check, for example, whether or not information referred with the query correspond to those recorded in the database (syntactic and semantic analysis). Queries are also normalized to facilitate further processing (e.g., transformation of $\neg(\neg p_1)$ to $p_1$). The last phase of the query decomposition consists of rewriting the query in an algebraic form. This involves (i) straight transformation of the query from the relational calculus into algebra, and (ii) restructuring of the relational algebra query to improve the performance. Details about these transformations can be found at [83].

- During the *data localization step*, relations are replaced by their corresponding fragments. Different techniques of query reduction can be used: reduction for primary horizontal fragmentation (where a relation is replaced by a union of its fragments), reduction for vertical fragmentation (where a relation is re-constructed by joining its different fragments), and reduction for hybrid fragmentation (where a relation is rebuilt with horizontal and vertical fragments).

- The last step is the *optimization* of the query by using appropriate techniques and producing appropriate execution plans. A query optimizer will contain different components such as a *search space*, a *cost model* and *search strategy*. A search space consists of alternative execution plans for a query. The cost model basically is used to evaluate the cost of each execution plan and the search strategy explores the search space and select the best execution plan.

---

[1]This will involve: the cost of transferring each fragment to $S_5$ + cost of making the union between fragments of Staff + cost of making union between Department + cost of making join between the complete relations Staff and Department.

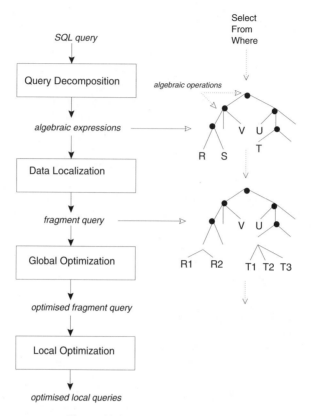

**Figure 11.6**   Query processing steps.

## 11.2.4   Join Operators

This section discusses a specific algebraic operator, the join operator (or $semi-join$ for distributed databases), because the design of such an operator can have a large impact on the performance of an optimizer. Here we overview some of the work done in the context of this area.

### 11.2.4.1   *Nonjoin Queries.*

Every operation, including scanning a relation and selecting data, is affected by the fragmentation of relations. If we assume that a relation A is horizontally fragmented, with half of all tuples at a site $S_1$, and the other half at a site $S_2$, the database system must be able to process SELECT queries by evaluating it at both sites and taking the union of the results. If the SELECT clause contained AVG, the results cannot be combined by simply taking the union. The database system must compute the sum and count of a field value at the two sites, and use this information to compute the average of all tuples. If the WHERE clause contained that all tuples related are stored at one site, on the other hand, the database system should recognize that this query can be answered by just executing it at the site $S_1$.

To better illustrate the difficulties related to query processing, let us consider a different scenario. In this case the relation A is vertically fragmented with the attributes $A_1$ and $A_2$ recorded in the site $S_2$, and the attributes $A_3$ and $A_4$ at site $S_1$. Because no attribute is stored at both sites, this vertical fragmentation would therefore be a poor decomposition. The database system has to reconstruct the whole relation A by joining the two fragments on the common tuple-id field and execute the query over this reconstructed relation. The other case is when the entire relation A is stored at both sites ($S_1$ and $S_2$). In this way, queries can be answered by executing them either in site $S_1$ or site $S_2$. Usually, to improve the performance of the query evaluation, the cost of shipping and the cost of executing the query are considered as criteria for evaluating the queries. The local processing costs may differ depending on what indexes are available on relation at the two sites.

### 11.2.4.2  *Joins.*

*Join* is an algebraic operation used to retrieve information from different database items (e.g., as relations, files and objects). This operator is the most difficult one to implement efficiently, especially if there is no predefined link between different database items [65]. Usually, the remaining algebraic operators (e.g., *Select* and *Project*) are implicit operations with the Join operation. There are different types of join operations (e.g., *equijoin, semijoin, outerjoin*) and most of their implementations [33] use the theta join operators (i.e., $=, \leq, \geq, <, >$, and $\neq$). Such implementation techniques include different join methods such as nested-loop, sort-merge-join, and hash-join. In the case of hash-join method various hashing techniques such as simple-hash-join, hash-partitioned-join using divide-and-conquer (i.e., grace-hash-join, hybrid-hash join and hash-loop-joins), and simple hash-partitioned-join can be implemented.

Let us consider a simple example to show the complexity of the join operator. Suppose that the relation A is stored at $S_1$, and that the relation B is stored at $S_2$. The cost of joining the two relations A and B should take into account various strategies. Fetch can be done with a page-based nested loop join in $S_1$ with the relation A as the outer, and for each relation A page, fetch all relation B pages from $S_2$. If the fetched relation A pages are cached in $S_1$ until the join is complete, pages are fetched only once. But if the query site is not $S_1$ nor $S_2$, the cost of shipping the result is greater than the cost of shipping both relations to the query site. Thus, it would be cheaper to ship both relations to the query site and compute the join there. Alternatively, an index nested loops join in $S_1$ can be built, fetching all matching B's tuples for each A's tuple. This is not a good idea because the cost of shipping tuples dominates the total cost, even for a fast network. An extreme solution is to ship the relation A from $S_1$ to $S_2$ and carry out the join, ship the relation B to $S_1$ and carry out the join there, or ship both to the site where the query was posed and compute the join there.

### 11.2.4.3  *Semijoins.*

The basic idea behind distributed query processing using the semijoin operation is to reduce the number of tuples in a relation before transferring it to another site. Intuitively, to send the joining column of one relation R to the site where the other relation S is located, then the column is joined with S. Consider the strategy of shipping the relation B to $S_1$ and computing the join at $S_2$. Some of

B's tuples do not join with any tuple in Sailors. If we could somehow identify B's tuples that are guaranteed not to join with any tuples in the relation A, we could avoid shipping them.

Two techniques have been proposed for reducing the number of A's tuples to be shipped. The idea is to proceed in three steps:

- At $S_1$, compute the projection of the relation A onto the join columns, and ship this projection to $S_2$.
- At $S_2$, compute the natural join of the projection received from the first site with the relation B; the result of this join is called the *reduction* of the relation B with respect to key field. Only those B's tuples in the reduction will join with tuples in the relation A. Therefore, ship the reduction of the relation B to $S_1$, rather than the entire the relation B.
- At $S_1$, compute the join of the reduction of the relation B with key field.

## 11.3   OQS LANGUAGES

OQS is designed to be independent of any specific query language. Therefore, a particular Query Service implementation can be based on a variety of query languages and their associated query processors. However, in order to provide query interoperability among the widest variety of query systems and to provide object-level query interoperability, OMG's requirements are that the OQS must support one of the following two query languages: SQL (e.g., SQL-92) or OQL (e.g., OQL-92).

As mentioned earlier, queries are transformed into an algebraic expression for query optimization and execution purposes. Because OMG is dealing with the object-oriented paradigm, the most appropriate algebra to be used is an object-oriented algebra. OMG does not provide details on the type of the algebra to be used because it relates to the implementation of the OQS, and therefore it is for the those who are building such a service to make the appropriate choices.

This section provides an overview of an object-oriented algebra and OQL to help the reader understand the way distributed objects are used.

### 11.3.1   Object Query Language

OQL is an SQL-like query language but with more abilities. The major difference with SQL is that OQL acts on the objects and not relations. OQL supports associative query and update on collections of IDL objects. Specifically, it is possible to define an object query language for any of the existing object models such as C++, Smalltalk, and SQL3. OQL, which queries over IDL specified collection objects, may be expressed. OQL deals with complex objects and collections. It allows querying objects starting from their names, where a name may denote any atomic, structure, collection, or literal objects, and acts as entry point into the database. Some of the differences are: (i) includes operation invocation in queries; (ii) feature of inheritance; (iii) ability to invoke operation provides the inserts, update and delete capability without violating encapsulation.

An OQL expression over a set of variables X is recursively defined as follows:

| | |
|---|---|
| const | constants |
| \|var | variables from X |
| \|lambda_var | if inside of a select or quantifier |
| \|expr.method_name() | method call |
| \|expr->field_name | field selection |
| \|[field_name = expr [, field_name = expr]*] | tuple constructor |
| \|set([expr [, expr]* ]) | set constructor |
| \|bag( [expr [, expr]*]) | bag constructor |
| \|list( [expr [, expr]*]) | list constructor |
| \|select [distinct] expr from lambda_var in expr [, lambda_var in expr]* [where expr] | selection |
| \|exists lambda_var in expr : expr | existential quantifier |
| \|for all lambda_var in expr : expr | universal quantifier |

The following is an example of OQL query.

```
select distinct p.name
from    p in Person
where p.own.manufacturer.location.name = "Detroit"
        and Person.own.drivetrain.engine.cylinder >= 6
        and Person.own.color = "blue"
```

where p, declared in the FROM clause, is a range variable over member objects of the set named Patients of type Set stored somewhere in an object services architecture instantiation. The function *name*() used in the WHERE clause is a public member function of Person inherited by Patient and Physician. Inheritance of function interfaces is as defined by IDL. The SELECT clause indicates that the objects returned by the query are Patient objects. The expression *p.family_doctor.name*, called a *path expression*, allows navigation through the object composition graph, which enables the formulation of predicates on nested objects. The function *family_doctor*() is of type Physician; therefore, we use the dot notation (following C++ convention) to invoke the function name of physician.

The previous query can be extended to return the name and the age of the person who owns a car which is manufactured by a company located in Detroit. These cars are blue and their engines have six cylinders.

```
select distinct struct (a: p.name, z: p.age)
from    p in Person
where p.own.manufacturer.location.name = "Detroit"
        and Person.own.drivetrain.engine.cylinder >= 6
        and Person.own.color = "blue'
```

But things can be complicated. For example, instead of returning the age of p, we may specify z as a result of another select statement. The following QQL query extends the result of the above query and adds to each returned tuple the name of the president of the company which manufactures the car owned by the person. In addition, this president must earn more that 100,000.

```
select distinct struct (a: p.name, z: age,
                    w: (select y.name
                        from y in employee
                        where y in x.own.manufacturer.president
                        and   y.salary > 100000))
from  p in Person
where p.own.manufacturer.location.name = "Detroit"
      and Person.own.drivetrain.engine.cylinder >= 6
      and Person.own.color = "blue'
```

### 11.3.2 OQL Algebra

An algebraic expression is used in query processing for the execution of queries in a "uniform model," and therefore independent of specific language or syntax. Because query processing aims at optimizing the execution of queries, properties of algebraic operations, such as permutation of selection and joins, are well suited for building different execution plans for the same query, and depending on a specific criterion (e.g., time execution, cpu) later select the most appropriate execution graphs. Access methods, such as indexes on available data, are used to compute the cost of each of the execution graphs.

There are several object-oriented algebras, such as [90]. Here we describe some of the basic common algebraic operators of these algebraic expressions. In most of these algebras, the results of object algebraic operators are collections of objects whose member may be different types like set, bag, list, and so forth.

- *get(monoid, extent_name, range_variable, predicate)*: It captures the OQL query *select * from range_variable in extent_name* with predicate. It creates a collection, where each tuple has only one component, range_variable, bound to an object of this extent. The predicate is in a form of $(p_1, \ldots, p_n)$ to indicate the conjunction of the predicates $p_i$. The predicates are not allowed to contain nested queries (all forms of querying nesting are eliminated).

- *reduce (monoid, expr, variable, head, predicate)*: For each tuple in the collection *expr* that satisfies the predicate, it evaluates the head. Then it reduces the resulting collection to a value (bound to a variable) or a collection (where each tuple binds variable to the value of head), depending on the output in monoid.

- *join (monoid, left, right, head, predicate, keep)*: It relates to the relational join operator. It concatenates the tuples of the left and right inputs if they satisfy the predicate. If keep=left, then it behaves like a left-outer join (it concatenates the left tuple with null values), if keep=right it behaves like a right-outer join, while if keep=none, it is a regular join.

- *unnest(monoid, expr, variable, path, predicate, keep)*: It unnests the inner collection path of the outer collection *expr* and filters out all tuples that do not satisfy the predicate. For example, if *expr* is of type set ($<$ $x$ $:<$ $name$ : $string, children$ : $set(person)$ $>>$) and path=x.children, then the output of this operation has type set ($<$ $name$ : $string, children$ : $set(person), variable$ : $person$ $>$). If there are no values, or no value satisfies the predicate, and keep=true, then the tuple is padded with a null value.

- *nest (monoid, expr, variable, head, groupby, nestvars, predicate)*: It groups the *expr* by the variables in *groupby* (which has the form: $vars(v_1 v_n)$, where a $v_i$ is a variable defined in *expr*.) Then, for each different binding of the *groupby* variable, it creates a tuple extended with the binding of variable to the value.

- *map (monoid, expr, variable, function)*: maps the function (that depends on the variable) over *expr*. It is simpler versions of reduce.

- *merge(monoid, left, right)*: merges the (union-compatible) input expressions.

As explained earlier, in order to perform optimization of the user queries, OQL queries will be translated into algebraic expressions. Here we will only illustrate these translations on a few examples of OQL queries.

```
SELECT distinct struct (E: e.name,
                        M: (SELECT c.name
                            FROM c in a e.children
                            WHERE c.age > 18 ))
    FROM e in Employee   WHERE e.name="Smith"
```

has the following algebraic form:

```
reduce(set,
       nest (bag,
             get(set,
                 employees,
                 e,
                 and (eq(project(e,name), "Smith"))),
                 c,
                 project(e, children),
                 and (get(project(c, age), 18), true),
                 x,
                 project(c, name),
                 vars(e),
                 vars(),
                 and()),
             y,
             struct(bind(E, project(e,name)), bind(M,x)),
             and () )
```

The following example returns a struct instead, where the names of employee and their departments are returned.

```
SELECT struct( E: e.name, D: e.dept.name )
FROM e in Employees;
```

This OQL query is translated into the following algebraic expression

```
reduce(bag,
       join(bags,
            get(bag,Employees,e,and()),
       get(bag,Departments,x,and()),
       and (eq(OID(project(e,dept)),OID(x))),
       none),
y,
struct (bind(E,project(e,name)),bind(D,project(x,name))),
and( ))
```

The last example about the translation of OQL queries is the following:

```
SUM( SELECT e.age
     FROM e in Employees);
```

is transformed to

```
reduce(sum,
       get(sum,Employees,e,and( ) ),
       x,
       project(e,age),
       and( ) )
```

## 11.4   OQS COMPONENTS

OQS provides query operations on collections of objects. Queries are predicate-based and may return collections of objects, and include all conventional manipulation operations, such as selection, insertion, updating and deletion on collection of objects. Objects involved in queried collections may be of any type. Figure 11.7 shows the overall OQS's architecture. QueryEvaluators represent the main components of such a service and allow nesting and federation of queries over a set of distributed objects. Such objects may participate in a query in two ways, either as an object as it is, or as a part of a collection of objects (either implicit or explicit). The first is more general because any CORBA object is supported; however it may have optimization problems. In the second, a query is passed to lower level Query-Evaluators (see Figure 11.7(b)(c)). The result of these subqueries should be combined and passed to the client; however, this is an implementation issue and not part

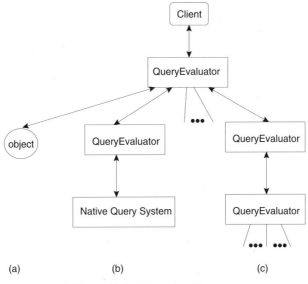

**Figure 11.7**   General architecture.

of the specification. This second way allows the use of optimizations provided by existing native database systems. As shown in Figure 11.7(c), queries can be nested to an arbitrary number of levels.

Figure 11.8 provides some details of the OQS's interfaces, and Table 11.2 describes the role of these interfaces. This framework provides two levels to accomplish

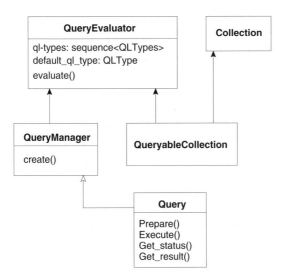

**Figure 11.8**   Query framework interface hierarchy/structure.

**TABLE 11.2   OQS Interface**

| Interface | Purpose |
|---|---|
| CollectionFactory | To create collections |
| Collection | To aggregate objects |
| Iterator | To iterate over collections |
| QueryLanguageType | To represent query language types |
| QueryEvaluator | To evaluate query predicates and execute query operations |
| QueryableCollection | To represent the scope and result of queries |
| QueryManager | To create query objects and perform query processing |
| Query | To represent queries |

this. The first level consists of the basic abstractions involving minimal functionalities related to the query service: QueryEvaluator and Collection interfaces. The next level can be considered as the advance level, which consists of QueryManager and QueryableCollection interfaces. They provide an extensible functionality for dealing with all aspects of a query.

### 11.4.1   QueryEvaluator

This module specifies the functionalities of query evaluators. QueryEvaluator evaluates queries predicates and executes query operations, and they are required to support queries expressed in various languages, including SQL-92 and ODMG's OQL. Each QueryEvaluator publishes the query functionality through its evaluate operation and performs all query processing by invoking operations on that object through the IDL interfaces. The specification proposes QueryEvaluators to support OQL or SQL dialects as query language.

```
module CosQuery {
   ... // list of exceptions
   enum QueryStatus {complete, incomplete};
   typedef CosQueryCollection::ParameterList ParameterList;
   typedef CORBA::InterfaceDef QLType;
   interface QueryLanguageType {};
   interface SQLQuery : QueryLanguageType {};
   interface SQL_92Query : SQLQuery {};
   interface OQL : QueryLanguageType {};
   interface OQLBasic : OQL {};
   interface OQL_93 : OQL {};
   interface OQL_93Basic : OQL_93, OQLBasic {};

   interface QueryEvaluator {
      readonly attribute sequence<QLType> ql_types;
```

```
    readonly attribute QLType default_ql_type;
    any evaluate (in string query, in QLType ql_type, in
      ParameterList params)
      raises(QueryTypeInvalid, QueryInvalid,
            QueryProcessingError);
  };

  . . .

};
```

A user can read the attribute default_ql_type to find the default query language for the QueryEvaluator or the other attribute ql_types for a list of other supported query languages. The query is submitted as a string in the chosen query language and passed to the QueryEvaluator, specifying the language and a list of parameters. When the query completes successfully, it returns the result of type Any. The returned result is a generic type and the most common return type will probably be a collection of objects. If the evaluator meets an error, then it throws an exception. For example, if the query language type specified is not supported by the QueryEvaluator, then it throws QueryTypeInvalid exception. If the query syntax or semantics is incorrect or if the input parameter list is incorrect, then, the QueryInvalid exception is thrown. If any error is encountered during query processing, the QueryProcessingError exception is thrown. The *evaluate*() operation evaluates a query and performs required query processing. The IFR (Interface Repository) contains the details of the data types and methods in it, the evaluate operation evaluate query predicates by referring this IFR. If the predicate type is not similar to the one in the Interface Repository, then, the evaluate function returns a QueryTypeInvaild.

### 11.4.2   Collections and Iterator

Collections of objects may be used both as the scope and result of a query. Collections are not typed; objects of different types can be part of the same collection. The Collection interface specification provides standard operations for retrieving, adding, deleting and replacing objects in collections. Associated iterators are used for traversal.

Collection and Iterators are abstract object types. The Collections module of the OQS describes classes for handling arbitrary collections of CORBA objects, and includes support for adding and deleting objects and for iterating over collections. The QueryEvaluator passes the query predicate to the collection. The objects that are present in the Collections are called elements. The Collection interface defines operations to add, replace, remove and retrieve elements (see `CosQueryCollection` interface). Elements of collections are generally of type any. In a heterogeneous distributed database environment, depending on the underlying types of data, these elements could be relational tuples, objects or images.

```
module CosQueryCollection {
    exception ElementInvalid {};
    exception IteratorInvlaid {};
    exception PositionInvalid {};
    ...
    interface CollectionFactory {
            readonly attribute long cardinality;
            void add_element (in any element)
                raises(ElementInvalid);
            void add_all_elements (in Collection elements)
                raises(ElementInvalid);
            void insert_element_at (in any element, in Iterator where)
                raises(IteratorInvalid, ElementInvalid);
    };
    ...
};
```

The attribute *cardinality* stands for the number of objects in the collection, and the function *next*() of the Iterator interface returns the object of the collection to the Iterator it is pointing to and advances the iterator position. The function *more*() of the Iterator interface returns true, if there are more elements left to be retrieved by a call to *next*(), and false otherwise.

Wrapper maps the given OQL to the respective query language; hence when the client receives the result he/she does not know whether it is from a relational or from an object database. It is often difficult to obtain a specific object without navigating through the Collection, as it is not always possible to get the result in the first instance. CORBA Query Service provides an interface to over come the above difficulty, by providing an interface called *Iterator*. The operation Iterator *create_iterator*() and creates an iterator.

```
Module CosQueryCollection {
    ...
    interface Iterator {
        any next() raises ( IteratorInvalid, PositionInvalid );
        void reset( );
        boolean more( );
    };
    Iterator create_iterator ();
};
```

An Iterator is a movable pointer into a collection. Iterator is a cursor implementation in database systems. For a client to navigate through the member elements in the collection uses this Iterator. In an Ordered Collection, an Iterator points to the beginning or the first element of the Collection. The operation *next*() moves the pointer through subsequent elements until it reaches the last element in the Collection. If the Collection is unordered then the Iterator visit in a random order. Each element in

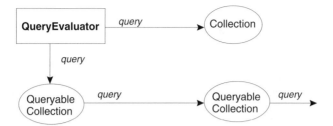

**Figure 11.9**   Query framework interface hierarchy/structure.

this is reached only once. The Iterator interface provides an operation called *reset*() which is used for restarting the iteration. We can have multiple iterator to traverse through the same or different collections.

### 11.4.3   QueryableCollection

It combines the query functionality of the QueryEvaluator with the data management functionality of Collection. Then after evaluating the predicate and the operation on the query it receives results and returns the result to the caller. This Collection is nothing but a QueryEvaluator by itself, as shown in Figure 11.9; that is, the Collection can itself be both results of a query and as a scope for another query. QueryableCollection interface provides a mechanism for nesting queries to any number of levels. The collection then serves as both result of a query and as a scope for another query. This type of collection is known as QueryableCollections.

```
module CosQuery {
   ...
   interface QueryableCollection : QueryEvaluator, CosQueryCollection::
     Collection {};
   ...
```

The interface `QueryableCollection` inherits from both `QueryEvaluator` and `Collection`. Though it is an implementation issue and not specified by CORBA, the result of a query on a `QuerableCollection` should be another `QueryableCollection` that can be queried again. To be able to use local optimization techniques, the `QueryableCollection` may raise an exception when new objects are replaced or added that are out of scope of the Query Evaluator section (like most ordinary CORBA objects will be).

### 11.4.4   QueryManager and Query Object

Query managers and Query objects are useful for complex and time consuming queries. Complex queries may be optimized before execution and saved for later use with a different set of parameters. By using Query Managers, a client is able to execute a time-consuming query in an asynchronous manner, that is, it's not blocked by the call and can perform other operations while waiting for the result.

When the client generates a query, no feedback regarding the query will be returned until the client receives data from the query. In these situations, QueryManager allows clients to monitor and manage the queries that have been generated. It returns the status of the operation of the query. QueryManager is more powerful than QueryEvaluator because QueryManager contains pointers to the set of object in a database through the wrapper, on which the queries can be specified. In other words, QueryManager contains the universal collection of objects. A wrapper then has the pointer to the object in the database containing the index. Any query to be accessed is represented by the Query Object, which operates on the subset of the collections present in the QueryManager.

```
module CosQuery {
    . .
    interface QueryManager : QueryEvaluator {
        Query create (in string query, in QLType ql_type, in
            ParameterList params) raises(QueryTypeInvalid, QueryInvalid);
    };

    interface Query {
        readonly attribute QueryManager query_mgr;
        void prepare (in ParameterList params) raises(QueryProcessingError);
        void execute (in ParameterList params) raises(QueryProcessingError);
        QueryStatus get_status ();
        any get_result ();
    };
};
```

The attribute ql_types is a sequence of query languages supported by the Query Evaluator and the attribute default_ql_type is the default query language used if not specified in a call to. The function *evaluate*() takes a string representation of a query, a query language type and a sequence of parameters and runs the query if possible and returns the result. The function of QueryManager is similar to evaluate function of the Query Evaluator, except that it returns an object of type Query. The attribute *query_mgr* of Query stands for the associated Query Manager and the function *prepare*() prepares a query with a different set of parameters (that are passed as an argument). It should optimize a query for faster execution. Finally, the function *execute*() executes a query. A list of parameters can be passed as an argument.

The QueryManager interface works in tandem with a Query object in managing overall query processing and monitoring the query execution. A Query object is created for each query. Once the Query object is created, the first step of query processing, the query language type and the query syntax are checked. If the Query Manager does not support the query language then a QueryTypeInvalid exception is thrown. If the query syntax or semantics is incorrect or if the input parameter provided is incorrect, the QueryInvalid exception is raised. The QueryManager obtains the information of the attributes and its data type, methods from the Interface repository to check whether the input parameter list is correct or not. Assuming that the syntax, semantics and the parameters are correct, the next step is to decompose the query. The objective of decomposing is to break up a given query into subqueries. The subquery is expressed in terms of the actual or conceptual databases into its component parts or subqueries and finds a strategy that indicats the sequence of primitive or fundamental operations and their corresponding processing sites in the network necessary to answer the query. The operation $prepare()$ defined in the Query Interface goes into different stages of query processing.

## 11.5 DOK QUERY SERVICE

This section describes the design and implementation of the OQS service in the context of the DOK project [102]. In this project, a loosely coupled approach similar to ODMG's C++ OQL binding [19] is used. A user's queries are written in the ODMG OQL syntax. The loosely coupled approach was chosen because it is much simpler to implement. The focus in this section is on the DOK Query Service, which is a CORBA compliant. Because the syntax of the CORBA Object Query Service has already been covered in the previous sections, the focus here will be on the details of the design and implementation of the DOK query processing engine.

The global query processing is composed of a set of phases: query preprocessing, query decomposition, query optimization, and query evaluation. After the global query is parsed and semantically is correct, the query preprocessor module translates a global query against the integrated schema into an internal representation in terms of external data sources objects to be next utilized by query optimizer. Because of the heterogeneity nature, a relational algebra tree (B-tree) is used to express the operations and semantics concepts for all possible external data sources (i.e., relational and object-oriented). The query tree internal nodes represent query operations (i.e., select, join, project, outer-join, etc.), while the leaf nodes are used to represent both tables in the case of relational databases and functions for object-oriented databases. The leaf nodes may contain both columns specifications, functions' parameters constraints and some other performance related operations such as scan and sort.

### 11.5.1 Query Execution Engine

Execution of queries is based on different algorithms (sorting and hashing). The DOK Query execution engine manages elements of large sets of items such as relations, records, tuples, entities, or other objects. The implementation of query processing algorithms is based on the iteration over their input items sets. Sets are represented by sequences and used to represent one-dimensional lists, arrays and time series bulk types. Algorithms are algebra-type operators that consume zero or more inputs and produce one or more outputs.

Query processing algorithms are based on algebra concepts categorized as logical and physical algebra algorithms. Logical algebra considers the data model (relational, and object-oriented) and defines what queries can be expressed in the corresponding data model such as a relational algebra. Physical algebra is a system-specific feature; different systems may implement the same data model (i.e., logical algebra), but they may use different physical algebras. The query execution engine may use one or more logical algebra algorithms such as the use of only nested-loops join algorithm, or both nested-loops join and merge-join algorithm, or entirely rely on hash join algorithm. It may also use the physical algebra algorithms such as cost functions that are associated only with physical algebra operators of the corresponding system. In a real environment the mapping process can be complex because it involves choices and frequently logical and physical operators do not map directly to each other. For-example, one physical algebra operator may implement multiple logical algebra operators (i.e., to join two tables we may implement into two steps: (i) projection without duplicate removal, (ii) then remove any duplication.

Here we define the implementation of the query execution module (execute) and the protocol used to invoke each query processing component to process a user query. As shown earlier, the second argument to the query execution module is an OQL statement, and the subsequent host language expressions are input operands of the query. Furthermore, the query string may contain place holders for its operands using some binding notations that transfer the required information (query statements and its operands) to a corresponding execution formula.

First, all operands of the host language are evaluated, and their values are converted into a string and inserted into the corresponding place in the query. Then the whole query is sent to the execution module component as a single string in a single message. The corresponding execution module parses the transferred query string and computes the values of operands. If the corresponding operand is an object, its handle number is passed. Suppose that we have the following user query invocation in a client program:

```
query(result, "binding notation not finalised",mysql);
```

Assuming that mysql has a handle number 3, based on that the host language program places the operand values in the corresponding places in the parse tree. The query statement must be scanned in the host language program to find out the number of operands and their types. The type information is necessary because the host language program may call different procedures to transmit values of different types.

## 11.5.2 Query Optimization

The abstraction of the query optimization process is divided into (a) query parsing and (b) searching stages. First, the parsing module applies some transformations in a submitted query based on some rules and produces equivalent queries that are intended to be efficient. The query parsing process may depend on some declarative information of the queries' operands and the related operations. Such information is related to some statics and characteristics of queries without concern for specific cost. The parsing of a query is performed on the form of standardizing queries sampling techniques and flattening the nested queries. Second, is the searching and planning stage of the query processing that is performed by the optimizer. This stage is employed in order to perform a search strategy which explores the space of all access plans that are determined by logical and physical algebra in terms of the required methods and structures.

After the initial query processing stage is completed and a parse tree generated, it is necessary to decompose a query by applying integrated decomposition rules into local sub-queries based on the global anthology.[2] This decomposition process is based on a optimized tree query representation that is produced during the transformation process. In the context of the DOK project, for the optimization purpose, an algebraic approach to global query optimization is considered. With this approach, a query is decomposed into operations of an object algebra form. Based on some heuristics, then for each operation an execution site is chosen, and the corresponded operations are sent to each local site through an interface utility based on CORBA object management architecture. Finally, local objects are computed locally in response to sub-queries initiated on a federated level.

In the optimization process, the most relevant and important question is to clarify the way the results of the first operator are passed to the second one. The answer to this question is closely related to the techniques implemented by the optimizer. Such techniques may be (i) by creating and accessing a temporary file that may be kept in the buffer or not. (ii) Creating one process for each operator, then using interprocess communication mechanisms (i.e., pipes) to transfer data between operators, leaving it to the operating system to schedule and suspend operator processes if pipes are full or empty. (iii) The above two solutions create or introduce an extra cost; to avoid a temporary file and scheduling, a rule-based translation program can be used. These programs transform a plan represented as a tree structure into a single iterative program with (a) nested loops, (b) or other control structures [38]. The required rules set in [33] are not simple, especially for algorithms with complex control logic such as sorting, merge-join, and hash join. (iv) The most practical alternative is to implement all operators in such a way so that they can schedule each other within a single operating system process. This solution defines a single record and iterates over all records comprising an intermediate query result. This technique is employed in the Volcano prototype system [39]. Each time an operator needs another Record, it calls its input operator to produce one output. This is called a simple procedure call, which is much cheaper than interprocess communication since it does not involve the operating system. This approach is very close to production systems such as System R/SQL.DS and DB2, Ingres, Informix, Oracle.

## 11.6  SUMMARY

In previous chapters we covered some of the main important services of distributed systems, such as the Naming Service, the Trading Service, the Event Service and the

---

[2]A collection of different component databases information provided by the corresponding database administrator.

Transactional Service. The service described in this chapter, the OMG Query Service, is not a "standard" service of conventional distributed systems. Indeed, it is a service for databases, centralized or distributed. Because CORBA is object-oriented instead of process-oriented, CORBA objects may contain persistent data, and therefore will be stored in persistent storage. We believe that this aspect of persistency is a very important advantage of CORBA over existing distributed systems.

If CORBA deals with persistent data, then appropriate database services need to be provided. One of these services is the Query Service, which offers query facilities over multiple (data) repositories. Another service is the OMG Object Transaction Service. However, the reader may notice that CORBA and database systems have different views when dealing with these services. Database systems are generally centralized, at least the commercial ones, and all their functions, including query processing, are done in a centralized manner. CORBA systems are distributed by nature. Their objects, even though they are persistent, can be stored in different systems (relational database systems, object-oriented database systems, files). Therefore, the query processing techniques for CORBA systems may differ from the database systems.

This chapter provided details of the OMG Object Query Service. Background on query processing in distributed databases was also described. We hope that this has helped readers to understand the issues and the complexity related to query processing. Later on, we described the architecture and the components of the OMG Query Service, including QueryEvaluator, QueryCollection, and QueryManager. Finally, we described an implementation of such a service within the context of the DOK system.

## 11.7   REVIEW QUESTIONS

- Explain the differences between query processing in distributed databases and CORBA environments.
- What are the issues that need to be addressed when dealing with the management of data in CORBA environments?
- Explain some of the advantages of CORBA and database technologies integration.
- Explain the steps involved when using OQS in distributed environments.
- What does the efficiency of a query manager practically depend on? Briefly explain two main components of a query manager.
- Compare different types of query optimization strategies. What are the problems in optimizing nested queries?
- What are the two techniques in storing relations across multiple sites in distributed database systems? Explain how the cost of transferring data over the network influences query processing in distributed databases.
- Explain the steps performed in a typical query processing system.

- Explain how semijoin is used to reduce the number of tuples in a relation prior to their transfer to another site.
- Briefly explain each of the functions of each OQS component interfaces.

## 11.8  EXERCISES

- A query optimizer in OMG query service finds the "best" Global Execution Plan (GEP) before sending its comprising Local Execution Plans (LEP)s to the object adaptors. Later, the object adaptors translate the LEPs to specific query language to the relevant database servers on the network. Discuss the nature of this "best" GEP.
- Discuss the benefit and the drawback of OMG Query Service. *Hint*: Relate the explanation to database schema and query manipulation language

# References

1. M. Abrams, C.R. Standridge, G. Abdulla, S. Williams, E.A. Fox, "Caching Proxies: Limitations and Potentials," *Proc. Fourth Int. World Wide Web Conf.*, Boston, 1995.

2. M. Atkinson, F. Bancilhon, D. DeWitt, K. Dittrich, D. Maier, and S. Zdonik, "The Object-Oriented Database System Manifesto," *Proc. Int. Conf. on Deductive Object-Oriented Databases* (DOOD), Kyoto, Japan, 1989, pp. 40–57.

3. M. Ahamad and R. Kordale, "Scalable Consistency Protocols for Distributed Services," *IEEE Trans. Parallel and Distributed Systems (PDS)*, 10(9), 1999, pp. 888–903.

4. C. Aggarwal, J.L. Wolf, P.S. Yu, "Caching on the World Wide Web," *IEEE Trans. Knowledge and Data Engineering (TKDE)*, 11 (1), 1999, pp. 94–107.

5. S. Baker, *CORBA Distributed Objects Using Orbix*, Addison-Wesley, Reading, MA, 1997.

6. A. Barak, S. Guday and R.G. Wheeler, "The Mosix Distributed Operating System, Load Balancing for UNIX," 1993.

7. M. Bearman, K. Duddy, K. Raymond, and A. Vogel, "Trader Down Under: Upside Down and Inside Out," *Int. J. Theory and Practice of Object Systems (TAPOS)*, 3(1), 1997, pp. 15–29.

8. A. Beitz and M. Bearman, "An ODP Trading Service for DCE," *Proc. 1st Int. Workshop on Services in Distributed and Networked Environments*, Los Alamitos, CA, 1994.

9. A. Beitz and M. Bearman, " Service Location in an Open Distributed Environment," Technical Report 21, CRC for Distributed Systems Technology, 1995.

10. P. Bernstein, V. Hadzilacos, and N. Goodman, *Concurrency Control and Recovery in Databases*, Addison-Wesley, Reading, MA, 1987.

11. K.P. Birman, "The Process Group Approach to Reliable Distributed Computing," Comm. *ACM (CACM)*, 36(12), 1993, pp. 36–53.

12. K.P. Birman and R. van Renesse (eds.), "Reliable Distributed Computing with the ISIS Toolkit," *IEEE Comp. Soc. Press*, 1994, pp. 558–565.

13. Boeing, "Joint Computer Systems Technical Committee and Software Systems," Report of Technical Committee Meeting, May 1998.

14. G. Booch, *Object-Oriented Analysis and Design with Applications*, Addison-Wesley, Reading, MA, 1994.

15. M.A. Blaze, "Caching in Large-scale Distributed File Systems," Ph.D. Thesis, Princeton University, 1992.

16. M. Carey et al., "Storage Management for Objects in EXODUS," In *Object-Oriented Concepts, Databases, and Applications*, W. Kim and F. Lochovsky (eds.), Addison-Wesley, Reading, MA, 1989.

17. M. Carey, M. Franklin, M. Livny, E. Shekita, "Data Caching Tradeoffs in Client-Server DBMS Architectures," *Proc. ACM SIGMOD Conf. on Management of Data, Denver*, 1991, pp. 357–366.

18. T.L. Casavant and J.G. Kuhl, "A Taxonomy of Scheduling in General-Purpose Distributed Computing Systems," *IEEE Trans. Software Eng. (TSE)*, 14(2), February 1988, pp 141–154.

19. R.G.G. Catell et al., *Object Database Standard: ODMG 2.0*, Morgan Kaufmann, 1997.

20. P.E. Chung, Y. Huang, S. Yajnik, et al., "DCOM and CORBA Side by Side, Step by Step, and Layer by Layer," C++ Report, Vol 10, No. 1, January 1998, pp. 18–30.

21. G. Cornell and C.S. Horstmann, *Core Java*, Sun Microsystem Press, 1996.

22. G. Coulouris, J. Dollimore, and T. Kindberg, "Distributed Systems, Concepts and Design," Addison-Wesley, Reading, MA, 1994.

23. G. Craske and Z. Tari, A Property-based Clustering Approach for the CORBA Trading Service, *Proc. Int. Conf. on Distributed and Computer Systems (ICDCS'99)*, Texas, June 1999, pp. 517–527.

24. J.P. Deschrevel, "The ANSA Model for Trading and Federation," Architecture Report, ANSA, July 1993.

25. A.B. Downey and M. Harchol-Balter, "A Note on Limited Performance Benefits of Migrating Active Processes for Load Sharing," Technical Report, No. UCB/CSD-95-888, University of California, Berkeley, Computer Science Division, November 1995.

26. D.L. Eager, E.D. Lazowska, J. Zajorjan, "Adaptive Load Sharing in Homogeneous Distributed Systems," *IEEE Trans. Software Eng. (TSE)*, 12(5), May 1986, pp. 662–675.

27. D.L. Eager, E.D. Lazowska and J. Zajorjan, "A Comparison of Receiver-Initiated and Sender-Initiated Adaptive Load Sharing," *Performance Evaluation Journal*, 6(1), March 1986, pp. 53–68.

28. D.L. Eager, E.D. Lazowska and J. Zahorjan, "The Limited Performance Benefits of Migrating Active Processes for Load Sharing," *SIGMETRICS*, May 1988, pp. 662–675.

29. R. Elmasri and S.B. Navathe, *Fundamentals of Database Systems*, Addison-Wesley, Reading, MA, 1994.

30. D. Faensen, A. Hinze and H. Schweppe, "Alerting in a Digital Library Environment: Do Channels Meet the Requirements?," *Proc. European Conf. on Digital Librairies (ECDL)*, Heraklion, 1998, pp. 643–644.

31. B. Fan, K. Kumar and Z. Tari, "An Efficient Trader Using Attribute Clustering Technique in Distributed Object Systems," *Proc. Int. Conf. on Parallel and Distributed Processing Technique and Applications (PDPTA)*, Las Vegas, 1998.

32. M. Franklin, M.J. Carey, and M. Livny, "Transactional Client-Server Cache Consistency: Alternatives and Performance," *ACM Trans. on Database Systems*, 22(3), 1997, pp. 315–363.

33. J.C. Freytag, "Rule-Based View of Query Optimisation," *Proc. ACM Int. Conf. on Management of Data (SIGMOD)*, 1987, pp. 173–180.

34. J. Garbis, D. Slama, and P. Russell, *Enterprise CORBA*, Prentice-Hall, Englewood Cliffs, NJ, 1999.

35. D.S. Gill, S. Zhou, and H.S. Sandhu, "A Case Study of File System Workload in a Large-Scale Distributed Environment," *Proc. ACM SIGMETRICS Conf. on Measurement and Modelling of Computer Systems*, 1994, pp. 276–277.

36. A.S. Gokhale and D.C. Schmidt, "Evaluating the Performance of Demultiplexing Strategies for Real-time CORBA," *Proc. IEEE Global Telecommun. Conf. (GLOBECOM)*, Phoenix, 1997, pp. 1729–1734.

37. A.S. Gokhale and D.C. Schmidt, "Measuring and Optimising CORBA Latency and Scalability Over High-speed Networks," *IEEE Trans. on Computers*, 47(4), 1999, pp. 391–413.

38. G. Graefe and D. J. DeWitt, "The EXODUS Optimiser Generator," *Proc. ACM SIGMOD Int. Conf. on Management of Data*, 1987, pp. 160–172.

39. G. Graefe, "Volcano—An Extensible and Parallel Query Evaluation System," *IEEE Trans. Knowledge and Data Engineering (TKDE)*, 6(1), 1994, pp. 120–135.

40. G. Graefe, "Query Evaluation Techniques for Large Databases," *ACM Computing Surveys*, 25(2), June 1993, pp. 73–170.

41. G. Graefe and D. J. DeWitt, "The EXODUS Optimiser Generator," *Proc. ACM Int. Conf. on Management of Data (SIGMOD)*, 1987, pp. 160–172.

42. G. Graefe and K. Ward, "Dynamic Query evaluation Plans," *Proc. ACM Int. Conf. on Management of Data (SIGMOD)*, 1989, pp. 358–365.

43. J. Gray and A. Reuter, *Transaction Processing: Concepts and Techniques*, Morgan Kaufmann, 1993.

44. E. Gamma, R. Helm et al., *Design Patterns: Elements of Reusable Object-Oriented Software*, Addison-Wesley, Reading, MA, 1995.

45. I. Gunaratne and G. Fernandez, *Building New Applications and Managing Legacy Applications with Distributed Technologies: Principles and Techniques*, Springer-Verlag, New York, 1988.

46. T. Harder, "Observation on Optimistic Concurrency Control Schemes," *Information Systems*, 9(2), 1984, pp. 11–20.

47. M. Henning, "Binding, Migration, and Scalability in CORBA," Technical Report, DSTC, University of Queensland, 1997.

48. M. Henning and S. Vinoski, "Advanced CORBA Programming With C++," Addison-Wesley, Reading, MA, 1999.

49. Y. Hoffner, G. Thomas, and M. Beasley, "Data Management for an Enhanced Trader," Technical Report, ANSA, 1994, APM.1162.01.

50. J.H. Howard et al., "Scale and Performance in a Distributed File System," *ACM Trans. Comp. Systems*, 6(1), February 1988, pp. 51–81.

51. IONA Technologies, "Orbix Database Adapter Framework Release 1.0," 1997.

52. IONA Technologies, "OrbixWeb Programmer's Guide," 1997.

53. IONA Technologies, "OrbixWeb Programmer's Reference," 1997.

54. P. Krueger and M. Livny, "The Deverse Objectives of Distributed Scheduling Policies," *Proc. IEEE Int. Conf. on Distributed Computing Systems (ICDCS)*, 1987, pp. 242–249.

55. P. Krueger and N.G. Shivaratri, "Adaptive Location Policies for Global Scheduling," *IEEE Trans. Software Eng. (TSE)*, 20(6), June 1994.

56. R. Kordale, M. Ahamad and M. Devarakonda, "Object Caching in a CORBA Compliant System," *USENIX Computing Systems Journal, Computing Systems*, 9(4), 1996, pp. 377–404.

57. O. Kremien and J. Kramer, "Methodical Analysis of Adaptive Load Sharing Algorithms," *IEEE Trans. Parallel and Distributed Systems (PDS)*, 3(6), November 1992.

58. L. Lamport, "Time, Clocks and the Ordering of Events in a Distributed System," *Commun. ACM (CACM)*, 21(7), 1978, pp. 558–565.

59. ITU/ISO, "Reference Model for Open Distributed Processing," Committee Draft ISO/IEC/JTC1/SC21 N807, October 1994.

60. S. Landis and S. Maffeis, "Building Reliable Distributed Systems with CORBA," *Journal of Theory and Practice of Object Systems (TAPOS)*, Volume 3, 1997, pp. 31–43.

61. R.G. Lavender and D.C. Schmidt, "Active Object: an Object Behavioral Pattern for Concurrent Programming," In *Pattern Languages of Program Design*, J.O. Coplien, J. Vlissides, and N.L. Kerth (eds.), Addison-Wesley, Reading, MA, 1996.

62. A. Leff, P.S. Yu, "Performance Study of Robust Distributed Load Sharing Strategies," *IEEE Trans. Parallel and Distributed Systems (PDS)*, 5(12), December 1994.

63. E. Maderia and L. Lima, "A Model for Fedrative Trader," *Proc. Int. Conf. on Open Distributed Processing*, Brisbane, 1995.

64. S. Maffeis, "Run-Time Support for Object Oriented Distributed Programming," Ph.D. Thesis, University of Zurich, Switzerland, 1995.

65. P. Mishra and M.H. Eich, "Join Processing in Relational Database," *ACM Computing Surveys*, 24(1), March 1992, pp. 63–113.

66. J.M. Morrissey, W.T. Bealor and S. Kamat, "A Comparison of Static and Dynamic Strategies for Query Optimisation," *Proc. 7th IASTED/ISM on Parallel and Distributed Computing Systems*, Washington, 1995, pp. 55–53.

67. T.J. Mowbray and R.C. Malveau, *CORBA Design Pattern*, Wiley, New York, 1997.

68. K. Muller-Jones, M. Merz and W. Lamersdorf, "The TRADER: Integrating Trading Into DCE," *Proc. 3rd Int. IFIP TC6 Working Conf. on Open Distributed Processing (ICODP)*, Brisbane, 1995.

69. Y. Ni, "Resource and Service Trading in a Heterogeneous Large Distributed System," *Proc. IEEE Workshop on Advances in Parallel and Distributed Systems*, New Jersey, 1993.

70. OMG, "Common Object Request Broker: Architecture and Specification," Revision 2.0, 1995.

71. OMG, "ORB Portability Enhancement RFP," June 1995.

72. OMG, "Naming Service Specification," December 1997.

73. OMG, "Trading Object Services Specification," December 1997.

74. OMG, "ORB Portability Joint Submission (Final)," May 1997.

75. OMG, "Transaction Service Specification," July 1997.

76. OMG, "Concurrency Control Service Specification," July 1997.

77. OMG, "Common Object Request Broker: Architecture and Specification," Revision 2.2, 1998.

78. OMG, "Common Object Request Broker: Architecture and Specification," Revision 2.3a, 1998.

79. OMG, "The Portable Object Adaptor," Revision 2.2, 1998.

80. OMG, "Persistent State Service 2.0," April 1999.

81. Open Group, "Event Management Services (XEMS)," Technical Report, X/Open Document, 1997.

82. R. Orfali and D. Harkey, *Client/Server Programming with Java and CORBA*, Wiley Computer, New York, 1998.

83. T. Ozsu and P. Valduriez, *Principles of Distributed Database Systems*, Prentice-Hall, Englewood Cliffs, NJ, 1991.

84. J. Pompeii, "Secant Persistent Object Manager: A Technical Overview," Secant Technologies, 1998.

85. G. Rackl and T. Schnekenburger, "Dynamic Load Distribution for CORBA Applications: Integration and Evaluation," Component Users's Conference, Munich, 1997.

86. K. Raymond and K. Raymond, "Federating Traders: An ODP Adventure," *Proc. IFIP TC6/W2.6 Working Conf. on Open Distributed Processing*, Berlin, 1991, pp. 125–141.

87. F. Reverbel, "Persistence in Distributed Object Systems: ORB/ODBMS Integration," Ph.D. Thesis, University of New Mexico, 1996.

88. W. Ruh, T. Herron and P. Klinker, "IIOP Complete: Understanding CORBA and Middleware Interoperability," Addison-Wesley, Reading, MA, 1999.

89. SAMS.net, "Java Unleashed," 1996.

90. I. Savnik, Z. Tari, and T. Mohoric, "QAL: A Query Algebra for Complex Objects," *Int. J. Data and Knowledge Eng. (DKE)*, 30(1), May 1999, pp. 57–94.

91. D. Schmidt, T. Harrison, C. O'Ryan, and D. Levine, "The Design and Performance of a Real-Time CORBA Event Service," *IEEE J. Selected Areas in Communications*, August 1999.

92. D. Schmidt, D. Levine and S. Mungee, "The Design of the TAO Real-Time Object Request Brokers," *Computer Communications*, 21(4), April 1998.

93. D. Schmidt and S. Vinoski, "Comparing Alternative Programming Techniques for Multi-Threaded CORBA Servers—the Thread-per-Request Concurrency Model," C++ Report, SIGS, 8(2), February 1996.

94. D.C. Schmidt and S. Vinoski, "Introduction to Distributed Computing (Column 1)," SIGS C++ Report, 1995.

95. S. Setiawan, "CODAR: A POA-based CORBA Database Adaptor," Technical Report, no. TR-00-3, RMIT University, May 2000.

96. K.G. Shin and C.J Hou, "Design and Evaluation of Effective Load Sharing in Distributed Real-Time Systems," *IEEE Trans. Parallel and Distributed Systems (PDS)*, 5(7), July 1994.

97. A. Stepanov and M. Lee, "The Standard Template Library," Technical Report, Hewlett Packard, April 1994.

98. W.R. Stevens, *UNIX Network Programming*, Volume 1, *Networking API: Sockets and XTI*, Prentice-Hall, Upper Saddle River, NJ, 1998.

99. Sysnetics, "Persistence of Distributed Objects," http://www.sysnetics.com/persist/persistence.html.

100. O. Tallman and J.B. Kain, "COM versus CORBA: A Decision Framework," Distributed Computing Journal, July 1998. http://www.quoininc.com/quoininc/articles.html

101. A.S. Tanenbaum, *Modern Operating Systems*, Prentice-Hall, Englewood Cliffs, NJ, 1992.

102. Z. Tari, W. Cheng, K. Yetongnon, and I. Savnik, "Towards Cooperative Databases: The DOK Approach," *Proc. Int. Conf. on Parallel and Distributed Computing Systems (PDCS)*, Dijon, 1996, pp. 595–600.

103. Z. Tari and G. Craske, Designing a CORBA Trading Service with Query Routing Facilities, *Proc. Int. Conf. on Distributed and Computer Systems (ICDCS'00)*. Taipei, April, 2000, pp. 504–511.

104. Z. Tari, Q. Lin and H. Hamidjaja, "A Caching Approach to improve CORBA Performance," *IEEE Proc. Int. Workshop on Internet 2000 (IWI200)*, Taipei, April, 2000, pp. 59–60.

105. Z. Tari, Q. Lin and H. Hamidjaja, "Cache Management in CORBA Distributed Object Systems," IEEE Concurrency, Vol 8, No. 3, 2000, pp. 48–55.

106. J. O'Toole and L. Shrira, "Hybrid Caching for Large-Scale Object Systems (Think Globally Act Locally)," *Proc. Int. Workshop on Persistent Object Systems (POS)*, 1994. pp. 99–114.

107. X/Open Ltd., "Distributed Transaction Processing: The XA Specification," October 1991.

108. X/Open Ltd., "Distributed Transaction Processing: The TX Specification," October 1992.

109. A. Vogel et al., "Trader Down Under: Upside Down and Inside Out," Technical Report, CRC for Distributed Technology, Australia, 1996.

110. Y. Wang and L.A. Rowe, "Cache Consistency and Concurrency Control in a Client/Server DBMS Architecture," *Proc. ACM SIGMOD Conf. on Management of Data*, May 1991, pp. 367–377.

111. C.J. Wang, P. Krueger, and M.T. Liu, "Intelligent Job Selection for Distributed Scheduling," *Proc. IEEE Int. Conf. on Distributed Computing Systems (ICDCS)*, 1993, pp 517–524.

112. A. Waugh and M. Bearman, "Designing an ODP Trader Implementation Using X.500," *Proc. Int. Conf. on Open Distributed Processing*, Brisbane, Australia, Feb. 1995.

113. S. Williams, M. Abrams, E. Fox, and G. Abdulla, "Removal Policies in Network Caches for WWW Documents," *Proc. ACM SIGCOMM Conf. on Application, Technologies, Architecture for Computer Communications*, Palo Alto, 1996, pp. 293–305.

114. S. Zhou, X. Zheng, J. Wang, and P. Delisle, "Utopia: A Load Sharing Facility for Large, Heterogeneous Distributed Computer Systems," *Software-Practice and Experience*, 23(12), Dec. 1993, pp. 1305–1336.

# Index

Page references followed by italic *t* indicate material in tables.